HEARTBEAT,
WARBLE,
AND THE
ELECTRIC

HEARTBEAT, WARBLE,
AND THE
ELECTRIC POWWOW

AMERICAN INDIAN MUSIC

CRAIG HARRIS

University of Oklahoma Press : Norman

Also by Craig Harris
The Band: Pioneers of Americana Music (Lanham, Md., 2014)
(with Melanie Safka) *Melanie: Look What They've Done to My Song, Ma* (New York, 2016)

Library of Congress Cataloging-in-Publication Data

Names: Harris, Craig, 1953 December 20–
Title: Heartbeat, warble, and the electric powwow : American Indian music / Craig Harris.
Description: Norman : University of Oklahoma Press, [2016] | Includes bibliographical references and index.
Identifiers: LCCN 2015036818 | ISBN 978-0-8061-5168-7 (pbk. : alk. paper)
Subjects: LCSH: Indians of North America—Music—History and criticism. | Indian musicians—United States.
Classification: LCC ML3557 .H38 2016 | DDC 780.89/97—dc23
LC record available at http://lccn.loc.gov/2015036818

The paper in this book meets the guidelines for permanence and durability of the Committee on Production Guidelines for Book Longevity of the Council on Library Resources, Inc. ∞

1 2 3 4 5 6 7 8 9 10

In memory of
Frank Taplin,
Geoff "Yippie" Meredith,
and Richard Bajorski,
mentors of my passion for music,
and with love and gratitude for my mother

CONTENTS

ILLUSTRATIONS

INTRODUCTION

"People think there are only a few Indians left, but there are millions of them. One day, they're going to be asking for their rights."
—John Lennon, *Mike Douglas Show*, 1971

Christopher Columbus was exploring the coast of Trinidad during his third voyage to the "New World" in August 1498 when he caught sight of a "large canoe of twenty-four [Native] men." Hoping to attract their attention, the once-lost navigator summoned for a tambourine and instructed members of his crew to play music and dance. When the Natives, misinterpreting the gesture to be a war dance, unleashed "a shower of arrows," Columbus responded by ordering "some crossbows to be discharged."[1]

This escalating exchange would not only exemplify the lack of understanding between European explorers and America's First People, but also emphasize the seriousness of music among the Indigenous. "There is not a phase of [tribal] life," said Alice Cunningham Fletcher (1838–1923) of the Peabody Museum of American Archeology and Ethnology, "that does not find expression in song."[2]

This book is the outgrowth of an article on powwow music that I wrote for the much-lamented folk and world music magazine *Dirty Linen* in 1995. As I conducted research and interviewed Drum (drum group) leaders, I became aware of how some musicians were remaining dedicated to preserving tribal traditions, while others melded these roots with a global range of influences to create an ever-evolving tapestry of great sounds. "I'm a member of a world culture," proclaimed two-time Grammy-winning American Indian flutist R. Carlos Nakai (Ute/Diné) in June 2012, "a mixture of every ethnicity that has come to this continent."

According to the United Nations' Department of Economic and Social Affairs, the average income for the more than five million American Indians who composed the 566 federally recognized tribes (and at least four hundred more without recognition) in the United States in 2009 was less than half the average of the country overall. Nearly one-fourth of the Amerindian population lived below the poverty level. Natives could anticipate a life span twenty-four years shorter than that of the general population, and a greater chance of dying from tuberculosis, alcoholism, a motor vehicle accident, diabetes, unintentional injury, homicide, or suicide.

Despite this severe poverty, and more than a half-millennium of cultural suppression, forced relocation, urbanization, stereotyping, and economic poverty, the creative spirit of Indigenous America refuses to be extinguished. Today's Indigenous soundscape radiates with the vibrancy of powwow drums and end-blown woodwinds, along with rock, jazz, country, folk, pop, reggae, blues, R&B, hip-hop, dance music, and symphonic influences.

In preparing this book, I interviewed singers, songwriters, instrumentalists, producers, record label owners, ethnologists, and educators. In addition to sharing insight into their music, and their experiences as musicians, they were eager to share what it meant to be American Indian.

Determining who was Native, however, was not, as I learned, a simple task. *A Declaration on the Rights of Indigenous People*, prepared by the United Nations' Permanent Forum on Indigenous Issues (UNPFII) in 2007, decreed that "Indigenous people have the right to determine their own identity or membership in accordance with their customs and traditions," while conceding that a "definition of Indigenous people on the global level was not possible at this time."[3]

Ancestry does not guarantee tribal relationship. Membership in the Cherokee Nation is not based on a specific blood quantum, but requires that at least one ancestor be listed on the Dawes Final Rolls, which were used to parcel out allotments of tribal land to individuals prior to Oklahoma's statehood in 1907.

There is also a question of how much blood is required to be American Indian. The first inductee into the Native American Music Hall of Fame, Jimi Hendrix, may have been four generations from his Cherokee great-great-grandmother, but Indigenous roots are reflected in everything from the clothes that he wore to the spiritual underlining of his songs. Peter LaFarge's claims of Narragansett ancestry may be debatable, but there is no question about the importance of his songs about broken treaties, environmental destruction, and the struggles of American Indians.

In writing this book, I used "American Indian," "Native," and "Indigenous" to generalize the people it represents, while emphasizing tribal affiliation whenever possible. The term "Native American" appears in direct quotes and in descriptions of the Indigenous woodwind, the radio talk show *Native America Calling*, and the Native American Music Awards Hall of Fame.

Each chapter (arranged chronologically) traces the steps leading from the earliest roots to musicians fueling today's Indigenous soundscape. The opening chapter ("The Heartbeat") explores the powwow, from sacred ceremony to intertribal gathering, while the second chapter ("The Warble") looks at the revival of the Native American flute. American Indian singers and songwriters are the subjects of the third chapter ("Tribal Voices"), while Indigenous rock, reggae, pop, and punk bands are featured in chapter 4 ("Rez Rockers, Guitar Heroes, and Rasta Men"). Chapter 5 ("Divas, Hip-Hoppers, and Electronic Dance Masters") focuses on artists who have broken into the mainstream through disco, electronic dance music, and hip-hop while retaining cultural connections. The concluding chapter 6 ("Depicting and Defying Stereotypes") looks at the pejorative imagery promoted by some non-Native music and celebrates Native and non-Native musicians who shatter inaccurate typecasting.

All quotations of musicians and music-industry personnel in this book are from my interviews with that person, unless otherwise indicated in a note citation. Interviews that are not listed individually in the bibliography are in my collection.

HEARTBEAT, WARBLE, AND THE ELECTRIC POWWOW

1 THE HEARTBEAT

"Picture a huge, resonant drum, which is situated in the center of a large circle. Place around this drum ten to fifteen men, all with sticks to beat out the peculiar rhythms of the Indian music. These men, then, begin to chant their spiritual thoughts. Then, around the circle, the light, rhythmic treading of the feet of hundreds of dancers begins."
—British journalist Melba Blanton

Combining tribal dance, music, crafts, food, and regalia, powwows provide opportunities for American Indians to reconnect with family and friends and offer non-Natives a way to experience Indigenous culture. "[Powwows] allow people to see us and our culture rather than assume," said George Thomas (Pequot).[1]

Powwows can include parades, rodeos, athletic competitions, gambling games, food courts, drum contests, and arts and crafts marketplaces. Some—including the Gathering of Nations in Albuquerque, New Mexico, the world's largest powwow—include a stage spotlighting Native rock bands; folk, country, and pop singers; and reggae groups. Dancing in the main arbor (dance arena), however, remains at the gatherings' core. "We know who we're singing and drumming for—the dancers," said Wayne Silas, Jr. (Menominee/Oneida), round-dance singer and leader of the intertribal Drum,* Tha Tribe. "If they're dancing their hearts out, we know we're doing our job."

Inspired by the opening processional in Buffalo Bill's Wild West show, most powwows kick off with a Grand Entry, during which dancers, following two lead dancers (one male and one female), enter the arena according to regalia and style of dance. "It's pretty amazing," said Gathering of Nations publicist Sarah Hattman. "Dancers come into the arena, and they just keep coming and coming. It keeps growing until the floor is packed."

*"Drum" refers to a group of drummers and singers.

Following a flag ceremony, the acknowledgment of armed forces veterans and special guests, and the recitation of a prayer, or invocation, a steady beat emits from a large buffalo-, deer-, or elk-skinned ceremonial drum. As eight to twelve singer-drummers answer the leader with punctuated cries and accented drumbeats (honor beats), the dancing begins. "You usually have men's traditional and the northern Plains style," said Black Swamp Intertribal Foundation director Jamie K. Oxendine (Lumber/Creek). "Sometimes you have men's straight, grass, and fancy dancing. You have women's traditional. Of course, there are the women's fancy and women's jingle dances. At some of the larger powwows, where there are hundreds of dancers, you are also going to see chicken dancers and Eastern Woodland dancers. I went to a powwow in North Carolina where they separated the men's dancing into men's northern fancy and men's southern fancy, with different speeds of music and different regalia. At some powwows, they may try to sneak in other dances like the snake dance. Tribes have been trying to push some of the older dances. We've been pushing Eastern Woodland dancing. In the upper Great Lakes, in Michigan and parts of Minnesota and Wisconsin, they've been trying to promote the old-time women's scrub dance."

"Northern traditional dancers often have lots of natural bird feathers in their outfits," said Patty Talahongva (Hopi), host of the radio talk show *Native America Calling*, "and [they] dance with quick steps, crouching low to the ground—resembling a prairie chicken's walk or a warrior in search of his enemy. Southern straight dancers have a regal air to them, standing upright, and dancing with short purposeful steps. At points in their song, they will bend over and dance in semicircles imitating how they surround their enemy. For ladies, there are the traditional buckskin or cloth dances, the jingle dress dance, and finally the ladies' fancy shawl dance, which is the equivalent to the men's fancy dance."[2]

Powwow songs, sung in English or tribal languages, relay a variety of messages. "They tell people to have a good time," said Terry Paskemin (Cree), leader of the Saskatchewan-based Blackstone Singers, "to not be shy, to be happy, to not waste time sitting around, and to get up and dance. Some are comical. A lot of them tell the dancers to be respectful to themselves and to their regalia, to live every day the best that they can. Some are love songs. There are songs that I've made up about different animals."

More frequently heard are vocables, composed of nonliteral vocal sounds rather than actual words. "[Vocables] were used long before First Contact," explained Jamie Oxendine. "They've been used in music all over the world, Native or not. A very easy way to understand it is to think of the Christmas carol 'Deck the Halls.' The entire chorus—'fa la, la, la, la'—is vocables."

"The story taught to me," said Wayne Silas, Jr., "was that [vocables] were more powerful than any other language because they're the way that we communicate to our Creator when we're infants, before we learn language."

Various drums play during a powwow. "The hand drum, or frame drum, is the dancing drum," said New Mexico–based drum maker Yolanda Martinez (Apache/Comanche/Hispanic) of Yolanda's Spirit Drums, "and the ceremonial powwow drum is the grandmother drum."

Martinez has been making drums since 1987. "I get the hides and soak them overnight," she explained. "Then, I cut them, burn the holes, and soak them again. I prepare the hoops and cut the cylinders. The hide is stretched and left to dry. Then, I do the final wrapping with leather. There is another process to make the beaters. You're looking at about a week for a drum."

Traditional symbols are incorporated into the designs that Martinez uses to decorate her drums. "The first symbol that I used was the spiral," she said. "It represents life. Energy moves in spirals, not in a straight line; the ancients knew this. Then, the symbol for Grandmother Spider came to me, the bringer of creativity, designing and creating her web. I also do a spirit cactus with an image of a person whose arms are stretching up, a starburst in the four directions, and a medicine wheel."

Many believe that a drum is endowed with special power. "A drum is more than a drum," said round-dance singer Jay Begaye (Diné). "It gives you a good feeling and it can bless you like a god. Before a powwow, every singer burns cedar for the drum. When a drum is happy, we can jam. If somebody feels sick, they can touch the drum and bless themselves."

"Not only does it set a rhythm and tone for the song," added Silas, Jr., "but [the drum] also carries our belief that, when we sing, we're singing for our people. Our songs are for healing and prayer lifting. The heartbeat of the drum lifts those prayers to the Creator and the spirits. You hear a drum beat and it does something to your heart, whether you are a dancer or not. It has a lot of power."

Powwows connect, according to most researchers, to a nineteenth-century ceremony of the Poncas' Hethuska (heh-THOO-shka) Society. Societies were responsible for organizing entertainment and providing outlets for celebrating honors and special distinctions, and could be religious, military, or social. Composed of warriors who had gained honor in battle, the Hethuska Society was governed by "a roster of officers, including a drum keeper, eight dance leaders, and two whip men who started each dance episode and who whipped reluctant dancers across the legs to make them get up and perform."[3]

"The dance was received through a vision by a man named Crow-Feather," explained UCLA ethnomusicology professor and author Tara Browner. "While

Crow-Feather was in a trance-like state, the spirits gifted him with a porcupine and deer-hair roach and a crow bustle or 'belt.' A roach is a crest of stiff porcupine guard hairs with a deer-hair center that male dancers wear on their heads; a bustle is the spray of feathers worn on their backs. Crow belts, a specific type of bustle made from the carcass of a crow, wings spread, are the precursors of the more formalized eagle-feather bustles used today."[4]

"Shortly the singers about the drum struck up one of the songs belonging to the society," recalled Alice Fletcher, "a song suitable for dancing, and whoever was so moved rose, and, dropping his robe in his seat, stepped forth nude, except his embroidered breech-cloth, and decoration of grass or feathers. Bells were sometimes worn about the ankles, or bound below the knee, and added a castanet effect, marking the rhythm of the song and dance, and adding to the scene, so full of color, movement, and wild melody."

The songs, dances, and rituals of the Hethuska ceremony spread to other groups during the nineteenth century. "The Ioways and Otoes have their own Hethuska music," said Fletcher, "and [they] call the society by that name. The Yanktons, a branch of the Dakota group, were old friends of the Omahas; [they] adopted the Hethuska, but did not call it by that name; they give it the descriptive title of 'the Omaha Dance,' or 'the Grass Dance,' the latter name referring to the tuft of grass worn at the belt."[5]

As it continued to evolve, the ceremony transformed into a secular celebration honoring elders and returning veterans, with speeches, gift giving, a feast, and social dancing replacing its original spirit-based rites.

By 1880, at least thirty tribes were organizing public-invited gatherings, increasingly referred to as "powwows"—a designation many attribute to the Narragansett Eastern Algonquins' "pau-wau," referring to a spiritual person or to a healing ceremony conducted by medicine men or spiritual leaders. "The words, 'pau wau,' translate literally into 'he, she, or they who dream,'" explained John Brown, director of historic preservation for the Narragansett tribe, in June 2011. "It referred to a title, not a place. The people who are called 'medicine men,' or 'medicine women,' today were the pau wau."

The Flathead Indian Reservation in Arlee, Montana, was the site of a massive powwow in 1898. The Wisconsin Winnebagos (now known as Ho-Chunk Wazijacis) became the first to charge admission in 1909.

The proliferation of powwows defied non-Native attempts to suppress tribal ceremonies. Sometimes lasting more than a week, these ceremonies had ritualistically commemorated the important events of life—birth, reaching adulthood, marriage, and death. They appealed to the spirits for leniency during harvests, astronomical phenomena, and periods of sickness. During times of drought, special ceremonies pleaded for rain. "Raindrops would be drawn toward the big drum," said British journalist Melba Blanton, "as if aiming at a bull's-eye."[6]

Ceremonial traditions differed from tribe to tribe. Among tribes of the Eastern Woodlands and the Southeast, including the Cherokee, Creek, Choctaw, Chickasaw, and Seminole, the Green Corn, or harvest, Ceremony commemorated the ripening of corn (maize) in late summer and marked a time when all personal offenses (except rape and murder) were forgiven. The Muskogee Creeks called it "Posketv" (Bus-get-uh, or "Fasting to Fast"), and considered it the beginning of a new year.

A Stomp Dance on the third evening climaxed the four-day Green Corn Ceremony. During an interview conducted on November 26, 1937, by L. W. Wilson for the Writers Project Administration (WPA), Lucy Cherry (Choctaw) recalled a Green Corn stomp dance, probably in Maryland, in the late nineteenth century. "In a secluded spot sits an Indian beating out a thump, thump, on his tom-tom," remembered the mother of sixteen, "denoting that the hour of the dance is at hand. The participants of the dance are in readiness, with turtle shells filled with gravel or little flint rocks attached to the ankles of the women and above the knees of the men."

After the recitation of a prayer of gratitude in the Choctaw language, Cherry remembered, "The man with the tom-tom again strikes up and the dance starts— all singing and chanting as they strut, and stomp, making rhythm with the rattling of the shells, as they circle around and around the glowing embers in the center of the circle."[7]

Pacific Northwestern tribes, including the Haida, Salish, Tlingit, Tsimhian, and Kwakwaka'wakw (roughly, QUAWK-wawk-ee-wawk), marked life's momentous steps with a potlatch (Chinook for "gift"). Organized by a host family, potlatches provided opportunities for the tribe to gather for joyous celebrations and funerals. Potlatch host families were required to provide a great feast and present gifts—including blankets, carved decorations, and baskets—to everyone in attendance.

Accompanied by whistles, rattles, hand drums, and spontaneous, nonliteral vocal punctuation, potlatch songs were especially powerful during funerals. "The family has to go to the songwriter," said Rosanne Mancuso to Alaska's *New Miner*, "so the songwriter can help the family write a song for the person who died. The songwriter sings at potlatches and it's a way to bring [the deceased person's] spirit alive."[8]

Among most tribes in the Great Plains and southwestern Canada, the Sun Dance (Wiwanke Wachipi or the Gazing-at-the-Sun Dance) represented an important step in one's vision quest. "It is sacred," said Oglala Lakota spiritual leader Frank Fools Crow (ca. 1890–1998), the intercessor for more than seventy-five Sun Dances, "and the highest way to honor [the Great Holy Mystery] Wakan Tanka."[9]

"The rationale for the Sun Dances of the several tribes varied," explained anthropologist Fred William Voget (1913–1997) in *Shoshoni-Crow Sun Dance.*

"It included the themes of seasonal renewal, growth, and replenishment, and the acquisition of mystical power."[10]

Most researchers agree that the Sun Dance originated among the horse-riding, buffalo-hunting tribes of the Great Plains (Oglala Lakota, Arapaho, Blackfoot, and Cheyenne) and spread to the Kiowa, Comanche, Cree, Crow, Gros Ventre, Hidatsa, Mandan, Pawnee, Plains Ojibwe, Ponca, Shosone, and Ute. In the autumn 1970 issue of the University of Pennsylvania's Museum of Archeology and Anthropology's *Expedition* magazine, Jeffrey Zelitch explained that, according to Lakota tradition, a buffalo had transformed into a woman and presented the ceremony to a Lakota man to share with his people at a time of hunger. "[The Sun Dance] represents," explained Zelitch, "the fulfillment of the ritual cycle of the sacred pipe which was brought to the Lakota by the White Buffalo Woman."[11]

Sun Dances incorporated spiritual purification through a steam bath, fasting, and the ritual cutting and placing of a sacred tree (sometimes topped with a buffalo head) in the center of a circular arbor, or medicine lodge. The top of the arbor was open, enabling participants to stare into the sun. "There were originally seven songs," explained Howard Bad Hand (Brulé Lakota), a Sun Dance singer and song maker, spiritual healer, and producer of the annual High Star-Sun Eagle International Sun Dance for Peace in Red Valley, Arizona. "After I started singing at Sun Dances, I found that the seven songs are not all the same. Our group is the Brulé and the tribe next door is the Oglala. We are all Lakota—we speak the same language—but, when I sang for the Oglala Sioux Nation Sun Dance, Max Blacksmith said, 'I'm going to teach you the seven original Oglala Sun Dance songs.' The seven that he taught were different from our seven. It was the same thing when I went to sing at a Sun Dance at the Cheyenne Butte reservation in the northern part of South Dakota. An old man there claimed to know the original seven Sun Dance songs. He taught them to me. They were different too. The message, the meaning, and sometimes, even the rhythm [were different]. The older forms had a peppy beat, almost staccato."

Some (but not all) tribes incorporated piercing into their Sun Dance. "Each one of the young men presented to a medicine man," recounted Lt. Frederick Schwatka in 1899, "who took, between his thumb and forefinger, a fold of the loose skin of the breast—and then ran a very narrow-bladed, or sharp, knife through the skin. A stronger skewer of bone, about the size of a carpenter's pencil was inserted. This was tied to a long skin rope fastened, at its other extremity, to the top of the sun-pole in the center of the arena."[12]

The Sun Dance is a "strictly religious rite," Alice Fletcher told the American Association for the Advancement of Science in 1883, "entered voluntarily, and performed in fulfillment of vows made in sickness or trouble in order to secure health and prosperity. . . . [It is the dancers'] recognition of supernatural powers and their dependence upon them."[13]

A drum "made of a hide dried for this occasion" and a "whistle, which is made from the wing bone of an eagle, ornamented at one end by a peculiar, soft feather used in religious ceremonies" accompanied Sun Dance songs. The Sun Dance concluded "when a certain song is started" and a dancer "must put his whistles to his mouth, and bracing himself, pull up with all his force until he shall tear the flesh loose."[14]

"The Sun Dancer has to reckon with the spiritual world by himself," said Southern Ute spiritual leader Eddie Box, Sr., to *American Indian Today*, "and cope, with rigors and pains of the spiritual quest alone, summoning his utmost physical and mental resources . . . the 'success' of his quest is purely a matter between him and the Great Spirit. And the gained 'medicine power,' if indeed obtained, is given to him to use or abuse according to his private vision."[15]

In the late 1880s, a messianic religious movement, known by many as the Ghost Dance, swept through the Great Plains, prophesying the restoration of tribal land, resurrection of departed ancestors, and return of the buffalo in exchange for believers' participation. "They kept dancing until fully one hundred persons were lying unconscious," said Pine Ridge Reservation, South Dakota, schoolteacher Z. A. Parker, recalling a June 1890 Ghost Dance on the banks of White Clay Creek. "Then, [the others] stopped and seated themselves in a circle, and as each recovered from his trance, he was brought to the center of the ring to relate his experience. . . . After resting for a time, they would go through the same performance, perhaps three times a day. They practiced fasting, and every morning those who joined in the dance were obliged to immerse themselves in the creek."[16]

"The sacred pole about which the people danced was set some distance from the houses," said James McLaughlin, the BIA agent who would order the arrest (leading to the death) of Hunkpapa Lakota chief/spiritual leader/song maker Sitting Bull in December 1890. "Around this pole, a ring of men, women, boys, and girls, about one hundred in all, were dancing. Some of the younger ones had been pupils of the reservation day schools until within a few weeks. The dancers held each other's hands, and [jumped] madly, whirling to the left about the pole, keeping time to a mournful crooning song that sometimes rose to a shriek as the women gave way to the stress of their feelings. There was nothing of the slow and precise treading, which ordinarily marks the time of the Indian religious dance."[17]

The Ghost Dance originated in a vision experienced during an 1889 New Year's Day solar eclipse by a Northern Paiute ex-ranch worker in Mason City, Nevada. In his "dream," Wovoka ("The Cutter," aka Jack Wilson) claimed that he had had a long discussion with God. "When the sun died," he recounted to James Mooney of the Bureau of American Ethnology, "I went up to heaven and saw God and all the people who had died a long time ago. God told me to come back and tell my people they must be good and love one another, and not fight, or steal, or lie. He gave me this dance to give to my people."[18]

Wovoka considered an earlier sage, Tavibo, or Tii'vbo ('white man"), to be his father. "[Tavibo] was a petty chief," he told Mooney, "but not a preacher or prophet." On three occasions during the 1860s, Tavibo had ascended the Sierra Mountains "to speak with the Great Spirits." After his first climb, he returned with the prediction that a massive earthquake was going to split the Earth, with white people consumed. After his second ascension, Tavibo amended his prophesy. Although the earthquake would swallow all human beings, American Indians would rise again. The third climb brought the stern warning that true believers would be the only ones saved; nonbelieving Indians would join whites in eternal damnation. "The new world would be covered with green grass," said Mooney, "and herds of deer, elk, antelope, and buffalo, and the Indians would live in a paradise, untroubled by disease, wars, or famine."[19]

Word about Tavibo's revelations spread. Shoshoni and Bannock Indians from Oregon and Idaho visited the Paiute sage to learn about and partake in this "new religion." Tavibo instructed followers to dance, at night, around a circle (with no fire in the center)—a dance that the Shoshonis claimed they had been doing for fifty years, calling it "the Father's Dance," or "[the dance] with joined hands."[20]

Tavibo's death, around 1870, kept his religion from spreading further, but his prophesies would be expanded upon, nearly two decades later, by his "son," Wovoka. Indoctrinated into the New Testament while living with a devoutly religious, non-Native rancher, David Wilson, and his family, and familiar with the Shaker religion, Wovoka combined tribal and Christian beliefs in his Ghost Dance. "Do not tell the white people about this," Mooney recalled Wovoka telling his followers. "Jesus is now upon the earth. He came once long ago beyond the waters and the white people killed him. Now he is come to the Indians who never did him harm."[21]

The dance was given many names. The Kiowas called it "the dance with clasped hands," while the Caddos referred to it as "the prayer of all to the Father." To the Lakotas, Dakotas, Nakotas, Arapahos, and some other Plains tribes, it was known as the "Spirit," or "Ghost," Dance.

Drums, rattles, or other musical instruments were not played—unless by "an individual dancer in imitation of a trance vision"—but the Ghost Dance inspired a vast repertoire of songs. "There is no limit to the number of these songs," observed Mooney, "as every trance at every dance produces a new one. . . . A single dance may easily result in twenty or thirty new songs."[22]

"As with church choirs," said Z. A. Parker, "the leaders, both men and women, frequently assembled privately in a tipi to rehearse the new or old songs for the next dance."[23]

Rather than providing relief, the Ghost Dance intensified Native misery when BIA officials, and the U.S. government, attempted to crack down on participants. Tension regarding a Ghost Dance on Sitting Bull's land, on the Standing Rock Reservation, led to the shooting death of the Hunkpapa Lakota spiritual leader on December 15, 1890. Recruited to secure Sitting Bull's arrest, Buffalo Bill Cody, who had featured him in his Wild West show only a year before, had his orders rescinded when James McLaughlin sent a letter to the BIA commissioner, incorrectly assuring that he had "matters well in hand, and when proper time arrives can arrest Sitting Bull by Indian police without bloodshed."[24]

Two weeks after Sitting Bull's death, members of the reconstituted Seventh Cavalry Regiment, still fuming over Custer's defeat fourteen years before, cut down as many as three hundred Miniconjou Lakota men, including Chief Big Foot (Spotted Elk), women, and children in the Wounded Knee Massacre. "Who would have thought that dancing could make such trouble," asked the Sicangu Lakota (Brule) medicine man, and Ghost Dance leader, Short Bull (ca. 1845–1915), "for the message that I brought was peace."[25]

"I did not know then how much ended," remembered Oglala Lakota holy man Black Elk, an eyewitness to the massacre, forty years later. "When I look back now from the high hill of my old age, I can still see the butchered women and children lying there heaped and scattered all along the crooked gulch as when I saw with eyes still young. And I can see that something else died there in the bloody mud and was buried in the blizzard; a people's dream died there—it was a beautiful dream."[26]

Christian proselytizing predated the First Encounter. Forty-seven years before Columbus's first voyage, Pope Nicholas V granted Portugal's King Alfonso the authority to "capture, vanquish, and subdue all Saracens and pagans whatsoever and other enemies of Christ wheresoever placed."[27]

By 1636, the Plymouth, Massachusetts, colony established laws encouraging the preaching of the Gospel to Natives. With the Board of Indian Commissioners advocating the further indoctrination of American Indians into Christianity, Congress passed the Civilization Fund Act of 1819, calling for the assimilation of Indians into the "standards of Euro-American society" and financing religious groups willing to teach on the reservations. A rider added to the Indian Appropriation Act in 1871 eradicated the right of Native tribes to be sovereign nations, thereby ending the negotiation of treaties, and enabling the United States to prosecute federal crimes committed by American Indians.

In 1882, the U.S. government escalated its assault on tribal religion. Promising to put an end to "heathen dances and ceremonies," Henry M. Teller, secretary of the interior under Pres. Chester A. Arthur, approved a Code of Indian Offenses that made it a crime to practice Indigenous religion, including traditional dances and feasts. The so-called Five Civilized Tribes—Cherokee, Chickasaw, Choctaw, Creek (Muscogee), and Seminole—were exempt. A decade later, Thomas Morgan, the commissioner of Indian Affairs, instituted penalties of up to six months in prison, and the loss of government-provided rations for thirty days, for participating in religious dances or acting as a medicine man.

Missionaries railed against the potlatch for centuries. Anglican preacher William Duncan (1832–1918) called the ceremony "by far the most formidable of all obstacles in the way of Indians becoming Christians, or even civilized."[28]

Canada became the first country to ban the potlatch in 1885, with the United States following shortly afterwards. Anyone caught participating, or assisting, in the ceremony was subject to "imprisonment for a term not more than six or less than two months in a jail or other place of confinement."

"One of the reasons the Canadian government outlawed potlatches," said Chief Dan Cranmer (Kwakwaka'wakw), "was based on information from missionaries that our people would be involved in debaucheries at these events, and no work would get done. But potlatches were held in the wintertime and our people used to work so hard the rest of the year to gather up gifts to give away."[29]

Prohibitions banning the potlatch did not lift until 1934 in the United States, and 1951 in Canada, though many families continued to gather in secret. Police raided a Kwakwaka'wakw potlatch in 1921, arresting forty-five participants. "They were charged with really criminal things," said Cranmer Webster, whose father hosted the raided ceremony, "like dancing, giving speeches, and distributing gifts. They were given a choice. If they gave up all their treasures, their masks, and regalia, they wouldn't have to go to jail."[30]

The boarding school system attempted to drive another nail into Native culture. Within a quarter of a century after the 1879 opening of the U.S. Training & Industrial School in Carlisle Barracks, Pennsylvania, there were more than 150 Indian boarding schools scattered across the United States. Forced to adopt Euro-American values, students, who often attended schools far from their reservations and families, faced punishment if caught speaking Native languages, wearing traditional clothes, or practicing tribal rituals. In his official report to the Nineteenth Annual Conference of Charities and Correction in 1882, Capt. Richard H. Pratt, founder of the Carlisle school, declared, "A great general has said that the only good Indian is a dead one . . . all the Indian there is in the race should be dead. Kill the Indian in him and save the man!"[31]

Despite restrictions, traditions continued to be observed. "Groups of families kept the songs and the music alive," said Howard Bad Hand. "Most of the traditions that we have are song-based. There had to be someone who remembered them. The songs got passed on."

Some sacred ceremonies transformed into secular experiences. "Social celebrations were not outlawed," said Bad Hand, "just the practice of the rituals. Families and friends got together to sing at celebrations. Singing was part of life's expression. In South Dakota, you attended a wachipi (dance). [It] served the purpose of gathering the people together without creating a political mess. It was a time to celebrate, a time to name kids, a time to honor achievements."

Despite an offer of citizenship to the 9,000 American Indian veterans of World War I, few Native Americans were citizens until 1924, when the Indian Citizenship Act bestowed citizenship on "all Indians born within the territorial limits of the United States." Forced assimilation of American Indians, however, had begun to lose its grip with the ascendency of the Kiowa 6, a group of artists whose brilliantly colored "Kiowa style" paintings of tribal life and rituals became a worldwide phenomenon. Thirty-five of their watercolors were exhibited at the First International Art Congress in Prague, Czechoslovakia, in 1929, and their artwork was published in France as a folio. Two of the Kiowa 6—Jack Hokeah (1900–1969) and Spencer Asah (1906–1974)—were also skilled powwow dancers. The senior member, Stephen "Painted Robe" Mopope (1898–1974), played Native American flute.

Appointed commissioner of the BIA under Pres. Franklin Delano Roosevelt in 1933, John Collier (1884–1968) ushered in a progressive (as opposed to assimilationist) policy popularly known as a "New Deal for American Indians." A year after taking office, the Atlanta-born son of a banker persuaded Congress to pass the Wheeler-Howard, or Indian Reorganization, Act. Though compromising on some of Collier's proposals, it terminated the Dawes Act allocations, which had divided communally owned tribal land into individually owned plots; returned remaining surplus land to tribal ownership; restored limited sovereignty; and repealed prohibitions against Native languages and traditions. "For nearly three hundred years," Collier explained in the *Annual Report of the Secretary of the Interior for the Fiscal Year Ended June 30, 1938*, "white Americans, in our zeal to carve out a nation made to order, have dealt with the Indians on the erroneous, yet tragic, assumption that the Indians were a dying race—to be liquidated. We took away their best lands, broke treaties [and] promises, tossed them the most nearly worthless scraps of a continent that had once been wholly theirs, but we did not liquidate their spirit."[32]

The appointment of Dillon Seymour Myer (1891–1982) as commissioner of Indian Affairs in May 1950 threatened progress spurred by Collier's efforts. As director of the War Relocation Authority (WRA) during World War II, Myer—whose 1987 biography by Richard Drinnon was entitled *Keeper of the Concentration Camps*—had overseen the internment of more than 120,000 Japanese Americans. A proponent of assimilating Indians into the dominant (white-controlled) culture, Myer now promoted the adoption of Indigenous children by non-Native families and lobbied for the Indian Termination Act, which ended the U.S. government's recognition of tribal sovereignty and subjected Natives to state and federal taxes and laws.

Under Myer's leadership, the BIA instituted a policy of encouraging American Indians to relocate to urban centers, providing a one-way bus ticket and promising assistance in finding employment and free medical care for a year. Although more than 35,000 Natives accepted the offer between 1952 and 1960, many grew frustrated by the lack of work and the challenges of ghetto neighborhoods, and nearly one-third returned to the reservations.

Myer's tenure as BIA commissioner ended in March 1953 after Dwight Eisenhower became president, but his successor, former banker Glenn L. Emmons, who would remain in office until 1961, was connected to the non-Native business community and continued most of his predecessor's policies.

Proscriptions against tribal religion began to lift after Richard Nixon, a member of the Religious Society of Friends (Quakers), a group with a long history of supporting Native rights, became president in 1968. Over the next decade, Nixon and subsequent presidents would affix their signatures to the Indian Civil Rights Act (1968), the Alaska Native Claims Act (1971), the Indian Education Act (1972), the Indian Self-Determination in Education Assistance Act (1974), the Indian Health Care Improvement Act (1978), the Indian Child Welfare Act (1978), and the American Indian Religious Freedom Act (1978).

Piercing would remain illegal until the ratification of the Religious Freedom Restoration Act in 1993, but the Sun Dance was resurrected in a modified form. "[Sun Dancers] mimicked the tradition by trying ropes around their waists," remembered Howard Bad Hand. "It was the same way with other traditions. It looked like we were just re-enacting, but we were using it as a basis to revive songs, the use of language, the prayer process, and healing."

The Kiowas, who held their last Sun Dance in 1890, continue to organize a weekend-long Gourd Dance on or near the Fourth of July. Originating in the 1700s, and nearly extinct by the 1930s, the gathering's popularity has continued to rebound since its revival in 1955. "The hottest part of the year," said Walter Ahhaitty, director of Oklahoma's Kiowa Tribe and a skilled Gourd Dance singer, "that's when the Kiowa come together. It has nothing to do with the independence of the colonies."

The roots of the Gourd Dance, explained Ahhaitty, trace back to a "group of warriors on a raiding party. They met up with an enemy that had superior firepower and they were overpowered. The enemy set fire to the plains. During the firefight that broke out, one of the warriors separated from his men and became lost. During the night, he could hear singing. He followed the sound of the songs and came to the top of a hill, where a wolf was singing these songs, and shaking a gourd rattle. After a few songs, the wolf told the warrior that he was giving the songs to the Kiowa. He knew where the warrior's people were and told him. He said, 'Bring this dance to your people; it'll help them.' From that point on, we've had this dance."

Despite its name, the Gourd Dance does not utilize gourds. "We use a metal can with rocks inside of it," said Ahhaitty. "We save the actual gourds for our Native American Church services."

THE COZAD SINGERS

The host Drum at the Kiowas' Gourd Dance, the Cozad Singers build on the teachings of song-maker Leonard Cozad (1916–2005), who started the group in the early 1940s. Now composed of Cozad's sons, grandsons, nephews, daughters, and other extended family members, the Oklahoma-based group "carry on what [my father] left us," said Charlie Cozad, the second-youngest of Cozad's five sons, in July 2011. "My dad's elders taught it to him and he passed that legacy on to us."

In addition to songs by their progenitor, the Cozad Singers' repertoire includes tunes passed down for centuries. "There are prayer songs," said Cozad, "and old, traditional songs that came south with us a long, long time ago. They came with [our ancestors] when they came down from western Montana: the Blackstone and the Yellowstone Mountains. They didn't have names. The 'long time ago dance' is what they usually called them."

WAYNE SILAS, JR., AND THA TRIBE

Many Drums incorporate modern sensibilities while remaining embedded in tradition. "We're taught that we live in two worlds," said Menominee/Oneida round-dance singer, and leader of Tha Tribe, Wayne Silas, Jr. (1973–). "I don't like to call it 'the white man's world,'" he said, "but we live in this modern world full of technology and advancement. You have to get an education, become an active member of your community, and be a positive role model. Our other world is our identity as Native people: everything passed down to us as far as our language, culture, heritage, traditions, songs, and dances. We have a double responsibility to keep that alive and not let it die. We're taught to live in both of these worlds simultaneously and to do the best that we can."

Formed by classmates at the intertribal Haskell Indian Nations University, in Lawrence, Kansas, in 1997, Tha Tribe has increasingly focused on the roots. "We've gone from a contemporary style with lots of words," explained Silas, Jr., "to a more vocable style, which some people call 'the old style,' and others, 'the straight, original style.' It was the popular style when I was a kid in the 1970s and '80s. Most groups on the powwow circuit sang in that [vocable] style, language was reserved mainly for special honoring songs and family songs."

Although they represent a diverse range of tribal backgrounds, members of Tha Tribe share a "common interest in powwow singing." "[When we first got together] and started going over songs that we all knew," remembered Silas, Jr., "we had a really good sound, better than we had expected or anticipated. It was exciting to think that all these people, from different groups, different areas of the country, and different styles of powwow singing, could get together and harmonize."

Belonging to the Bear Clan, Silas, Jr., was born in Chicago to a Menominee mother and an Oneida father. "They're definitely not the same," he said. "The Menominee is an Algonquin band and the Oneida is an Iroquois band. In different wars, we fought on opposite sides. The languages are different, and there are cultural differences, but we've become a close community. Our reservations are only thirty miles from each other. As far as powwow culture, we follow the same etiquette and believe in the celebration of life through song and dance."

Though raised in the inner city, Silas, Jr., grew up with powwow music. "We went to a lot of powwows," he recalled, "and I looked at drum groups as though they were celebrities. I'd think, 'Someday, that's what I want to do.' It was as important as the pop music that you would hear on the radio or see on MTV. That's how serious I took it."

"My father started giving me serious teachings about etiquette, songs, and all of the respectful and traditional ways to be around the drum," he recalled, "when I was eight."

He continued, "He would sit me by his drum group, singing instead of just watching. I had to learn as I went."

In addition to recording with Tha Tribe, Silas, Jr., has released three solo albums (*Unconditional*, *Infinite Passion*, and *True*) of round-dance songs. "I didn't want to do an album with me singing by myself," he explained, "so I've had guests doing duets and trios with me."

MALCOLM YEPA AND THE BLACK EAGLE DRUM GROUP

Embracing, while expanding upon, tradition has also been a goal for Malcolm Yepa (Kiowa/Tanoun) and the Black Eagle Drum Group. After their sixth album,

Flying Free, received a "Best Native American Album" Grammy award in 2003, Sen. Tom Udall of New Mexico proclaimed that the twenty-plus-member group should be "applauded for their musical achievements" and "commended for their loyalty to the history of the powwow." "Our music is as good as anything that you hear on the radio," Yepa told me in June 2012.

Raised in the Pueblo of Jemez, New Mexico (about fifty miles north of Albuquerque), speaking the Tiwa language, Yepa had little connection to the powwow as a child. "I grew up with Pueblo music," he said, "not the Plains Indians' powwow. We sang Pueblo songs and danced Pueblo dances. Plains music has high-pitched singing. Pueblo style is a low, chanting-like style. It's much different."

Attending his first powwow in Lame Deer, Montana, in 1989, Yepa found himself transfixed by the drumming, singing, and dancing. When a family friend, Jimmie D. Little Coyote, spoke to him about the protocols of the powwow, he absorbed every word that the Northern Cheyenne chief had to say. "He told me what the powwow drummers were singing about," he recalled, "and explained, step by step, about the different categories of dancing and the songs that were appropriate for those dances."

Returning to the Pueblo, Yepa persuaded his brother, David Yepa, Jr., and several cousins, to join him in a powwow drum group. More than a decade later, the Black Eagle Drum Group has grown into one of the leading forces of powwow music. "We sing for the people," said Yepa, "to make them feel better and to give them hope for tomorrow."

THE WOOD BROTHERS AND THE NORTHERN CREE SINGERS

The sounds of the powwow have gotten a boost with the masterful drumming and spirited singing of the Saddle Lake, Ontario-based Northern Cree Singers, a group composed mostly of singers and drummers from the Treaty 6 area in central Saskatchewan and Alberta. "I remember watching rock-and-roll bands," said Steve Wood, who formed the six-time Grammy nominee with his three brothers—Charlie, Randy, and Earl—in 1982, "and thinking that powwow music should be as good."

As youngsters, the Wood brothers harbored no aspirations of becoming musicians. Their entry into show business came as the result of needing to raise money quickly. "We used to play a stick game," explained Wood, "a gambling game. It's about hiding a bone in your hand and the other person trying to guess which hand it's in. We started singing after losing all of our money gambling. We were far from home [visiting our brother Earl in Idaho] and had no way to get back. Earl remembered the songs and dances that we had been doing since we were kids and suggested that we get a gig at a local powwow."

Northern Cree has brought masterful drumming, and spirited singing, to the powwow.
Photo by Robert Doyle.

Securing the gig, the group still did not have a name. As the powwow emcee asked how to introduce them, Wood noticed his brother Randy removing a ceremonial drum, borrowed from a local museum, from a blanket. Reading the words etched into the drum skin, he quickly replied, "What about Northern Cree—it says it right here on the drum." "It was the first time that we used the name 'Northern Cree,'" he remembered, "but I think that the idea of the group was formed back in the '60s. I remember a man who would visit us, and, after eating, he would pull out a drum. He would play and the kids would dance. That's where the spirit of Northern Cree evolved from."

Northern Cree's discography includes more than three dozen albums. They shared the inaugural "Best Native American Album" Grammy award in 2001 for *Gathering of Nations Powwow 1999*, with Southern Cree and High Noon (and producers Tom Bee and Douglas Spotted Eagle). Their music was included in the Lord Richard Attenborough–produced and directed film *Grey Owl*, starring Pierce Brosnan, in 1999.

Entering eleven competitions in 2000, Northern Cree won nine and placed second twice. That same year they were crowned Aboriginal Contemporary Singing World Champions, Julyamsh Champions, and Canadian National Champions. They continued their climb a year later, scoring a Native American Music Award (NAMMY) for "Best Pow-Wow Album" for *Rockin' the Rez*. "We have to sing and play harder," said Wood, "because people are not listening to the Earth's heartbeat. She's telling us that she's sick. She hurts and she's going to cleanse herself—there's nothing that we can do about it."

Leaving Northern Cree and relocating to Saint George, Utah, Randy Wood scored Grammy and Juno nominations with his debut solo album, *Round Dance the Night Away*, in 2002. His third album, *Round Dance Blues*, received a NAMMY as "Best Traditional Album of 2005," while his fourth album, *Our Love Will Never Die*, a year later, garnered his second Grammy nomination. *The Gift of Life: Round Dances and Songs of the Native Road* followed in 2010. "With his blend of powwow rhythms, Native melodic lines, and songs that flip between English and vocables," said *No Depression*, "he's created a powerful form of Native singing that's as accessible as it is compelling."[33]

ROUND DANCE

A gender-free style of social dance (originating among the First Nations of Canada), the round dance adds to many powwows. "It stays with a triple beat," said Canyon Records owner and producer Robert Doyle, "which helps to lock people into the step. The syncopation on the third beat makes it easy for non-dancers."

"Round-dance songs are traditionally sung at wintertime dance parties that could go on for as long as three or four days," said NAMMY-winning round-dance singer Jay Begaye (Diné). "People dance all night long until the sun comes up. They go home to sleep during the day and return towards evening to dance again."

"A round dance is a ceremony where everybody comes together to pray for somebody," added Begaye's daughter, Tiinesha, also a NAMMY-winning round-dance singer. "People will hold round dances as memorials or for people that are sick. They believe that, when they sing these songs, and do the round dance, the holy people, or our grandmas and grandpas that passed, come down to dance with us."

"The round dance is different from nation to nation," explained Jamie Oxendine. "For some, it's very social. For others, it's very formal. For some, the round dance is not part of the powwow. It's completely separate. Others have round dances before the powwow. They may do several hours of round dancing before the Grand Entry. Some round dances come after the Grand Entry, before the intertribals and competitions."

JAY BEGAYE

A former rodeo rider, Jay Begaye helped to introduce the round dance to the United States. "[The round dance] came to me in a vision," he claimed. "It wasn't something that I forced myself to do. It just happened. It was the Creator telling me to seek my traditional ways of singing."

A member of the Arizona-based White Eagle Singers from 1982 until 1986, Begaye spent the late 1980s and early '90s in British Columbia, where he recorded four solo albums and an album with the Cathedral Lake Singers, a group formed with his ex-wife. Returning to the United States in 2002, he continued to add to the round-dance repertoire. In addition to five solo albums (*Honoring Our Ways, The Beauty Way, Round Dance in Beauty, Song of Colors*, and *The Colorful World*), he recorded an album with Native American flutist Everitt White (*The Long Walk*), and two CDs with his daughter, Tiinesha (*Night of the Northern Lights* and *Horses Are Our Journey*). "I have so many round-dance songs honoring our elders, our warriors, and our chiefs," said Begaye. "They're mostly for healing. When people are having a hard time, we tell them to come out and dance. I sing, and use my drum, for the people—not just our people, but people around the world. I sing to make them feel good, to make them happy, to get them out of loneliness, and to help them out of sickness. . . . I tell people that the songs are not mine. They are the Creator's songs."

Begaye grew up on the Navajo Reservation in Steamboat Canyon, Arizona. "Our reservation is in four states: Utah, Colorado, New Mexico, and Arizona," he said. "Our elders, chiefs, and holy people say that it is a holy place. They knew about the four sacred mountains, and it is where we settled as the Navajo nation."

Moving to Utah after high school, and attending his first powwow in Salt Lake City, Begaye found himself mesmerized when he heard the Snake River Singers. "The song that I heard," he recalled, "was played by a bunch of good singers, sitting around a big drum, and it really got to me. It took me back to the old days, when our people sang in a free country, before any other nationality came, when we could ride horses and go fishing."

Inspired by the experience, Begaye turned to music. "I started singing just like [the Snake River Singers]," he said, "and I learned many of their songs. It brought me to where I could compose my own songs, in my own language, with the same rhythm and style. I didn't have to take any lessons; I just started doing it."

Begaye became emotionally lost after his mother—a renowned horse breeder—died in 1981. "I had nowhere to go," he remembered. "I just wanted to feel comfort and happiness. I wanted to get away from thinking about how my mom used to be, so I left home and headed north [to Canada]." As soon as he arrived, Begaye felt at home in the Great White North. "An elder showed me around when I first got to Canada," he remembered. "He pronounced the words of some songs and they sounded like words in the old Navajo language. The main tribe had come down [from Canada and settled in what became the United States], but some families had remained behind in the mountains. When the elder was telling me these words, I was amazed. It was just like being home on the Navajo reservation."

In early 1982, Arlie Neskahi, leader of the White Eagle Singers, a group that had formed in Cortez, Colorado, eight years before, invited Begaye to sit in. He soon became a full-fledged member, remaining until 1986. "They were the kings of powwow singers among the Navajo Nation," he said.

Although he returned to Canada, married, and started a family, Begaye had a hard time leaving music behind. "He missed singing," said his daughter, "because he wasn't around anyone who knew how to sing. He would be downstairs practicing. Soon, my mom started joining in, along with my auntie, and all my cousins. That's how the Cathedral Lake Singers were formed."

"I really liked the name 'Cathedral Lake,'" said Begaye, "because my clan is water people. I want to do anything that has to do with water and my drum. There were four lakes way up in the mountains that were sacred lakes. [American Indians] had a name for the lakes in their own language, but the white men called them 'the Cathedral Lakes.'"

Begaye's first collaboration with his daughter, *Night of the Northern Lights* (2008), drew some attention, but its follow-up, *Horses Are Our Journey*, a year later, was a true masterpiece. Father and daughter scored NAMMYs as the year's "Best Male Artist" and "Best Female Artist," respectively. "I watched Tiinesha when she was a young, beautiful girl growing up," said Begaye, "but I never paid attention to what I wanted her to be. I wanted it to be the Creator's choice how she would grow up. If the Creator puts you on the planet with a talent, that talent will come out; but I remember, when she was only three years old, she was already singing."

A passion for horses thematically linked songs on *Horses Are Our Journey*. "My dad and I love horses," said Tiinesha, "and we have horses of our own. [Before we recorded the album], we thought about how they have helped us throughout our journey—from warhorses to packhorses—but did not have a voice of their own. We wanted to [provide] that for them."

TIINESHA BEGAYE

The younger Begaye recorded two solo albums of her original round-dance songs—*Rhythm of Love* in 2005, and *Melodies of the Purple Horizon* in 2011. "It took me two days to record [*Melodies of the Purple Horizon*]," she said, "but it represented me as a person. It had songs that told of my life and what I have gone through. I composed 'Where Are You?' for my boyfriend [African American rapper/producer Kelvin Ternoir] when I was going to school. He was in Chicago and I was in Arizona. It was hard for me to be in that kind of long-distance relationship, so I wrote the song."

Begaye wrote her first round-dance song at the age of nine. "We were on our way to my favorite powwow," she recalled, "the Arlee, Montana, celebration near Missoula. It was my cousin, my dad, and me. We were listening to [R&B group] Destiny's Child on the radio. I started listening to the lyrics. I looked at my cousin and told her, 'I think we should make a round-dance song.' We came up with this song and sang it for my dad. He said, 'That's a really good song.'"

Participating in a hand drum contest, Begaye and her cousin caught the ear of a Canyon producer with their harmonies. "He pointed to the stage," she recalled, "and asked my dad who was singing."

Begaye released her first solo album, *Night of the Northern Lights*, shortly after her fifteenth birthday in 2005. "When I was nine, I came to the studio to record," she said, "but it didn't work out. They told me to come back, but I was in school and had to wait." Six years passed between Begaye's debut and her second solo album, *Melodies of the Purple Horizon*, in 2011. "I make songs every day," she said, "and I have tons. They were just building up. I figured that I needed to put them down on an album."

Begaye's relationship with Ternoir, whom she met when he visited his mother in Phoenix, has expanded her musical scope. "He's teaching me to write R&B and hip-hop songs," she said. "I've always wanted to do it. I have always been into hip-hop. Most of my cousins and the people that I grew up with listen to hip-hop, R&B, and pop. I love to listen to Beyoncé. Rhianna is my favorite. I love their lyrics and the stories that they tell."

The relationship has been a mutual cultural exchange. "I'm the first aboriginal First Nations person that Kelvin has been with," said Begaye. "He had never been to a powwow before, had never heard this kind of music, and knew very little about Native American culture, but he's really interested and he's learned a lot."

The greatest influence on Begaye's songwriting has come from her two children. "Being a mom has been a great experience," she said. "It's been tough at times. I was such a young mother—I had [my oldest son] when I was nineteen—but to experience all of those feelings and to put them into my songs, that's my inspiration."

It is that hope for the future that continues to fuel powwow music. "We were encouraged to learn the Indian ways," said Charlie Cozad, "and we're teaching our grandchildren the little that we know."

"We're not a stagnant culture," added Jamie Oxendine. "We're constantly evolving, while hanging on to as much tradition as we can."

2 THE WARBLE

"The flute has magic to it. It touches people in a special way. It reaches into the heart and touches the soul."

— Douglas Blue Feather (Cherokee)

Woodwinds and whistles provided Turtle Island's earliest melodies. Known as the Breckenridge flute, a two-chamber duct flute, made of river cane and dating to between A.D. 1020 and 1160, was found along the shores of northwest Arkansas's Beaver Lake. An archeological expedition led by Dr. Earl H. Morris discovered four wooden, end-blown flutes, dated to between A.D. 620 and 670, in a northwestern New Mexico cave. Images of the humpbacked, flute-playing fertility god Kokopelli, who took his name from the Hopi word for "wooden backed," can be seen on petroglyphs drawn by the Anasazi as early as A.D. 1000 and on pottery dating to between A.D. 750 and 850, attributed to the Hohokams, ancestors of the Pimas and Tohono O'odhams.

Cabeza de Vaca (1528), Hernando de Soto (1539), and Jacques Le Moyne (1564) observed flutes, whistles, and "simple cane flageolets" in Florida. In his report on Francisco Vázquez de Coronado's 1540–1542 expedition to what is now New Mexico, Pedro de Castaneda recalled watching women grind corn. "A man sits at the door playing on a fife," he remembered, "[while the women], moving the stones to the music, [sing] together."

The flute served a variety of functions. "Some tribes used it strictly as a courting instrument," said J. Bryan Burton, professor and department chair of music education at West Chester University of Pennsylvania, "and some incorporated it into healing, rain, or fertility rituals."[1]

"The pipe or flute is called 'Cho-tan-ka,' which means literally, 'big-pith,'" explained Christian missionary/linguist Stephen Return Riggs (1812–1883):

It has two varieties, one made of wood and the other of bone. The first is the most common, and much resembles the flageolet. It is made by taking the sumac—a wood which has the requisite "big-pith"—a straight piece nineteen or twenty inches long, and, when barked and smoothed down, an inch and a quarter in diameter. This is split open in the middle. The pith and inner wood [are] carefully hollowed out to make a bore of five eighths of an inch diameter, extending through the whole length, except that it grows smaller at the mouthpiece, and, at a point four inches below, it is interrupted entirely by a partition three eighths of an inch thick, which is left to form the whistle. The halves are glued together. Finger holes, one quarter of an inch in diameter, and usually six in number, are burnt along the upper face. On the same face, the whistle is made by cutting a hole, three-eighths of an inch square, on each side of the partition. Then, over these, and connecting them, is laid a thin plate of lead, with a slit cut in it, a little more than an inch long and three eights of an inch wide. On top of this is a block of wood, two inches long and three fourths of an inch wide, flat on the bottom, and carved above into rough likeness of a horse; and a deerskin string binds the whole down tight. A brass thimble for a mouthpiece, some ribbon streamers, a few lines of carving, and a little red and yellow paint, and the instrument is complete.[2]

Each tribe had its distinct style of woodwind, based on available resources. New England tribes bore out the pithy core of white cedar, or sumac, while southern tribes used the naturally bored river cane or bamboo. Tribes on the northwestern coast used bone and cedar whistles. Believed to have originated with the Northern Ute tribe, and crafted from the wood of a juniper tree, the "Plains flute" possessed a distinctively resonant tone. Easy to play, its influence spread through the Southwest.

Although the woodwind's popularity waned by the turn of the twentieth century, a handful of musicians kept the tradition alive. A student of Kiowa flute player Oldman Turkey in the late 1800s, Belo Cozad (Kiowa) recorded solo flute tracks for the Library of Congress in 1941. The recordings were reissued by Rounder Records fifty-six years later. Author and activist Mary Brave Bird, aka Mary Crow Dog (1954–2013), recalled her Lakota grandfather, Richard Fool Bull (ca. 1880–1976), a survivor of the Wounded Knee Massacre, as "the last man to make flutes in the shape of a bird's head which had the elk power, the power to lure a young girl into a man's blanket."[3]

Oklahoma-born Joyce Lee "Doc" Tate Nevaquaya (1932–1996), a Comanche, sparked "a whole wave of new interest [in the flute]" with his debut album, *Comanche Flute*, in 1978. "He played in the old style," said composer and flutist

Jerod Impichchaahaaha Tate (Chickasaw). "It was more shrill [compared with more recent flutists]."

"[Nevaquaya] had a powerful sound," his biographer and University of Oklahoma American Indian Studies and music professor Dr. Paula Conlon said. "He called it 'a mature sound.' It was very assertive and rounded, very solid."

A skilled visual artist, Nevaquaya acquired his first woodwind by trading one of his paintings with flute collector and maker Dr. Richard Payne (1918–2004), who, in turn, had acquired his first flute from Belo Cozad. Amassing a collection of flutes that included more than a thousand instruments, Dr. Payne, whose childhood interest in the flute was enhanced while he served as an army medic in Central and South America, became one of the first non-Natives to make Indigenous-style woodwinds. "[He'd] give them back to the Indians," said the founder of fluteopia.com and flute player Clint Goss, "and tell them, 'Here, play your music.' He was quite a character."

Navaquaya's five sons and four daughters continue to build on his legacy. "Sonny is very active as a flutist in Florida," said Dr. Conlon. "Edmund plays flute, and sings, and he worked with Kevin Locke. Timothy does a lot of artwork; I have two of his paintings. He also plays and makes flutes. Joseph is involved with gourd dancing. Calvert, the youngest son, plays flute and does art. The girls express themselves by quilting and doing beadwork."

R. CARLOS NAKAI

R. Carlos Nakai (Ute/Diné) set the standard for solo Native American flute playing with his debut album, *Changes: Native American Flute Music* (1982), and his million-selling Grammy winners, *Earth Spirit* (1987) and *Canyon Trilogy* (1989). Born in 1946, Nakai has continued to adapt the woodwind to a variety of formats. His discography includes trio, quartet, and quintet recordings, as well as collaborations with a slack key guitarist from Hawaii, Keola Beamer; a Philadelphia Orchestra cellist from Israel, Uri Bar-David; a flutist/vocalist from Tibet, Nawang Khechong; a New Age pianist from Germany, Peter Kater; a classical composer from Minnesota, James DeMars; and the Wind Traveling Band from Japan. The soloist when the Omaha Symphony premiered Philip Glass's *Piano Concerto N0.2: After Lewis & Clark* in 2004, he has been a featured guest of more than a dozen symphony and chamber orchestras.

Nakai's atmospheric melodies are featured on the soundtracks of *Geronimo* (1993) and *New World* (2005). Modern dance choreographer Martha Graham used tracks from his second album, *Cycles*, in her final work, *Night Chant*. "The

R. Carlos Nakai (Ute/Diné) leads the expansion of the Native American flute with melodic improvisations and spirited playing. *Photo by Craig Harris.*

rumbling heard at the beginning is electronic," said Anna Kisselgoff in her *New York Times* review of the Martha Graham Dance Company's performance at City Center in New York in October 1988, "suggesting the 'subsonic vibrations' Mr. Nakai says he has felt on the northern plains and in the southwest."[4]

"[Nakai] draws inspiration from mountains, valleys, canyons, wind, rains, sunsets, the scent of juniper, from wildlife, and from the earth itself," said Society of Ethnomusicology cofounder David Park McAllester. "His music describes the Southwest particularly and has a vivid sense of his ancestors moving through this landscape. Anasazi ruins, immigration routes, and intertribal cultural references all have an important place in the liner notes of his recordings."[5]

Nakai's earliest exposure to the woodwind came in early 1957. As he placed the phonograph needle on the 78-rpm disc—one of many that he was auditioning for his parents' daily Navajo language radio show—he was immediately transfixed as the flute playing of William Hornpipe (Lakota), from the Pine Ridge Reservation's

Medicine Root District, wafted from the speaker. When he learned that the school he attended on the Colorado River Indian Reservation, in La Paz County, Arizona, was planning to offer music instruction, he was ecstatic. Auditioning for the music teacher at the beginning of the school year, however, he felt his heart sink when the instructor told him that he would be playing cornet instead of the flute. "I hated being suited for the brass," he remembered. "I thought brass instruments were like plumbing—pipes that you'd put under a sink."

Despite the youngster's pleading, the music teacher refused to change his mind. "He told me that [the cornet] would open me to a wide variety of instruments," recalled Nakai, "the trumpet, the baritone sax, and, maybe even, the valve trombone."

Reluctantly, Nakai dedicated himself to mastering the cornet, and later the trumpet. By his late teens, he had begun attracting attention as solo trumpet player for the Navajo Tribal Band. "The University of Arizona bandmaster and the Northern Arizona University bandmaster tried romancing me," he remembered. "They'd say, 'Why don't you join our music program? We'd love to have you.'"

On the verge of accepting one of the scholarship offers, Nakai received his draft notice. The marines rejected him for being underweight (at only ninety-eight pounds), but he was accepted by the navy and spent two years, studying electronics and communications, in Hawaii and the South Seas. Hoping to keep his "chops as a trumpet player up," he auditioned for the Royal Hawaiian Band at the suggestion of the bandmaster at the Pearl Harbor Naval Base. "I passed the audition," he remembered, "but they said, 'We'd love to have you, but there's one problem—you're not Hawaiian.' I said, 'Every place I go, people think I'm Hawaiian.' 'We know, but we're funded by the state and, if they found out that we had an American Indian, it would be the end of our money.' 'What if I just come down and play with you on the weekends?' 'No, we can't do that either.'"

Returning to the Navajo Reservation in 1971, Nakai encountered a reception far short of what he had hoped. Instead of being hailed for his heroism, he became the target of eggs and rotten tomatoes as he walked the streets of his hometown. "All of my classmates were in the ground [having lost their lives in Vietnam]," he said, "and people resented me for coming back. All of the girls were already married and having families of their own. It was very disheartening."

Turning to alcohol and drugs, Nakai came close to spiraling out of control when a near-fatal auto accident forced him to re-evaluate his life. "I damaged my embouchure," he said, "and thought that my world had ended. After the physician put my teeth back, they weren't in the right order anymore."

Unable to play the trumpet, Nakai grew frustrated without music. A girlfriend's flute provided an outlet. "I had years of music theory and practice behind me," he said, "and thought that I could transfer that knowledge to the flute. I began working on it from a disciplined perspective."

Purchasing a woodwind, which was suited more for a wall display, in a Cortez, Colorado, tourist shop, Nakai committed to learning about the instrument. "'I couldn't allow it to be lost to museums and private collections,'" he said, "so I tried to find out as much as I could about what remained of the traditions."

Nakai acquired his first well-built flute in 1974 from Dr. Oliver Wendell "O. W." Jones, a medical doctor and flute maker, from La Jolla, California. Initially sparked when he noticed a flute in a painting of an American Indian, Jones's fascination with the woodwind was further whetted after he heard a tape that ethnologist Frances Densmore had recorded in the early twentieth century on the Cheyenne Reservation in South Dakota. "It had this distinctive sound," Jones recalled, "what we call a 'warble.' It really intrigued me. I wanted to learn more about it. I wanted to be able to create that sound."[6]

"It was a goal of [Native American] flutes to 'warble,'" Clint Goss later explained. "If you close all of the holes, and breathe into it with a steady breath pressure, the flute itself will begin to vibrate—between two octaves. It's not vibrato; the flute is oscillating between the lower and upper octave (or warbling)."

Absorbing as he much as he could about the woodwind from Dr. Payne and Nevaquaya, as well as Comanche flute makers and players Carney Saupitty and George "Woogie" Watchetaker, Jones sought outlets to express his passion. "I would take two or three flutes," he remembered, "and stroll around [and play]. Inevitably, somebody would ask me about it. We would talk, and maybe share some ideas. Sometimes, it would end up in a trade."[7]

Nakai was working as a vendor selling moccasins, chokers, and beadwork at the Santa Fe Indian market in New Mexico, when he met Jones in the early 1970s. "This fellow from Oklahoma walked over to me with a bag of flutes," Nakai remembered, "and told me that they were Southern Plains flutes. Then he said, 'I'd like to trade a couple of these flutes for those moccasins.' I said, 'Well, I'd like to hear those flutes.' After I heard him play, we traded and I got two flutes—one in the key of F-sharp minor and the other in the key of G minor."

Nakai continues to acquire flutes from Jones. "He's probably been the biggest influence on my playing," he said, "because, through him, I've been able to obtain flutes in different keys."

Other flutes in Nakai's arsenal have come from the late Hawk Littlejohn (1941–2000), a Cheyenne, and non-Native flute makers Ken Light and Butch Hall. He also continues to make his own woodwinds. "The instruments make themselves essentially," he told *New Visions* magazine. "What I do is either carve or work on tools in a machine shop and turn out the instruments, but how the instrument will sound is entirely determined by where the visual cues are to place the finger holes and sound-producing mechanisms. Even in that sense, they aren't keyed as the flute in the orchestra is. They play whatever pitch or range they might have. Otherwise, I would just go down and buy a recorder."[8]

The scarcity of sheet music, or early recordings, of Native American flute music required alternate sources for material. "I went to meet the nephew of one of the last surviving flute players of the Comanche tribe," said Nakai, "and he informed me that I had to learn vocal music. He said that, when you can sing the music, you could play the flute. I had learned a number of traditional songs of the Kiowa tribe, when I was in the service, and had always wondered why I had spent my time learning to sing them. Here was the answer. I started playing those songs on the flute and, lo and behold, it was very easy."

Nakai's repertoire continued to expand. "I started making my own songs," he said, "and listening to powwow singers. I would ask, 'Do you mind if I turn your song into a flute song?' They would say, 'Well, let us hear it first.' I would play, and then the head singer would go, 'That sounds really good. You can use it.'"

Possessing an undergraduate degree in graphic design and a master's degree, from the University of Arizona, in American Indian Studies, Nakai taught graphic arts at a high school on the Navajo Reservation until 1983, when he found himself one of Arizona's many laid-off teachers. "I was bemoaning my situation," he remembered, "and wondering what I could do now that I couldn't teach anymore. A friend who played with a bluegrass band in Utah said, 'You play flutes on the weekends, why don't you do music?'"

Taking his friend's advice, Nakai purchased a pair of Panasonic cassette recorders. "I recorded fifteen songs on one recorder," he said, "and made copies with the other. I gave them to friends and asked them which songs I should keep."

Paring the list down to a dozen tunes, and making cassette copies, Nakai tried hawking them to trading posts surrounding the Navajo Reservation, in Albuquerque, Durango, Cortez, New Gallup, Farmington, and Flagstaff. "I would walk in with the cassettes," he remembered, "and say, 'Would you take a couple of these—on consignment?' 'What is it?' 'It's American Indian flute music.' 'We've never heard flute music. Is it Japanese?' I would say, 'No, I made them; take a couple. Sell them for ten dollars and I'll take half back.' They'd hem and haw and then they would say, 'Nobody's going to buy flute music,' and send me away."

Faced with disappointing cassette sales, and the scarcity of work on the reservation, Nakai realized he needed to find employment elsewhere. After receiving a $1,500 check for unused vacation time accumulated as a teacher, and talking it over with his wife who was still teaching and needed to finish the school year, he set off to seek work in Phoenix, a little over two hours away.

Although the change of scenery did little, at first, to ease his frustrations, an announcement of an exhibition at the Heard Museum of Native Culture and Art helped to change Nakai's luck. Armed with his cassettes, he headed to the museum and sought out the woman who was organizing the show. When he caught up with her, and asked for permission to sell his cassettes, he met resistance. "She was getting angry," he remembered. "She told me that it was a juried show and that she didn't know me. I tried telling her that I was an unemployed teacher from the Navajo Reservation and I went through my whole history. Then I said, 'I'll buy my own table and come here.' She said, 'You can't do that. Quit bothering me.' I said, 'Okay, but a card table would work.' She said, 'Let me think about it,' and walked away."

When she returned, three hours before the end of the show, the disgruntled organizer told the flute player to set up in a corner of the museum. After placing a blanket atop a card table, and setting up his display of cassettes, Nakai began to play his flute. "People started coming over to listen," he remembered. "I had a really good time for two and a half hours."

Nakai's impromptu appearance represented his first step toward a contract with Canyon Records, for whom he continues to record more than a quarter of a century later. As the exhibition was nearing its conclusion, the label's marketing director, Bob Nuss, approached him. "I've been listening to your music," Nuss told the flute player. "One of my employees bought a cassette. Do you have another?'" Nakai looked into the empty box and said, "No, I'm all sold out and probably won't be able to make any more until next month."

Watching Nuss's smile turn to a frown, Nakai remembered that he did indeed have one cassette left. "I had one in my van," he recalled, "so I ran out to get it. I cleaned off the dust and the beer marks and gave it to him."

Nakai's performance also caught the attention of Heard Museum administrators, who phoned him a few days later, asking if he would be interested in helping to set up a new presentation, *Native People: Our Voices, Our Hands*. Nakai eagerly accepted, and continued to work for the museum for the next three years.

The reversal of fortunes continued. A few weeks after accepting the museum's offer, Nakai was visiting his wife when he got a message that Canyon was trying to reach him. "One of the people from the school came to our apartment," he remembered, "and told me, 'There's somebody from Phoenix calling and they want you to call them right away. They want to talk to you about the flutes that you've been playing. Here's their phone number.'"

Walking to the school where he had taught, Nakai went into the office, picked up the telephone, turned to the bewildered staff, and said, "I know I'm not supposed to be here, but I need to use the phone."

Although he brought the master of his cassette to his introductory meeting with the Canyon executives, Nakai had left it in his car, and heat and humidity had rendered it unplayable. Jack Miller, a veteran engineer of rock-and-roll singles and film soundtracks, came to the rescue. "[Miller] took that master," remembered Nakai, "and fixed it. Then he copied it onto another cassette and said, 'Listen to this.'"

Miller continues to engineer the flute player's recordings. "I don't go to the studio to fix things," said Nakai. "I know that Jack can get the job done. I know nothing about what the general population likes to hear. It's the engineer and the producers who make me sound as good as I do."

"[Our interest in Nakai] had to do with [label founder Ray Boley's] not coming to Native music with fixed ideas about what it was supposed to be," said Robert Doyle, who purchased Canyon Records in 1992. "His approach was very individual, a person-to-person relationship. There was no stereotyping. He could look at somebody, like Nakai, who was outside of what American Indian music was considered to be, and played in a style that was not like the older flute styles, and his response would be, 'I like this music. Let's do something with it.'"

Nakai's early albums intersected with the ascent of the minimalistic, ambient, and spiritually healing New Age music of the 1970s and early '80s. "Paul Horn (1930–2014) essentially started the New Age movement in 1969," said Clint Goss, "after meditating for three months. He took his silver flute and started playing it in the Taj Mahal [in Agra, Uttar Pradesh, India]. [It sounded like] a huge echo chamber. He recorded it and put it out as a whim. People loved it."

Enthusiasts of New Age music embraced Nakai's gentle melodies and atmospheric textures. "The sound [of the flute], the sine-wave pattern of the instrument itself, will move people on different levels," Nakai told Kristine Morris, of *Spirituality & Health*. "There are chakras, or sound centers, in our human body, and, I think, the Native American flute works in a way to effect a kind of healing, a kind of relaxation—a meditative or reflective state. The Native American flute allows me to speak from my soul, from my heart, in a language that can be understood by anyone at any moment in time."[9]

Nakai's music, however, defies categorizing. "My music has nothing to do with New Age," he explained, "but a lot to do with my perspective of being in the world at the moment. Seeing the beauty and even the ugliness of life, you've got to keep your perspective about being a participant in the world as it grows and changes all the time."

Nakai's unprecedented success proved a boon for Canyon Records, who used profits from his albums to become the leading source for new traditional and contemporary American Indian recordings, celebrating its sixty-fourth anniversary in 2015. The label's catalogue includes recordings by powwow Drums, flute players, Tohono O'odham polka (Waila) bands, classical guitarists, round-dance singers, peyote harmonizers, singer-songwriters, and rock bands. "[Nakai's success] allowed us to work with a generation of talented, young Native artists," said Canyon Records producer Stephen Butler, who began working with the label in the mid-1980s. "He was exploring his cultural identity, which was what a lot of musicians were also doing at the same time."

"We were successful in crossing over to the mainstream," added Canyon owner Robert Doyle, "and reaching out to the bigger market. Every retail store was stocking Native music in their music departments. Borders Books came on line, then Best Buy. There was a lot of profitability for all of the Native record labels existing in that economic ecosystem. Cash flows were big enough for retailers to go deeper into the catalogues."

In 1988, with Canyon's encouragement, Nakai began to stretch out, recording an album, *Carry the Gift*, with master guitarist/luthier William Eaton. "The panoramic harmonies of Eaton's guitars, and haunting melodies of Nakai's flute," said the *All Music Guide*, "conjure visions of the mesas, canyons, and plains of the American West."[10]

"[Eaton] expanded my musical world," said Nakai, "and enabled me to add to the tradition of the flute. We met by accident. He heard me play my flutes when I was an artist-in-education and we met again at a conference of people working for the Arizona Commission on the Arts at Central Arizona College. I had heard the sound of his guitars and really liked it. I walked over to him and asked, 'Can you play something in G minor? I'd like to play my flute with your guitar.'"

"We talked about a lot of things," recalled Eaton of their first meeting, "a lot of philosophy. To a large extent, we didn't talk about music as much as we did about ideas and the ways of the world."

During a telephone conversation with Thomas Houlon, director of Phoenix-based arts organization Spirit of the Senses, a few weeks later, Eaton suggested that he and Nakai perform at one of the organization's events. Houlon told the guitarist to put a show together. After telephoning the flute player and getting him to agree, Eaton expanded on the performance. "My partner at the time, Christine, was a dancer," he said, "and we got one of her friends to come and dance with her. We improvised the soundtrack for them."

Eaton and Nakai connected immediately. "Music is a response to what's around you," said Eaton, "and improvised music has a vocabulary that both of us has learned. We respond to each other in the way that birds, animals, the wind, or water would respond. There's a mystical component; it becomes a conduit for people to discover their own roots and apply them in a modern world context."

Nakai was so enthused by the collaboration that he called Ray Boley to tell him about it. With the label owner suggesting that they record an album, the duo was soon in the studio, recording *Carry the Gift* in two three-hour sessions. "There's a sense of space and presence on that recording," said Eaton.

Influenced by the finger style guitar picking of John Fahey, Leo Kottke, and Stephen Stills, Eaton was inspired just as much by the natural environment. "I lived in the desert for a couple of years," he said, "sleeping under the stars every night and discovering my humanity in relation to the more-than-human natural world. Birds have an important role in communicating sound and music. As you listen, you get to know a bird's voicing, phrasing, and language, because they are not only communicating with each other, but also with other animals and humans. Those few years forever changed my concept of music; it became a dialogue with the natural world."

A skilled guitar builder, and cofounder/director of the Roberto-Venn School of Luthiery, Eaton has created a variety of unique stringed instruments. "The instruments come to me in many ways," he explained. "Sometimes, I want the strings to have certain pitches or certain sounds. On other occasions, I see a shape in nature or architecture and think how it could be adapted into an instrument. Many references are historical. I have a whole series of multistringed instruments that I consider contemporary shaman bows. They're inspired by the hunter's singing bow, which many ethnomusicologists consider the first stringed instrument: I have a Lyra harp guitar and an electric harp guitar that incorporate that bow shape."

Joined by percussionist Will Clipman, Nakai and Eaton's collaboration reached its apex in 1995. Their first trio album, *Feather, Stone, and Light*, topped the New Age charts for thirteen weeks. "[Eaton and I] felt that something was missing [as a duo]," said Nakai. "I told him that what we needed was not a drummer, but a percussionist, and he said that he knew this percussionist who lived not too far away."

Eaton and Clipman had already begun playing together. "We met through the Arizona Commission on the Arts," said Eaton, "and became really good friends. I invited him to be in the William Eaton Ensemble. He's an outstanding player, and good percussionists are hard to find. We were looking for somebody whose palette had a lot of variety, not just somebody who could lay down a rhythm. We wanted somebody who could stop on a dime and change direction, apply texture to some areas, and Will is a master of all of it."

"The sound of the Earth as it moves is what I equate percussion to," said Nakai. "If you meditate in a quiet spot, you can hear the Earth as it breathes. That is where, I believe, percussion sound comes from. Being trained by people like [late Nigeria-born percussionist] Babatunde Olatunji, [Clipman] got that philosophy. The three of us have our own awareness of being in the world. Together, we create a painting in sound. There's a canvas above the heads of the audience and we paint with our musical brushes."

Nakai, Eaton, and Clipman's first trio album in nine years, *Dancing into Silence*, scored a Grammy award as "Best New Age Recording of 2010." "Pure intuitive improvisation as it morphs from ethereal ballets to percussion trances," said the *Arizona Network News*.[11]

The unofficial house drummer for Canyon, Clipman has appeared on more than two dozen albums by Indigenous artists, as well as recording with ARC, a trio that he briefly shared with classical guitarist Gabriel Ayala and Native American flutist Vince Redhouse. Along with multi-instrumentalist/composer/producer Amo Chip Dabney and electric bassist, flutist, acoustic guitarist, keyboardist, and vocalist Mary Redhouse, he was a charter member of Nakai's quartet.

Gifted with a five-octave vocal range, uncanny ability to recreate the sounds of birds and animals with her voice, and extraordinary instrumental skill, Mary Redhouse (Diné) is a former accompanist of Joy Harjo, Keith Secola, and blues/ rock vocalist Star Nayea (Anishinaabe). She's collaborated with African American jazz saxophonist, flutist, composer, and poet, Oliver Lake (1942–). A charter member—along with Eaton and Clipman—of the William Eaton Ensemble, a world music band shared with Claudia Tulip (flute and panpipes), Allen Ames (violyra and violin), and Keith Johnson (percussion), Redhouse also plays with violinist/flute player Arvel Bird (Paiute/Scottish), Eaton, and Clipman in a Native-fusion band, Ananeah. She continues to perform with her sister Charlotte and her brothers, Vince, Tony, Lenny, and Larry, as the Redhouse Dancers, an intertribal social dance-and-song group, founded by their father, Rex Redhouse, in the late 1960s.

Nakai has consistently sought new musical forums. "I like to hear how the flute blends with instruments from other parts of the world," he said, "as well as the human voice. I was in Morocco last summer and heard an African griot [oral historian]. I went over to him and said, 'I have been listening to you chant and I want to do something with you onstage that will bring our cultures together.' I told him, 'I'm going to chant in my traditional language and then, I want you to join me in your language. Let's see what we could do.' His chanting was much louder, but we kept the same timbre. We just went on and on and he started crying. When we finished, we hugged each other so tightly. I said, 'It worked.' He said, 'It more than worked. It brought us together.' It's those instances of working with other musicians that are quite important to me."

A quest to unite musical traditions motivated Nakai to record with Japan's Wind Traveling Band in 1994. The resulting album (*Island of Bows*), recorded in Kyoto's Hounji Temple, combined Nakai's flutes with the Japanese *shakuhachi*, an end-blown flute, three-stringed *shamizeen*, and thirteen-stringed *koto*. "Our experiences in music are so similar," he said, "because we sing with our souls

Mary Redhouse (Diné) applies multioctave vocals and instrumental proficiency to a growing of list of projects.
Photo by Craig Harris.

and we share the ability to bring ourselves together in such a way that we're not in conflict. We're singing to God."

Two albums with Tibet-born, and Colorado-based, flute player/vocalist Nawang Khechong—*Winds of Devotion* in 1998, and *In a Distant Place*, two years later—brought Nakai in touch with Buddhist traditions. Raised in India, where he moved with his family following the invasion of Tibet by the People's Liberation Army of China in 1949, Khechong studied meditation and Buddhist philosophy as a youngster, and spent eleven years as a monk, including four years in the Himalayan foothills under the supervision of the Dalai Lama. "It was kind of tricky, having two melodic instruments like the flute," Eaton, who participated in the recording sessions, remembered, "but it worked. [Khechong] was a monk, and he still has plenty of quiet, meditative time, but there's a lot of mirth, humor, and fun in him, too."

An album (*Our Beloved Land*) and world tour with Hawaiian slack-key guitarist Keolamaialani Brockenridge "Keola" Beamer (1951–) provided Nakai with a further opportunity to expand the Native American flute. The great-grandson of a songwriter and hula dancer, and one of two sons of an influential composer, dancer, and educator, Beamer had been half of one of Hawaii's most successful musical acts of the 1970s and '80s, with his brother Kapono, and had written "Honolulu City Lights," the lush, string-laden title track of the duo's best-selling album *Honolulu City Lights*. *Honolulu* magazine placed it at the top of its list of the fifty most important albums of 2004. "I heard [Beamer] and his brother when I was still in the navy," said Nakai. "I really liked their music and the way that they told stories between songs about their heritage and family."

Nakai took the flute to an even higher plateau when he joined Israeli-born Udi Ben-David, cellist with the Philadelphia Orchestra, to improvise on American Indian, Jewish, and Arabic melodies. "The beautiful deserts of the Southwest," said Ben-David, "remind me of southern Israel."

First playing together during a concert that included American Indian and Middle Eastern music and an interpretation of Antonin Dvořák's "American String Quartet," which incorporates Native themes, Nakai and Ben-David went on to record an album (*Voyagers*) and tour the United States in 1997. The climax of the tour came with a concert shared with the Philadelphia Orchestra. "I put together a program about American Indian and African American influences on Dvořák's *New World Symphony*," said Ben-David. "[Nakai] played with me and an ensemble. We had a Native American storyteller narrate it."

Nakai and Ben-David returned to the recording studio in early 2012. "We purposely tried not to take anything from either of our cultures," said Ben-David. "It was a creation of the two of us, an improvised musical dialogue."

Since 1990, when they collaborated on their first duo album (*Natives*), Nakai has periodically re-established his musical partnership with German-born pianist, composer, producer, and New Age pioneer Peter Kater. Their first four albums reached the top twenty on the *Billboard* chart of top-selling New Age recordings. *Migration* received a "Best New Age Recording" award from the National Association of Independent Record Distributors (NAIRD) in 1992.

Silver Wave Records founder and owner James Marienthal had no prior experience with Native music when Kater approached him in the late 1980s. "He wanted to do an album [with Nakai]," remembered the pianist, flute player, and record executive. "I was aware that Nakai's flute music was selling well in the New Age music market, and I was confident that his recording with Peter would fit well with everything else that Silver Wave was doing."

Emigrating from Germany with his parents at the age of four, and settling in New Jersey, Kater studied piano before his eighth birthday. After sharpening his skills with a series of top-forty cover bands in New Jersey and New York, he moved to Boulder, Colorado, at eighteen, and built a following with his improvisational piano playing. Releasing his debut album, *Spirit*, in 1983, he went on to record a series of top-ten contemporary jazz albums.

Inspired by Nakai, Kater began incorporating Indigenous melodies into his music, composing the orchestral score, and playing solo piano, for the thirteen-hour Discovery Channel miniseries *How the West Was Lost* (1993).

Released on the independent Mysterium Music label in April 2014, *Ritual* was Kater and Nakai's first album in a decade. Recorded with Paul McCandless, formerly with the Paul Winter Consort and its world music offshoot, Oregon (reeds), Trisha Bowden (vocals), and Jacques Morelenbaum (cello), the album was, according to *Spirituality & Health*, "deeply satisfying, emotionally moving, and beautifully dynamic."[12]

Nakai joined with New Age/jazz flutist Paul Horn (1930–2014) to record a pair of albums—*Inside Canyon De Chelley* (1997) and *Inside Monument Valley* (1999)—in southwestern caves. "Caverns have sympathetic vibrations," said Eaton, "and resonant peaks. There's a feeling that you're one with the Earth itself, and that it's speaking back to you in your own tongue."

Retaining ties to Western classical music, Nakai composed lighthearted orchestral pieces with two-time Grammy Award–winning producer and arranger Billy Williams and worked extensively with composer James DeMars. He coauthored a book, *The Art of the Native American Flute*, with David P. McAllester and Ken Light, and he played on recordings of DeMar's compositions—*Spirit Horses*, the first concerto composed for Indigenous woodwind, *Two World Concerto*, recorded with the Canyon Symphony Orchestra and the Black Lodge Singers, and an intercultural opera, *Guadeloupe, Lady of the Roses*. "[Working with DeMars] is a link to the serious, or fully composed, music that I've always wanted to do," said Nakai. "I have a whole history of disciplined music behind me. When I perform improvisations, the melodies that I play go by, in my brain, like a long composition."

Formed as part of the "Classical Native" series at the Smithsonian Institution's National Museum of the American Indian, in Washington, D.C., in November 2006, the North American Indian Classical Cello Project brought Nakai together with percussionist Steven Alvarez, Native flute players Timothy Archambault and Ron Warren, and cellist/vocalist Dawn Avery. "Our music, though all very unique, perhaps [comes] from a similar place," suggested Avery in a program booklet for one of the group's concerts, "one of being with nature, with conflict, with reparation, with heart and mind."

In the fall of 2013, Nakai joined with Uganda-born and Oakland, California–based didgeridoo player Stephen Kent and two Mongolians—throat-singer Shinetsog "Shinee" Dorjnyam and *yatag* (twenty-one-string zither) player Munkh-Erdene

Chuluunbat—to create the Earth Sounds Ensemble. Funding for the three-show project came through a grant arranged by Aziz Rahman, president of the Indo-Mongolian Society of New York. "All four musicians draw inspiration from the same source," said Rahman, "the natural environment and the sounds of nature. They have a deep respect for the traditional roots, and they're committed to preserving the culture of their people, but they take the initiative and go beyond the traditions, bridging cultures through their work."

A duo album, *Awakening the Fire*, with Will Clipman, in late 2013, was nominated for a Grammy (in the "Best New Age Recording" category) and led to an "Artist of the Year" NAMMY nomination for Nakai. "The communication between the two creates music they call 'passionate and calm,'" said John Malkin of *Spirituality & Health*. "*Awakening the Fire* is an expression of balanced harmony."[13]

"Subdued soundscapes that resonate beyond the ears," added Asheville, North Carolina's *Mountain Xpress*. "Songs like 'Meeting at Twilight,' 'Invoking the Elements,' and 'Dream Dances' verbally suggest the sense of wonder and earthy tranquility that each piece conjures sonically."[14]

ROBERT MIRABAL

The son of a farmer, Robert Mirabal (1967–), of the Taos Pueblo, expanded the scope of the flute by incorporating musical theater, rock, jazz, hip-hop, world music, and avant-garde influences. Although he met Nakai as a youngster, the only flutist that he knew when he began to play woodwinds at the age of nineteen was Adam Turjillo, "an old man, in his eighties, who lived on the Pueblo and made flutes."

When one of Turjillo's woodwinds was auctioned at a local powwow, Mirabal, who played clarinet, saxophone, piano, and drums in school, made the winning bid, paying with money borrowed from his grandmother. "That's how I got connected to this instrument," said the two-time Grammy-winner and Native American Music Hall of Fame inductee as we sipped coffee in a Burlington, Vermont, hotel, "but the first flute that I played was a clay instrument from South America. I was already prolific; I knew what to do with it."

Bringing the flute that he bought at the auction home, Mirabal took it apart. Carefully studying the instrument's construction, he was soon building woodwinds of his own. It didn't take long before he was going beyond traditional flute making. "I started out as a rock and roller," he said, "so I pushed it really hard—creating my own instruments, my own scales, and my own tonalities."

Raised on the Cheyenne River Indian Reservation in South Dakota, Mirabal grew up speaking Tiwa, along with English and Spanish. "The majority of our experiences were environmental," he recalled. "We [were] immersed in our culture,

Robert Mirabal (Taos Pueblo) builds on Native American flute traditions with musical theater, rock, jazz, hip-hop, world music, and avant-garde influences. *Photo by Craig Harris.*

but it didn't seem so important. It was just the way that we lived, the way that everyone around us lived."

Moving to New York in the late 1980s, Mirabal "spent a lot of time on Ninth Avenue and Forty-third Street." "There were artist apartments in that area," he explained. "Hell's Kitchen—that was some funk. I enjoyed it. I was young and New York seemed to be my city. I loved that there was so much vibrancy and so much competition." Mirabal's experiences in New York broadened his music. For a while, he played with a band that included a keyboardist from Haiti, a drummer from Cape Verde, and a guitarist from Senegal.

Missing the natural environment of the Southwest, Mirabal left New York in the early 1990s, and settled in Taos Pueblo, New Mexico. He soon connected with equally enlightened musicians, including Reynaldo Lujan (Taos Pueblo), a percussionist with whom he would play for a decade. "[Lujan] was dabbling in a lot of things," Mirabel said, "and trying to push the envelope, whether it was with music, art, or his political stance."

Mirabal also developed a musical kinship with Mark Andes (of Spirit and Firefall), a Philadelphia-born bass player he met through singer-songwriter Eliza Gilkyson. "I was spending a lot of time in Santa Barbara, California," he explained, "because I had a girlfriend there. Mark lived close by; I'd visit him and we'd jam. We started working on twenty different pieces at the same time."

Signed by WEA-distributed Warner Western in the early 1990s, Mirabal had already begun experimenting with his music. "I had done a really eclectic album, *Land*, using traditional [American Indian] instruments," he said. "It was very avant-garde. I composed it for [a dance production by Japanese modern dancers] Eiko and Koma [inspired by their trip to New Mexico]. It was weird, but it had a strange brilliancy."

On their first album (*Mirabal*), Lujan, Andes, who had relocated to Taos Pueblo, and Mirabal were augmented by British lead guitarist Andy York and Kenny Aranoff, one of the all-time great session drummers. "I had a band that was world-class," said Mirabal. "They established '80s pop rock. That gave me some profound humbleness. How they expressed themselves was what I wanted to emulate; they knew what they were doing."

Mirabal's neotraditionalism resonated with Native and non-Native listeners. "I was at the right place at the right time," he said. "There was a huge resurgence of Native imagery and a demand for what we were doing. There were very few other people doing it. I was young and I had hair down to my ass. It was a novelty and I just played into it."

"He had a lot of energy," remembered James Marienthal, whose Boulder, Colorado–based Silver Wave Records label has released most of Mirabal's albums since 2001, "and he could certainly be intense at times because he focused so much on his music and art; there was a seriousness to what he was doing. He's such a diverse performer and so gifted, so much fun to work with."

Mirabal's performances were tailor-made for television. In 1988 he participated in a musical spectacular, *Spirit: A Journey in Dance, Drums, and Song*, broadcast by PBS, and coproduced by billionaire Warren Buffet's son, Peter. "It was around the *Dances with Wolves* breakout time," he said.

After broadcasting a musical special, *One World*, which was filmed during Mirabel's world tour with New Age pianist and composer John Tesh in 2000, PBS invited Mirabal to prepare a program of his own. Premiered two years later, *Music from a Painted Cave* spotlighted the flute player's diversity. Some tunes featured solo flute, while others added an electric band (the Rare Tribe Mob), intertribal dancers, cowboy poets, and Hawaiian chanters. "[Mirabal] really broke through when he took that rock energy," said Marienthal, "and turned it into a performance art. He did some of the same rock songs that he had been doing, but brought it back to the traditions with intertribal dancers and drumming. He did everything in that show. He played soulful flute music, sang singer-songwriter-style folk songs, and rocked out."

The exposure gained from *Music from a Painted Cave* propelled Mirabal's career to global proportions. "We were selling out five-thousand-seat theaters," he said. "I had two tour buses, twenty-two musicians and dancers. We were always traveling and being gypsies all over the place. It became crazy. We were doing two-and-a-half to three-hour shows each night. It burned a lot of people out."

A featured player on the 2006 "Best Native American Recording" Grammy-winning album, *Sacred Ground—A Tribute to Mother Earth*, Mirabal scored his own Grammy—under the pseudonym Johnny Whitehorse—for *Totemic Flute Chants* two years later. "Crafted of Native American flute (many that Mirabal makes himself), keyboards, tribal drums, and an array of world music instruments," said Sandra Hale Schulman in *Indian Country Today*, "this enchanting music interprets animal spirits that have the power to transform."[15]

"It was the tail end of the *Music from a Painted Cave* lifestyle," explained Mirabal, "and I started to dabble in computers and keyboards, creating rhythms. [Crediting the album to Johnny Whitehorse] gave me opportunities to collaborate with people and create sounds that I would not have had as Mirabal, the rock-and-roller."

After portraying Tony Lujan, the Taos Pueblo husband of wealthy art patron Mable Dodge Lujan, in the 2009 bio-flick *Georgia O'Keeffe*, Mirabal toured with a one-man show, *Po'pay Speaks*, about the leader of the Pueblo Revolt of 1680. "I don't like film as much as I love theater," he said. "*Po'pay Speaks* comes from creating expression through agriculture. That's who we are—corn people."

In late 2011, Mirabal renewed his collaboration with ETHEL, a New York–based avant-garde string quartet featuring cellist Dorothy Lawson, violinists Cornelius Duffalo and Jennifer Choi, and led by violist/violinist Ralph Ferris, who had been the assistant conductor of the Broadway production of *The Lion King* and musical director of Roger Daltry's 1994 tour, *A Celebration: The Music of Pete Townshend and The Who*. Mirabal and ETHEL first played together as part of a new-wave music festival at the Brooklyn Academy of Music in 2008. "They're an amazing group," said Mirabal. "Too many times, we get stuck in our own genre. Anything out of that realm is bound to be profound. Just getting out of the box is the most important element."

MARY YOUNGBLOOD

Stepping out of the box has also been the key to Mary Youngblood's flute playing. "I'm not playing traditional music," said the Kirkland, Washington–born, and northern California–based, three-time Grammy winner. "They're not Zuni sunrise songs or old Navajo tunes, but my own compositions."

Adopted at the age of seven months by a non-Native family, Youngblood (1958–) grew up as Mary Edwards. "I was very aware [of my Aleut/Seminole heritage] when I was growing up," she said. "I was brown and [my adopted family] was white. My adopted parents, who are both alive, are retired schoolteachers, and we would go to the library and find books about the Aleuts. I only knew only about the Alaskan side of my family, but, later, when I met my birth mother, I discovered that I was Seminole, too."

Raised in mostly Caucasian communities, Youngblood was subject to intense racism. "I was really bullied," she remembered, "and my early childhood was pretty painful. Kids were mean. They would point to me and say, 'She's not your real mommy. Your mommy gave you away.' They were just horrible. I stuck out like a sore thumb, not only in my family, but also in the community. I was very aware of being different, and of being Native, from a very early age."

Music came naturally. By the age of four, Youngblood could pick out tunes on her adopted family's piano. "My adopted parents weren't musical or creative," she said, "and they didn't know that [a four-year-old playing piano] was an unusual thing until friends told them. They tried looking for a piano teacher for me, but couldn't find anyone who would teach [someone so young]."

Performing in her first recital shortly after starting piano lessons at the age of six, Youngblood felt at ease playing in public. "That exposure was awesome," she remembered. "It validated that creative side of me and helped to save my spirit as an adopted young person who was brown in a white world."

Temporarily moving to Tucson, while her adopted father worked on his PhD dissertation and taught at the University of Arizona, Youngblood felt an immediate kinship with the area. "I really fell in love with the desert," she said, "and the beauty of Arizona."

Youngblood's glee, however, quickly turned to sorrow. "It was tough to move around," she reflected. "I had to acclimate to a new community, and it was weird that people thought that I was Hispanic. Thankfully, we didn't stay there too long. I had some racial things happen, which surprises me when I look back. There were many Natives and Hispanic people, but I went to a mostly white school and faced a lot of discrimination. I was chased home from school a lot and beaten up."

Despite the attacks, Youngblood looked forward to the fourth grade. "That's when you could play music," she said. By the time that she joined the school band, however, classical flute was the only instrument left. "You could rent [any instrument]," said Youngblood, "but coming from a frugal family of teachers, I was going to use whatever they had available. If they had had a tuba, I would have been all over it."

The metallic woodwind was, at first, extremely difficult for the youngster to play. "Classical flute is a complicated animal," said Youngblood, who had played piano at six, violin at eight, and guitar at ten. "You play it transversely to the side and you can't see the fingering or the holes. [My adopted parents] tried to discourage me from playing it. They thought it was too complicated. You can't just blow into it. You have to develop an embouchure, but I didn't care; I wanted to be in the band. I just went for it. Whenever my dad would be in class, I'd be at the music department, with a graduate student, taking a private flute lesson."

A turning point in Youngblood's musical growth came with her discovery of Scottish singer, songwriter, and multi-instrumentalist Ian Anderson. Thirty-five years later, the Jethro Tull frontman would add his flute to an instrumental ("Passions to Ignite") on her 2004 album, *Feed the Fire*. "[Anderson] blew the whole flute myth out of the water," she said. "When I was in high school, playing the classical flute was cool because of Jethro Tull. He is still my mentor and muse. I do a lot of embellishments that remind me of him."

Youngblood's enthusiasm made her an important member of the American Trucking Company, the cover band that she joined after moving with her adopted family to Sacramento, California, in 1971. "We were pretty well known," she said. "We did songs by the Doobie Brothers, Chicago, and hits of the '70s. I added classical flute to their rock thing, sang backup vocals, and played a little guitar."

Along with the American Trucking Company, Youngblood had a regular booking at a local club before her eighteenth birthday. "My parents weren't too happy about me hanging out with twenty-year-olds in bars," she said. "I'd tell them that we were going to play at a high school dance, as we headed off to the Holiday House, where the band would sneak me in."

Being in a band was thrilling. "This was different than playing in the high school's marching band or concert band," Youngblood said. "This was people jumping up and down and dancing—a whole other scene. We were playing at this little dive, but to a teenager, it meant 'I'm out in the world now!'"

Married at twenty-three, and soon divorced, Youngblood balanced raising three sons—Benjamin, Joseph, and Christopher—and a daughter, Elizabeth, with living-room jam sessions. "My kids remember weekends filled with music," she said.

Experimenting on a flute at the Native American Crafts Association store, where she worked on the weekends, Youngblood, then in her mid-thirties, found that the techniques developed on classical flute were adaptable to the wooden instrument. "With all of my skill and training," she said, "I was able to do things that hadn't been done before. I hadn't listened to anyone else's flute recordings or hunted down R. Carlos Nakai. I didn't even think of going out and hearing how it was supposed to be played—I just picked it up and went for it."

Improvising on the woodwind as she worked at the crafts shop, Youngblood attracted large crowds with her playing. "It was good for business," she said. "The flute had a quality that drew people. [The manager of the shop] told me to keep playing."

Youngblood's big break came within weeks, when she made a guest appearance on a locally produced PBS TV show, *American Indian Circles of Wisdom*. "It gave me some exposure on a local level," she said, "and allowed me to have a promotional video to give Silver Wave so that they could see what I could do. It was a valuable tool. It was good timing. I was ready. I was prepared. I just knew that I would find the right entity, or it would find me, and that's what happened."

"She sent me a demo tape of her original flute songs," remembered Marienthal. "Joanne Shenandoah had suggested that she send it. As soon as I heard her playing, I knew there was something special about it. She has such a magical touch. It raises the flute to a much higher level. I heard that right away and knew that I wanted to work with her."

Recorded solo in the Moaning Cavern, California's largest single-chamber public cave, in September 1997, Youngblood's debut album, *The Offering*, explored the sonic possibilities of the Native American flute. "The acoustics of playing in such a place—a long, tubular cave—were incredible," she said. "My producer [Marienthal] was concerned that the sound would bounce all over the place. I didn't need to add reverb; it was natural. You could hear the plunks of water as they hit the rocks."

Silver Wave handled Youngblood, the first woman to record an album of solo Native American flute music, with caution. "They wanted to test the market," she said, "and didn't want to add instrumentation [to my first album]. I was devastated because what I had visualized were the kinds of things that I am doing now with full instrumentation."

Releasing a more-arranged album, *Heart of the World*, in 1999, Youngblood lifted the bar even higher with *Beneath the Raven Moon* in 2002, winning a "Best Native American Recording" Grammy and a "Best New Age Recording" NAMMY. "I was in a very romantic place in my life," she remembered, "and thinking about the raven as being like the trickster. As the daughter of an English professor, I love play on words. A raven moon is a moonless night, a dark night. During my concerts, before playing 'Beneath the Raven Moon,' I talk about how, traditionally in some tribes, this instrument was used for courting. I set up an image of a young man playing his flute, playing a special song for his ladylove who follows the music down to the river where they go for a walk, beneath the raven moon, the dark, romantic moon."

Youngblood dedicated the title track of *Beneath the Raven Moon* to her birth mother, who she managed to track down after a two-and-a-half-year search. "It was a very long process," she said. "I wrote to organizations that help adoptees, asking if they had any information. I have a whole notebook of my journey. Ultimately, a secretary with the Chugach Corporation did some research and found the connection. I got a manila envelope in the mail in 1986, and pulled out an extra-long piece of paper folded all up. It was my family tree. I read my grandmothers' names, my grandfathers', my siblings', aunts', uncles', and my mother's name—Nadia. I was overwhelmed."

"When I called my mom in Bothell, Washington," she continued, "I was shaking. Her husband picked up the phone. The first thing that she did was try to explain why she had given me up for adoption. It just broke my heart. That was not why I was calling, but, in her mind, all that guilt and shame came to the forefront. I was just so happy to find her. I had to interrupt and say, 'It doesn't matter.'"

Six months later, Youngblood's adopted parents bought her a plane ticket so that she could meet her biological family. "It was a very emotional roller coaster of a ride," she recalled. "[My mom] had had a really tough life. She had run away from government school in Sitka, Alaska, and ended up in Seattle, where she gave birth to twelve children. It's a long, crazy story."

As she spoke with her birth mother, Youngblood learned that she had been the product of a short-lived affair. "Her husband didn't know that she had had an affair with my father," she said. "He was a commercial fisherman and often out at sea. By the time that he came back from a trip to Alaska, she had had a baby and given it up for adoption. He didn't even know about it until I knocked on the door, but he didn't hold it against her, and there was no weirdness. It was just something that had happened a long time before."

Boosted by the enthusiastic reception received by *Beneath the Raven Moon*, Youngblood took another step forward with *Feed the Fire* in 2003, mixing flute instrumentals with original songs that she sang with Bill Miller and Joanne Shenandoah. "[Miller] recorded his part when he was in Albuquerque to perform at the NAMMY," she said. "The vocables that he put on that song were recorded in his hotel room."

Feed the Fire paid tribute to the women in Youngblood's life. "There are so many," she said, "especially since I found my birth family. I have eight sisters between my birth family and adopted family, and I have two mothers. I am the mother of four, the matriarch of my family, and I have worked hard to keep my family together. There were times when I would work during the week as a childcare provider, and at the crafts gallery on the weekend, and stay up all night working on music. That was the only time that I had to myself. That was the inspiration behind *Feed the Fire*. I would get up after everyone had gone to bed, light a couple of candles, and work on material. It was my time to feed the fire."

Youngblood continued to build on her relationship with her biological mother. "I hand-delivered a copy of *Feed the Fire* to her a week before she died," she said. "It really lifted her spirits. Even after all those years, she still felt that she had to explain why she had given me up. For me, that was a moot point. When I wrote [the title song], I wanted to tell her story in a way that would be beautiful. I wanted her to be proud. The guilt and shame had caused her so many problems. I wanted her to know that it was okay, and that everything had happened the way that it was supposed to happen."

"My sisters told me that she was a different person [when she listened to the song]," she continued. "It lightened the heavy load that she had carried and really did heal her spirit. I talk about her at every concert, and adoptees and birthmothers come up to me afterwards in tears and tell me, 'That's my story.'"

Youngblood continued to deal with deep concerns on *Dance with the Wind*, the recipient of her second "Best Native American Recording" Grammy award. "I was having identity and abandonment issues as an adoptee," she said, "and they were so devastating. They stick with you forever and you become fearful of people leaving you. You sabotage things in order to keep people in your life. For me, *Dance with the Wind* encompassed a lot of challenges: the ending of a relationship and the learning to go with the flow."

A rainstorm near Youngblood's home in Sacramento inspired the title track. "I saw trees thrashing around in a storm," she said, "being plummeted by rain, sleet, hail, and wind. They were really at the mercy of the elements. They were rooted in the ground, and they couldn't go anywhere, but they seemed like they were dancing. I thought, 'Aha, they adapt to the wind, maybe they like to have the rain brush off the dust, maybe it feels good to have the wind shake off those old limbs, maybe I need to learn how to bend and be more pliable during these tough storms in my life.'"

Sacred Place: A Mary Youngblood Collection (2008) compiled tracks from the flutist's previous four recordings. "It looked like the ending of a chapter," she said, "but a lot of that had to do with the timing of the universe and the decisions made by the label."

Youngblood's collection of flutes includes more than 250 woodwinds made of cedar, red oak, pine, redwood, bamboo, cane, alder, and PVC pipe. "Maybe twenty are in concert pitch," she said. "There're a lot of variables involved—temperature, where the flute maker made the flute, where I'm playing it. I put a lot of breath into a flute, and I need wiggle room to push it into tune. With most flutes, I have to play so softly I can't give it that last attack. Then, everything sounds too sharp. I have perfect pitch, so I can really hear when the tone is off; it drives me crazy. Once I started listening to Native flute music, I realized that flutes were hardly ever in pitch; that was the typical sound until R. Carlos Nakai, who was a trumpet player."

With an eye toward her next album, Youngblood is planning a trip to Charlotte, North Carolina, to work on a flute-and-percussion album with Jim Brock (Cherokee). "He's played with Hootie & the Blowfish, Janis Ian, and, most recently, Kathy Mattea," she said, "and he's been producing the Indigo Girls. I've got a lot of new vocal pieces that will just have to wait."

BRYAN AKIPA

Imaginative, genre-bending musicians have dominated the revival of the Native American flute, but some woodwind players have remained committed to the instrument's roots. "[The flute] is a traditional instrument," said flute maker and player Bryan Akipa (Sisseton-Whapeton Dakota), "and there are traditional songs for it."

As a youngster, Bryan Akipa was steeped in powwow music and dance. "My aunts and uncles would try to wear me out [by beating on a powwow drum and making me dance]," he recalled, "but I outlasted them."

Painter, muralist, and teacher Oscar Howe (1915–1983) helped to shape Akipa's aesthetic vision. Born on the Crow Creek Indian Reservation, Howe had overcome childhood sickness, temporary blindness, and a boarding school in Pierre, South Dakota, to become a leader of the American Indian Fine Arts movement. "The first time that I met him, I was in the sixth grade," remembered Akipa. "The next time, I was sixteen. I was doing some illustrations for a program. The third time, I was a senior in high school and studied under him for a semester. Then I went and joined the army. Every leave, I would come back and visit him in his studio. After I got out of the army, I worked with him until he got sick. His art was in a very traditional style that went back to the art of the Dakota."

Akipa's life changed forever when he noticed a wooden flute on a shelf in Howe's studio. "There was no flute tradition at the time," he recalled. "It wasn't like it is today. Much of our culture was made illegal by the government; you could be punished for practicing it."

The first songs that Akipa learned came from the repertoire of Richard Fool Bull (Rosebud Lakota) (ca. 1880s–1976). "[Fool Bull] used to sing at the University of North Dakota's National Music Museum," said Akipa, "where Oscar Howe's paintings were exhibited."

After teaching himself to play, Akipa started to build flutes of his own. "I had no idea how to do it," he said. "The first one took a long time; I couldn't get it to play. My grandmother told me that I should ask her cousins. One knew a lot about the culture and songs, and the other one had played flute when he was younger. He had some old flutes in a trunk, including one that his father had given to him in 1918."

Akipa's art apprenticeship came to a sudden end when Howe succumbed, after a long illness, in October 1983. "I didn't know what to do," he remembered. "I tried studying Fine Arts [at the University of South Dakota], but, with so many white people there, I didn't fit in. I was wondering what to do. My aunt had been a teacher for over thirty years and she encouraged me to go into teaching. I talked to my dad about it. He said that I should listen to my aunt."

Securing a teaching position at the Pierre Indian Learning Center, Akipa spent the next eight years working with youngsters. "I taught kindergarten to the eighth grade art for two years," he said, "Dakota studies for a couple of years, fifth grade for a couple of years, second grade, and kindergarten."

Akipa used the flute to relieve stress in his classroom. "They were the most talented artists that I've ever worked with," he remembered, "but they were, at the same time, the most difficult. Most had been court-ordered to be there for some reason or another. For others, their home life had been impossible."

Word of Akipa's flute playing spread, and he began performing at art shows and museums. "At the Northern Plains Indians Arts Market," he said, "I met [traditional painter and dancer] Jim Yellowhawk (Lakota Sioux/Onondaga/Iroquois). He encouraged me to go into music and art full-time."

On his debut album, *The Flute Player*, released independently in 1993 and reissued by SOAR three years later, Akipa fused the natural sounds of birds and rivers with flute melodies that reached back to the distant past. "People kept asking me if I had a tape," he said. "Kevin Locke told me about a sound studio [Makoché] in Bismarck, so I went there and recorded some music. I was able to work out some deals to pay for it."

Just when it looked like he was on the threshold of success, Akipa's daughter died following heart surgery, two weeks before her sixth birthday. "It was a very sad time," he said. "I went into a very deep depression."

In the decade and a half since, music has helped Akipa find solace. In addition to releasing four additional albums—*Mystic Moments* (1995), *Thunderflute* (1998), *Eagle Dreams* (2001), and *Song of Aspen* (2005)—he's performed as a soloist and with the Lakota Sioux Dance Company. Albums by Peter Rowan, Brulé, and Mary Louise Defender have also featured Akipa's playing.

KEVIN LOCKE

The woodwind's roots remain entrenched in the playing of Kevin Locke (1952–) (Hunkpapa Lakota/Anishinaabe). "I started out by learning the traditional songs, the songs that were once spread throughout the prairies, the woodlands, the Great Lakes area, Northern Plains, and Southern Plains," said the Southern California–born, and Standing Rock Reservation–raised, great-grandson of Mdewakanton Dakota chief Little Crow (1810–1863). "In English, they're called 'courting songs,' but, in the Lakota language, there were different words to describe songs of heartbreak and unrequited love—some of them genuinely romantic."

Locke began playing flute at the age of twenty, eleven years before Nakai's debut. "The baton was passed to me," he said, "by the greatest promulgator of the Native flute, Richard Fool Bull [Lakota]. He was my mentor, the one who got me started."

Many of Locke's compositions pay homage to White Buffalo Calf Woman, who, according to oral tradition, presented the Lakotas with seven ritualistic ceremonies—the Keeping of the Soul, the Inipi (sweat lodge), the Hanblecia (vision quest), the Sun Dance, Making Relatives, Puberty Ceremony, and Throwing of the Ball—and the smoking of the Canupa Wakan, or sacred pipe. "She's considered the revelator," explained Locke. "She established social laws, which change according to the contingencies of the current times, but she also established spiritual laws, which are immutable."

Locke had begun to build his reputation as a flute player when Arlo Good Bear (Mandan/Hidatsa) taught him the hoop dance, a traditional storytelling dance in which as many as fifty hoops twist and turn to symbolize animals, abstract shapes, and other elements of a story. Locke's hoop dancing incorporates speed and agility as he maneuvers hoops into the shapes of birds, animals, butterflies, flowers, trees, the stars, and the sun. "It requires a lot of training," he said. "I ran four miles today, five yesterday. I do weight training, too."

Since 1983, Locke has recorded extensively for Bismarck, North Dakota–based Makoché Records. "Kevin had some cassettes [of flute music] from the Library of Congress," remembered Makoché co-owner David Swenson. "Frances Densmore recorded them in the early 1900s. He wanted to use them for his master's thesis and asked if I could enhance the sound. I worked on them as fast as I could."

Locke's commitment to tradition was encouraged by his mother, Patricia Locke (1928–2001), a highly respected educator who was instrumental in the preservation of the Lakota language. A devotee of the Baha'i faith for the last ten years of her life, she served as an officer of the national governing body of the Baha'i community in the United States. The National Women's Hall of Fame would induct her posthumously. "She was a master of the science of sociability," recalled her son, "and very persuasive. She had a great skill for bringing people together."

Sharing her devotion to Baha'i, Locke continues to follow his mother's footsteps. He has served as a cultural ambassador for the U.S. Information Service since 1980, and he was a delegate to the Earth Summit in Brazil in 1992. Four years later, he performed and spoke at the United Nations Habitat II Conference in Turkey. "Our ancestors had prayers, dreams, visions, hopes, and aspirations," he said. "We can express their prayers and hopes through our music and the way that we live our lives."

KEITH BEAR

For Keith Bear (ca. 1960–), of Mandan and Hidatsa heritage, the flute provides a way to converse with the natural environment, "I'll sit by a river and play," said the Fort Berthold, North Dakota–based father of eleven. "I'll hear birds and try to make that sound—the doves, the owls, a loon, or a meadowlark—on my flute. People ask me how I make a trill. I tell them, 'That's what a bird does.' 'How do you bend a note?' 'That's what the wind or a wolf does.' I'm just imitating nature."

A descendent of Chief Bullseye, the adopted father of Sacagawea, the Lewis and Clark Expedition's translator and guide, Bear inherited his love of music from his father, who played with Tommy Dorsey and Glenn Miller in the 1950s. "He could play anything," Bear said, "guitar, bass, banjo, fiddle, piano, tuba, and trumpet."

Prior to playing the flute, Bear remembers being "pretty ripped up." "I was into drugs and alcohol," he said, "a mess. I went through a tough divorce, hit the bottom, and stayed there for four years." The serenity of childhood had ended before Bear's seventh birthday. "My father passed on," he said, "and my mother had a drinking problem. [My brothers, sisters, and I] were placed [with foster families]. In those days, they would not send you to live with an Indian family. They'd place you with white people, and—I don't know what the idea was—you could only stay for three, six, or nine months before they'd move you again."

Joined by one of his ten sisters, Bear ran away from their foster home and headed back to the reservation. "I had never been to that part of town," he remembered. "It was on the other side of town—the east side—where white people lived, but as soon as a woman took us to the playground, I knew where we were. I waited until she took her eyes off us. As soon as she did, I grabbed my sister's hand, and we took off and ran home. I could see that woman watching us. We finally ran up the block where we lived. She watched us go right to our house. Soon they came with their little black car and picked us up. A lady with blue hair, a social worker, came and got us and took us to another place."

Over the next twelve years, Bear, whose Mandan name—Omashi Ryu Tã— translates as "Northern Lights" or "He Who Makes the Sky Burn with Great Flame," lived with fourteen non-Native families. "With some, I was just a farm-hand," he said. "There were some who I wouldn't even turn my head to spit in their direction, they treated me so bad. I got wicked beatings from a couple of those people. I had other [foster parents] whom to this day I still call 'Mom' and 'Dad.' I have brothers and sisters whom I love dearly, because they treated me so good."

Doc Tate Nevaquaya's son, Sonny, provided Bear with his first flute. "We worked together in the oil fields," Bear remembered. "I watched him make it, and then I heard him play it. I said, 'I want to buy that from you.' A few days later, he came back and said, 'Your wish has come true. You could have it if you could play it.' I offered him cash, four hundred dollars, and he said, 'No.' I laid this quilt on the floor with a bunch of feathers and said, 'This is the best that I have. You could have whatever you want.' He picked up some feathers, shook that blanket, and everything went flying. I thought he was offending me and being rude. I looked up at him. I was ready to fight. He said, 'Well, you said I could have whatever I want.' I didn't know what to say. The flute was lying on the floor. I picked it up and carried it for a couple of years before I even tried to play it."

Relocating to Flagstaff, Arizona, after the closing of the oil field, Bear re-assessed his life, and he has not had a drink in the decade and a half since. "I had my daughter and my son there," he said, "and I didn't want them to see me in that shape. I wanted to sober up. The only thing that I could think of doing was going up on a hill, by myself, and praying the Indian way. I took the flute with me. My grandparents told me that it was a sacred branch. It heals people."

Unfamiliar with the traditional flute repertoire, Bear taught himself to play. "My first song was 'Itsy Bitsy Spider,'" he said. "I remember my family telling me that the spider was a warrior, a tricky guy, but powerful. They're just like human beings. They come in all colors—red, white, black, brown. They're fat, skinny, hairy, and bald. They're ugly and they're beautiful. They're amazing."

Bear's flute melodies resonated with patients that he encountered as a physician assistant, at the Flagstaff, Arizona, Medical Center. "I worked with people who had gotten into bad accidents in the desert or the Grand Canyon," he said. "They were all bandaged up with pulleys all over the place. I knew they were hurting. I only knew one song, but I improvised and made something up on the spot. It was soothing. [The hospital] asked me to come back."

Bear further observed the flute's potential while teaching a karate class. "I played while students did a relaxation exercise," he remembered, "and I could see them moving, swaying a little bit, as I played. I could see them close their eyes. Some would make their fingers into little circles like yoga. Some would cry. They'd come up to me afterwards and say, 'I've been thinking about this'; 'I've been thinking about that'; 'I just lost a loved one'; 'You touched my heart.' I could see that power. To bring out tears is part of the healing process. The water of life comes from the human being and goes back to the earth."

Guided by his uncle, Carl "Blacky" Whitman, Sr., Bear was soon making woodwinds of his own. "[My uncle] was a tribal council chairman on our reservation, a very well educated man who taught at Harvard University." Bear said, "He could use White Man words and tear you apart. He'd curse you and make you smile about it and nod in agreement. He was a wonderful man."

In the early 1990s, when his uncle was invited to participate in a buffalo ceremony at the Smithsonian Institution's Folklife Festival, Bear accompanied him to Washington, D.C. "[My uncle] heard me playing [during the ceremony]," he remembered, "and he asked me if I knew a particular song. He sang this little piece of it, and I said, 'Yeah.' He said, 'OK, play it for me.' I had never tried that song. I was just improvising before that—I only had five songs—but over the next few days, I kept thinking about it. When I found the notes, I went back to that big ballpark. There were hundreds of people walking around. I started playing a couple of songs, and then I broke into that song. Uncle Carl was with a couple of people on my right. He leaned forward, nodded his head, and pointed. He recognized the song. It made me feel good."

Upon his return to North Dakota, Bear visited his uncle. "When an elder asks you to come to see them," he said, "it's a big thing. I took some groceries, some tobacco, a little bit of money, and went to his place in Lucky Mound. We walked around his house and he said, 'I want to show you something.' He handed me this flat piece of wood and a pencil. 'Here, mark that.' He showed me how to hold my fingers. 'Put your hand right here and put your finger there.' I marked it wherever he told me. We drilled it out. He gave me a knife and we cut it out. I did the side with the holes and he did the other side. We let it sit for a couple of days. We'd eat and sleep and come back to work on it. After three days, we had it all sanded and rounded. We tied it together with leather and tried it—to hear that first note was exciting."

Bear's aunt Naomi Black Hawk offered encouragement. "She said, 'Those [flutes] are really pretty when you put those beads on them,'" he recalled, "'but they're sacred instruments. They touch the spirit of people. When the old people hear that sound, they become young again. When children hear it, they can have dreams of being somebody.'"

At first, Bear's flute making left him frustrated. "Whenever I'd make flutes that didn't sound like the flute that I made with my uncle," he said, "I'd throw them into a bucket. I would take them to the river and burn them. They smelled good, kept the mosquitoes away, and attracted the fish. When I went back to visit my uncle, he said, 'I've heard that you've been making flutes.' I said, 'Yeah, but, Uncle, it's crazy. I show the flutes that I have hanging on my wall to people, and they turn around, look at that bucket with the ones I don't like, and say, 'What about that one?' Then, they want to buy it. He said, 'What's the matter with that?' I answered, 'It doesn't sound like yours,' and he said, 'Do you sound like me when you sing? Do you sound like your grandmother? These are spirits—you have to remember that. They're not just pieces of wood. They sing for you.'"

JOSEPH FIRE CROW

"Our flutes come from the Earth," explained Joseph Fire Crow (1965–), Cheyenne. "We look for the hardwood—not the limbs or the main trunk, but the hardwood. We ask a tree for permission to use its wood. Then we give the heart of that tree a new voice. We split it into two pieces, carve our flute, and it goes back together. The true connection is heard, and, for people who are aware of their environment and where they come from, their own history, it really touches them."

Raised on the Northern Cheyenne Reservation in southeast Montana, Fire Crow endured a difficult childhood. "It was a very poor life," recalled the Connecticut-based, multiple-NAMMY recipient. "Terrible things were always happening—not just rampant alcoholism, but domestic violence and police brutality too."

The sound of the woodwind helped to ease tension. "I'd hear flute music late at night," Fire Crow recalled, "and become unafraid about the uncertainty of reservation life. The sound healed my heart. It was an awakening from the fear and uncertainty to a place where I felt that I belonged."

A transcription of the oral history of Fire Crow's grandfather, John Stands-in-Timber, as told to anthropologist Margot Liberty, was published as *Cherokee Memories* in 1956. "When you hear stories through oral tradition," Fire Crow explained, "they're still vibrant and strong, even today. They connect to our environment, to the Earth, and to all of us who are in that circle."

Forcibly removed from his childhood home shortly after his ninth birthday, Fire Crow grew up with a non-Native Mormon family. "We weren't allowed to listen to rock and roll," he said, "but I was exposed to a lot of big-band, classical music, and world music. I remember falling in love with Herb Alpert and taking

Joseph Fire Crow (Cheyenne) balances solo Native American flute recordings with fully arranged productions.
Photo by Bob Magee, courtesy Joseph Fire Crow.

on the trumpet in school band. At the same time, I yearned for the sound of the meadowlark and the magpie. There was this flip-flop thing going on. It made me a strong person. I had to make adjustments in both places."

Discovering the Native American flute during his senior year of high school in 1977, Fire Crow became enchanted with the instrument. He became further immersed in his Native heritage during a music class taught by the Taos Pueblo flute player, and adjunct professor of music, John Rainer. "I learned four traditional songs," he remembered, "an intertribal song, a lullaby from the Hopi, a Navajo song, and a round-dance song."

With his adopted parents encouraging him to become a priest, Fire Crow spent three-and-a-half years studying at Brigham Young University in Provo, Utah. "It was a wonderful opportunity," he said. "With it, came the theology and the gospel of the Mormon Church and I became immersed in it."

Fire Crow expanded his repertoire as a member of the Leymanite Choir, an Indigenous student choir that took its name from the Mormon word for Native people. "It was an eye-opener for me," he recalled. "Blending chants with a piano or playing a powwow drum with a jazz beat; there was always something new. We listened to a lot of country music and crossed over to that too."

A year before graduation, Fire Crow began to question his commitment to the church. "My friends were all leaving on a mission," he remembered, "and I went to my bishop and told him, 'I don't feel right about this.' He kept telling me to pray about it. Finally, I said, 'You know what, I truly don't believe in this church and I want to leave.' They excommunicated me for having 'an unforgiving heart,' but that was all right with me. On the night of excommunication, I felt this immense weight lifted off my shoulders; I felt free."

Releasing a pair of independent albums, *The Mist* (1992) and *Rising Bird* (1994), and a self-titled album, with Makoché, in 1995, Fire Crow broke through in 2000 with *Cheyenne Nation*, a rich mix of traditional and contemporary influences. His fifth outing, *Legend of the Warrior*, in November 2003, fared even better, and he received a "Songwriter of the Year" NAMMY and a "Best Flutist" Indian Summer Music Award. "We picked it up a notch," he said, "and I worked with a band in the studio. We had Brazilian percussionist Jovino Santos Neto, guitarist Jon Nyrborg, bassist John Scalia, drummer Dale Heib, and [Makoché co-owner and president] David Swenson on additional percussion and keyboards."

With his next outing, *Red Beads*, Fire Crow returned to his roots. "I wanted to make it more authentic," he said, "without as much keyboard in the background. I went to my elders and asked for permission to start the project. I wanted to sing Cheyenne songs; half of the album is flute playing and the other half is singing."

Fire Crow returned to more-contemporary music with the heavily electrified *Face the Music* in 2010. "I want [my music] to be tight," he said, "and I want the transitions to flow. I want to be able to tell a story. The best advice that was ever given to me came from [jazz musician, world music multi-instrumentalist, and composer] David Amram, who told me that beautiful music is about knowing when to play and when not to. I knew exactly what he was talking about; they were simple words but they said a lot."

Fire Crow's composition, *Symphony No. 2: Parmly's Dream*, cowritten with classical composer James Cockey, recounted a Cherokee legend about the flute's origin. It was premiered by the Billings Symphony Orchestra in September 2002, and the Cape Cod Symphony and the Waltham, Massachusetts, Symphony subsequently performed it as well. Cockey's album, *Signature*, with the composition as its centerpiece, scored a "Best Instrumental Recording" NAMMY. "It's twenty-seven minutes long," said Fire Crow. "[Artistic director and conductor] Jung-Ho Pak guided us through the whole thing. I had to memorize all of my parts. This was the very first time, as far as I know, that that legend had been the subject of a symphony. It has spoken word, drumming, and the Cheyenne language, as well as the flute."

DOUGLAS BLUE FEATHER

Douglas Blue Feather (Douglas Bunnell) has tapped the woodwind for its healing abilities. With fourteen albums since his debut in 1998 with *Seventh Fire*, the drummer-turned-flute-player has used the atmospheric melodies of his woodwind not only to celebrate his Cherokee heritage, but also as a tool for relieving stress. "The flute is considered a heart instrument," he said. "Its music is soothing, relaxing, and meditative. People tell me that it touches them in a heartfelt way and that it has a spiritual meaning for them."

Blue Feather recorded with the rock band Magic Days in the early 1980s, but he had been away from music, working for the Dayton, Ohio, police department, for a decade and a half when he noticed some flutes on a shelf in a music store. "I inquired about what they were," he recalled, "and the salesman demonstrated one. I was immediately attracted to it, as so many people are the first time that they hear it, and I bought it."

Teaching himself to play by listening to albums by R. Carlos Nakai and Douglas Spotted Eagle, and quickly going on to create his own melodies, Blue Feather balanced his police work with performances at local powwows, outdoor festivals, and nursing homes. Off-duty head and eye injuries forced Blue Feather to leave the police department in 2000, but he had already taken the first steps to resurrecting his musical career. "I had my first two CDs—*Seventh Fire* and *Arrival*—out when I was injured," he said. "When the disability came and I left the police department, it opened the door to pursuing music full-time again."

Blue Feather's recordings alternate between solo outings and more-arranged productions. "If I'm playing solo flute," he explained, "I just want to close my eyes and improvise. A lot of my music is more contemporary, though. I like to use keyboards, guitars, drums, and bass guitars. Natives don't just play drums and rattles. We're modern people working with modern sounds while still trying to keep the spirit of Native music."

Blue Feather has been collaborating with classical guitarist Danny Voris since 2009. Their debut CD, *Rollin' Like Thunder*, reached number eleven on the international New Age charts and scored a "Best New Age CD" award from the Coalition of Visionary Resources (COVR), a nonprofit organization dedicated to supporting independent retailers, manufacturers, distributors, wholesalers, and publishers of futurist books, music, and merchandise. The duo renewed their collaboration with *Earth Songs: Music for Meditation and Relaxation* in April 2011.

MICHAEL GRAHAM ALLEN

Among the first non-Natives to master the Indigenous woodwind, Alabama-born Michael Graham Allen learned about the instrument by studying artifacts in museums and private collections. Meeting "Doc" Payne in 1981, he continued to study with the anthropologist and flute maker until Payne's passing in 2004. Allen's woodwinds include the first pentatonic, multikeyed, and bass Plains-style flutes. Forming a New Age/electronica duo, Coyote Oldman, in 1986 with Barry Stamp, a classically trained flutist he had met five years earlier at an Oklahoma City fair, he continued to spread the popularity of the Indigenous woodwind, selling nearly a million copies of their albums, including *Tear of the Moon* and *Night Forest.* NPR producer and host of the music show *Echoes* John Diliberto described it as "A sound that could have come from some mythical gathering in a prehistoric kiva or a cyberspace meeting twenty minutes into the future."[16]

◇◇◇

The popularity of the Native Americana flute continues to grow. "There are hundreds of flute circles," said Clint Goss. "It's a social thing, and there's a correlation with community drum circles. My wife and I have traveled extensively around the world and, when we've gone to developing countries, we've seen everybody playing music. It's not about performance but about the whole family, and community, getting together."

O. W. Jones could recall only "a dozen or so" flute makers in the 1970s, but that number has multiplied exponentially. One Yahoo newsgroup for flute makers includes more than 3,600 registered members. To differentiate between products—including woodwinds—made by American Indians and those made by non-Natives, the U.S. Congress passed the Indian Arts and Crafts Act in 1990. Augmented by an amendment a decade later, it made it a felony to sell art or craftwork as "Native American" unless it had been created by a member of one of the country's 562 federally recognized tribes, bands, nations, pueblos, and Native villages. Non-Native flute makers have subsequently labeled their instruments as "Native American style flutes."

Greek/Italian-American flutist and composer Gary Stroutsos believes that it's a matter of respect. "Some of the elders recognize what I've done," he said, "and that means a lot. Would you rather have a New Age Grammy nomination, a *Billboard* Critics' Choice award, or an eighty-six-year-old matriarch of the tribe telling you that your music reminds her of relatives from days gone by? I think the answer is obvious."

Influenced by American jazz flutists, including Herbie Mann, Rahsaan Roland Kirk, Yusef Lateef, Paul Horn, Frank West, Frank Moody, and Charles Lloyd, Stroutsos was a student of African-American jazz and classical flutist James Newton. Relocating to Seattle in 1978, he was taken under the wing of Afro-Cuban flutist Roland Lozano, and his son, Danilo, and Cuban conga player Mongo Santamaria.

Starting out with a cedar flute, made by Clayton Brascouple (Mohawk), that his mother purchased for him in a tourist shop in Santa Fe, New Mexico, Stroutsos turned his focus to the Indigenous woodwind. His discography now includes improvisations based on traditional Mandan/Hidatsa, Zuni, Dakota, Diné, and Taos Pueblo melodies and his flute playing furnished much of the soundtrack of Ken Burns's PBS documentary *Lewis and Clark: Journey of the Corps of Discovery.* "I have a way of bringing the past to life," he said. "You can hear the roar of the river and the blowing of the wind in my playing and it brings tears to your eyes."

3 TRIBAL VOICES

"We look to our songs for healing, protection, storytelling, and acknowledgment to all life forms; they establish our relationship to what's greater than us."

—Radmilla Cody (Diné/African American)

From the call-and-response singing of the Eastern Woodlands to the high-pitched, octave-jumping chants of the Great Plains, American Indians were singing long before the First Encounter. "Song nerves the warrior to deeds of heroism and robs death of its terrors," reported Alice Fletcher to the Peabody Museum of American Archaeology and Ethnology in 1893. "It speeds the spirit to the land of the hereafter and solaces those who live to mourn. Children compose ditties for their games and young men, by music, give zest to their sports. The lover sings his way to the maiden's heart and the old man tunefully evokes those agencies, which can avert death."[1]

"There are songs made by the mind of man to please the ear," Dakota elders Huhuseca-ska (White Bone), Zintkala Maza (Iron Bird), and Mato-Nakin (Standing Bear) told Natalie Curtis Burlin, "and songs that come in dreams or in visions through the spirits from Wakan-Tanka."[2]

Songs, prayers, and rituals provided the foundation of tribal ceremonies. According to Henry Rowe Schoolcraft (1793–1864), author of a six-volume study of Native legends, rituals, and day-to-day life, and BIA agent to the Upper Great Lakes tribes, "The priests and prophets have, more than any other class, cultivated their national songs and dances and may be regarded as the skalds and poets. They are generally the composers of the songs, and the leaders in the dance ceremonies, and it is found, that their memories are the best stored, not only with the sacred songs and chants, but also with the traditions and general lore of the tribes."[3]

"The [Diné] must never make a mistake or miss a word in singing any sacred chant," reported Burlin. "If he does, the singing must stop, for its good has been blighted. . . . The [Diné] sing a Hozhonji song to purify or bless himself or others; or he will sing in order that his flocks and herds may thrive. If he makes no mistake, blessings will follow and evils will be warded off."[4]

Songs were important to one's personal journey. During their vision quest, Kiowa men hoped to acquire new songs. Cherokee boys and girls would sit on a tree stump, blindfolded and alone, waiting for a spirit—usually some kind of anthropomorphic animal—who would teach them special power songs. "My rite of passage was standing in a fierce storm at the age of nine," remembered Darlene Doll Dotson (Cherokee) of the history-based Facebook page Strong and Free Warriors. "[I was] sleep- and food-deprived, but I learned much about courage and endurance."

Songs provided Christian missionaries with a powerful tool in their evangelizing efforts. Arriving in New Mexico's Zuni territory in 1629, Franciscan Fray Rogue de Figueredo founded missions in Pueblos Hawikuh and Halona. In addition to preaching from the Bible, he instructed Natives in Gregorian chant, along with counterpoint, bassoon, and organ. Figueredo's work came to a sudden halt in 1632, when a group of Apache Indians, angered by the conquistadors' brutal treatment, attacked the Pueblo Hawikuh mission and killed him, along with two other priests. It was a temporary setback. Within a little more than a decade, the British-born Puritan minister John Eliot (1604–1690), the "Indian Apostle," was leading converted Natives in Nontaum (Newton), Massachusetts, as they sang hymns in the Algonquin language. Eliot's Algonquin translation of the catechism in 1646 would be the first book published in a Native tongue. His translation of the New Testament would follow in 1661, and the Old Testament two years later. Credited with the conversion of more than 1,100 Natives, Eliot would help to establish fourteen "Praying Indian" communities in eastern Massachusetts.

The Tahlequah, Oklahoma–based Cherokee National Youth Choir continues to use Christian hymns to preserve the Cherokee language. "It gives us a way to get youngsters interested in their language," said choir coordinator and language teacher Kathy Sierra. "We quit speaking it in our homes. Our children started going to English-speaking schools and there were intermarriages. I don't think they meant to [forget the language]. It just happened."

"We're not allowed to sing certain Cherokee songs outside of the stomp circle," added choir director Mary Kay Henderson, "but many Cherokees are familiar with the [Christian] hymns. European missionaries had a very big influence, and there were missionaries who married Cherokee women and learned the language."

Performing as Rainsong since 2000, Terry Wildman (Ojibwe/Yaqui) and his wife, Darlene (Irish American), interweave tribal traditions and Christian spirituality, setting biblical themes to contemporary pop arrangements accented by Native chanting and hand drums. "I try to write songs that Indians, no matter the tribe, can relate to," said Wildman, the Detroit-born, and Arizona-based, self-described "chief" of the nonprofit organization Rain Ministries and author of *Sign Language: A Look at the Historic and Prophetic Landscape of America.* "But I also try to write in a way that the dominant culture can also get. [My songs] help Natives to understand Christianity and Christian people to understand the Indian way of seeing the world. I want to bring people together in reconciliation and see walls come down."

Songs are essential to the all-night healing ceremonies of the Native American Church (NAC). Popularized by Quanah Parker (ca. 1845–1911), war chief of the Kwahadi Comanches of the Staked Plains, the last band to surrender in the South Plains war of 1874–1875, NAC now counts more than a quarter of a million devotees. "Singing occupies about sixty percent of the Church's devotional ritual," said retired anthropology professor Jay Fikes. "Each of about twenty-five worshippers has ample opportunity to sing to the accompaniment of a gourd rattle and small drum that is pounded rapidly. . . . Worshippers sing, drum, pray, meditate, and consume peyote, all night."[5]

"Members give an account of their past sins," said longtime University of Colorado anthropologist Omer Call Stewart, "and several of the members sing in a minor strain a very weird chant. During the singing, a number of the members hold a gourd in their hands which is shaken to the time of the singing and a little drum is beaten in rapid time."[6]

"Each male participant sings a set of four solo songs," added former University of Chicago associate professor James Sydney Slotkin, "accompanied, on a water drum, by the man on his right. The singing continues from the time of the starting song [when it begins] to that of the morning water song [at dawn]; the number of rounds of singing depends upon the amount of men present. On most occasions, there are four rounds, so that each man sings a total of sixteen songs."[7]

Founded in 1966, Taos, New Mexico–based Indian House Records was one of the first labels to document the NAC's peyote songs. "At first, all peyote music sounded alike to me," admitted Indian House founder Tony Isaacs. "[All of the singers] have a water drum and a rattle, and they all play the same style of song. I recorded some of it, but it never really talked to me."

An opportunity to attend an NAC meeting provided a different perspective. "It was a wonderful experience," recalled Isaacs, "very powerful. They say that when someone goes in for the first time, you want it to be a good meeting. It colors their experience from then on. I began to understand the music, but it took a lot of listening. Now, when I hear good peyote singing, it grabs me by the throat.

I just love it. It's like developing any language. When you begin to acquire the vocabulary, the words start to mean something."

Scottsbluff, Arizona–born Verdell Primeaux (1966–) (Oglala Yankton/Ponca) has been harmonizing with Johnny Mike (Diné) as Primeaux and Mike since 1990. The duo brought the NAC's "healing song" tradition to the international stage. Their seventh album, *Peyote Songs of the Native American Church*, received a New Age Music Award and a NAMMY as "Best Traditional Native American Album of 1998," while their eleventh outing, *Bless the People—Harmonized Peyote Songs* (2002), scored a "Best Native American Recording" Grammy and a "Best Traditional Album" NAMMY in 2002. Robbie Robertson's *Music for the Native Americans* (1994) and *Contact from the Underworld of Redboy* (1998) featured their harmonies, gourd rattles, and water drums. The son of noted peyote singer Francis Primeaux, Sr., with whom he recorded four albums in the 1980s, Verdell Primeaux, who grew up on the Pine Ridge Reservation, is descended through his mother from chiefs Red Cloud (1822–1909) and Crazy Horse (ca. 1840–1877).

Performed by residents of the Uintah-Ouray Reservation in Utah in 1913, the first opera cowritten by an American Indian, *The Sun Dance*, featured a score by Brigham Young University music professor William F. Hanson and a libretto and songs by Gertrude Simmons Bonnin—Zitkala-Ša, or "Red Bird" (1876–1938). An esteemed Nakota author and Native rights activist, Bonnin taught at the Carlisle Industrial Boarding School—which she described as "a miserable state of cultural dislocation"—between 1899 and 1901. She would become secretary/treasurer of the Society of American Indians and editor of the society's journal, *American Indian Magazine*, in 1916. Five years later, she would organize the National Council of American Indians. The New York Light Opera Guild would restage *The Sun Dance* at the 1,761-seat Broadway Theater in 1938. "The opera does not depict the Indian in the dime novel fashion familiar on stage and screen," said Edward Ellsworth Hipsher in *American Opera and Its Composers*. "It is a sympathetic portrayal of the real Indian in a conscientious attempt to delineate the manners, the customs, the dress, the religious ideals, the superstitions, the songs, the games, the ceremonials—in short, the life of a noble people too little understood."[8]

Muskogee, Oklahoma–born mezzo-soprano Barbara McAlister (1941–) has sung with the Houston Symphony Orchestra and with opera companies in Alaska, New Mexico, and Colorado. She also spent a decade with the Flensburg, Germany, Opera Company. She sang in Cherokee, Chippewa, and Winnebago in Linder Chlarson's musical adaptation of Robert J. Conley's novel *Mountain Windsong* in 1995; received a Cherokee Medal of Honor for "dedication to the promotion of the Cherokee language"; and recorded an album of classically arranged Cherokee lullabies, *Songs of the Nightingale*, with arranger/pianist Timothy

Long (Muskogee Creek) in 2010. "There's nothing as exhilarating as being on a horse," said McAlister, "galloping along the roadway. Singing is that way, too."

The first woman to sing with a big band in the jazz world, Mildred Rinker Bailey (1907–1951), of Couer d'Alene and Irish descent, was one of the most successful vocalists of the pre-World War II–era, fronting orchestras led by Paul Whiteman, Eddie Lang, Frankie Trambauer, and her third husband, Red Norvo. Harmonies on her late 1920s and early '30s solo recordings were sung by the Rhythm Boys, featuring her brother Al Rinker, Harry Barris, and future crooning superstar, Harry Lillis "Bing" Crosby, who would credit Bailey with launching his career. Subsequent releases under Bailey's name featured the Dorsey Brothers, Benny Goodman, and members of the Count Basie Band. "She was the vocalist to beat," said Julia Keefe (Nez Perce), a Spokane, Washington–based jazz singer who has been spearheading a campaign to have Bailey inducted into the Jazz Hall of Fame. "There was a time when she was the most popular jazz vocalist, more popular than Billie Holiday or Ella Fitzgerald."

American Indians have played an often-overlooked role in the blues. Mississippi Delta blues pioneer Charley Patton (1891–1934) and David "Honeyboy" Edwards (1915–2011) were both Choctaw. Born on a reservation near Tulsa, Oklahoma, Lowell Fulson (1921–1999) was Creek. Scrapper Blackwell (1903–1962) was Cherokee, as is Chicago bluesman Eddie "The Chief" Clearwater, aka Eddie Harrington (1935–).

Country music also reflects Indigenous roots. "The King of the Cowboys," Roy Rogers (Leonard Franklin Slye) (1911–1998), and "the Hillbilly Shakespeare," Hiram King "Hank" Williams (1923–1953), counted Choctaw among their ancestral roots. Kitty Wells (Ellen Muriel Deason) (1919–2012), the first woman to score a chart-topping country hit—"It Wasn't God Who Made Honky Tonk Angel"—in 1952, claimed Cherokee ties, as do Willie Nelson (1933–), Loretta Lynn (1932–), her sister Crystal Gayle (1951–), Billy Ray Cyrus (1962–), and his daughter Miley (1992–). Country music's "reigning queen," Carrie Underwood (1983–), professes partial Muscogee Creek heritage.

Popular music resonates with the spirit of Indigenous America as well. Cherokee and African American roots converge through vocalist/actor Della Reese (Dellareese Patricia Early) (1931–) and the late sultry songstress Eartha Kitt (1927–2008). Las Vegas's "Mr. Entertainment," Wayne Newton (1942–), is the product of a part-Powhatan father and a part-Cherokee mother. Elvis Presley (1935–1977) was the great-great-great-grandson of full-blooded Cherokee Morning White Dove. A founding member of Frank Zappa's Mothers of Invention, Jimmy Carl Black (James Inkanish, Jr.) (1938–2008), who was Comanche, was respectfully identified as "the Indian of the group."

PRESERVING AND RECORDING THE MUSIC

The Havana, Cuba–born daughter of a New York attorney and a Boston socialite, Alice Cunningham Fletcher (1838–1923) was one of the first to document American Indian songs. Although she mostly focused on the Omaha tribe—with whom she resided for more than fifty years—the ethnologist for Harvard University's Peabody Museum of Archeology and Ethnology also transcribed songs by the Pawnees, Sioux, Arapahos, Cheyennes, Chippewas, Otos, Nez Perce, Ponces, and Winnebagos.

Conservatory-trained pianists and vocalists Natalie Curtis Burlin, née Natalie Curtis (1875–1921), and Frances Theresa Densmore (1867–1957) made some of the earliest recordings on the reservations. Guided by the belief that Native culture is "of great value to the history of the human race as well as the history of America," Burlin called Indigenous music "the spontaneous and sincere expression of the soul of a people."[9]

Songs, stories, and drawings collected from eighteen tribes between Maine and British Columbia were included in Burlin's *The Indians' Book: Authentic Native American Legends, Lore and Magic* (1905). The book's two hundred transcriptions cover "all aspects of life: love and war, victory and hunting, rejoicing and thanksgiving; there are lullabies and laments, corn-grinding and corn-dance songs, ghost-dance and snake-dance songs, and a great many others."[10]

Burlin adapted some of the melodies she collected into her own orchestral compositions. The publishers of a monthly Newton, Massachusetts–based magazine dedicated to "a nationalistic American music," the Wa-Wan Press published several of her pieces, including "Dawn Song," which was based on a Cheyenne melody. A melody she collected from the Pima—"Bluebird Song"—and one of the "hand-game" songs that she obtained from the Cheyenne, became a part of the 1911 composition of her former teacher, Ferruccio Busoni, "Indian Fantasy." Four years later, the Philadelphia Orchestra, under the direction of Leopold Stokowski, performed the piece with Busoni on piano.

Frances Densmore was responsible for thousands of field recordings of tribal music. During seventy-nine trips to fifty-four locations between 1907 and 1954, the Red Wing, Minnesota–born daughter of a civil engineer and iron foundry owner documented songs by the Chippewas, Mandans, Hidatsas, Sioux, Northern Pawnees, Papagos, Winnebagos, Menominees, Pueblos, and Seminoles. "I have met with much opposition in securing [songs]," she wrote of her early efforts, "some of the old men insisting that it were better to let the songs die than to sing them for any fee less than a horse, which was their value in the old days. Fortunately, there have been others willing to sing them, for a reasonable fee, in order that they might be preserved."[11]

As fascinated by birdcalls as she was by music, Laura Crayton Boulton (1899–1980) combined both of her passions. Traveling the world with her husband, Rudyard Boulton, Jr., an ornithologist and lecturer at the Carnegie Museum in Pittsburgh, she collected more than 30,000 songs between 1929 and 1970. During a trip to the Inupiat community in Barrow, Alaska, in the 1930s, she recorded 106 songs, sung by seven adult males and, at least, three children. These were combined with thirteen songs recorded during a previous trip to the Canadian Arctic, and an album, *The Eskimos of Hudson Bay and Alaska*, was released by Folkways in 1955.

Working with state-of-the-art recording equipment provided by the Library of Congress, Willard Rhodes (1901–1992) recorded 160 discs between 1940 and 1949, and 50 seven-inch tapes between 1950 and 1952. These featured songs of fifty tribes in fourteen states. Folkways released numerous albums featuring Rhodes's recordings, including *Music of the Sioux and Navajo* (1949). In his liner notes for *Music of the American Indians of the Southwest* (1951), he explained, "The music lover whose experience has been limited to western European music, its harmonic and polyphonic complexities, and huge tonal masses, resulting from the elaboration and development of essentially simple themes, will be puzzled at first by the seeming simplicity of American Indian music. Just as he is required to change his aural perspective in shifting from symphonic music to chamber music within his own culture, so he must adjust his scale of musical values in approaching this very special and strangely beautiful music."[12]

In the late 1940s, a San Juan Pueblo Indian from Gallup, New Mexico, Manuel Archuleta, or Tse-We Ant-Yen (Rain God), used his life savings to launch Tom Tom Records. It would be the first Native-owned record label. "We had enough milk for the baby," Archuleta told *Desert Magazine* in October 1949, "and a recording machine, and that was the most wonderful thing in the world."[13]

A stock and file clerk at the Albuquerque Indian School by day, Archuleta supplemented his income by lecturing about American Indian music at the University of New Mexico and singing traditional songs at public schools. Although he initially "had to ask permission of the Indians [to record them]," he soon had Natives approaching him. "While I was making songs of other tribes," he said, "the San Juan people were wondering why I wasn't making a recording of their songs—my own pueblo. I explained to them that it was due to lack of funds and distance. When I could, I would get there. [Otherwise,] it meant that I had to pick out my singers, haul them to Albuquerque to make the recordings, and feed them."[14]

Distributed primarily in the Southwest, Tom Tom's releases—originally on 78-rpm discs and later collected as a pair of twelve-inch albums, *Indian Chants, Volumes 1 and 2*—are remembered more for their historic importance than their commercial success. Archuleta's own songs, recorded with his Laguna Pueblo wife, Alycia, and their three daughters, and credited to the Tom Tom Family Singers, failed to sell.

With cultural preservation the goal, a Methodist minister from Carnegie, Oklahoma, Rev. Linn D. Pauahty (Kiowa), founded the American Indian Soundchiefs label in the mid-1940s. Traveling to tribal communities, and recording their songs, he would amass a collection of more than 4,000 tunes over four decades. Releases included intertribal surveys of the Grass Dance, Warriors' Dance, circle dance, round dance, Owl Dance, and Sun Dance. There were collections of Menominee, Winnebago, and Taos Pueblo songs, Tia-piah Society songs, and Kiowa, Comanche, and Apache peyote songs. "[Pauahty] saw that Indian people had lost their Native spiritualism," said his granddaughter, Mary Helen Deer, in September 2013, "and he realized that, after his generation was gone, a lot of the links to our old way of life would be lost. Thinking of his children, and his grandchildren, and their children to come, he wanted to preserve as much as he could."

Raised on a farm, Pauahty was neither a musician nor an anthropologist. After graduating from Oklahoma A&M (now Oklahoma State University), with an undergraduate degree in animal husbandry and agriculture, he turned to more spiritual concerns at the urging of a missionary who preached on the Kiowa reservation. "[The missionary] talked with Grandpa," said Deer, who, along with her brother Alvin Deer, grew up with her grandparents, "and saw that he was, as the Christians say, 'under the conviction of God.' He got him into the Perkins School of Theology, where he became the first Indian, and the first Kiowa, to graduate."

Pauahty's first assignment for the Methodist Church was to produce a movie about its relationship with residents of what was then the Oklahoma Indian Reservation. Although he had no experience with film, he took to the project with zeal. The experience led him to record the tribe's songs. "People wanted to buy the music," recalled his granddaughter. "I remember traveling with him to the big Indian fairs. He had vendors who would sell the records."

American Indian Soundchiefs' releases were aimed at Native listeners. "[Pauahty] wanted to give them the latest songs, the round-dance and peyote songs," said Tony Isaacs, founder and owner of Indian House Records, who purchased the label's catalogue after Pauahty's passing. "He started with 78-rpm discs, but once he got to albums, he would record whole albums of round-dance songs or war-dance songs. He's the one who pioneered that in-depth style."

Having previously worked with a Pittsburgh-based radio station, Canyon Records founder Ray Boley (1917–2003) had no connection to American Indian music when he, and his wife, Mary, moved to Phoenix, Arizona, in the mid-1940s. "He had gotten his first job," said Robert Doyle, "by telling station management, 'If you just give me car fare, I'll work for you.' He was quickly picked up as a regular employee, but that's how he got started—by volunteering his work."

The Pittsburgh radio station job led Boley into recording. "He'd record concerts on lacquer discs," said Doyle, "and then run them back to the studio and play them over the air." Moving briefly to Los Angeles in 1948, Ray and Mary Boley found the Southern California city overpopulated, congested, and unwelcoming. Remembering how much they had enjoyed driving through Arizona, they returned to Phoenix and set up a home. After a brief stint with KOY, Boley opened the city's first recording studio, Arizona Recording Productions. "They recorded all of the political commercials for the state elections of 1948," said Doyle.

Boley was still a novice in tribal music when the Phoenix Little Theater contracted him to record four songs to be sung by Ed Lee Natay (Diné) and used as the musical soundtrack for a play. Awed by Natay's smooth baritone vocals, Boley couldn't get the singer out of his mind after the session. Although he had little information about the vocalist—other than that he was a railroad worker in northern Arizona—he managed to track Natay down and set up another recording session at a local dance studio. "He wanted to record in a room that had a lot of natural reverberation," said Doyle. "His own studio was actually built to dampen the echo."

The resulting album, *Ed Lee Natay, Navajo Singer*, included Navajo, Hopi, Kiowa, Tewa, Zuni, and Pueblo songs and became Canyon Records' first release. Still in print, the album has continued to pay royalties for more than six decades. "It makes me feel good that my dad accomplished such things," said Natay's daughter, Cindy June Natay-Curley, "especially at a time when it was rare to find people who gave tribes an opportunity to show their talent. It opens doors in Navajo land because everyone knows my father's voice."[15]

Before his 1992 retirement, Boley produced more than three hundred albums. Recognized by the Phoenix Indian Center in 1995 for "Outstanding Contribution to the Indian Community by a Non-Indian," he received a "Native Heart" award from the Native American Music Awards in recognition for his contributions to Native music four years later. "Ray and Mary Boley met Native music on an equal ground," said Canyon Records producer Stephen Butler. "They saw it as musical expression, something that was living. There was continuity, but it was still going on. The music was not something to be left in a museum."

PETER LAFARGE

Although his repertoire included cowboy songs, American folk songs, love songs, and a playful ode to marijuana, Oliver Albee LaFarge, better known as Peter LaFarge (1931–1965), made his greatest impact by turning his pen toward broken treaties, environmental destruction, and the mistreatment of the Indigenous. Songs like "Custer" and "Trail of Tears" presented a Native perspective of history. "The Crimson Parson" recalled the November 1864 Sand Creek Massacre, when Ohio-born Methodist missionary and army colonel John Chivington led a force of seven hundred men in an unprovoked attack on a peaceful encampment of Cheyenne and Arapaho Indians in southeastern Colorado territory, killing between 70 and 138 Natives, nearly two-thirds of them women and children. "As Long As the Grass Shall Grow" chronicled the building of the Kinzua dam in Pennsylvania's Alleghany Mountains in 1960, and the resultant flooding of Seneca land—despite treaties dating back to George Washington.

LaFarge offered more than history lessons. He sang of disenfranchisement as an American Indian ("I'm an Indian, I'm an Alien" and "Johnny Half-Breed") and addressed racist-provoked heartbreak ("White Girl"), lamenting that "she who said she loves me will not wed an Indian man." He sang of environmental concerns, pleading "don't poison the mesas, don't poison the skies" ("Coyote, My Little Brother"), and satirizing nuclear proliferation ("Radioactive Eskimo").

LaFarge's most enduring Native-themed tune, "The Ballad of Ira Hayes," told the heartrending tale of the Pima Indian who had been one of five marines to raise the U.S. flag on Iwo Jima's Mount Suribachi on March 26, 1945, at the conclusion of a fierce thirty-five-day battle. Pete Seeger, Patrick Sky, Kinky Friedman, Hazel Dickens, Townes Van Zandt, and Bob Dylan—with whom LaFarge reportedly shared a girlfriend—would cover it. Johnny Cash included it as one of five LaFarge-penned tunes on his groundbreaking 1964 album, *Bitter Tears: Ballads of the American Indian*. Released as a single, the Man in Black's recording would reach number two on *Billboard*'s country music album charts and break into the pop top-fifty.

Hayes's tale was indeed tragic. Acclaimed a hero in the United States, he was extremely uncomfortable in the spotlight. Although he presented an upbeat portrayal of himself in the 1949 film, *Sands of Iwo Jima*, he grew exceedingly bitter and drank heavily. At a rally in Boston in May 1945, he snarled at a *Boston Globe* reporter and asked, "How can I feel like a hero when only five men in my platoon of forty-five survived?"

Hayes would offer similar sentiments seven months later, at the dedication of the Iwo Jima Monument in Arlington, Virginia. When a reporter asked him how he liked the ceremony, he snapped that he didn't and turned away. It would be his last public comment. Within ninety days, he would be dead, at the age of thirty-two, from exposure and alcohol poisoning.

Originally recorded for topical song magazine *Broadside*, "The Ballad of Ira Hayes" provided the centerpiece of LaFarge's first (and only) album for Columbia

Records. Folkways would release his others. Amid songs like "St. James Infirmary," "John Henry," and "John Brown's Body," the tune stood out with its Native theme.

LaFarge's next recordings took things further. All of the songs on *As Long As the Grass Shall Grow* (1963) and *Peter LaFarge Sings of the Indians* (1964) addressed the lives, history, and struggles of North America's First People.

Although he claimed Narragansett ancestry, LaFarge's Native heritage remains a subject of debate. The biological son of noted author, anthropologist, and Native Rights activist Oliver Hazard Perry LaFarge (1901–1963), and not adopted as he sometimes claimed, he was the great-great-great-grandson of Benjamin Franklin, the great-great-grandson (on his mother's side) of Commodore Oliver Hazard Perry, and the great-grandson of stained glass pioneer Jean LaFarge. His uncle Christopher LaFarge wrote novels, including *Hoaxie Sells His Acres* (1934) and *Each to the Other* (1939), and collections of short stories, including *East by Southwest* (1944). LaFarge's interests in American Indians can be traced to his grandfather, Christopher Grant LaFarge, a Beaux Arts designer and archeologist who conducted research in Central America and the North American Southwest.

Born in New York, LaFarge "came from a pretty privileged background," said Sandra Schulman, who spent nearly a decade researching the songwriter's life. "His father was a Pulitzer Prize–winning writer, and his mother (Wanden Matthews), who raised him, was a wealthy heiress who twice became mayor of Fountain, Colorado. It was quite an unusual family. His mother paid for everything and he didn't have to work." His father did more than write about Americans Indians. Helping to form the Eastern Association on Indian Affairs (EAIA) to "protect the basic rights of American Indians," he became president of the organization in 1933. Six years later, he merged the group with the New Mexico Association on Indian Affairs (NAIA) and the American Indian Defense Association to create the American Association on Indian Affairs. "He was very intellectual," said Schulman, "and very highly regarded in the Native community. The power of the American Indian fascinated him, but he was also into the cowboy lifestyle. He had that dual thing going on."

The American West had as much of an allure for LaFarge's mother. Born into New York's elite, Wanden LaFarge studied with tutors while traveling around Europe with her family and completed her education at Columbia University. She married Oliver LaFarge in New York in December 1929. Though the family expanded with the birth of Peter and his sister, Povy, the marriage had fallen apart by 1935.

After his parents' divorce, LaFarge and his sister moved with their mother to a sprawling, 4,000-acre ranch in Fountain, Colorado. "We moved to Colorado for very definite reasons," Povy LaFarge told Antonino D'Ambrosio. "My brother was very ill with a series of ear infections and they didn't have antibiotics or penicillin at the time to treat him. The doctors told Mother that he would be deaf if he had another serious infection."[16]

An ex-professional rodeo cowboy and horse breeder who had been hired to run the ranch, Andy Kane, would become Wanden's second husband—and Peter and Povy's stepfather. "It was much harder for my brother," Povy LaFarge told D'Ambrosio. "[Peter] didn't get along well in public school in Fountain. He didn't make friends . . . and he didn't get along with our stepfather almost immediately; they never did get along."[17]

LaFarge began earning money as a professional rodeo cowboy—first as a bareback rider and then as a saddle bronc rider—before finishing high school. Serving aboard a navy aircraft carrier as an undercover antinarcotics operative for the navy's Central Intelligence division during the Korean War, he narrowly escaped with his life following an onboard explosion. Although he resumed his career with the rodeo after returning to the United States, an injury ended his days as a cowboy. "He got really beaten up in the rodeo," said Schulman. "He almost lost a leg because his knee got tangled very badly. He had to stop, as most people [who compete in the rodeo] do. By their late-twenties, they're usually all beaten up."

Compounding his injuries as a boxer, LaFarge was forced to take a respite from the rodeo and the ring. While recuperating, he studied acting at the Goodman Theater School of Drama in Chicago. Remaining in the Windy City for two years, he acted in supporting roles in stock theater and Shakespearean plays.

Although he married a fellow cast member, Suzanne Becker, the romance was brief. When an opportunity to perform in an off-Broadway show in New York arose, he jumped at the chance. Once back in the Big Apple, he immersed himself in Greenwich Village's burgeoning scene of bohemians and artists and began singing in folk music coffeehouses. "He had been playing guitar and singing since he was in high school," said Schulman." Cisco Houston mentored him and blues artists like Big Bill Broonzy and Josh White used to stop by his house. He spent six months in Harlem studying black music and the blues."

LaFarge kept his wealth hidden. "He was living in the Dakota, one of the most magnificent apartment buildings in New York City," said Schulman, "but he didn't want to be known as a rich kid and had to get away from there. He moved to Hotel Earle, which was a horrible, sleazy place on Washington Square, and he lived in various other Village apartments. He was a roommate of [folksinger] Patrick Sky (1940–) (Creek/Irish) for a while. He had to appear to be one of them."

Attracting some minor attention as a singer and songwriter, LaFarge's career went into overdrive after Johnny Cash discovered his songs. During an interview for Beth Harrington's documentary film, *The Winding Stream: The Carters, the*

Cashes, and the Course of Country Music, Antonino D'Ambrosio spoke about the significance of Cash's album. "It's not a simple tale of Cash and a few musicians making a little-known, controversial record," he said, "but, rather, a compelling example of how art and culture can be a powerful exercise in democracy."

LaFarge met Cash on May 10, 1962, after the country music superstar's concert at Carnegie Hall—his debut appearance in New York. "Irish folksinger Ed McCluskey suggested [to Cash] that they go down to the Gaslight Café in Greenwich Village," said Schulman, "and hear LaFarge. [Cash] met Bob Dylan there the same night."

Fresh from a chart-topping country—and crossover pop—hit, "Ring of Fire," and equally successful album (*I Walk the Line*), Cash's decision to record American Indian protest songs (*Bitter Tears: Ballads of the American Indian*) represented a bold move for the Kingsland, Arkansas–born country singer. Recorded three days after the March 15, 1964, arrest of actor Marlon Brandon for participating in a protest for Native fishing rights in the state of Washington, the album received a cold reception when released five months later. Radio stations banned it from airplay and critics refused to review it. It took a full-page open letter in *Billboard*, paid for by Cash, before the resistance eased and both the single, "The Ballad of Ira Hayes," and the album became hits.

Bitter Tears: Ballads of the American Indian transformed LaFarge from an obscure folksinger to one of Greenwich Village's hottest young tunesmiths. "It absolutely separated him from the rest of the pack," said Schulman. "Suddenly, he was big-time."

LaFarge, however, was unprepared to live up to the hype. "His shows were very stilted," said Schulman, "and he had a hard time keeping up with [the more modern approaches] that other singer-songwriters were taking."

Although LaFarge organized a nonprofit organization, FAIR (Fairer Nation for American Indian Rights), with Buffy Sainte-Marie and Patrick Sky, to raise awareness of the suffering on the reservations, it received little public support and quickly fell apart. "People thought that he was posing," said Schulman, "and he got a bit of ridicule for it. It really upset him. He was very fragile."

In the October-December 1976 issue of *Broadside*, Gordon Friesen alleged that FBI agents paid an unexpected midnight visit to LaFarge's apartment. "They scattered and tore up his papers," claimed Friesen. "They put him in handcuffs and dragged him to Bellevue [the state psychiatric hospital, in Manhattan] in his pajamas. They put pressure on Bellevue to declare him insane, but Bellevue couldn't find anything wrong with him and they turned him loose."[18]

Dismissing Friesen's report, Schulman explained, "I contacted the FBI through the Freedom of Information Act. If they had had a file on him, they would have been legally obligated to give it to me, but they had no file. I think that it was the New York City police, not the FBI. He was planning rallies at a time when there were radicals and Black Panther groups. The police were getting very uneasy with all of it."

Schulman blamed psychological problems for LaFarge's sometimes-erratic behavior. "In his writings, he talked about manic highs and sudden, horrible lows," she said. "One minute he'd be down in the gutter and the next, he'd be flying with eagles. It was classic manic-depression, with all of the mood swings, and manic-depressives self-medicate. They cannot control which way their brain is going, or their moods, so they drink alcohol, take pills, and smoke pot. He was very frightened. He was going through very strange treatments and was in the hospital a lot. The rodeo had beaten him up. It was all taking a toll on him."

"He was treated for schizophrenia," continued Schulman, "and terrible, experimental things were done to him. They gave him drugs and subjected him to shock therapy. His mother kept all of it secret. She never let on to any of it and she paid for everything."

LaFarge and his girlfriend, Danish singer Inga Nielsen, had a daughter, Karen, but they were unable to wed. "He couldn't get married," said Schulman, "because he was already married to this girl [Suzanne Becker] who [had had a nervous breakdown and] was in a mental institution in Michigan. They were never legally divorced. In those days, you had to wait seven years to get an annulment from someone who was institutionalized."

LaFarge's unexpected death, on October 16, 1965, may have put the problems eating at his psyche to rest, but it only contributed to the mysteries of his life. Although the cause of death was officially listed as a stroke brought on by an overdose of Thorazine, an antipsychotic drug that Cash had allegedly introduced to him, LaFarge's neighbor, Liam Clancy—of the Irish folk group, the Clancy Brothers—claimed that he had slit his wrists. "I can't imagine that it was suicide," countered Schulman. "He had a baby that was three months old and he was planning to leave New York and go back to Santa Fe. I can't imagine that he would have killed himself."

"It is too easy to feel sorry for a poet who dies young," said Julius Lester in his obituary for LaFarge in the *Village Voice*. "'If he had only lived' is the pathetic plaint of those who stand at the grave, but he did live and our sorrow and our tears are wasted on him now. He is beyond us—the audiences that never quite understood him, and the friends who pitied him. None of them can hurt him anymore—those who used his face for a mirror and those, filled with the wisdom of their press notices, who thought his lack of success was a reflection of his mettle, just as they thought their own acquisition of success was a reflection of theirs.

Their tongues and pens can no longer hurt one who was too gentle to retaliate and not strong enough to resist."[19]

In 2010, Schulman brought Keith Secola, Blackfire, John Trudell, and Felipe Rose (the Village People) together with non-Natives, including Hank Williams III, John Densmore (The Doors), and Sarah Lee Guthrie and Johnny Irion, to record tracks for a tribute album, *Rare Breed: The Songs of Peter LaFarge*. A forty-six-minute-long documentary filmed during recording sessions, *The Ballad of Peter LaFarge* told the singer-songwriter's story through still photos and rare video clips, including ones of Johnny Cash and June Carter Cash singing "The Ballad of Ira Hayes" and LaFarge performing uncomfortably on a TV show hosted by folklorist Alan Lomax. "The fact that [LaFarge] made an impact on so many brilliant people says a lot," said Schulman. "Those kinds of people are not easily impressed."

BUFFY SAINTE-MARIE

Beverly "Buffy" Sainte-Marie (1941–), who met LaFarge in 1963, would carry a similar message to the highest levels of the entertainment business. Born of Plains Cree heritage, Sainte-Marie would be inducted into the JUNO Hall of Fame (1994) and Canadian Country Music Hall of Fame (2009). She would also be designated an officer in the Order of Canada, that country's highest civilian honor. "This complex young Indian girl is full of the arrogance of the very shy (a very Indian trait)," wrote LaFarge in the liner notes of her 1965 sophomore album, *Many a Mile*, "gentle with a wealth of compassion for the world and its people."[20]

"I've had no desire to copy other singers," said Sainte-Marie from the Kauai, Hawaii, goat farm she's called her home since 1967. "Instead, I've tried to give audiences things that they couldn't find elsewhere—not only songs about my life, which was different from my peers in folk music, including the Indian part, but also unique melodies and attitudes, and well-thought-out treatises or protest songs. Most singers are like a Volkswagen; I am more like a 747. I go longer, farther, stronger, and higher—combining rock and roll with the power of Plains Cree singing. I invented Powwow Rock forty years ago."

Born on the Piapot Cree First Nation Reserve, Saskatchewan, and raised by non-Native adoptive parents in Maine and Massachusetts, Sainte-Marie addressed Indigenous America with many of her songs. Dedicated to LaFarge, the opening track of her 1964 debut album, *It's My Way*, "Now That the Buffalo's Gone," built on the story that he had told during "As Long As the Grass Shall Grow" about the flooding of Seneca land by the Kinzua Dam in Pennsylvania. Sainte-Marie would re-record the song twice. "Seneca and the Chippewa" would change to "Chippewa

Buffy Sainte-Marie (Plains Cree) has taken the American Indian experience to the highest levels of entertainment. *Courtesy Buffy Sainte-Marie.*

and the Cheyenne" on *I'm Gonna Be a Country Girl Again* (1968), and to "Inuit and the Cheyenne" on *Up Where We Belong* (1996).

The songstress turned the heat even higher with "My Country Tis of Thy People, You're Dying," on her third album, *Little Wheel Spin and Spin*, in 1966. Over the course of a little more than six-and-a-half minutes, she delivers a near-spoken word recap of injustices experienced by American Indians—broken treaties, loss of land, smallpox-carrying blankets, and parents forced to send their children to boarding schools "where they're taught to despise their traditions." Sainte-Marie left no doubts as to how she felt, singing, "Hands on our hearts, we salute you your victory—choke on your blue, white, and scarlet hypocrisy."

"My early protest songs tried to reach out to everybody," said Sainte-Marie, "but, later on, they were for the people on the reservations. They didn't need songs about how terrible conditions were. They needed to be able to look around and dig themselves. It was partly an educational project—I was a teacher before I was a singer. I believed that if the public understood our reality, they would help. I worked towards that by writing the most accurate, emotionally moving songs that I could."

Sainte-Marie also spoke out against war. Included on her 1964 debut album, *It's My Way*, "Universal Soldier" became an unofficial antiwar anthem after Donovan turned it into a worldwide pop hit in 1967. Although he was later to pen folk-pop hits, including "Mellow Yellow," "Sunshine Superman," "Hurdy Gurdy Man," and "Season of the Witch," the Scottish folk-rocker had yet to make the break from troubadour to international stardom. "Universal Soldier" provided that springboard.

Sainte-Marie penned "Universal Soldier" in the basement of the Purple Onion, a folk-music coffeehouse in Toronto, after speaking with American soldiers returning from the conflict in Vietnam. "I was in the airport in San Francisco," she recalled, "and saw some soldiers in wheelchairs and stretchers. They were in horrible shape. The government had been telling us that there was nothing going on in Vietnam, but I could see for myself how they were trying to deceive us. Later, when I thought more about it, it hit me that it was not enough to yell at the generals or the power structure. Who elects the politicians? Everyone has a responsibility for democracy."

"Universal Soldier" became one of the best-selling songs of the 1960s protest era, but Sainte-Marie gained little financially. "I didn't know what publishing was," she told Winnipeg-based writer John Einarson. "I had only been in town for a very short time, a matter of weeks or months, I can't recall."[21]

At Bob Dylan's suggestion, Sainte-Marie had gone to a Greenwich Village nightspot, the Gaslight, to pitch the song to the Highwaymen, who were seeking a follow-up to their chart-topping gospel-folk hit, "Michael Row the Boat Ashore." "I sat with them at the Gaslight," Sainte-Marie recalled, "and one of the people at the table said, '[Y]eah, we're going to record that song, who's the publisher?' I said, 'What's that?' and [pianist/musical supervisor] Elmer Jared Gordon, damn his soul, said, 'Oh, I can help with that, we'll have to do it legally, though.' He wrote up the contract right there and then and I signed it. There went 'Universal Soldier.' I sold it for one dollar. I didn't know any better."[22]

Sainte-Marie would reacquire the worldwide rights to "Universal Soldier" for $25,000 ten years later, but the saga was not yet over. "I learned a few weeks ago," the songwriter wrote me in a July 2014 e-mail, "that Gordon misled or otherwise failed to let foreign associates know that the song had returned to me; for the past forty years they have been keeping my royalties."

Donovan also covered Sainte-Marie's "Co'dine." One of the few hip antidrug songs, it detailed the songwriter's addiction and withdrawal from prescription drugs. After signing to record her first album, she had accepted a stint at a small coffeehouse in Key West, Florida, to prepare for the recording. Contracting bronchitis partway through the engagement, she became extremely sick. Seeking relief, she went to a doctor who prescribed codeine. Although it helped to make her well, she found herself addicted to the drug and had to go through a difficult withdrawal. The Charlatans, Quicksilver Messenger Service, Jimmy Gilmer, Gram Parsons, Janis Joplin, and Courtney Love would cover the tune.

Affairs of the heart proved an equally potent theme. More than two hundred artists—including Elvis Presley, Barbara Streisand, Neil Diamond, Cher, and the Boston Pops—covered Sainte-Marie's "Until It's Time for You to Go." "I was falling in love with someone that I knew couldn't stay with me," wrote the songwriter in the liner notes of her first greatest hits album in 1970. "The words are about honesty and freedom inside the heart."

Written with her former husband and record producer, Jack Nitzsche, and Texas-born songwriter Will Jennings, "Up Where We Belong" became an international hit. Sung by Joe Cocker and Jennifer Warnes in the 1982 film *An Officer and a Gentleman*, it scored a Golden Globe, and an Academy Award, as the year's "Best Song." Cocker and Warne's performance earned them a Grammy for "Best Pop Performance by a Duo or Group with Vocals." British vocalist Cliff Richard later recorded it as a duet with Canadian pop/country singer Anne Murray, and Alvin and the Chipmunks sang it with the Chippettes.

A semiregular on *Sesame Street* from 1977 to 1981, Sainte-Marie—often accompanied by her son, Dakota "Cody" Starblanket—taught viewers about sibling rivalry and breastfeeding, and shared what it meant to be a modern-day American Indian. The PBS program was broadcast from Sainte-Marie's Hawaiian home for a week in December 1977. "I wanted to show that Indians existed," she explained, "that we're not all dead and stuffed in museums like dinosaurs." *Sesame Street* aired three times a day, in seventy-two countries, including the United States, enabling Sainte-Marie to reach out to longtime fans and youngsters. "I did the same thing for little kids and their caregivers as I had always tried to do for adults," she said, "use my music to help them to know about Native reality."

Although she emerged at the peak of the folk-music revival, Sainte-Marie remained on the cutting edge of technology. She used a synthesizer on her 1969 album, *Illuminations*, the first quadraphonic album ever, and multitracked her mouth bow on the soundtrack of the 1970 film, *Performance*, which was directed by Nicolas Roeg and starred Mick Jagger. Recording her music and creating digital art on Macintosh computers since 1981, she transmitted (via modem) tracks that were recorded in her Hawaiian home for her 1992 album, *Coincidence and Likely Stories*, to her producer Chris Birkett in England. Internet exchange of music has since become commonplace, but, at the time, it was groundbreaking.

Following the album's release, Sainte-Marie embarked on a traveling exhibition of her digital paintings. A list of museums and galleries that exhibited her work included the Glenbow Museum in Calgary, the Emily Carr Gallery in Vancouver, the Winnipeg Art Gallery, and the American Indian Arts Museum in Santa Fe, New Mexico.

Adopted shortly after her February 20, 1941, birth by Albert and Winifred Sainte-Marie, who were non-Native relatives of her biological parents, Sainte-Marie discovered the family piano at the age of three. "It became my favorite toy," she recalled. "I still 'play' music. I knew that I was a musician before I knew that I was American Indian. I'm a natural musician—that is, the music comes from inside of me, not from a teacher or a desire to have a career in showbiz."

Writing songs and playing acoustic guitar since her teens, Sainte-Marie, who earned a bachelor's degree in Oriental Philosophy and Religion from the University of Massachusetts in 1963, and a PhD twenty years later, supported her schooling with weekend performances at the Saladin Coffeehouse in Amherst. A career in music was the furthest thing from her mind. "I thought that I was on my way to a graduate degree in India," she said, "studying creativity and the Creator."

When she arrived in Greenwich Village following her graduation in 1963, the downtown Manhattan neighborhood was a hotbed of creativity with art galleries, hip clothing stores, jazz clubs, and folk-music coffeehouses. Sainte-Marie's protest songs found a very welcoming audience. "People thought that it was unusual for an Indian woman to be singing about the war," she said, "so I guess it stuck in their minds."

The power of Sainte-Marie's vocals helped her to stand apart from the many folksingers competing for attention. "Critics, rivals, and unknowledgeable people scolded me," she said, "and warned me that I was going to ruin my voice because of how strongly I sang—in ranges, volumes, and timbres that they'd never heard before. They had never been around powwow singers who sang all night with strength and power."

Sainte-Marie's early repertoire included traditional British folksongs, including "Lord Randall" and "Reynardine—a Vampire Legend," and Appalachian fiddle tunes like "Cripple Creek," which she converted to mouth bow. But she never felt comfortable with the label "folksinger." "I felt like a fraud," she said. "I wasn't singing folksongs. I was writing my own songs."

Although she remembers being told that she "couldn't be an Indian, because all of the Indians are dead," Sainte-Marie continued to reconnect with her heritage. When she returned to the Piapot Cree First Nations Reserve for a visit in 1964, the youngest son of the chief and his wife adopted her. During the trip, she collected the chokeberry branches that she would use to make the mouth bow that would flavor much of her early music. Patrick Sky (Cree/Irish), a Georgia-born folksinger she met when they shared billing in a nightclub in Miami, Florida, built her first mouth bow and introduced her to the single-stringed instrument. "A mouth bow is probably the oldest musical instrument in the world," she would write in *The Buffy Sainte-Marie Songbook*. "It's basically a hunting bow and I guess somebody one day figured out that you can make music on a weapon. Maybe there will be virtuoso concertos to be played on M-1s and tanks."[23]

Vanguard Records, the New York–based, folk-oriented label cofounded and operated by producer Maynard Solomon, released Sainte-Marie's early albums. The label had previously issued recordings by Joan Baez, Odetta, and Pete Seeger's folk group, the Weavers, and it would go on to release albums by the Kweskin Jug Band and political acid-rockers Country Joe (MacDonald) and The Fish. "I couldn't even sing on pitch," recalled Sainte-Marie. "In those days, I just wanted to write. I was scared and inexperienced."

As the 1960s faded into the '70s, Sainte-Marie expanded into film. She composed the theme song for the Ralph Nelson–directed film, *Soldier Blue*, about the 1864 Sand Creek Massacre, and her cover of Joni Mitchell's "The Circle Game" played during the opening of Stuart Hagmann's *Strawberry Statement*. Her original score was featured in a 1979 documentary (*Spirit of the Wind*) about celebrated dogsled driver George Attla—and was one of three American entries, along with *The China Syndrome* and *Norma Rae*, at that year's Cannes Film Festival. A decade later, *Where the Spirit Lives*, Bruce Pittman's heartbreaking documentary about Canada's Indian boarding schools, featured Sainte-Marie's songs.

The Indian narrator of *Broken Rainbow*, the Academy Award winner for "Best Feature-length Documentary" in 1989, Sainte-Marie provided the unseen voice of a Cheyenne woman in a made-for-TV movie, *Son of the Morning Star*, two years later, about the events leading up to Custer's massacre at Little Bighorn. In 1993, she made an onscreen appearance in *The Broken Chain*, a TNT film about two Iroquois brothers during the American Revolution.

An internationally acclaimed artist, with increasing sales of her records in Europe, Asia, Australia, and Canada, Sainte-Marie experienced a different response in the United States. By the early '70s, radio stations had stopped playing her music, sales of her recordings had plummeted, and she was no longer being booked into concert halls that she had previously sold out. Unsure of the causes for such a rapid shift in public opinion, she didn't get an answer until a radio station interviewed her more than a decade later. "The interviewer apologized," she recalled, "for having gone along with letters that he'd received in the 1960s from then–Pres. Lyndon Johnson's administration commending him for suppressing my music."

Sainte-Marie instructed her attorney to obtain her FBI files under the Freedom of Information Act. "The FBI insisted that I go to their offices in Washington,

D.C.," she said, "but he refused. He said that he would allow them to be present in the room, but I would look at the files in his law office, which is what we did."

As she and her attorney gazed at the documents, Sainte-Marie discovered how severely the government had blacklisted her. "I was flabbergasted," she said. "I didn't want to believe it, but it explained the sudden drowning of what had been a huge career—the disappearance of big-time national television shows, movies, record sales, and major magazine stories. I did not know that politicos in the Johnson and Nixon White House were making nasty phone calls behind my back to sink my career. Who would think something like that? I just thought that people's tastes had changed."

Sainte-Marie put things in perspective. "I was just one person put out of business," she told *Indian Country Today*. "John Trudell is another whose [career] was nearly put out of business. Anna Mae Pictou-Aquash died for speaking out, and Leonard Peltier is still in prison for murdering two FBI agents [during a shootout at the Pine Ridge Reservation], though the prosecutor's star witness recanted her testimony. They were made ineffective, too."[24]

Realizing that there was little that she could do after two decades, Sainte-Marie turned to where her success had continued to flourish. "I re-evaluated my life and my career," she said, "and decided to keep on with my original goals: to be a complete artist in two worlds: Native America and the great stages and concert halls of the world. I went where I could work. My records and concert appearances abroad kept me very busy. I was selling hugely everywhere except in the United States."

"[The blacklisting] was for very stupid reasons," added Michel Buyere (Ojibwe), drummer, background singer, grass dancer, and the anchor of Sainte-Marie's band since 2009, "for being American Indian and outspoken with music. They were afraid of what she was saying. It's funny how words could freak out the government."

Sainte-Marie took steps to recapture her recording career in 1992, releasing *Coincidence and Likely Stories*, her first album in sixteen years. "My so-called return to recording," she said, "was a misnomer. I never left, so I never came back. All through my career, I have often taken time off from recording, and when that happens, the public thinks that I must have retired. I am more of an artist than a careerist, though, and I have always tried to fit my career into my real life instead of the opposite. There's no sense in recording unless you're willing to tour, so whenever I feel like touring, I make a record of what I've been stocking up in my home studio."

Response to *Coincidence and Likely Stories* was overwhelmingly positive. *Rolling Stone* called it "a winning comeback—eleven songs that have deep thematic resonance and that are among her most appealing work."[25] The *Toronto Star* proclaimed that "the music's well up to date, Buffy being no slouch when it comes to composing with the Apple Mac . . . and being relevant as she is, this is a piece of work that'll hold its own in the commercial arena."[26] The acclaim was international. France awarded Sainte-Marie the prestigious Grand Prix Charles de Gaulle as the year's "Best International Artist."

The Indians of All Tribes (IAT)/American Indian Movement (AIM) occupation of the town of Wounded Knee on the Pine Ridge Reservation in North Dakota (February 27–May 8, 1973) spurred Sainte-Marie to write one of her angriest tunes. She dedicated "Bury My Heart at Wounded Knee" to Leonard Peltier, Joseph Killsright, or "Little Joe," Stuntz—the only American Indian killed during the "Incident at Oglala" shootout—and Anna Mae Pictou-Aguash. The song told Pictou-Aquash's tragic tale with graphic detail. One of the top women involved with the American Indian Movement, the Nova Scotia–born mother of two had been thirty years old when she was murdered and her body thrown below a cliff in the northwest corner of the Pine Ridge Reservation. Reported missing before the start of 1976, her lifeless body would be found on February 24, 1976. Law officials and agents of the FBI, including Dave Price, who had arrested her eight months before, arrived on the reservation to investigate. Claiming that they did not recognize her, FBI agents had Pictou-Aquash's hands cut off and sent to headquarters for "fingerprint analysis." The BIA pathologist determined that she had died from frostbite, despite an obvious bullet hole in the back of her head. She was buried in a grave marked "Jane Doe," but memories of her refused to fade. After the FBI opened their files, the Wounded Knee Legal Offense Defense Committee and her family requested a second autopsy. The independent pathologist who examined her found the .32 caliber bullet, still embedded in the back of her skull.

Folk-rock duo the Indigo Girls would cover Sainte-Marie's "Bury My Heart at Wounded Knee" in 1996, including live and studio versions, on their album, *12:00 Curfews*. The same year, Sainte-Marie digitally re-recorded some of her best-known songs and released the results as *Up Where We Belong*. In addition to the title track (with Patrick Crockett on slack-key guitar), she included a reworking of "God Is Alive, Magic Is Afoot," the Leonard Cohen poem that she had set to multitracked, improvised, avant-garde music and used to open her album, *Illuminations*. *Up Where We Belong* also included a new round-dance song, "Darling, Don't Cry," recorded with the Red Bull Singers, a family round-dance group from the Little Pine Creek Nation near North Battleford, Saskatchewan, and written with the group's leader, Edmond Bull.

It would take a dozen years before the release of Sainte-Marie's next album, *Running for the Drum*, in December 2008, but the wait was worth it. One of her strongest outings, the twelve-song collection earned the songstress her third JUNO award as "Album of the Year." Mixing Indigenous, electronica, rock, R&B, and folk influences, *Running for the Drum* surveyed the vast range of Sainte-Marie's songwriting. With Jennifer Kreisberg and Soni Moreno, of Ulali, singing harmonies, she harkened back to her coffeehouse days, accompanying herself on acoustic guitar during "Still This Love Goes On," and sharing a duet with Taj Mahal on a New Orleans R&B-flavored tune, "I Bet My Heart on You." The album's climax came with two newly written songs, "Cho Cho Fire" and "No No Keshagesh," the former a celebration of American Indian spirit recorded with the Black Lodge Singers, and the latter a powerful indictment of corporate greed. When released in the United States in August 2009, a biographical DVD, *Running for the Drum: A Multimedia Life*, accompanied the CD.

Although her appearances in the United States have been limited primarily to reservation concerts, AIM events, and political benefits, Sainte-Marie continues to make her presence felt in her adopted homeland. She sang at the Kennedy Space Center in Cape Canaveral, Florida, for John Herrington, America's first American Indian astronaut, in 2002, and served on the committee for Save America's Treasures, a nonprofit organization that filtered hundreds of millions of dollars toward the restoration of nationally important sites.

Despite a demanding schedule as a musician and artist, Sainte-Marie continues to share her passion for education. She taught digital music as an adjunct professor at several Canadian colleges, served an artist-in-residency at the Institute of American Indian Art in Santa Fe, New Mexico, and was the spokesperson for the UNESCO Associated Schools Project Network in Canada. A founder of the Nihewan Foundation for American Indian Education, a private nonprofit foundation dedicated to improving the education of and about American Indian people and culture, she spearheaded the organization's Cradleboard Teaching Project, helping to develop a multimedia curriculum, *Science: Through Native American Eyes*, for kindergarten through high school–aged students. She has received honorary doctorate degrees from the University of Regina (1996), Lakehead University (2000), University of Saskatchewan (2003), Emily Institute of Art and Design (2007), Carleton University (2008), University of Western Ontario (2009), and Ontario College of Art and Design (2010).

Entering her seventh decade as a performer, Sainte-Marie remains as committed to her music as ever. "I make enough concert money internationally," she said, "that I can support my incredible band. They are all rockers from First Nations reserves in Manitoba, Canada, and they have become my best friends. It's a great life and it just keeps getting better and better."

ANTHONY "A." PAUL ORTEGA

LaFarge and Sainte-Marie were not the only ones reflecting Indigenous America in their songs. A medicine man from Riconda Valley, New Mexico, Anthony "A." Paul Ortega (1937–), of Mescalero Apache lineage, composed folk and blues songs about Apache life, rituals, and beliefs. His two solo albums—*Two Worlds* (1964, reissued in 1973) and *Three Worlds* (1974)—remain, according to Canyon Records producer Stephen Butler, "absolutely required listening. They're incredibly beautiful, traditionally rooted albums, just as revolutionary today as when they came out. They express American Indian culture through the experiences of a man, living in the 1960s, whose roots went back to a traditional lineage, with very strong tribal ties, but was welcoming enough of the world of guitars and harmonicas."

Not all of Ortega's songs reached into antiquity. One of the strongest pieces on *Two Worlds*, "What Is an Indian," was a spoken word, acoustic guitar, and chant-accompanied piece by Oklahoma-based attorney and songwriter Ralph Keene. Responding to the stereotyping of American Indians, Ortega addresses the pejorative view of Natives as "lazy," "drunkard," and "a person who doesn't work but gets a monthly check from the government," and asserts that Natives have proven to be "the best in their chosen profession, whether it be law, medicine, politics, athletics, or fighting for freedom."

Descended from a long line of medicine men on his mother's side, Ortega trained in the ritual songs, visual arts, and healing traditions. "I was given to my grandfather when I was five," he said, "to learn the ways of life. He lived across the road from where my parents and I lived."

Despite scoring numerous awards for traditional dancing and artwork as a teenager, Ortega committed to pursuing a career in medicine. After a stint in the army, he settled in Chicago, hoping to secure an x-ray technician's job at Cook County Hospital. As he waited for an opening, he decided that, instead of looking for other work, he would enroll at the Allied Institute of Technology and Design. "I had done some surveying work," he said, "so I went into drafting."

The school quickly recognized Ortega's talents. "They contracted students out to do remodeling and renovating of old buildings," he explained, "and I was very good at inking [architectural drawings]. They immediately put me to work. Nowadays, you just type something into your computer and it draws a line for you, but back then, there were no machines. Everything was done by hand."

Taught to play guitar by his father (an amateur mariachi musician), Ortega became a fixture in Chicago's club scene. "There was an Indian lady, from Oklahoma, who owned a club (Mother Blues) in Old Town," he said. "Whenever a band needed a bass player, she'd tell them about me and I'd get the gig. I used to go to

Wells Street in downtown Chicago, where the blues clubs were, and, on Sundays, I would go over to the University of Chicago. There was a place on campus where musicians would play for donations. Some of them were the best that I've ever heard."

Ortega found a connection between the blues and Native music. "American Indian music comes from the heart," he said. "It's the same with the blues."

A turning point came as Ortega watched the performance of an American Indian comic. "He dressed in buckskin and made jokes about Indians," he recalled. "He threw water into the air and stood underneath it. After he was wet, he looked up and said, 'I'm now called "Chief Rain in the Face."'" Ortega decided to confront the unfunny humorist. "He was smaller than me," he said. "I figured that I would take him on. I told him that what he was doing was wrong, that the songs and prayers, that he was making fun of, were important." When the comedian replied, "Show me," Ortega set on the path that led to his groundbreaking recordings. "I started devoting my life," he said, "to getting people to understand that Indian songs are not just guttural sounds and chants, that they mean life, giving, blessing, and everything in the world to the American Indian."

It took a while before Ortega was ready to fulfill his plan. "I tried to find a musician who played similar to what I was looking for," he said. "I was going to hire him to show me what to do, but I couldn't find anybody."

Relocating to Palm Springs, California, in the late 1950s, Ortega found the mentor that he was seeking. "I knew this man who was blind," he said. "He lived three or four buildings away from me and I could hear him playing music. I went over one day to see what was going on. He was playing the harmonica and the guitar at the same time. I started doing that."

Continuing to hone his skills in folk music coffeehouses in Southern California, and in San Francisco where he moved in the early '60s, Ortega prepared to record his debut album, *Two Worlds*. Unable to afford time in a recording studio, he sought alternatives. "The only place that I could find," he said, "was in the basement of a church where a friend of mine preached. That's where we recorded." Ortega's involvement with the church continued to grow. "I started playing on Sundays," he said, "and people started coming to hear Indian music and share philosophy as a way of life."

Signed by Canyon in 1973, Ortega's relationship with the label continued for the next two decades. In addition to the reissue of *Two Worlds* in 1973, and the release of the similar-minded *Three Worlds*, a year later, he collaborated on albums with Sharon Burch (*Blessing Way* in 1984) and Joanne Shenandoah (*Loving Ways* in 1991). "I met Sharon (Diné/German) in Phoenix," he said. "She wasn't doing Indian songs yet, but coffeehouse-type tunes with a loud beat. I approached her [about doing something together], but she didn't think that I was sincere."

Reunited a few years later, when both were performing in Albuquerque, Ortega and Burch began work on *The Blessing Ways*. "It took four or five years to finish it," said Ortega.

Ortega's introduction to Shenandoah (Oneida) came as a traditional healer for the BIA Health Services in New Mexico, a position he held from the early 1970s until his retirement in 1998. "Some people that I worked with were related to her," he said, "and they told me that she had been singing Indian songs. I made it a point to go to listen to her. She was as good as they said she was. I approached her and she told me that she had heard about me. We started recording right away."

Loving Ways took more than five years to complete. "Nowadays, people put lyrics together, record it with a musical background, and that's it," said Ortega, "but I try to convey a message. The songs mean a way of life, a philosophy. People have died for it."

FLOYD "RED CROW" WESTERMAN

Floyd "Kangha Duta (Red Crow)" Westerman (Dakota) (1936–2007) shared Ortega's belief in the power of song. As he declared with the opening words of the title track of his debut 1969 album, *Custer Died for Your Sins*, the South Dakota–born singer, songwriter, actor, and activist addressed "all of the lies that were spoken, all of the blood that was spilled."

Songs on *Custer Died for Your Sins*, whose title derived from Vine Deloria, Jr.'s best-selling book, responded to the exploitation of America by anthropologists ("Here Come the Anthros"), proselytizing mercenaries ("Missionaries"), and the Bureau of Indian Affairs ("B.I.A."). "Red, White, and Blue" equated the American Indian struggle with the African American Civil Rights Movement. "I remember when *Custer Died for Your Sins* came out," said Joseph Fire Crow. "We'd listen to it in our sleep, all night."

Westerman would record three additional albums—*Indian Country* (1970), *The Land Is Your Mother* (1982), and *A Tribute to Johnny Cash* (2006)—and re-record *Custer Died for Your Sins*, in 1982, and appear in more than fifty movies and television shows. His portrayals of Sioux leader Ten Bears in *Dances with Wolves* in 1990, and the shaman in Oliver Stone's biopic, *The Doors*, the following year, were watershed events in the history of American Indian cinema. He made memorable appearances in *Renegades* (1989), *Hidalgo* (2004), and *Tillamark Treasure* (2006), guested on television shows (*Northern Exposure, L.A. Law, MacGyver*, and *Murder, She Wrote*), and appeared in the reoccurring roles of Uncle Ray Firewalker (*Walker, Texas Ranger*) and George Littlefox (*Dharma and Greg*).

Despite his fame, Westerman, who spent his later years in Southern California's Marina Del Rey, never lost touch with Native people, wherever they lived. A schoolmate of AIM cofounder Dennis Banks at the Wahpeton, North Dakota, boarding school, he provided guidance and assistance to the Indian Rights organization from its inception and participated in the occupation of the Pine Ridge Reservation in 1973. He toured with Sting in the early 1990s to raise awareness of the struggles of the Kaiapo people of the Brazilian rainforest, and founded and served as executive director of the nonprofit Eyapaha Institute. Taking its name from the Lakota word for "messenger" or "town crier," the institute's mission was to speak out against "racism, discrimination, depredation, and genocide, of indigenous people the world over."

Westerman's activism went beyond Native issues. He performed with Harry Belafonte, in protest of nuclear power, in 1977, and joined with Jackson Browne, Willie Nelson, Bonnie Raitt, Joni Mitchell, Kris Kristofferson, and Buffy Sainte-Marie at benefit concerts for a variety of causes. He spoke at the 1992 World Uranium Hearings in Salzburg, Austria, and chaired the executive board of the National Coalition on Racism in Sports and Media.

Forced from his birthplace on the Lake Traverse Reservation, home of the Sisseton-Wahpeton Oyate branch of the Dakota tribe in northeastern South Dakota, shortly after his second birthday, Westerman spent his early years in a Catholic boarding school. Speaking to NPR in 1996, he remembered watching his mother as he boarded the bus that would bring him to the school. "It was hurting her, too," he recalled, "and it was hurting me to see that. I will never forget it. All of the mothers were crying."[27]

Moved even farther from home at the age of ten, to the Wahpeton Indian School, eighty miles from the reservation, Westerman's problems continued. "When his mother was in her forties," said Chenoa Westerman, the second-youngest of his four daughters, "she was murdered—much too young. He wrote the song 'Thirty-Five More Miles' for her."

After finishing high school, where he learned to play the guitar, in Flandreau, South Dakota, and serving a year with the U.S. Marine Corps reserves, Westerman studied speech, theater, and art, and earned a degree in secondary education, at Northern State Teacher's College, in Aberdeen, South Dakota.

At the time of his passing—from leukemia—at the age of seventy-two, in December 2007, Westerman was at his creative peak, having released his fourth album, *A Tribute to Johnny Cash*, just two years before. In addition to reworked Cash classics, including "Big River," "Folsom Prison Blues," "Don't Take Your Guns to Town," and "Tennessee Flat Box Top," the album included a rendition of Peter LaFarge's "Drums," recorded with John Densmore of the Doors. *A Tribute to Johnny Cash* received a NAMMY for "Best Album of 2005." "He was the greatest cultural ambassador that Indian America ever had," said Dennis Banks, "a real national treasure."[28]

JOANNE SHENANDOAH

Joanne Lynn Shenandoah (1955–) was working as a computer programmer and architectural systems engineer in Washington, D.C., when she met Westerman in the early 1980s. He would continue to mentor her until his passing, and she would pay homage to his memory two years later (2009), with *Bitter Tears, Sacred Ground*, an album that also recalled the influence of Peter LaFarge and Johnny Cash. "I don't want to say that Floyd gave me my start," the Oneida singer-songwriter told me in October 2011, "but he certainly inspired me. He always encouraged me and invited me to sing with him. I remember the first time that I sang 'Thirty-Five More Miles.' I didn't realize that he had written it for his mother. He stood there and cried. I thought to myself, 'I'm going to stay strong so that he can see that I'm paying honor to him.'"

Shenandoah last saw Westerman at a memorial service for a mutual friend. "He came over to me," she remembered, "and said, 'I read that you told somebody that A. Paul Ortega was one of your major influences. Now, you damn well know that it wasn't [Ortega], it was me.'" The songstress was shocked. Gazing at her mentor, Shenandoah could see the hurt in his eyes. "Floyd, you have always been an inspiration to me," she remembered telling him, "and I hugged him."

Inclement weather prevented her from attending Westerman's funeral, but Shenandoah listened to it via cell phone, and, several months later, visited his widow in California. A dream helped to provide closure. "I dreamt that I had performed a big show," she remembered. "We were packing up afterwards, and [Westerman] walked in with these two huge bodyguards. He came over, put his arms around me, and whispered in my ear, 'I just want to make sure that every-thing's okay with you.' I said, 'Everything's okay with me, Floyd. Is everything okay with you?' Then he said, 'Oh, yes, everything's all right,' and hugged me for a long time. He turned around and they left. It seemed so real. We dream about people, not always when we need closure, but when there's something that needs to be said."

Combining country, folk, and pop influences with the stories, history, and musical traditions of the Iroquois, Shenandoah has risen to the upper echelon of Indigenous music. In addition to sharing a Grammy with Bill Miller, Robert Mirabal and the Little Wolf Band for her participation on *Sacred Ground: A Tribute to Mother Earth* in 1995, she's garnered an unparalleled fourteen NAMMYs, including

Joanne Shenandoah (Oneida) is the recipient of an unprecedented fourteen Native American Music Awards (NAMMYs). *Photo by Craig Harris.*

"Lifetime Achievement." "I just knew, in my heart of hearts," Shenandoah said, "that it was my responsibility to put out music that was healing. The Iroquois believe that everyone on this Earth is here for a specific purpose. We all have a special gift that, if we use it in the right way, will make the whole world a better place. For me, it's music."

Belonging to the Wolf Clan of the Haudenosaunee Six Nations Iroquois Confederacy Oneida Nation, Shenandoah is a descendant of John Skenardo (Skenandoah or Shenandoah), the George Washington compatriot for whom Virginia's Shenandoah River and valley are named. Her mother, Mary "Maisie" Shenandoah, collected American Indian art and operated a trading post. Selected as clan mother in 1977, she served as "Matriarch of the Oneida people" for the next three decades.

Joanne's father, Clifford Shenandoah, a chief of the Onondaga Nation, played guitar for jazz great Duke Ellington. "We sang songs every night of the week," she remembered, "my brother, five sisters, mom and dad, and me, everything from Sam Cooke to Hank Williams and Patsy Cline. My mom and dad both played guitar, and, when I got old enough, I'd join them on piano. That was all we did. I thought it was a natural thing, that everybody played music."

Singing from the age of five, Shenandoah was steeped in Iroquois song. "There are songs for when a new baby is born," she said, "and songs for when someone is passing into the spirit world. We sing for the plants, the medicines, the animals, and the harvest. There are hundreds and hundreds of songs."

Pop music also drew Shenandoah's attention. Competing in a school-wide talent contest as a third grader, she took the grand prize with a heart-melting rendition of Harry Warren and Al Durbin's "September in the Rain." "I remember not wanting to go onto the stage," she recalled, "but my dad was there with his guitar. He made it so easy. He whispered to me, 'C'mon, sing it like you've always sung it,' and I did."

Debuted in the 1935 film *Stars over Broadway*, "September in the Rain" was subsequently covered by Bing Crosby, Doris Day, Lionel Hampton, George Shearing, Nelson Riddle, and Frank Sinatra. Rod Stewart included a version on *Fly Me to the Moon: The Great American Songbook, Volume 5*, in October 2010. "Some people have told me that I was way too young to know that song," said Shenandoah, "but it's a song that my dad taught me."

Sent to a boarding school in her teens, Shenandoah, whose Oneida name, Tekali Wha Khwa, translates as "She Sings," studied Western classical music and learned to play clarinet, flute, cello, and piano. "I went to school half a day," she recalled, "and worked half a day. Fortunately, I got to work in the music department, setting up the rehearsal room for the school band. I would pick up every instrument, try to play, and read every book on how to play anything. It was a blast."

Shenandoah took a job in Washington, D.C., following her graduation. "I worked in the design field," she said. "I had top-secret clearance and made a lot of money." Music's lure, though, proved too great to resist. "One day, I saw this beautiful tree being cut down," Shenandoah remembered, "and it uprooted me. I was stunned. I realized that I had been working eighteen-hour days and asked myself why I was working so hard. I wanted to sing."

An opportunity arose when Buddy Red Bow (1949–1993), who was born Wakefield Richards, into the Oglala Lakota tribe, and would become the second inductee to the Native American Music Hall of Fame, invited her to perform at the July 1980 Paha Sapa (Black Hills) festival in South Dakota. "The whole idea completely riveted me," she recalled. She was one of many American Indians and politically aware non-Native musicians participating in the six-day series of workshops and concerts. The event drew people from as far away as Nicaragua, northern Europe, Canada, and South America. According to Roger Moody in *The Indigenous Voice: Visions and Realities,* "Redneck-ranchers rubbed shoulders with radical 'redskins,' white 'green movement' activists with native practitioners of alternative technology, militant left-wing political adherents with anarchist pacifists."[29]

Encouraged by the enthusiastic response her songs received at the festival, Shenandoah returned to her Oneida, New York, birthplace and turned her full-time focus to music. "I felt a bit of pressure," she remembered. "I wanted to represent Native people in a good light and be known as a human being, not as someone who was superhuman. It was a huge responsibility."

Shenandoah's eponymous-titled debut album, released by Canyon Records in 1988, featured the kind of country music she had sung since childhood. She refers to the recording as her "cowboys and Indians album." "It was sort of a test drive," she explained. "I didn't think that I would be doing any more recordings so I sang everything."

Although the lyrics of most of Shenandoah's songs are in English, many include words in the Algonquin-based Iroquois language or vocables. "Some people ask me for the translation of songs," she said, "but I tell them that they're about a nonliteral place. I don't want to call it a 'trance,' but it's a ritual, not something that we need to define or dissect, just a way to put ourselves into a circle of well-being."

One of Shenandoah's earliest compositions, "Make No Mistake, He's Mine," had gone on to be covered by both Barbara Streisand (with Kim Carnes) and Kenny Rogers. She had failed to copyright it, however, before the pop singers recorded it. "I was at a meeting of the Songwriters' Association, in Washington, D.C., sitting next to Mary Chapin Carpenter," she said, "and we started talking about it. She advised me not to sue. Since that time, I've written more than four hundred songs, including many that I still haven't put out yet."

Shenandoah has recorded with pianist and composer Peter Kater (*Lifeblood*), resonant-voiced singer Lawrence "Happy" Laughing (*Orenda*), a Mohawk, and guitarist Michael Bucher (*Bitter Tears—Sacred Ground*), a Cherokee. Robbie Robertson's *Contact from the Underworld of Redboy* featured her harmonies on several tracks. "We've become really good friends," she said of Robertson. "He's an incredible artist and I totally love working with him."

Shenandoah's tunes about respecting the land, and love between all people, made her a natural choice to open Woodstock '94. "My mom was there," she remembered. "We opened with a song that I wrote, 'America,' about the tree of peace, the four directions, and people of all colors coming together."

With her eighth release, *Peacemaker's Journey* (2000), a concept album based on Haudenosaunee legends about the immaculately conceived unifier of the Iroquois

Nations, Shenandoah scored the first of her three Grammy nominations. "Going to the Staples Center [for the Grammy Awards ceremony] was a dream come true," she said. "I never thought about winning, but knowing that people around the world were hearing my message of peace was profound."

For her next album, *Eagle Cries*, a year later, Shenandoah set Native-themed lyrics, in English, to contemporary folk and country music arrangements. "It was my most expensive album," she said. "I had Neil Young and Bruce Cockburn on it, as well as Bill Miller and Mary Youngblood." When the album was nominated for a Grammy, in the "Best Folk Recording" category, Shenandoah took a realistic view of its chances. "It was in the same category as Bob Dylan," she said, "and I don't have the clout that he has."

A treatise on the ancient spiritual pact between the Iroquois people and Mother Earth, Shenandoah's twelfth album, *Covenant* (2003), became her third consecutive Grammy-nominated release. Her studio expertise proved helpful when she produced an album, *Sisters: Oneida Iroquois Hymns*, by her mother, "Maisie" Shenandoah, and aunt Elizabeth "Liz" Robert. "We had an absolutely divine time," she said, "but it was one of the most difficult recordings that I've ever done. Those two bantered like sisters."

"They sang harmonies beautifully," she continued, "but they had never recorded professionally before. We didn't go into a studio; we went to friends' homes to record. The album sounds gorgeous, though. People ask me why we did an album of hymns. They were the songs that their mother [Joanne's grandmother] had taught them—the songs that are part of who we are. I didn't want to lose that memory."

Shenandoah's daughter, Leah, who often accompanies her mother in concerts and recordings, is a cum laude MFA graduate of Rochester Institute of Technology (RIT) in jewelry and metalsmithing. Releasing a debut solo album, featuring blues, jazz, and electronica originals (*Spektre*), in 2013, Leah scored a "Debut Artist of the Year" NAMMY. Leah continues to perform, with her mother and Aunt Diane, in the Joanne Shenandoah Trio. "She sang on stage, with me when she was a baby," said her mother. "She was singing solos when she was five for 2,000 people. Yesterday, when we performed in Kansas City, people were screaming for more. I'm so proud of her."

Along with R. Carlos Nakai, Bill Miller, Margo Thunderbird, and Joseph Fire Crow, Shenandoah and her daughter represented Indigenous America when folksinger Pete Seeger celebrated his ninetieth birthday at Madison Square Garden in May 2010. Bruce Springsteen, Dave Matthews, Richie Havens, Emmylou Harris, Arlo Guthrie, Bruce Cockburn, Ani DiFranco, and Kris Kristofferson also performed.

A few months after recording the title track of *Path to Zero*, a compilation of never-before-released poetry by the Doors' Jim Morrison set to music, the mother and daughter embarked on one of their most unforgettable experiences. Traveling to Israel in November 2011, they joined Sting, Bono, Sinead O'Connor, and Robert Downey, Jr., for a six-hour-long concert, broadcast internationally, from a stage in front of the Church of the Nativity in Bethlehem. They had ample time to explore the land of milk and honey. In addition to visiting the birthplace of Jesus Christ, they harmonized on an Iroquois women's song at the Church of Mary Magdalena in Jerusalem.

Released in January 2012, Shenandoah's thirteenth album, *Lifegivers*—her first independent recording—featured songs, sung in her Native tongue, about the life cycles of a woman.

Movies and television have provided additional outlets for Shenandoah's music. The soundtracks of PBS documentaries, *Warrior in Two Worlds: The Life of Ely Parker*, and *Dancing on Mother Earth*, featured her songs, and she joined R. Carlos Nakai and Bill Miller for a PBS musical, *Sky Woman: Legends of the Iroquois*. Since making her acting debut with a major role in *The Last Winter*, a 2006 flick starring Ron Perlman about global warming, she's remained active with cinema. "I've just written some songs for a film, *The Year of the Rat*," she said. "It's about a bad drug deal where a baby gets killed in the crossfire."

Possessing an honorary doctorate from Syracuse University, Shenandoah serves on the board of directors for the school's Hiawatha Institute for Indigenous Knowledge (HIIK). "The institute is the fulfillment of a dream first envisioned by the Oneida leader Shenandoah two hundred years ago," she said. "His wish was to provide a place of learning where the essence of Native knowledge would be shared with the world in a school of higher learning. The institute plans on making available traditional knowledge, taught by elders, about everything from sustainability and agriculture to music, dance, language, and culture."

Shenandoah continues to find new ways to heal with her songs. She donated an original song and video, "I Feel Your Love," to the children's grief camp of the Hospice of Central New York. "I wrote it because one of my daughter's friends died," she said. "It was her first and only time trying heroin. Leah asked me to come to the funeral and sing. It was a beautiful summer day. I said, 'Let's go to the lake.'"

When they reached their destination, Shenandoah sat by the lake's shore, thinking. "I asked myself," she recalled, "'How can I write a healing song for these young people?' The Iroquois think death is a natural thing and I have sung at hundreds of funerals. It's not odd unless someone goes unnaturally, and that's difficult."

Shenandoah dedicated a video of "I Feel Your Love"—filmed with a background chorus of youngsters under the direction of Syracuse University professor Larry Ellin—"to those who are suffering from grief." "We're giving all the profits to the Hospice Council," she said. "It's not about the money. It's about the love."

Shenandoah's 2013 album, *Nature Dance*, scored a "Best World Music Recording" NAMMY. In the album's liner notes, she reiterated her approach to music. "As I make this journey in life," she wrote, "I've found that most people around the world are compassionate about our Mother Earth and concerned about the environmental changes affecting all living things. We are told to remain eternally grateful for the blessings of life, to use only what we need and to respect the rights of those unborn until the seventh generation. We believe balance and harmony are realized when the natural world has a voice in the affairs of human beings and each one of us is free to live in accordance with our Creator given talents."[30]

KEITH SECOLA

"The Bob Dylan of American Indian music," Keith Secola (1957–), who is of Anishinaabe and Italian descent, was a University of Minnesota Native Studies student and aspiring singer-songwriter when he met Floyd Westerman in 1979. "He was coming to play a concert [at the school]," recalled Secola, "and I was asked to open the show. I was excited about it. I really liked his music and his activism."

Picking Westerman up at the airport, and bringing him back to his apartment, Secola suggested that they play some music. From the moment that they began jamming, he sensed a strong connection with the Dakota singer-songwriter/actor/activist. "We locked in from that moment," he remembered. "Whenever he would come through town, I'd back him up. A few times, he even gave me some cash—two or three hundred bucks. To a college student, that meant a lot."

Secola retains plenty of fond memories of Westerman. "One time, he was sleeping at my house," he said, "and we put a mattress on the hardwood floor in the living room. He was lying down, listening to me playing the piano. He said one of the most complimentary things that I ever heard him say, 'Keith, you are pure music energy.' That inspired me. We had many moments like that. We would talk about things. I remember once one of my little nephews came up to me while I was playing my guitar. He started putting his hands on the strings and having fun dancing around. Floyd looked at him and said, 'Yep, that's what it's all about.'"

By the time that he met Westerman, who was twenty-one years his elder, Secola was a seasoned musician. Raised in a family that included fiddle players and powwow singers, he had grown up singing. Teaching himself to play guitar and flute, he accompanied his four sisters, brother, and parents at family sing-alongs.

Keith Secola (Anishinaabe/
Italian) has been called the
"Bob Dylan of American
Indian music."
Courtesy Keith Secola.

"If you have good ears," he said, "you can find a pitch as easily as you can find the
pitch of a mountain stream or crickets at night. I've pitched a tent by a mountain
stream and found the right flute. I've learned that crickets are in D minor. I've
always been at that intersection—life and imagination, music and dreams."

Writing his first songs as school assignments, Secola learned the craft quickly.
One of his earliest tunes, "Fry Bread," remains a much-loved staple of his concerts.
"When I first performed it," he remembered, "I would invite volunteers from the
audience onto the stage and tell them to lie down as though they were fry bread
dough. In the middle of the song, I would stop singing and tell a story about how
fry bread had once been illegal. I would talk about the Fry Bread Removal Act,
the Trail of Grease, and military people like Major Rip-off, Major Alcoholic, Major
Asshole, and Major Delay. I would say that there had been a fry bread messiah,
born to the people, who taught that the strongest ingredient that we have is love.
I would get the audience charged up, singing 'fry bread' back and forth with me.

The people on the floor would start to rise. Sometimes, Floyd [Westerman] would come onto the stage, as the messiah, and tell the dough to rise. He had fun with it. He would get everyone on his or her feet singing."

The two musicians remained friends until Westerman's passing. "Towards the end, he was taking a lot of medication," said Secola. "I remember the last time that I saw him. I had heard that he was sick, so, after playing a show in San Francisco, I went to see him in the hospital in Los Angeles. There were so many people there—musicians, movie stars, and friends—waiting to see him a final time. When I went into his room, I brought my guitar. That was the best thing that I could have done. Instead of talking to him, a few of us sang. That made him happy. Playing for him, on his dying bed, was reminiscent of Bob Dylan playing for Woody Guthrie, seeing what he was going through, and knowing that I had never gone through anything like it."

Arranging songs into a rock, blues, country, folk, and tribal-inspired mix that he calls "Alt-Native" and "Native Americana," Secola, who hails from the Iron Range city of Cook, Minnesota, about forty miles from Bob Dylan's birthplace, has continued to explore cultural fusion. "I've always been into blending things," he said, "the powwow drum and the kick drum, the guitars tuned to a traditional flute. It's an understanding of the relationship between pitch and beat, the intersection of Minnehaha and Hiawatha."

Having studied trombone since grade school, Secola approached the brass instrument with enthusiasm. "Playing in a marching band," he said, "was like being in a rock-and-roll band with uniforms. I thought that the trombone was the guitar of the marching band."

"My band director was an old Italian man from Joliet, Illinois," he continued. "He had been an athlete, but he really believed in my music. I would look at the sheet music, but I would not stay on the page. I would try to incorporate my sound into the sound of the band. The trombone is very much a 'hearing' instrument. You could slide up to notes and pitches. It is not in a fixed position like a cornet, trumpet, saxophone, or flute. That comes in handy when you're mixing traditional and modern Native music."

Secola's tenure as a marching-band trombone player ended when a freak accident left him with a broken leg. "After football games, one of the linesmen and I would race back to the bus," he explained. "[The last time], I slipped on the sidewalk. Ironically, I fell one hundred yards from the entrance to a hospital. All they had to do was bring out the gurney, pick me up, and carry me in."

Hitchhiking to Dylan's hometown of Hibbing, a few months later, Secola bought his first new electric guitar and amplifier. "Once I had the electric guitar," he said, "it made all my dreams real."

While studying for a public service degree at Mesabi Community College in Virginia, Minnesota, Secola continued to build on his musical skills, performing every weekend with a local rock band, the Schwartz Brothers. "We played cosmic Americana music," he said. "I wasn't singing lead, yet—we had a female singer who helped to get us in the doors. She could sing Bonnie Raitt tunes and the blues."

Despite the group's local popularity, Secola had different ambitions than his bandmates. "The guitar player always said that, if you can't find happiness in your backyard, you can't find it," he remembered, "and I would tell him, 'You define your backyard—mine is the world.'"

Briefly attending the University of Colorado, in Boulder, Secola not only met his future wife, Patricia McKinley (Ute), but also broadened his musical vision. "I heard all kinds of music," he said, "especially bluegrass, folk, and acoustic music. I had gone through my rock-and-roll phase, and learned to play electric guitar, but I really dove into the acoustic. I really learned to play. I learned about fingerpicking and alternate tunings. Oh, man, did it sound good."

Returning to the Iron Country, Secola continued to balance school and music. In addition to pursuing a degree in American Indian Studies at the University of Minnesota—he graduated in 1982—he resumed his role in the Schwartz Brothers Band. He also began performing with the group's offshoot, the Dog Soldiers. "We were punks," he remembered, "into antigovernment anarchy through music."

Meeting two female singers at a guitar repair shop, Secola became the third member of their acoustic trio, Sweetwater. "We called ourselves 'Rusty Well Water,' 'Crystal Clear Water,' and 'Luke Warm Water,'" he remembered. "It was a joke, but, for me, [playing in the group] was a reprieve. I started to learn folk songs and the importance of vocals."

An early Secola composition, "NDN Kars" has gone on to be one of contemporary Native America's best-loved anthems. Featuring a different version on each of his albums, Secola has adopted the song to rock, country, blues, and dance music. His 2012 album, *Life Is Grand*, included a punk rock version, recorded with his son, Keith Michael Secola, on drums, his son's musical partner, Joe Dougherty, on guitar and vocals, and longtime Wild Band of Indians member Jimmy Vickers on bass and vocals. "Two young punks and two old punks," Secola joked. "We're like the Indian Ramones."

Written while he was still in school, "NDN Kars" originated during what Secola recalled as a "beer-drinking road trip." "We were in Winton, Minnesota," he remembered, "and stopped at the end of Highway 169, one of the longest highways in America. There was a municipal liquor store by a beautiful lake/marsh area and the road turned to dirt after that, five miles into the wilderness. It was a very romantic setting. I remember going to the restroom and seeing that somebody had written 'NDN Kars' as graffiti. I said, 'That would be a good name for a song.' When I came out, I had a couple more drinks and started chanting. I got a pretty riff going by the end of the night. A few days later, I translated it to the guitar. I wrote the song in minutes, but took another fifteen years to learn how to play it."

With its despite-all-odds optimism, "NDN Kars" resonated with nearly everyone who heard it or read its words. "I sent the lyrics to an American Indian magazine in Minneapolis, *The Circle*," said Secola, "and they immediately published them. That excited me. The idea that a bumper sticker can hold a car together is the same premonition that people have of juju or magic, the essence of life. 'NDN Kars' is all of that."

Moving to Tempe, Arizona, in the early 1980s, Secola supported his musical career, and family, by working at the Indian Resource Center. Releasing his debut album, *Indian Cars*, on his independent label, Akina, in 1985, he refocused the spotlight on his music. "An entertainment lawyer, who had broken many big acts, called me," said Secola, "and told me that people at A&M had picked a couple of acts that they believed in. One was a band from Seattle (Nirvana) and I was another. I didn't know anything about contemporary music or have management behind me. There was nobody saying that they would invest $50,000 in me, but I had raw talent, and a song that could cross over. It changed things so much, allowed me this underground notoriety."

Secola's ascent continued after the Grateful Dead added "NDN Kars" to their preconcert playlist. "Jerry Garcia told me not to worry," he recalled, "good music slips through the cracks. He was right—that song opened doors."

As his influence spread, mainstream acts (David Bowie, Pearl Jam, Nirvana, and the Neville Brothers) invited Secola to open shows, and he traveled with the Indigo Girls as part of their *Honor the Earth* tour. "We all have some very common songs," he said, "things that people could relate to right away, with roots in power chords, pentatonic scales, and four-four time."

Signed by German-based Normal Records in 1982, Secola, and his bands (the Wild Band of Indians, the Wild Javelinas), have toured Europe on a semiregular basis. "It's where I really cut my teeth," he said, "where I learned to use music to entertain people. The novelty wears off fast in Europe; there's a sense of musical integrity."

Secola was forced to put his dreams on hold when a routine medical exam in 1989 detected an acoustic neuroma extending from his right ear canal to his brain. "It was devastating," he remembered, "a life-and-death thing. I had health insurance, lived next to a neurological institute, and went to see doctors, including the world-renowned surgeon Dr. Ralph Spencer, but I also went to see three healers."

Secola's loss of hearing alarmed doctors. "One doctor wanted to hook me up with a hearing aid," he recalled, "but another put a tuning fork to the base of my ear. I couldn't hear it. They examined me closer and discovered that there was a tumor growing inside my head. They had to get it out. I didn't have much time to wait, only about a month to prepare. I went to my medicine society, saw an Apache healer, and gave blood. Then, I went through a two-day surgery, where they opened my head like a pumpkin and carved the tumor out."

Recuperation was extremely rough. "I had palsy for a year," said Secola, who lost the hearing in his right ear, "and I couldn't smile. I felt like a monster. I'd go out in public and people would say, 'What's wrong with that guy?' I staggered a little bit. People thought that I was drunk."

The experience had a lasting impact. "I learned to hear with my heart," said Secola. "When I lost hearing in my ear, I learned to hear that pitch that hits the heart."

Releasing a career retrospective, *Circle*, in 1992, which was compiled from his first three albums—*Indian Cars* (1985), *Time Flies Like an Arrow, Fruit Flies Like a Banana* (1990), and *Acoustic Aroma* (1991)—Secola followed with critically acclaimed albums, *Wild Band of Indians* in 1996, *Finger Monkey*, three years later, and *Life Is Grand* in 2012.

When we spoke, in October 2012, the recent Native American Music Hall of Fame inductee had just returned from recording a four-song EP to raise funds for the struggle against strip mining in coal-rich Black Mesa (Big Mountain), Arizona, sacred to American Indians for over 7,000 years. One of the tunes was a flute-accompanied spoken-word piece inspired by childhood dreams. "I dreamt of three ghosts," Secola recalled, "the ghost of the Iron Range past, the ghost of the present, and the ghost of the future. The past showed me a forest in its prime, with two-hundred-year-old pine and cedar mountaintops, streams, beaver ponds, rivers. Warriors fought over this area. When people first drilled there, there was enough iron ore to feed every furnace in the world for one hundred years. The next ghost showed me the present. When I was growing up, in 1973, everyone was prospering—the boom years. There was more wealth than there was during the Gold Rush. Kids out of high school could get twelve-dollar-an-hour jobs. Everybody's pockets were full, and everyone had a new car. Then, the last ghost, the ghost of the future, took me to this huge mine dump and had me look down into the world's largest man-made hole, almost a mile deep, five miles wide, and sixty miles long. I looked around, and saw empty stores and abandoned mines."

Another song on the EP was a rendition of "This Land Is Your Land" by Dylan's inspiration, Woody Guthrie, in the Ojibwe language. Secola had previously included it on his 2007 album, *Native Americana—A Coup Stick*. "It reflects a worldview," he said, "of being a part of the world and not detached from it. Woody was into people creating their own stories about the dynamic life that they were experiencing. That's what I got from him—how to apply this strategy, this procedure of songwriting, to the topics that affect American Indians."

Humor has been a key to some of Secola's best songs. "Drum in My Car" poked fun at a familiar aspect of contemporary life—Native and non-Native. "It's about the hilarious things that people say," said Secola. "The expression, 'I've got my drum in my car,' may seem tongue-in-cheek, but people tell me that all of the time."

The oddest tune in Secola's repertoire, "ND Waza Bat," mashed characters from Andy Griffith's classic TV show, *Andy of Mayberry*, with horror film imagery. "That was one of Robbie Robertson's favorite songs," said Secola. "It came out of the romantic, pre–Annie Rice, vampire era, but you could look at it on a socioeconomic level, too. ND could be a giant corporation, sucking the blood out of the Earth. It was a collision of being unemployed and watching TV reruns, and having a guitar in my hands. I put together a story that followed A, B, C, and D, but removed part B, so people had to jump to conclusions."

Not all of Secola's songs are so lighthearted. "Innocent Man" spoke out for more than the falsely imprisoned. "It's a cry to each of us shackled by society," he said, "with the complexity of modern-day society entrapping our innocent child, never allowing dreams to come out. That song is very cathartic, getting rid of all of that misery and suffering. Of course, it has connections with Indians imprisoned, Leonard Peltier being the poster child, but that is a whole other story. The song is, not so much about individual rights, but about our rights as human beings."

With the release of *Life Is Grand*, his first album of new material in a dozen years, Secola not only picked up where he left off, but also re-emerged as an artist still evolving. "There were a lot of things that I wanted to say," he explained. "Some songs are straight-up acoustic, just me and slide guitar, some are more produced with background vocals and other instruments. I started some of the songs when I was in my twenties and only finished them now. There's even [a soon-to-be Yuletide classic] 'Christmas Time.'"

Several songs on *Life Is Grand* originated in *Seeds*, a rock opera completed in 2012. "It's a play about virtues," explained Secola. "Creation sends seeds down to the Earth, brought down by an angel. There are actually forty-nine seeds, forty-nine virtues, given to the human race. There are three characters [in the play]. One is an Earth sage, a singer. The hero is a mountain lion. His nemesis is Grey Wolf. [The play] is not only about disenfranchisement but also about inheriting the Earth by the meek, a prophecy that will come true. When the seeds come down, they land in the hands of 'the good,' but they lose them through their vanity and an eagle starts misappropriating the seeds. Love turns to hate, prosperity to greed. It's a very simple story."

The hardest-hitting tune on *Life Is Grand*, "Open the Door," surveys more than five centuries of atrocities committed against American Indians. "That was a Floyd Westerman–influenced song," said Secola. "The scary part of understanding the complexity [of Native America] is how deep you have to dive."

ACTIVISM IN THE SIXTIES

The struggle for tribal sovereignty and Native Rights has steadily gained steam. Building on the efforts of earlier organizations, including the Society of American Indians and the American Indian Federation, the National Congress of American Indians (NCAI) began meeting in 1944. A champion fancy dancer and song leader, known for his large repertoire of tribal songs, Clyde Merton Warrior (1939–1968), a Ponca, helped to launch the "Red Power Movement" when he cofounded the National Indian Youth Council (NIYC) in 1961. Two years later, the group became involved with fish-in protests against the loss of tribal fishing rights in the Pacific Northwest. Actor and activist Marlon Brando, who accompanied Warrior to the NIYC's annual meeting in 1963, became increasingly involved with the group's efforts, culminating in his March 2, 1964, arrest for participating in a fish-in protest on Washington State's Pallyup River. "I was very happy when Marlon Brando stood up for us," recalled singer/songwriter/flutist Bill Miller (Mohican). "I was impressed when he showed up at Wounded Knee, in 1973, and when he had a Native woman (Sasheen Littlefeather) accept the Academy Award for him and speak on behalf of Indians. It was powerful."

Warrior would succumb to liver failure, at the age of twenty-nine, in 1968, but the NIYC's struggle would continue to inspire similar groups, including AIM. "There was something in the air," remembered poet and songwriter Joy Harjo (Muskogee Creek/Cherokee/Irish). "It followed, naturally and directly, from the [African American] Civil Rights Movement, and was one of many community movements; people were starting to stand up. There was a visibility, a questioning, and a reclaiming of our arts, literature, and sovereignty."

Alcatraz Island, located off the coast of San Francisco, became the center of American Indian activism on November 20, 1969, after seventy-nine Natives—including students, married couples, and children—took over the former federal penitentiary. The group, which became Indians of All Tribes (IAT), cited the Treaty of Fort Laramie (1868), which called for retired, abandoned, and unused federal land to revert to its original tribal ownership. A smaller group had attempted a similar takeover in March 1964, but they had retreated from the inhospitable island after a brief four hours. This time, occupants remained for nearly nineteen months before the federal government forcibly removed them on June 11, 1971.

JOHN TRUDELL

John Trudell (1946–2015), of Santee heritage, was studying radio broadcasting, under the GI Bill, at San Bernardino Valley College and working as a reporter for the campus radio station, when he arrived on Alcatraz Island in December 1969. He would remain at the embattled site for the rest of its occupation, serving as spokesperson for the AIT and being placed on the FBI's "ten most wanted" list. Using a relayed feed to the campus station at the University of California, Berkeley, his on-site "Radio Free Alcatraz" broadcast news and interviews, providing an important link between occupiers and the outside world. Trudell's activism, and ability to speak eloquently, connected with the goals of AIM, and he would serve as its national chair from 1973 until 1979.

Born in Omaha, Nebraska, and raised on the Santee Sioux Reservation, Trudell was the grandson of a compatriot of the Mexican revolutionary general Pancho Villa, who had kidnapped (and married) Trudell's grandmother from the northwestern Mexican state of Chihuahua. His mother, raised as Mexican in Kansas, died before his seventh birthday. Dropping out of high school at the age of seventeen, he served four years in the U.S. Navy, including two stints aboard a destroyer off Vietnam, before his honorable discharge in 1967.

Trudell's activism reached a critical point on February 12, 1979, when he burned an American flag during a protest demonstration on the steps of the FBI building in Washington, D.C. Less than twelve hours later, as his pregnant wife, Tina Manning (Paiute/Shoshone), a water rights activist, their children—daughters Ricardo Star (five) and Sunshine Karma (three), and son, Eli Changing Star (one)—and Manning's parents slept, Trudell's in-law's house on the Duck Valley Indian Reservation near the Idaho/Nevada border caught fire. All but Tina's father, Arthur Manning, perished. BIA officials denied any connection, but Trudell believed that the fire was the result of arson. Kris Kristofferson would recount the events in his song "Johnny Lobo," while Trudell would reflect on his loss during "Tina Smiled," the closing track of his second album, *AKA Graffiti Man*. "What happened to my family," Trudell told Robert Baird of Phoenix, Arizona's *New Times*, "tells me that I was closer to the truth than even I knew."[31]

Trudell had seen the lengths that the federal government would go to muffle him many times. When he attempted to attend the Leonard Peltier trial in Fargo, North

Dakota, in March 1977, guards prevented him from entering the courtroom. An argument ensued and security evicted him from the building. Shortly afterwards, he was arrested and charged with contempt of court. After a brief hearing, the judge sentenced him to sixty days in jail. Constantly kept on the move, he spent time in five prisons, in three states, including the federal prison in Springfield, Missouri, where an inmate warned him that his family would be in danger if he did not give up his political activities. Heartbroken, and spiritually crushed, Trudell spent four years driving across North America trying to find himself. Six months into the journey, his thoughts were begging for release. Pulling to the side of the road, he grabbed a pen and let the thoughts pour onto the paper—his first poems.

Encouraged by his early efforts, Trudell continued to write. Reciting his poems at festivals and benefit concerts, he was soon stirring attention with the intensity of his words. In 1982, a seventy-one page booklet of his poems, *Living in Reality: Songs Called Poems*, was published by Haymarket Press/Society of People Struggling to Be Free.

At the suggestion of singer and songwriter Jackson Browne, Trudell began reciting to ceremonial drums (played by Milton "Quiltman" Sahme) and tribal chanting. "Jackson is one of the people who, what I'm going to call spirits, put in my life," he told the Honolulu, Hawaii *Star Bulletin*. "He appeared in my life at a time when I needed this ally. I mean, I'm coming out of an activist world, my whole is completely wrecked, I'm wrecked, everything is messed up, just destroyed, and I'm trying to figure out, 'how do I stay, how do I stay.' He took me into a completely different world of music and I had no restrictions, no rules put on me. I just had access. He gave me sanctuary; he gave me shelter when I needed it. I wouldn't be doing what I'm doing without Jackson."[32]

Trudell's debut album (*Tribal Voice*), produced by Browne, was released on cassette in 1983. When a copy reached Jesse Ed Davis (Kiowa), the session guitarist whose slide guitar solo had propelled Browne's 1973 hit, "Doctor My Eye," Davis was awestruck. Tracking down the poet/activist, Davis convinced him to combine their talents—and their Native heritages.

Trudell and Davis hit the mark with their first collaboration, *AKA Graffiti Man*, a Grammy nominee, in 1986. Declaring it the best recording of the year during an interview with *Rolling Stone*, Bob Dylan played it before shows on his world tour. A 1992 reissue included new material and remastered tracks. "Sometimes if people hear that Jesse or I are Indian," Trudell told the *Los Angeles Times*, "they have images in their mind of what musically we would be and I wanted to escape that preconception. It was a challenge to lay it right out there. . . . [T]hese are an accumulation of our feelings and views and for this one, we didn't put on the beads and feathers. We just used the communication of music, thought and words."[33]

Their next outings, *Heart Jump Bouquet* and *But This Isn't El Salvador*, presented Trudell's spoken word and Davis's slide guitar in more commercial, full-band arrangements, but Davis's drug addiction proved too difficult an obstacle to overcome. On June 22, 1988, an overdose took the guitarist's life, three months before his forty-fourth birthday. Trudell reflected on Davis's death during "The Needle," one of the songs on his cassette-only 1991 release, *Fables and Other Tragedies*.

Forced to regroup, Trudell accepted an invitation to join Midnight Oil's *Diesel and Dust to the Big Mountain* tour. The Sydney, Australia–based rock band's sixth album, *Diesel and Dust*, had focused on the struggles of the Indigenous people of Australia's Outback. Using the pseudonym Graffiti Man, Trudell set his spoken words to tribal drumming, chanting, and Martin Rotsey's screaming electric guitar.

In 1990, Trudell participated in the recording of British pianist/keyboardist/synthesizer player Tony Hymas's tribute (*Oyate*) to Barney Bush (Shawnee/Cayuga), the Illinois-born poet, songwriter, AIM member, and founder of the Institute of the Southern Plain, a Cheyenne Indian school in Oklahoma. Trudell recited several of Bush's poems and his own spoken-word piece, "Crazy Horse," with Jeff Beck on guitar.

Trudell's resurgence continued three years later, when he participated with Ziggy Marley, Crowded House, the Drummers of Burundi, and Sheila Chandra in Peter Gabriel's WOMAD tour. His fifth album, *Johnny Damas and Me*, released in February 1994, renewed his collaboration with Mark Shark, a producer, guitarist, and mandolin player whom he had met through Davis. The album sold briskly, shipping 25,000 copies in the first three weeks that it was available and becoming a top-forty hit in England. "This is not only an 'extremely eloquent' protest album," proclaimed *The New Industrialist*, "but one you can dance to."[34]

The recipient of a "Living Legend" NAMMY in 1997, Trudell picked things up a notch with his sixth release, *Blue Indians*, two years later. The title track received a "Song of the Year" statuette at the 2000 NAMMY ceremonies, with Trudell also receiving "Producer of the Year" and "Artist of the Year" honors.

Trudell's words cut even deeper on *Bone Day* in 2002. Executive-produced by Academy Award–winner Angeline Jolie, the thirteen-track CD looked at the state of the world at the dawn of the twenty-first century. Trudell told a *Billboard* reporter that both the album's title track and the band's name (Bone Days) reflected on "hard times." "You know, 'no meat, down to the bone,'" he explained. "The average human being in America is going through some sort of hard times—physical, emotional, psychological. Everybody's carrying a bit of bone days in them."[35]

As his notoriety grew, other American Indian musicians sought Trudell's services. He appeared on Native-reggae singer Casper Loma-Da-Wa's album, *Sounds of Reality*. Leech Lakes Reservation–based singer and songwriter Annie Humphrey bookended her second album (*The Heron Smiled*) with two versions of Trudell's "Spirit Horses," one featuring the poet's spoken recitation. The album went on to garner NAMMY nominations for "Songwriter of the Year," "Recording of the Year," "Best Folk/Country Recording," and "Best Female Artist of the Year."

Trudell's influence spread into motion pictures and made-for-TV films. He starred in *Thunderheart*, a 1992 murder mystery set on the Sioux Reservation, and he had a major role in *Smoke Signals*, a Chris Eyre–directed 1998 comedy about reservation life. He also appeared on Hallmark's made-for-TV, four-hour-long drama *Dreamkeeper*, in 2003.

Trudell was the subject of an eighty-minute documentary film, produced and directed by Heather Rae (Cherokee), that premiered during the 2005 Sundance Film Festival, and aired nationally in April 2006 on PBS-TV's *Independent Lens*. Rae had spent a dozen years (1992–2002) researching and filming the poet's life.

Continuing to record gutsy, musically accompanied, spoken-word discs, Trudell released an Internet-only double-CD, *Madness and the Moremes*, in 2007, composed of new pieces and ghost tracks recorded with Jesse Ed Davis, and a seventeen-track collection of new tunes and reworked pieces, *Crazier than Hell*, came four years later. Recorded with Swiss multi-instrumentalist and producer Kwest, Trudell's fourteenth album (*Through the Dust*) released in April 2014. "When I first started doing this," Trudell told Anthony Goulet six months later, "I wanted to see if I could kind of influence the next generation and the community to look into the arts and the culture versus the political activist way of expression. I felt that, through our culture and our art, we could express the truth, authenticity, and reality of who we are."[36]

HIGH-STAKES MEDIA AND CASINOS

Trudell was not the only AIM leader to branch out to film and recording. Dennis Banks made cameo appearances in several films, including *The Last of the Mohicans* (1992), and he sang/chanted on Peter Gabriel's *Les Musiques des Monde* (1994) and Peter Matthiessen's *No Boundary* (2009). He collaborated with Japanese New Age keyboardist, composer, and producer Kitaro, in 2012, on an album (*Let Mother Earth Speak*) of songs and spoken words set to tribal-meets-electronica arrangements.

Inducted into the Native American Music Hall of Fame in November 2014, Russell Means (1939–2012), an Oglala Lakota, was one of AIM's most colorful figures. The organization's first national director in 1970, he was instrumental in the occupations of the BIA building, in Washington, D.C., and the Pine Ridge Reservation. He appeared in *Natural Born Killers* (1994) and *Cowboy Up* (2001), portrayed Mohican Chief Chingachook in *The Last of the Mohicans* (1992), and provided the voice of Chief Powhatan in Disney's *Pocahontas* (1995) and *Pocahontas II: Journey to a New World* (1998). He starred in *Pathfinder* (2007), which recalled the brutal, pre-Columbian relationship between Vikings and the Natives of "Vinland," along the northeastern seaboard of North America.

A charismatic orator, Means was equally gifted as a writer. His autobiography, *Where White Men Dare Not Tread* is an essential read. Musically, Means delivered some of America's sharpest recordings, combining rock-edged arrangements and sharp-tongued diatribes. On his two albums, *Electric Warrior* (1993) and *The Radical* (1996), the Pine Ridge Reservation–born activist held nothing back in songs like "Nixon's Dead Ass," "Indian Cars Go Far," "Conspiracy to Be Free," "Waco: The White Man's Wounded Knee," "Wounded Knee Set Us Free," and "Remember Wounded Knee."

On December 14, 1979, the Seminole tribe opened a high-stakes bingo hall in Hollywood, California. Authorities attempted to shut it down, which led to a slew of lawsuits and, finally, a Supreme Court ruling that federally recognized tribes could indeed operate casinos outside of state jurisdiction. The Indian Gaming Regulatory Act, signed by Pres. Ronald Reagan in 1988, established federal jurisdictional guidelines for reservation gambling.

For some tribes, gambling has provided a much-needed source of income. Four hundred twenty three casinos, run by 233 tribes, in twenty-eight states, brought in more than $26 billion in 2009. Since the opening of a casino in 1992, the Stockbridge-Munsee Reservation in Wisconsin, where much of the Eastern Algonquin Mohican tribe relocated in the 1830s, has seen a new gym, an expanded health center, and newly paved roads. The forest has resuscitated, with deer, bear, waterfowl, and wild turkeys returning.

BILL MILLER

It was a much different setting when three-time Grammy-winning Mohican singer, songwriter, guitarist, and Native American flute player Bill Miller (1955–) was a child. "I saw alcoholism, domestic violence, and suicides," he remembered, "so many harsh images."

Racism was part of Miller's early life. "I was spit at," he told the *Los Angeles Times*, "called 'Timber Nigger,' 'Brown S—t,' this and that. I saw my dad attacked by white racists . . . saw it turn him into an alcoholic and kill him. I got my life threatened a couple of times at truck stops. These guys grabbed me by the back of the hair and said, 'You want a haircut, Indian?' People would do weird, violent things to us. I grew up with a lot of pain and hatred."[37]

Bill Miller (Mohican) is a three-time Grammy winner who expands the traditions of country and American folk music with tribal chants, flutes, and rhythms.
Photo by Craig Harris.

Miller—whose Mohican name, Fush-ya Heay Aka, means "Bird Song"—never lost his sense of optimism and hope. "I could see that the beauty far outweighed the negatives," he said. "It amazed me that nobody else saw the trees. Nobody else saw the sky. We have this beautiful painting, with plains, woodlands, and mountains, and we take it for granted. When I thought about the beautiful things in life, and the beauty in people, I could heal, I could go forward, and I could write. I could put it into my songs and not give darkness a place in my life. I could deal with depression through music, with not having friends by playing guitar, with an alcoholic father by writing songs, and with racism with words. I let music into my heart and allowed it to lift me."

Personal experiences infuse Miller's songs. "I take notes on what I see coming out of the sky," he explained, "and what I hear coming out of the mouths of people in a restaurant or on a reservation. What I observe, I apply to the page and add music. It's as simple as that."

Miller's spiritual journey also reflects in his tunes. "I've had problems in my life," he said, "based on fear and abuse in my past. I suffered, when I was younger, from posttraumatic stress. My older kids will tell you that they saw their dad breaking down. I couldn't escape from the shame of growing up in a home of violence, but, to get to the truth, and the deeper roots, you have to go to the depths—the depths of writing, the depths of seeing, and the depths of relationships. I bridge the natural and the supernatural worlds and that's my job until I die."

Miller's songs connect with his heritage. "I've heard drums, flutes, and rattles at sacred ceremonies and powwows since I was young," he said. "I can't get them out of my head."

Inspiration came from non-Native sources as well. "I loved that the Eagles were using imagery from Native America," recalled Miller, "and doing songs, like 'Witchy Woman,' with a Native sound. I thought it was wonderful that Neil Young named his band Crazy Horse. They were touching on the Native backbone."

Playing electric guitar from the age of twelve, Miller spent the first two years with rock-and-roll cover bands. Trading his electric guitar for an acoustic six-string in 1969, he turned to American folk, country music, and bluegrass. A Pete Seeger concert at the University of Wisconsin, where he was studying art, inspired Miller to write about his experiences as an American Indian. "I had seen Buffy Sainte-Marie at a festival," he recalled, "kicking butt, and being a beautiful woman. She knew what she was doing and her music spoke to me. Redbone also gave me inspiration. Songs, like 'Custer Died for Your Sins' and 'We Were All Wounded at Wounded Knee,' filled me with hope."

Acquiring a Native American flute at a bluegrass festival on the Mole Lake Indian Reservation in 1975, Miller added another hue to his musical palette. "[My first flute] was made by Louie Webster," he said, "an incredible flute maker, from northern Wisconsin. I saw him trying to sell his flutes for gas money and bought one for fifty bucks. It was a beautiful, hand-carved, loon's head flute. I hadn't thought about becoming a flute player before, but I started playing a little, night after night. After about a year, it became natural to me. I started including it in my concerts, not having any idea of how popular the Native flute would become. I was just playing it for peace, comfort, and enjoyment."

The first break in Miller's career came through Dallas, Texas–born Michael Martin Murphey, a former folk-singing camp counselor who had become one of America's most successful young songwriters. The Monkees included his "What Am I Doing Hangin' Round" on their 5-million-copy-selling 1967 album, *Pisces, Aquarius, Capricorn & Jones, Ltd.* His songs were covered by Flatt & Scruggs ("Carolina in the Pines") and Bobbie Gentry ("Greyhound Goin' Somewhere"). Kenny Rodgers recorded an entire album of his tunes, *The Ballad of Calico* (1972).

Modeling himself on the cowboys of the American West, Murphey wore ten-gallon hats, fringed outfits, and leather boots, and sang original tunes based on Hollywood's cowboy songs of the 1940s and '50s. An equestrian and rancher, he had his greatest success with a ghost song about a woman and a horse. "Wildfire" reached number three on *Billboard*'s best-selling singles chart in 1975, topping the Adult Contemporary Charts, and becoming, according to BMI, one of the songs most frequently aired on the radio ever.

"It's kind of surreal [how Murphey and I met]," Miller remembered. "I had been listening to his music for years and he was a musical hero of mine. One night, I was playing with a friend in a coffeehouse at the University of Wisconsin. There might have been seven people there, playing pool and drinking coffee. Four of them—two men and two women—came over to the stage and waited until we finished playing a song. I thought they were going to request something. They were some far-out looking hippies. I was thinking, 'Who are these people?' when the leader goes, 'Do you know who Michael Martin Murphey is? Your destiny is to meet him. You need to cross the Mississippi River and go to Winona, Minnesota.' Then they turned around and walked out of the coffeehouse."

Miller and his accompanist looked at each other, shook their heads, and went back to playing their songs. When they finished their set, they looked in the local newspaper, and, sure enough, Murphey was performing in Winona, as opening act for country-rockers, the Ozark Mountain Daredevils. Looking at their watches, and seeing that they had enough time to make it before the end of the show, they decided to embark on the prophesized journey. "It was only forty miles away," recalled Miller, "so we got in the car and drove. We got inside the church, where the show was going on, without a ticket, thanks to the bad security. The Ozark Mountain Daredevils were playing, and they sounded great. I went backstage and asked, 'Is Murphey around?' They said, 'No, he left,' but then they said, 'He's staying at the Holiday Inn, just down the road.'"

Driving to the hotel, Miller found the cowboy singer's room. "He was sleeping," he remembered, "but his road manager said, 'Murphey loves meeting Indian people. Hang out. You can meet him when he gets up in the morning to run.'"

Manically driving back home, Miller gathered some of his more recent paintings and sample recordings and rushed back to wait for Murphey to wake. "I literally sat by his door from midnight on," he said, "waiting for him to get up." But Murphey didn't stir until noon. "I was still waiting outside his door," said Miller. "When he saw me, he went, 'Whoa, who are you?' I said, 'I'm Bill Miller. I was told that I was supposed to meet you.' He invited me in and we talked for a while. Then we went for a six-mile run together. I brought him to my house and my family made him dinner. Within a week, I was touring with him. We became lifelong friends."

With Murphey's endorsement, Miller gained entry into the American folk-music community. He opened shows for Richie Havens and Arlo Guthrie and cowrote songs with Peter Rowan. The oldest of three Massachusetts-born brothers, Rowan had played with Bill Monroe and the Bluegrass Boys in the mid-1960s, before going on to explore psychedelic rock with mandolin wiz David Grisman in Earth Opera in 1967, and with fiddler Richard Greene in the equally adventurous Seatrain, two years later. Returning to bluegrass, he played with Muleskinner, a short-lived supergroup featuring Greene, Grisman, banjoist Bill Keith (also a Bill Monroe alumni), guitar flat-picker Clarence White, and Old and in the Way, an all-star band shared with fiddler Vassar Clements, Jerry Garcia of the Grateful Dead (on banjo), upright bassist John Kahn, and Grisman. A tenor-voiced singer and songwriter, Rowan would introduce such now-classic tunes as "Panama Red," "Midnight Moonlight," and the American Indian–inspired "Land of the Navajo."

Writing together, Miller and Rowan penned several tunes, including "Tumbleweed" (about a reservation elder), which was included on Rowan's Indie Award–winning album, *Dust Bowl Children* in 1991, and Miller's first album for Warner Western (*The Red Road*). Alison Krauss covered it on *Paper Airplane* in 2011.

After a series of albums on independent labels, Miller broke through with his first major label release in the summer of 1993. Produced by Bob Johnston, *The Red Road* interwove chanting, Native American flutes, full-band arrangements, and original songs, including "Dreams of Wounded Knee" and "Reservation Road." One of the most powerful tunes, "Trail of Freedom" took a somber look at alcoholism on the reservation. "When I was making the album," Miller told the *Los Angeles Times*, "my dad called to tell me he was dying, so I had to go back and forth between Nashville and the reservation. . . . [A] lot of priorities changed in my life by doing that. I think it really changed my writing, changed the attack of the album. I was home with the singing style I grew up with, the powwow singers, the area that influenced me not only musically, but [also] life wise. I buried my father a week after I finished the album. It was very intense—it's a piece of my life I'll never forget."[38]

Shortly after the album's release, alt-rock pianist and songwriter Tori Amos tapped Miller to be the opening act for her 1994 *Under the Pink* tour. Born in North Carolina, and raised in Maryland, Myra Ellen "Tori" Amos had been captivating audience members with stark lyricism, and hard-rocking piano playing, since her debut album, *Little Earthquakes*, two years before. "She heard about me, oddly enough, through an article in the *Irish Times*," said Miller. "When we went to dinner to talk, she told me that she had listened to hundreds of demo tapes and couldn't stand any of them. No one was unique enough to stand on stage with her. She told me that she had spoken about it with a journalist, who had done an interview with me, and he recommended me. Her manager called me the next day and asked if I'd do a 280-date tour across the United States and Canada."

Miller went on to open shows for Pearl Jam's Eddie Vedder and the Bo-Deans. "They're all very down-to-earth people," he said, "very concerned with causes, and it was a blessing to be in their presence, but I want to be able to do my own thing."

Releasing a collection of Christian worship music, *Hear Our Prayer*, in 2000, Miller took many of his longtime fans by surprise. "Gospel producer Chris Harris asked me to do it," he explained. "I relate to prayer and worship—it's what we do with the powwow drum—and I was glad to get involved. What I believe is God-centered. I have the spirit inside of me. Whether I'm playing blues, singing a song, or jamming with a jazz band, it doesn't matter."

Miller's greatest musical challenge came with *The Last Stand*, a thirty-five-minute-long orchestral piece reflecting on Custer's 1879 defeat at Greasy Grass (Little Bighorn). Working with Joshua Yudkin, a Philadelphia-based pianist, keyboardist, composer, songwriter, and producer of Miller's 2004 "Best Native American Recording" Grammy-winning album, *Cedar Dream Songs*, and Kristin Wilkinson, a Nashville-based composer, Miller based the piece on a childhood visit to the Montana site of the massacre. "I remembered going there with my grandfather when I was nine," he said, "and spending time with historians, and Crow Indians, who were talking about the battle. You could still find arrowheads from Crazy Horse's warriors, and bullet shells, on the field. Tourists were picking them up and taking them."

Premiered by the La Crosse, Wisconsin, Symphony Orchestra, with Amy Mills conducting, in April 2008, *The Last Stand* would be performed throughout Israel by the Kibbutz Orchestra, with Miller featured on Native American flute and guitar. Among their performances was a much-publicized show at the Tel Aviv Museum of Art. The Holy Land had a profound effect on the songwriter. "Music was suddenly more than just songs," he told Mark Crawford of *Cowboys & Indians* after returning to the States. "I wanted to raise the awareness of peace, to share my own experiences about moving from victim to victory—whether it's for one person or an entire culture. I knew I could shine a light on this path through my heritage and my music."[39]

Miller's singer-songwriter albums intersperse with recordings spotlighting instrumental Native American flute playing. His first, *Loon, Mountain, and Moon*, was released in 1991, while a four-CD series (*Spirit Wind*) was bookended by Grammy-winning albums, *Cedar Dreams*, in 2005, and *Spirit Wind North*, five years later. "I wanted to recognize the four directions," Miller said, "and the traditions of the tribes who live in those directions. It represented a period of years of writing, playing my flutes, and praying in different areas of the United States. It was a nice journey."

Miller's 2010 album, *Chronicles of Hope*, reflected deep personal introspection. In the liner notes, he explained, "[This album] covers a period of three and a half years. In those times of searching, perseverance, and healing, I gained clarity and answers to questions I had turned away from for years. I questioned life and death. I cried out from the wilderness in my own personal storms. I whitewater rafted down the dark rivers into the eternal."[40]

Much of Miller's energy is reserved for his wife, Renee, and their three biological children, their adopted son, and their wheelchair-bound adopted daughter, who was born with spina bifida, a birth defect in which the bones of the spine (vertebrae) fail to form properly around the spinal cord. "It's an honorable role to be a father," he said, "and it's definitely made my outlook on life different."

Residing in Franklin, Tennessee, about twenty miles south of Nashville, since 1984, Miller has been collaborating with the offspring of some of country music's most influential musicians. "I've been working with [Johnny Cash's son] John Carter Cash, [Roy Orbison's son] Wesley Orbison, and [Waylon Jennings's son] Shooter Jennings," he said. "We're writing songs and making a record together. This is a great place to do it."

Miller's watercolor paintings have been exhibited in the Smithsonian's National Museum of the American Indian in Washington, D.C., the Trickster Gallery in Chicago, the Barbara Able Gallery in Santa Fe, and the American Indian Community House in New York City. "I love to paint," he said, "but I don't separate the painting from the music. When I write songs, I am always sketching. When I paint, I'm always listening to music. It gets me fired up. If I use my mind in a painterly sense, I can compose. I can bring life to a song."

JOY HARJO

An established poet when she turned to music, Joy Harjo, née Foster (1952–), was the recipient of a William Carlos Williams Award from the Poetry Society of America (1991), a "Lifetime Achievement" award from the Native Writers Circle of the Americas (1995), and a New Mexico Governor's Award for Excellence in the Arts (1997). She received a Guggenheim Fellowship for Creative Arts in 2014. Her publications include five poetry collections—*What Moon Drove Me to This* (1980), *She Had Some Horses* (1993), *In Mad Love and War* (1990), *The Woman Who Fell from the Sky* (1994), and *A Map to the Next World: Poetry and Tales* (2000)—and a memoir, *Crazy Brave* (2012).

Setting words to music was a natural extension of her poetry. "When I write poems, I don't always think there should be music," Harjo told me in July 2011, "but I'm very aware of the rhythms, sounds, and language. Poetry has to do with

Joy Harjo (Muskogee Creek/Cherokee/Irish) expresses the Native experience through award-winning poetry and song. *Photo by Paula Abdoo, courtesy Joy Harjo.*

word and sound choices, how you maneuver within lines, within a sequence, and how that culminates into emotional streams. It's very similar with music."

Harjo, who is of Muskogee Creek, Cherokee, and Irish lineage, released her first musical project, *Furious Light*, on cassette in 1986. "I invited some of the best jazz players that I knew to play with me as I recited my poetry," she said. "Laura Newman was on sax. Eric Kennison, who used to play with Carmen MacRae, was on keyboards."

Featuring spoken word set to Caribbean, African, and Indigenous-influenced arrangements on her first two albums, *Furious Light* (1989) and *Letter from the End of the Twentieth Century*, Harjo introduced her singing voice on *Native Joy for Real* (2004) and continued to sing on *Winding through the Milky Way* (2008) and *Red Dreams: A Trail beyond Tears* (2010).

Harjo purchased a tenor saxophone in the mid-'80s, but it went unused for a decade. "The first song that I learned," she recalled, "was 'A Song for Annie Mae

Pictou Aquash.' It came out on [my band] Poetic Justice's album, *Letter from the End of the Twentieth Century* (1997)."

Although she yearned to play saxophone as a youngster, Harjo's aspirations were nearly squashed. "My junior high school band teacher wouldn't let me play the saxophone," she recalled. "He said, 'Girls can't play saxophone.' So I quit. Music became very painful for me. I felt like it had been taken away from me."

Rediscovering the brass instrument as an adult, Harjo took to it with passion. "The saxophone is like a human voice," she said, "it can sing the way that my voice wants to sing."

Harjo wasn't the first female saxophone player on her family tree. "My great-grandmother Naomi Harjo played the saxophone in Indian Territory," she said. "She died when my dad was a baby, of tuberculosis, which was common among Indian people. I didn't know that she played until I was in my forties, but it gave me a sense of having a personal history."

In addition to her great-grandmother's musical talent, Harjo inherited her passion for visual art. "I have a painting of [Seminole leader] Osceola that she did in 1916," she said. "Not only was he a warrior, but he was our uncle too."

On her father Allen W. Foster's side, Harjo is descended from a long line of great leaders. Her great-grandfather was a full-blooded Muskogee Creek Baptist minister. "I'm seven generations from [Muscogee Creek chief] Menawa," she said, "the leader of the Red Stick War, one of the largest uprisings in the history of the United States."

The oldest of four daughters, Harjo grew up in a musical family. "My mother's brother played guitar almost every night in a Pentecostal church," she said, "and my mother loved to sing ballads. She even recorded her songs. Ernie Fields, the bandleader, arranged them. They were mostly country swing and the kind of music that was hot around Tulsa, Oklahoma, in the 1950s."

Varied traditions helped to shape Harjo's musical growth. "I remember hearing a lot of hard-core Muskogee Christian music," she said, "and a lot of traditional ceremonial Creek music, but there was social music, too, like the stomp dances that were for gatherings. I grew up hearing powwow drums and chanting. I never became a powwow freak, but it's still a presence in my life. I'm usually at the Green Corn Ceremony, where I hear stomp dances, and I've gone to community stomp dances and love those, too."

School music classes provided grounding in musical rudiments. "I played clarinet for a few years," said Harjo. "Music was what sustained me, what motivated me."

Life at home was far from tranquil. Harjo's father, a heavy drinker, was physically and emotionally abusive to her mother. When his extramarital affairs became too blatant to ignore, and her parents divorced, Harjo had not yet reached her ninth birthday. At first things improved, but Harjo and her stepfather quarreled often. After a particularly harsh argument, she was told to leave the family home. She was sixteen years old. She would support herself with a variety of odd jobs. She also continued to study at the Institute of American Indian Arts, a residential high school—now a full-fledged college—for Native students in Santa Fe, New Mexico. "I never took music classes there," she said, "but the counselor that they assigned to me, Louis Ballard, was a very influential Cherokee classical composer. I spent a lot of time with him. He was a wonderful mentor."

Graduating in 1968, Harjo, who by then had married a fellow student and given birth to her first child, continued on to the University of New Mexico. Initially studying visual arts, she found her interests pulled elsewhere. "I was suddenly in the presence of a lot of poets," she said. "New Mexico seemed to be at the focus of what they now call 'the Native Literary Renaissance.' I was around people like Simon Ortiz [with whom she would have a daughter], Leslie Silko, and Jim Welch. There was this huge poetic force."

Switching her major to creative writing, Harjo found her true voice. Earning a bachelor of arts degree from the University of New Mexico in 1976, she went on to earn a master's degree from the University of Iowa two years later. "Poetry is like singing on paper," she said, "but, in a way, even more private. I used to be extremely shy. I could 'sing' on paper and not have to stand in front of an audience."

After serving as an artist-in-residency at Navajo Community College (now Diné College), in Tsaile, Arizona, and performing for youngsters as part of New Mexico's poetry-in-the-schools program in the early 1980s, Harjo began a two-year stint as an English professor at the University of Colorado. While in Boulder, she unwound from classes in the city's jazz clubs, listening to artists like James "Jim" Pepper (1941–1992). Saxophonist, flutist, and composer of the Free Spirits, one of the earliest jazz fusion bands in the mid-1960s, Pepper had gone on to work with jazz pianist Keith Jarrett and he had been a guest as a session player on Classic IV's top-forty hits, "Spooky" and "Stormy." Increasingly embracing his Kaw/Creek heritage, Pepper made his debut solo in 1970 with *Pepper's Powwow*. Produced by world music/jazz flutist Herbie Mann, the album included post-bop–meets–Native-America instrumentals ("Squaw Song" and "Rock Stomp Indian Style") and two tunes by Peter LaFarge—"Seneca (As Long As the Grass Shall Grow)" and "Drums." "[Pepper] was the first to integrate traditional forms of Native music and jazz," Joy Harjo has said. "He was prompted by [African American jazz trumpeter] Don Cherry to do it."

Harjo joined a long list of artists, including folk-pop duo Brewer and Shipley, jazz saxophonist Jan Garbarek, and world/jazz pioneers Oregon, who have covered Pepper's best-known piece, "Witchi-Tai Toe." Pepper's recording—with the short-lived jazz-rock band Everything Is Everything—of the Native American Church–based tune cracked the top seventy on the *Billboard* pop charts in 1969.

Accompanied by Larry Mitchell, a multi-instrumentalist and the Grammy-winning producer of *Totemic Flute Chants* (by Johnny Whitehorse, aka Robert Mirabal), Harjo introduced her one-woman show, *Winds of Night Sky, Wings of Morning Light*, in 2008. "I tell stories, sing songs, play music, recite poetry, and dance," she said, "but it's a dramatic show with a character and a story. It's the hardest thing I've ever done."

The impact that Native musicians have had on mainstream music continues to be a passionate subject for Harjo. Premiered in April 2009, as part of the New Mexico Jazz Workshop's Jazz Deconstructed series, her show, *We Were There When Jazz Was Invented*, included jazz, blues, and rock bands, a stomp-dance troupe, and a multimedia show. "It talked about the origins of jazz and blues," she said, "and how Indigenous people were there from the beginning."

A longtime resident of the Hawaiian island of Oahu, Harjo returned to the continental United States shortly before debuting *Winds of Night Sky, Wings of Morning Light*, settling in Albuquerque. "[Living in Hawaii] was too expensive," she said, "jet-lag wise and money wise. I make my living performing and need to be where I could be available."

With her autobiography capping the first three decades of her career, Harjo is eager to get back to her music. "There are two albums that I want to record," she said, "one with Barrett Martin, a wonderful drummer who was with [Ellensburg, Washington–based rock band] the Screaming Trees, and the other with music from the *Winds of Night Sky, Wings of Morning Light* show."

JAIME ROBERT ROBERTSON

At the February 8, 2002, Winter Olympics' opening ceremonies in Salt Lake City, dancers from dozens of tribes, and five Drums, each with twenty-four drummers, transformed Rice-Eccles Olympic Stadium on the campus of the University of Utah into an unprecedented showcase of Native American creativity. "I was almost in a dream state when we were on the stage," remembered pop/R&B singer Rita Coolidge (Cherokee/Scottish), who participated as a member of Walela, the Indigenous vocal trio shared with her sister, Priscilla, and niece, Laura Satterfield. "It was so cool. There were thousands of people in full regalia. I felt like I had crossed over. There was nothing more beautiful than what I saw that night. I was so swept up by that moment that, as I think about it, ten years later, my heart still takes wings."

At the core of the extravaganza was Toronto-born guitarist and songwriter Jaime Robert "Robbie" Robertson, or Jaime Robert Zlegerman (1943–) . Accompanied by the Red Road Ensemble, a supergroup of Indigenous musicians, including members of Walela, Kashtin, and Ulali, Robertson pushed the globally telecast celebration to another level. As the world watched, the only child of a Jewish father and a Mohawk mother led the large troupe through the Native-funk title track of PBS documentary, *Making a Noise.* Then came "Stomp Dance (Unity)," from Robertson's soundtrack for the Ted Turner–produced TV miniseries *The Native Americans.* "What a beautiful moment," Robertson recalled when we spoke in May 2013. "My music was being played [over the speakers] in the stadium when someone came out with an eagle and turned it loose. It flew over the audience, all around the stadium, and came back and landed on his hand. It was chilling. That was before we even performed."

As guitarist and songwriter of The Band (1968–1976), Robertson influenced popular music with songs—including "The Weight," "The Night They Drove Old Dixie Down," "Jemima's Surrender," and "Up on Crippled Creek"—that idealized the American South. The sounds of Indigenous America, however, didn't seem to be a hue in his musical palette. "I grew up with a philosophy from my mother," he told *Venice Magazine* in December 1998, "which was 'be proud that you're an Indian, but be careful who you tell.' . . . When my mother left the reservation to come to Toronto to live with her aunt, her aunt told her, 'Don't tell anybody you're from the reservation. Let them think whatever they want, that you're from another country, but don't tell anyone unless you absolutely have to.'"[41]

The first hint of Robertson's roots came with "Broken Arrow," the premiere single from his 1987 debut solo album. Rod Stewart, the Grateful Dead, and Phil Lesh and Friends later covered it. The eponymous-titled album, which featured such guests as Peter Gabriel and members of U2, also included tracks heard on the 1989 soundtrack of *Powwow Highway,* the Jonathan Wacks–produced adaptation of David Seal's novel about reservation life.

Reaching the thirty-eighth slot on *Billboard*'s "Hot 100" chart, Robertson's album spawned two top-ten hits—"Sweet Fire of Love" and an American Indian –influenced piece, "Showdown at Big Sky." In addition to JUNO awards for "Best Album" and (with Daniel Lanois) "Best Producer," Robertson received the award as the year's "Best Male Vocalist."

The experience opened Robertson further to his ancestral roots. When Turner Network Television (TNT) asked him to prepare a soundtrack for *The Native Americans* in 1994, he was eager to begin. "It was the door that I had been looking for," he said. "I had wanted to do something with Rita Coolidge for years. We had been talking about it for ages. I wanted to do something with Pura Fé, on and on, down the list of people that I wanted to bring into my group, which I called 'The Red Road Ensemble.' Jim Wilson, from the Choctaw Nation in New Mexico, helped me to produce it."

Interweaving his soundtrack with the narration of the six-hour, history-based miniseries fulfilled a lifelong dream. "Music was one side of my growing up," said Robertson, "storytelling was another. Big shows didn't come to the reservation. There was some radio, but no television. Everybody made their own entertainment, their own music, and storytelling was part of it. An elder would tell a story and it would stick with you in a way that gave you a chill. When I was very young, five years old, I can remember thinking, 'One of these days, I want to play music and tell stories.'"

Although he spent most of his childhood in Toronto's impoverished Cabbagetown neighborhood, numerous trips to the Six Nations Reserve in Ontario, where his mother was born and raised, deeply inspired Robertson. "[My mother's] relatives were there," he said, "so we would go there all the time. I've read things that say that I spent my summers there. It was much more than my summers. It was every holiday. It was my beginning in music. My cousins, uncles, and everybody played music. I just thought, 'I need to be in this club.'"

Robertson recalled that his relatives "listened to a lot of country music." "When I was a kid," he said, "Hank Williams, Lefty Frizzell, and Hank Snow were big on the Rez. Sometimes, someone would sing Slim Whitman's 'Indian Love Call.' Sometimes, it'd be a hybrid—country music and some kind of chanting—right in the middle of two worlds. I still think it's bizarre for Indians to be singing cowboy music."

Music for the Native Americans brought a new dimension to the Indigenous soundscape. "I tried to use everybody in ways that were really special and dignified," said Robertson. "On some of *Music for the Native Americans*, I used music that would fit into their world, but, with other pieces, I didn't care—I wanted sounds that were beautiful. It was somewhere between wanting to accommodate the documentary and going full circle in my life to where it began for me."

Before he embarked on a follow-up (*Contact from the Underworld of Redboy*), PBS asked Robertson to film a documentary, *Making a Noise: A Native American Musical Journey*, about his return to his mother's birthplace on the Six Nations of the Grand River Reserve, the largest First Nation in Canada. "I wouldn't trade it for anything else that I've done," he said. "Floyd Westerman went with me. We were just experimenting together. We didn't have a script or anything figured out ahead of time. It was a discovery process and there's something so beautiful in that."

A feature on Robertson's exploration into his Native roots had been included on a segment of VH-1's *Behind the Music*. "It showed me going to a peyote ceremony," he said, "although, obviously, you can't shoot footage during the ceremony, and some of the old peyote men weren't too keen about having cameras around. It was getting uncomfortable until one of the younger peyote men said, 'We've got to be part of the future. It's part of our heritage.' He convinced the others that we were not doing a terrible thing. We had respect for boundaries."

Partially recorded in New Orleans, Robertson's second solo album, *Storyville* (1991) celebrated the Crescent City's musical heritage. Appearances by New Orleans musicians, including Russell Batiste, Jr.; Aaron, Art, and Cyril Neville; the Meters' George Porter, Jr.; Leo Nocentelli; Zigaboo Modeliste; Big Chief Bo Dollis (the Wild Magnolias); Big Chief Monk Boudreaux (the Golden Eagles); and the Rebirth Brass Band, provided authenticity. Bruce Hornsby and Ginger Baker (Cream, Blind Faith) made invaluable contributions. The Band's Garth Hudson played organ on three tracks; Rick Danko sang backup.

Robertson continued to embrace his Indigenous roots as author of an American Indian–oriented book, *Peacemaker*, for young readers. "It's an enchanting, fantastic story," he said. "It takes place in the Haudenosaunee Nation. I grew up with the story. Everybody knows of Hiawatha through Longfellow's poem, but Longfellow got Hiawatha and another Indian mixed up, and his poem was completely wrong. I want to spread the real story of the giver of the Great Law of Peace. The Peacemaker was an amazing human being. Hiawatha was his spokesperson, his speechmaker. The Peacemaker had a speech impediment. They brought the five nations together, and, later, the sixth nation joined. Where they dug this tree out of the ground, the Indians threw their weapons into the cavity. They replaced the tree and called it 'the tree of peace.' The Six Nations have lived in peace ever since."

Sessions with Eric Clapton, Steve Winwood, bassist Pino Palladino, and drummer Ian Thomas, along with Robert Randolph, Tom Morello (Rage Against the Machine, Audioslave, the Nightwatchman), Trent Reznor (Nine Inch Nails), and Taylor Goldsmith (the Dawes), spawned Robertson's first new album in twelve years—*How to Become Clairvoyant*—in April 2011. It was his first non-Native–oriented album in two decades. "I haven't tried to intellectualize it," he explained, "but I'm doing the same thing that I did as a kid—walking between two worlds. Nobody says, 'You can't come in here and make that kind of music.' I feel privileged to be able to get away with it."

RITA COOLIDGE

The second of three daughters of a Cherokee Baptist minister (Richard Coolidge) and his Scottish schoolteacher wife (Charlotte), Rita Coolidge (1944–) was the first recruited when Robertson began working on *Music for the Native Americans*.

"We went to Village Recorders in New York," the two-time Grammy-winning pop/R&B singer told me in January 2012, "and spent many nights there, listening to stuff, and getting ideas."

At Robertson's urging, Coolidge assembled a vocal trio with her older sister, Priscilla (1941–2014), and Priscilla's daughter, Laura Satterfield. The group took its appellation from her Cherokee name, Walela ("Hummingbird"). "[Robertson] knew that I came from a family of singers," she said, "and he asked me to get in touch with them. We went [into the studio], did the background vocals, and became part of his Red Road Ensemble." The richness of the trio's harmonies was undeniable. "[Robertson] said that our voices were magical," remembered Coolidge, "that there's nothing like a family singing together."

After the release of *Music for the Native Americans* in October 1994, Coolidge watched its influence spread. "The response was overwhelming," she remembered. "I would speak with people after concerts, and they would tell me how much the music meant to them. There was one woman who told me that she had been playing the CD in her apartment and people kept asking her what it was. After she told them, they all went out and got their own copies. She said that, at one point, they all started the CD at the same time and it became like a choir of angels. The music had wings of its own and flew right into people's hearts. As a solo artist, I never felt that way before."

Released on Triloka, the world-music label owned by Krishna Das, a singer/chanter in the kirtan style of Indian bhakti devotional music, in July 1997, Walela's self-titled debut album mixed the trio's luscious harmonies with Native percussion and contemporary instrumentation. Along with such tunes as "Cherokee River," "Cherokee," and "Wounded Knee," it included the Coolidge-penned "The Cherokee Morning Song," also available on *Music for the Native Americans*, and "Amazing Grace" sung in the Cherokee language. At the NAMMY ceremony in November 1998, one of the album's most harmonious tunes, "The Warrior" received awards as "Song of the Year" and "Record of the Year." The "Debut Artist of the Year," Walela was also honored with a "Lifetime Achievement" award.

Walela recorded a second studio album, *Unbearable Love*, in 2000. The album included tunes like "Gathering of Eagles," "Cherokee Rose," and "I Have No Indian Name." The Sovereign Nation Preservation label released a live CD/DVD, *Live in Concert*, in 2004. A fourteen-track retrospective, with songs from the trio's first two outings, *The Best of Walela* followed (on Triloka) three years later. "I've been haunted that Walela wasn't able to do as much as we could have done," said Coolidge. "My father was terminally ill; all I felt like doing was praying and being with him as much as I could."

Raised in predominantly white communities, Tennessee-born Rita and Priscilla Coolidge grew up harmonizing with their younger sister, Linda, in church choirs. By their teens, they were veterans of state fairs and talent contests. "Priscilla and I used to put the radio between our beds," remembered Coolidge. "Late at night, when everyone else was asleep, we'd be awake, listening to the blues. That had more of an influence on us than anything."

The sisters' maternal grandmother, Mama Stewart, helped to shape their creativity. "She was a storyteller," said Coolidge, "and she wrote over five hundred songs. She would tell everything through song. She encouraged Priscilla and me to keep that going. She didn't live to see [Walela] happen, but we were able to use her voice."

Mama Stewart would make her recording debut at the age of ninety-five. "She flew to California [to have cataract surgery]," explained Coolidge, "and, afterwards, lived, in Malibu, with Priscilla and [her then-husband] Booker [T. Jones]. She wanted to make a record and Booker said, 'Okay,' and recorded her. One of the songs on the first Walela CD, 'I'll Turn My Radio On' starts with my grandmother's voice. We sang with her on that song."

As a youngster, Coolidge felt little connection to her Cherokee roots. "Daddy wasn't raised on a reservation," she said, "and he was never even near a reservation. He was born in California and grew up in Texas when Indian people experienced bad treatment. As a boy, he was spit upon and disdained in the eyes of prejudice."

"He learned to fly under the radar," she continued, "and didn't connect with other Indian people. Instead, he became an activist for all people and was very active in the Civil Rights Movement. He wanted people to realize that the color of our skin should not be what judged us. He was adamant to the people of his congregation, and the deacons of the church, that, if anyone of color walked into the church, they were to be welcomed—as all of God's children should be. There were many conflicts and times when churches said that they didn't want him there, but then they would change their mind. He started preaching once a year at an African American church, across town, and that pastor would come to our church and preach."

Coolidge's heritage, however, continued to pique her fascination. "In school, we were taught very little of the history of American Indians," she remembered. "The teacher would get up and say that Columbus discovered America, that he found savages in loincloths, and conquered them. That would be it and they would move on. As I got older, I would ask my parents questions and they would tell me what they knew. My mother was a schoolteacher, but the information was not available and hidden in the early 1950s."

"In the first town where we lived," she continued, "people called us 'Gypsies.' There were only white people there; I didn't even see a black person until I was six years old. Our experiences with ethnic diversity were limited to the 'Gypsies' and the white people, but we knew that we were Indians."

After Coolidge moved, with her family, to Florida at the age of fifteen, her passion for singing continued to grow. During the summer between high school and college, she sang regularly on a local music-variety TV show. Although she considered postponing her education and pursuing music, her parents made it clear that she had no choice. She would go on to earn a degree in art education from Florida State University in Tallahassee. "My father was a painter," she said, "an amazing visual artist. I have a painting that he did when my mother was carrying me and I feel the correlation between music and color. To get a degree in music from Florida State University, you had to spend a year with the marching band. I wanted to be watching the game, not waiting in the wings with a big hat and a baton, so I went for a degree in art, instead."

Coolidge continued to sing. "I had a rock band (RC and the Moonpies) with members of the Sigma Chi fraternity," she said. "We played at frat parties in Tallahassee or we'd go down to the University of Florida or any other university that wanted a band for a party. I also had a folk band and sang with a couple of other people. I was always singing."

Relocating to Memphis, Tennessee, following her graduation in 1965, Coolidge found work singing radio jingles and commercials at KDIA owner John Pepper's Pepper Records. At the time, Memphis was the epicenter of one of the few R&B scenes to challenge Motown Records in Detroit. As she sharpened her skills as a session singer, many of the city's musical elite befriended her, among them her future brother-in-law, Booker T. Jones. As leader of a multiracial, instrumental group, Booker T. and the MGs, the Memphis-born organist and producer backed up Otis Redding, Wilson Pickett, Sam and Dave, and others, as well as recording such hits as "Hip-Hugger," "Time Is Tight," and the R&B chart–topping "Green Onions," with Booker T. & the MGs.

Playing matchmaker, Coolidge introduced her (recently divorced) sister Priscilla to Jones in 1968. "I didn't see either of them for a long time afterwards," she remembered. "They moved to California, got married, and lived in a volatile environment. It wasn't acceptable for a black man and a white woman to be together, even though she was an Indian."

Coolidge, meanwhile, was continuing to draw attention with her singing. Encouraged by John Pepper, she recorded "Turn Around and Love You," a haunting tune about domestic abuse by Donna Weiss, who would later cowrite (with Jackie DeShannon) Kim Carnes's 1981 hit, "Bette Davis Eyes." Although the single went unnoticed locally, Coolidge discovered, after relocating to California, that it had indeed made an impact. "I walked into [a club in] Los Angeles," she said, "and everybody was singing this song."

The vocalist immediately felt at home. "Musicians in Memphis would sit around and fantasize about becoming California musicians," she said, "and musicians in California would fantasize about being studio players in Memphis. We were one big, happy family—there was no competition in our music."

Don Nix, a producer, arranger, songwriter, and saxophone player she met before leaving Memphis, introduced Coolidge to multi-instrumentalist Leon Russell (Claude Russell Bridges) (1942–). Playing in nightclubs from the age of fourteen, Russell had joined with guitarist and songwriter J. J. Cale (as the Starlighters) to help create Oklahoma's Tulsa Sound in the late 1950s. Moving to Los Angeles in the early 60s, the Lawton, Oklahoma–born pianist and guitarist played with Phil Spector's studio band (the Wrecking Crew) and became a much-in-demand session musician, recording with artists ranging from Doris Day and Frank Sinatra to the Byrds, the Beach Boys, and Bob Dylan. Between 1964 and 1966, Russell joined Mississippi-born guitarist Delaney Bramlett and future Redbone founders Pat and Lolly Vegas in the Shindogs, the house band for the ABC-TV music show *Shindig*. Producer Snuff Garrett's assistant and creative director, Russell scored his first success as a producer with "This Diamond Ring," a chart-topping hit for (comedian Jerry Lewis's son) Gary Lewis and the Playboys, in 1965, and went on to write (or cowrite) the group's top-ten hits "Everybody Loves a Clown" and "She's Just My Style." Together with Dallas, Texas–born guitarist Marc Benno, Russell formed a duo, the Asylum Choir, in 1967, releasing an album the following year. Though they recorded a second album in 1969, it went unreleased for two years, by which time Russell had established a career as a bandleader. "He was kind of a recluse," remembered Coolidge. "We drove to California together in his blue Thunderbird. He never got out of the car to deal with one single person. I think that was why I was there. When we would check into a hotel for the night, I had to do everything. He was terrified that everybody had a gun; he was a little paranoid."

At Russell's suggestion, Delaney Bramlett hired Coolidge to perform with him and his then-wife, Bonnie, along with a loose aggregate of rock elite that included Eric Clapton, Dave Mason, and George Harrison in their Southern rock band, Delaney & Bonnie and Friends. "Bonnie and I are still best friends," said Coolidge. "We talk to each other all the time. She's such an amazing singer."

Russell continued to guide Coolidge toward historic projects. Through his intervention, the songstress became involved with one of rock and roll's wildest tours. The backup band (under Russell's musical direction) for the gravelly voiced British singer Joe Cocker, Mad Dogs and Englishmen featured a huge array of musicians and singers and built on the communal "hippie" atmosphere that Cocker had experienced at the Woodstock Music and Art Festival a few months before. "For me, it was Rock and Roll University," said Coolidge. "I was just out of college. I can't say that I had lived a sheltered life, but I had been a 'good girl.' My mother was a teacher and my dad was a preacher. I had done everything exactly the way that I thought my parents wanted me to do it. When I toured with Delaney and Bonnie, and ended up on the Mad Dogs and Englishmen tour, there was stuff going on that I didn't even want to know about."

The Mad Dogs and Englishmen tour nearly fell apart before it got started. "Less than two weeks [before the first show]," said Coolidge, "Joe [Cocker] decided that he wasn't going to do the tour. [His manager] Dee Anthony told him, 'There's no choice. The halls are already booked and people have already bought tickets.'"

Five days before the tour, Russell asked Coolidge to put a vocal choir together. "We started rehearsing on the soundstage at A&M Records," she recalled, "fourteen hours a day for four days. Our throats wore out. We were exhausted by the time that we got on the plane."

On the first day of full-band rehearsals, Coolidge saw a different side of Russell. "Everyone was used to seeing him as laid-back and introspective," she said, "but when he got out of the car, wearing that top hat and striped pants, looking like the ringmaster at a circus, everybody's jaw dropped. He had come from being fearful to having to be out front and he forced himself into this role of being the leader. He talked a lot and laughed a lot, and he was bigger than life. Joe [Cocker] was always the same, a sweet man with an amazing voice. All he cared about was singing. Leon was in control of everything else."

Russell had written "Delta Lady," one of the songs Cocker performed at the Woodstock Music and Arts Festival, for Coolidge. He would later pen "Song for You" and "Hummingbird" for her. "'Song for You' is one of the most beautifully written songs that I've ever heard," Coolidge said. "It always makes me cry. He wrote it after we had broken up. There's a line in 'Delta Lady' that talks about me 'standing wet and naked in the garden.' I never did that. I didn't even have a garden. He said, 'It's poetry.'"

The high point of Coolidge's stint with Mad Dogs and Englishmen (as documented by the double album and film of the tour) came as she stepped into the spotlight to deliver "Superstar," a tender ballad she had helped to write—though she would be denied credit. On the B-side of Delaney & Bonnie and Friends with Eric Clapton's single, "Coming Home," "Superstar" had gone on to be covered by Bette Midler and Sonny & Cher. The Carpenters had their biggest hit with it, reaching number two on *Billboard*'s Hot 100 chart, and topping the easy-listening list. "I got the idea for a song about a guitar player," explained Coolidge, "during the tour that we did in Europe with Eric Clapton. It was Delaney and Bonnie's band, and Eric was a sideman, but, as we got to England and Germany, people started screaming, 'Clapton, Clapton.' At one theater, they ripped up the seats. I remember being in a bus and skinheads trying to turn it over. Bonnie and I started writing the song one night and Leon and Delaney came into the room. We told them what we were doing and sang what we had done so far. They went into the other room and finished it. When the record came out, my name wasn't on it and Delaney's name wasn't on it. It was credited to Leon and Bonnie."

Clapton would base the piano coda of "Layla," his million-selling love lament for then–George Harrison's wife, Patti, on a tune ("Time") that Coolidge had composed with Jim Gordon, but the credits again failed to acknowledge her contribution. "They just took the melody and used it," she said. "I called [Clapton's manager] Robert Stigwood's office and told them that I had cowritten the song and that it been taken away from me. They laughed and said, 'What are you going to do—sue us? We don't think so.'"

Gordon, who went on to play drums with Clapton's Derek & the Dominoes, had been Coolidge's boyfriend at the start of the Mad Dogs and Englishmen tour, but their romance soured when the drummer invited her into a hallway and, without provocation, punched her in the face. Coolidge sported a black eye for the rest of the tour. The incident marked the beginning of an uncontrollable slide for Gordon; doctors misdiagnosed his paranoid schizophrenia as alcoholism. His demons caught up with him on June 3, 1983, when he obeyed "voices" and killed his mother with a hammer and an eight-and-a-quarter-inch butcher knife. Sentenced to sixteen years to life, he remains, as of October 2015, at the Atascadero State Hospital in San Luis Obispo County, California (halfway between Los Angeles and San Francisco).

Coolidge had plenty of suitors. Stephen Stills wrote "Cherokee," "The Raven," and "Sugar Babe" for her. "He didn't play them for me," she said, "but, when I heard them later, I felt so honored. He's such a great musician and writer, and the cutest man. He was just so fabulous, a little bit wild."

Coolidge had barely gotten over her failed relationships when she met Brownsville, Texas–born singer-songwriter, Kristoffer "Kris" Kristofferson, who was then on the verge of becoming one of the deacons of modern country music. "I met him at the airport in L.A.," she remembered. "He was on his way to Nashville for an interview [with] Look magazine. I was on my way to Memphis to rehearse with my band, the Dixie Flyers. We sat together on the plane. When we got to Memphis, he got off with me."

"I loved Kris's music," she continued. "It was so honest and the songs so well crafted and heartfelt. When I'd go to his concerts, I could see how much his music moved people. It was a turnaround from what I had been doing with Delaney and Bonnie, and Joe Cocker, where the goal was to get people dancing in their seats. With Kris's audiences, he was going right for their hearts. People would be sitting in their seats with tears coming out of their eyes."

Married in 1973, Kristofferson and Coolidge struck gold with their first album as a duo. *Full Moon* topped the country charts and became a top-thirty pop hit. The husband-and-wife collaboration bewildered many of Kristofferson's longtime fans, however. While he had staked his claim with literate country rock, Coolidge's roots lie in more-commercial R&B and pop balladry. Sales of their subsequent duo albums, *Breakaway*, in 1974, and *Natural Act*, four years later, failed to match those of their first album.

The elation that Coolidge and Kristofferson felt after the birth of a daughter, Casey, in 1974, turned to heartbreak when the songstress suffered a miscarriage in the fifth month of her pregnancy three years later. "I was really taking care of myself," she told the *New York Times*, "watching my diet, sleeping right, and I was in excellent health. My baby was alive and kicking. I heard the heartbeat and, then, for some reason, no one knows why, it just stopped."[42]

Coolidge poured everything into song. The result was a ten-song collection (*Anytime . . . Anywhere*) that would sell more than a million copies and spawn three hit singles. A remake of the Smokey Robinson–penned, and Temptations-popularized, song, "The Way You Do the Things You Do" broke into the top twenty, while a Carpenters-like treatment of Boz Scagg's "We're All Alone" reached number seven. A slowed-down rendition of Jackie Wilson's up-tempo raver, "(Your Love Has Lifted Me) Higher and Higher," fared even better, peaking at number two.

Despite her commercial success, critics continued to scorn Coolidge. Robert Christgau claimed she was "halfway to becoming Andy Williams with cleavage."[43] "It's always been so hard for people to put me in a box," Coolidge countered. "I'm a lot like my favorite singer, Peggy Lee—it's all about the music. She sang jazz, pop, and recorded the most fabulous blues albums. She did Latin music. The record company would say, 'You can't do that,' and she'd just go to another label."

Coolidge recorded an album of jazz and R&B standards, *It's Only Love*, with pianist Barbara Carroll in 1975. Carroll, who was acknowledged by British music scribe Leonard Feather, in the 1940s, as "the first girl to play bebop," was fifty-three when she joined Coolidge and Kristofferson's 1978 tour. "[Carroll] is still performing in New York cabarets," said Coolidge more than three decades later, "and she's still gorgeous."

Although A&M recorded the singer and pianist, they refused to release the results. Coolidge bought the masters and released the album in Japan as *The Good Old Days* in 1984. Supplemented by a pair of previously unavailable songs, a CD version, *Out of the Blues*, followed twelve years later. Coolidge yearned to record more tunes from the Great American Songbook. The chance came with *And So Is Love* in 2010. "All I wanted to do was record another jazz album," she said. "When I signed with my current management [Nexis Entertainment], I told that to them. They shopped the idea for five years, and finally did it—United Masters in Japan and Concord Records in the U.S. Recording the album in Los Angeles, I had the thrill of my life."

Jazz singers had sparked Coolidge's early passion for music. "I loved Nina Simone," she said, "and Ella Fitzgerald lived in my neighborhood when I lived in Hollywood. Something about that music was crisp and unpredictable. I loved spontaneity in a different structure than pop music. I loved that jazz could go all over the place; it was such a challenge. When I recorded the jazz CD, I was in tears. I had thought, 'What have I gotten myself into—these people are in a whole other world,' but I found out that the jazz players [including drummer Terry Lynn Carrington, baritone saxophone player Ronnie Cuber, Spyra Gyra vibraphonist Dave Samuels, and special guest trumpeter, Herb Alpert] were like the rest of us, just making music."

Divorced from Kristofferson in 1980, Coolidge struggled to follow her own muse. Although she reached the top of the Adult Contemporary charts in 1983 with "All Time High," from the soundtrack of James Bond film, *Octopussy*, her contract with A&M expired a year later. Continuing to record for independent labels, including Critique, Permanent, and Varese Sarabande, she also acted in musical theater and sang on albums by Eric Clapton and Jimmy Buffett.

Two thousand eleven was a particularly challenging year. After her father succumbed to a long illness in February, Coolidge helped her sisters pack up the family home and move their mother into her house overlooking the Camp Pendleton Marine Base in Oceanside, California. Suffering a massive stroke six days after her arrival, Coolidge's mother passed less than three months later.

Music again provided solace. Coolidge released *A Rita Coolidge Christmas* on October 30, 2012, celebrating the Yuletide with ultra-warm renditions of classic tunes, including "Rockin' around the Christmas Tree," "Santa Claus Is Coming to Town," "Little Drummer Boy," and "Have Yourself a Merry Little Christmas." The album would lead to a "Best Female Artist of 2014" NAMMY for the songstress.

On October 3, 2014, a 9-1-1 call brought police to the Thousand Oaks, California, home that Coolidge's sister Priscilla shared with her third husband, Michael Seibert. According to their report, they found Priscilla the victim of a gunshot to her head and Seibert dead from a self-inflicted gunshot to the chest. "Words cannot express the devastation our family is feeling with the loss of my sister, Priscilla," Coolidge told the *Ventura County Star*.[44]

Now, a decade after the release of *Music for the Native Americans*, Coolidge, who married UC Irvine professor Dr. Tatsuya Suda in August 2012, dreams of renewing her collaboration with Robertson and reconnecting with their shared culture. "I love working with Robbie," she said, "especially the way that he becomes a mad professor in the studio. He's so free that he makes ideas come to fruition. He was the key to bringing Native music to the public's attention. There were other people, but he had the ability to bring all of these Native sounds together."

PURA FÉ

Vocalist and lap steel guitarist Pura Fé (Pura Fé Antonia "Toni" Crescioni) (1959–), of Tuscarora, Taino, and Corsican heritage, was singing with her cousin, Jennifer Elizabeth Kreisberg (Tuscarora), and Soni Moreno (born Carmen Carbonella) as Ulali, when they became members of Robbie Robertson's Red Road Ensemble in 1994. "[Robertson] came to us through the American Indian Community House in New York," Fé told me. "We toured with him in Europe, along with Buffy Sainte-Marie, John Trudell, and the Coolidge sisters, and we did some television shows and some filming together. It helped to open the door wider to American Indian music and brought it into the mainstream."

Music for the Native Americans featured Ulali's harmonies on two tunes— "Ancestor Song" and the album's first single, "Makh Jchi" ("Heartbeat Drum Song"). Performed with Robertson and the Red Road Ensemble on the *Tonight Show with Jay Leno* in the United States, *The Late Show* in the United Kingdom, and the *Joe Squares Show* in Brazil, it became a major hit in Italy. *Makh Jchi (Heartbeat Drum Song)* achieved platinum status for sales of 1 million copies.

Ulali, a name that comes from the Tuscaroran word for the sweet-singing wood thrush, continued to build on their success with extensive world touring and an appearance on the soundtrack for Cheyenne/Arapaho director and coproducer Chris Eyre's independent film, *Smoke Signals*. Collaborating with Jim Pepper on a three-part TV series about American Indian culture (*Remembrance*), which was left unfinished when the saxophonist/composer succumbed to lymphoma on February 10, 1992, they sang at his memorial service. "[Pepper] told me about stomp-dance music," said Fé, "and about all this music from the Southeast that comes out of Native culture."

Soni Moreno grew up working in the fields outside Sacramento, California, with her Mayan mother and Apache/Yaqui father. Songs on the radio helped her to learn English, and she later studied at the American Conservatory Theater in San Francisco. A member of the original cast of *Hair*—in the role of Chrissie—in 1968, she became involved with the Bay Area's Native community and participated

Pura Fé (Tuscarora/Taino/ Corsican) joined Soni Moreno (Mayan/Apache/ Yaqui) and Jennifer Elizabeth Kreisberg (Tuscarora) to create the Indigenous folk trio Ulali. *Courtesy Pura Fé.*

in the occupation of Alcatraz Island. Moving (with *Hair*) to New York in the early 1980s, she split her time between the Broadway stage and the gift shop of the American Indian Community House, where she met Fé.

The daughter of Nanice Lund (Tuscarora), a classically trained vocalist who sang in Duke Ellington's sacred concert series, and Puerto Rico–born Juan Antonio Crescione-Collazo (Taino/Corsican), Fé was primed for a career in music. In addition to studying dance at the American Ballet Theater Company, and (briefly) at a school operated by modern-dance choreographer Martha Graham, she attended a performing arts school—Lincoln Square Academy—in Manhattan. "Irene Cara was in the grade above me," she said, "and Ben Stiller was three grades below. I remember him running through the hall every morning. Gian-Carlo Esposito and his brother made fun of me. Robbie Benson was there, Robert Siegel is his real name, and Stephanie Mills. I had homework that I had to do on the road."

Music was a natural part of Fé's childhood. "My mother played recordings of Wagner, Vivaldi, and Verdi," she said, "and my [stepfather] played jazz. All of my aunts and cousins sang. I thought we were unique—until I moved to North Carolina and found that all Native communities sing in harmony. Many American Indians grow up singing in the church. We sing Christmas carols in big, full harmonies. I always tell people that singing is my first language."

Though she didn't meet her biological father until she was in her forties, Fé retained ties to his Hispanic roots. "I get everything from him and my mom," she said, "the features on my face, my attitude, and my love of music. I'm a mixture of both of them. My music comes from that cultural mix—blues, jazz, and gospel."

Fé stirred early attention with her dancing, winning several intertribal championships as a smoke dancer and participating in powwows as a fancy dancer. "The smoke dance comes out of the Iroquois social dance," she said. "I haven't done it in a while. My dance chops are a little rusty."

As a professional dancer, Fé appeared in the chorus line of touring productions of Gary William Friedman and Will Holt's *The Me Nobody Knows*, the futuristic *Via Galactica*, and *Uri*, which is based on Leon Uris's novel set in post–World War II Cyprus. "I got discouraged with dance," she said, "because I wasn't white. It brought me problems at a very young age."

Leaving the world of dance and musical theater in the late 1970s, Fé immersed herself in New York's burgeoning rock scene as a server at the legendary music club Max's Kansas City. "I remember the Hells Angels," she said. "Every night, when I'd go to the club, I would see their bikes outside and get really nervous."

Musicians left a more favorable impression. "I met so many bands," said Fé, "but the Sex Pistols stood out for me. I remember going up to the third floor, on my way to the office, and finding the whole band sitting in this little closet. There were long benches that came out of the walls, but they were sitting on top of each other. The florescent lighting made them look green, with green hair and green skin. They were all there including Sid and Nancy. They looked like the picture of unhealthy. They looked dead."

"I was waiting on tables when Devo came into town," she continued. "They bounced on the stage, in asbestos suits, singing, 'Are we not men? We are Devo—D-E-V-O!' I remember screaming at the top of my lungs, 'What would you like to drink?'"

Fé also worked part-time at what she remembers as "a hamburger bar." "Every morning, there would be this guy sitting there," she recalled, "looking really strange, with a pompadour hairdo and cowboy shirts. I'd take his order and serve him. He never said anything, not even hello. It was [American rockabilly singer] Robert Gordon. I used to serve him breakfast every morning."

Aspiring to sing, Fé took advantage of her mother's musical connections. "[My mom] called [Duke Ellington's son] Mercer Ellington," she recalled, "and asked, 'Would you please hire my daughter?' He said, 'Send her down.'"

At the audition, jazz-funk pioneer Roy Ayers accompanied the young singer on piano. "I didn't even know who he was," Fé recalled. "I remember, at the start of the audition, the phone rang and Mercer walked away to answer it. I looked at [Ayers] and said, 'I'm so nervous.' He said, 'Well, honey, you just keep on being nervous.'"

Fé debuted with the Mercer Ellington Orchestra at the opening of the Duke Ellington School in Washington, D.C. "In the second row was Lena Horne," she remembered. "My microphone wasn't working. She jumped out of her seat, and shouted, 'Go to the other mic!' She said it twice. I felt like she was my mom. I was very nervous that night; it was such a very exciting evening. I was only twenty-three years old."

Fé spent much of her childhood with Mercer Ellington's father, one of the most influential figures of early American jazz. "He was a really nice man, very friendly, very flashy," she recalled. "He used to live in our building on 106th Street. I remember that, in his apartment, he had a grand piano. I'd listen to him play and watch as he went through his record collection. He had one record that made an impression on me. On the cover, there were photographs of tribal people from around the world. I thought that was cool. It gave me a historical view of where our music was coming from. Duke talked a lot to me about his Indian ancestry."

Fé's musical interests continued to expand. She became a fervent attendee of St. Peter's Church—the jazz church—on Lexington Avenue. Once a year, the church would be the site for All Soul's Night, featuring a marathon thirty-eight hours of jazz performances. "I'd go to listen, fall asleep for a couple of hours, wake up, and listen some more," she said. "It was nonstop."

After she had sung on commercial jingles and radio IDs, trombone player and songwriter James McBride recruited Fé to sing on demo recordings. "We met through Mercer Ellington's piano player, George Cardwell," she said. "[McBride] had a small four-track recording machine and a microphone that looked like a ping pong paddle. After singing one of his songs, I said, 'This sounds like an Anita Baker song.' He said, 'I can't believe you said that—that's who I'm sending this to.' [Baker] wound up buying it, taking half of the writer's credit, and having a hit."

Fé continued to work with McBride, cowriting several R&B tunes, and singing with a large band that featured Cardwell on piano. McBride would produce her debut album, *Caution to the Wind*, in 1995. "It was mostly me singing McBride's songs," said the vocalist.

Hired to sing backup on one of Fé recordings, Soni Moreno began a decades-long collaboration with her. Their first concert together, a show with Joy Harjo and the

American Indian Dance Theater, marked the beginning of what would become Ulali. "I didn't want to waltz in with a jazz ensemble," said Fé, "so I told Soni, 'How about if we take songs that I wrote for the jazz band and bring them down to a hand drum and vocal harmonies?'"

Fé and Moreno's collaboration went through several changes. Performing under Fé's name, accompanied by a band, and joined by a third female vocalist (Matoaka Little Eagle), they mixed "a strong influence of the blues, the sound of the powwow drum, and the harmonies of three women singing."

Scaling down to three women—with Kreisberg replacing Little Eagle—the group became Ulali. Still in high school when Fé and Moreno met, Kreisberg was familiar with all of the vocal parts and easily fit. "[Ulali] relay the message of their ancestors with voices as sweet as honey," proclaimed the *Washington City Paper* on January 29, 1999, "but leavened with the biting crunch of reality."[45]

In addition to recording three independently released cassettes—*Corn Beans and Squash* (1991), *Ulali* (1992), and *In the Spirit* (1993)—and a CD, *Makh Jchi* (1996), Ulali appeared on the Indigo Girls' album, *Shaming of the Sun*, and participated in the feminist alt-folk duo's 1997 *Honor the Earth* tour. "Our blood and people are older than America will ever be," read the liner notes of Ulali's *Mahk Jchi* album, "and we don't recognize the borders. Our brothers and sisters run from North to South and into and under the waters for miles and years back."[46]

Fé remained involved with a variety of outside projects. Recorded with Ecuador-born, and Toronto-based, charango, panpipe, and Andean drum player Marcos Arcentalis and his band (Kanatan Aski), *Condor Meets the Eagle* scored a "Best Global Recording" JUNO award nomination in 1994. "There were no borders before First Contact," Arcentalis explained to me, "and [American Indians] traveled from north to south and east to west. There was a spiritual connection between all Indigenous people—whether they were in North, Central, or South America. We wanted to express that through music."

Sharing a workshop stage, in the late 1990s, with Washington-born, jazz/blues slide guitarist Kelly Joe Phelps at the Edmonton Folk Festival, Fé thought back to a powwow she had attended as a child. "There was a man, Chief Leon Locklear, the chief of the Tuscarora Nation, playing slide guitar," she recalled. "It had such a beautiful sound."

Purchasing a pair of guitars—one twelve-string and one six-string—in a California music store shortly afterwards, Fé put the instruments away in a closet after a few weeks. They remained unplayed until her move to Chapel Hill, North Carolina, after three years in Philadelphia, in 1994. "I locked the door," she remembered, "and taught myself to play my songs on guitar."

Three months later, Fé approached Tim and Denise Duffy, owners of Music Makers, a nonprofit record label in Hillsborough, North Carolina, and persuaded them to release a solo album (*Follow Your Heart's Desire*) showcasing her lap steel slide playing and connecting Indigenous music with jazz and the blues. "The roots aren't just in African music," she said, "but also in the Native communities of the Southeast."

Fé continued to reach out to an ever-widening audience, opening shows for Neil Young, Taj Mahal, Herbie Hancock, George Duke, and Al Jarreau. "Audiences were very receptive," she said. "They bought all of my albums."

French audiences provided an exceptionally warm reception; Fé received L'Academie Charles Cros "Best World Album" award for *Follow Your Heart's Desire*. "I hate that I have to travel so far," she said, "just to tour all the time."

Fé's return to her ancestral home in North Carolina in 2004 further connected her with her heritage. Although she temporarily moved to Seattle a year later, she became involved with North Carolina's Native community after returning in 2010. "I'm working with a women's society," she said, "and a tribal canoe society. We're looking forward to getting onto the water, singing our canoe songs, and journey songs, and having feasts and paddle dances. We're going to record our songs, a lot of which I write, and I've been encouraging people to share their own family songs."

Fé recorded a duo CD, *Hold That Rain*, with Seattle-based guitarist Danny Godinéz in 2007. Augmented by members of the Carolina Chocolate Drops, a more-arranged album, *Full Moon Rising*, followed two years later. "Sailing from traditional melodies to scorching blues with her usual grace and dedication," said bluesweb.com, "[Fé] adds a healthy sprinkling of rap and canoe chants to her music before leading us all the way to Southern America where the eagle meets the condor—pure magic!"[47]

Cary Morin (Crow), who replaced Godinéz before the completion of *Full Moon Rising*, has continued to play with Fé, bringing along his longtime percussionist and vocalist, Pete Knudson. "We worked so hard that [Godinéz] got burned out," said Fé. "I worked with [Morin] about seventeen years ago. He's a very accomplished and amazing musician, a great Piedmont blues fingerpicker. He's had his own band, the Atoll, for many years, playing reggae, jazz, R&B, and rock."

A double-disc CD, *A Blues Night in North Carolina*, released in the spring of 2011, documented the Pure Fé Trio's live show. "Those were two beautiful nights," said Fé. "The audience was hesitant to be too loud, because they knew it was being recorded, but we stirred them up and got them to be on their 'bad' behavior, shouting things between songs. It was lots of fun."

Since their days with Ulali, Moreno and Kreisberg have remained busy. Moreno has performed with Maori singers (from New Zealand) in a Native-fusion band

(Matou) and has continued to explore visual art, exhibiting many of her large-scale sculptures. She also coproduces the annual Roots and Rhythm Native American Performing Arts Festival in Albuquerque, New Mexico.

Kreisberg has balanced music with film, making her acting debut, and contributing a song, "Deer Song"—composed for an aboriginal Women's Project—to the soundtrack of Sherman Alexei's 2002 film, *The Business of Fancy Dancing*. Two of her songs were included in *Osinilshatin*, starring Michelle St. John (the voice of Disney's *Pocahontas*). She received an "Achievement in Music" Genie Award from the Academy of Canadian Cinema and Television in 2007 for an original song, "Have Hope," which she sang in Carl Bessai's film *Unnatural and Accidental*. Since releasing her solo debut album, *Wah Thye Ye Rak* ("She Mixed It"), Kreisberg has been writing a stage play about the murder of ten Native women in Vancouver, British Columbia, in the 1990s, and occasionally performing with Fé in a duo, Twoali.

FLORENT VOLLANT

One of the most striking tunes on *Music for the Native Americans*, "Akua Tuta" featured Kashtin, an Innu folk-pop duo composed of singer, acoustic guitarist, songwriter, and traditional drummer Florent Vollant (1959–) and electric guitarist, harmonica player, and singer Claude McKenzie (1967–). As the title song of their third album, with contributions by Robbie Robertson, it would become a hit in France, Belgium, South Korea, Bolivia, and the United States. "[Robertson] reached us in Montreal," remembered Vollant, "and asked us to do a recording session with him. He is very special, from another world. I am so proud to have been part of [*Music for the Native Americans*]. I really appreciated the time that we spent together."

Formed in 1987, Kashtin had risen to the upper echelon of Canadian entertainment when Robertson contacted them. Although slightly more than 8,000 people speak the Innu-aimun (or Montagnais) language that they sang, Vollant and McKenzie's soft-voiced, Paul-Simon-meets-the-Gipsy-Kings folk-pop tunes brought international fame and commercial success. Their 1989 self-titled debut album included a pair of top-ten singles—"E Uassiuian" ("My Childhood") and "Tshinanu" ("Dance of the Devil")—and attained double-platinum status, with sales of more than 200,000 copies in Canada. The Québécois Felix Awards named it "Album of the Year" and "Best Country-Folk Album." "We didn't have any experience in the studio [before we recorded the album]," said Vollant, "but we had a lot [of experience] on the stage and the spirit was familiar. [Toronto-based drummer] Claude Rangar, who produced us, was interested in our music, language, culture, and band."

Kashtin continued to spread their message of harmony, and Innu culture, around the globe. They made their United States debut at the New Music seminar in New York in 1990, and shortly afterwards toured Europe. Between 1989 and 1991, they toured France, where audiences considered them superstars, fifteen times, headlining and sharing stages with the Gipsy Kings. "It wasn't hard to play for their audiences," said Vollant. "We're gypsies, too."

The son of an ironworker (and amateur harmonica player), Vollant hails from the remote city of Labrador in the northernmost region (Newfoundland and Labrador) in Atlantic Canada. "My grandfather and grandmother worked as guides in the mines," he said. "All of my family worked there—my aunts, my uncles, my cousins."

The joys of Vollant's childhood came to a premature end. "We had to move from the north," he said, "because the mine had gotten too big and the lake [had been polluted]."

Forcibly removed from his parents' home at the age of five, Vollant found himself a "prisoner" in a residential school. "It was hard to be away from my father, mother, and clan," he said. "All of my brothers and sisters were there with me, and we tried to keep the spirit of my family, but it was tough to go from speaking the Innu language, and living the kind of life that we had up north, to becoming someone else. We tried to understand the French language, but it was a big shock."

Having spent countless hours, before his fifth birthday, listening to his grandfather sing Inuit songs and beat on a hand drum, Vollant continued to expand his repertoire. "I learned a lot of music from the church and [sang] prayers in French," he said. "I also got to watch music on TV at a time when there was a big wave all around the world called 'the Beatles.' All young Innu wanted to be in the Beatles. They had a new spirit and a new sound and we were very attracted by it."

Montreal-born filmmaker, playwright, singer, songwriter, and political activist, Willie Dunn (1942–2013), of Micmac, Scottish, and Irish descent, had a major impact on the young musician. They would cowrite "Son of the Sun," the only English-language song on Kashtin's second album, *Innu*. "[Dunn] was one of the first Native musicians that I met," recalled Vollant. "He was playing protest songs and I was against the system. I didn't like the way that American Indians were treated, and I was looking for a way to be part of that protest."

Louisiana-born Zydeco accordionist Zachary Richard (cousin of Michael Doucet of Cajun trad-rock band, BeauSoleil) also provided inspiration. Mixing Cajun French patois and English, the Cajun/Zydeco accordionist had been stirring enthusiasm on both sides of the United States/Canada border, as well as in France, since the early 1970s. He would become an honorary member of the Order of Canada in 2009 for contributions made as an author, composer, singer, and poet, and for his role in "defending and promoting the French language and Acadian identity." "I've always been a big fan of his music," said Vollant, "and the way that he's fought so hard for his culture and language. We worked together in my studio, in Maliotenam Reserve, Quebec, and traveled together for a while. I'm so happy to have him in my life; he's a good friend."

Initially singing English-language country music and pop songs, Vollant found his own voice through his native tongue. "I heard people from the Cree Nation singing country music in their language," he said, "so I started making songs in the Innu language."

An apprenticeship with "the father of contemporary Innu music," Philippe McKenzie (no relation to Claude) strengthened Vollant's musical skills, but his salary as a musician was insufficient for the then-new father to support a family. Seeking additional income, he founded an annual two-day celebration of aboriginal culture, Le Festival Innu Nikamu, in 1980, serving five years as director. His brother, Reginald Vollant, currently directs the festival, still held each year during the first weekend of August. "The first year was very difficult," remembered Vollant, who performed during the festival's inaugural weekend with Philippe McKenzie and Willie Dunn, "and it took a lot of time and energy."

When Philippe McKenzie's group temporarily disbanded in 1984, Vollant continued to collaborate with bandmate Claude McKenzie. "We had been playing music at my house," recalled Vollant, "when we got a telephone call. Music was needed for a program that was going to honor tribal elders." After Vollant agreed to play, the caller asked him for the duo's name. The vocalist thought for a minute before answering, "Kashtin," taken from an Innu word that translates as "tornado," but can also refer to the slang term, "cashing in," as a response to traditionalists' claims that they were "selling out" with their commercialized approach to Innu music.

Vollant and McKenzie reunited with Philippe McKenzie shortly afterwards, but the response elicited by their duo debut left them with enough confidence that, two years later, they handed in their resignation and returned their focus to Kashtin. "We started at Le Festival Innu Nikamu," said Vollant, "and kept traveling, playing at powwows and bars, and learning to be performers. We were kings of the road."

As word about their updated Innu music spread, Vollant and McKenzie received an avalanche of offers to record, especially after an appearance in a documentary about Innu life, broadcast by a Quebec television station, in 1988. "A lot of record company people tried to reach us," said Vollant, "but we didn't answer them. Claude and I were very happy with what we were doing. We were free and having a good time playing music. We had enough money to take care of our families."

Relenting to requests to document their music, Kashtin hit double platinum with their debut album, selling more than 150,000 copies in the six months following its release. As their popularity grew, they became the musical voice of the Oka Crisis, an oft-violent battle between Mohawk activists protesting the planned building of a housing development, and a nine-hole private golf course, on the site of an ancient Indian burial ground southwest of Montreal. Many radio stations banned their music during the standoff, which lasted from July 11 to September 26, 1990, but their heartfelt Innu-language songs remained symbols of cultural pride.

Continuing their ascent with a second album, *Innu*, which included "Son of the Sun," in 1991, Kashtin followed with *Akua Tuta* three years later. Shortly after its release, Vollant and McKenzie announced they would be separating. "We had played together for many years," said Vollant, "and had created a lot of great music, but I had spent more time with him than I had with my wife. It was time to move on."

Shortly after releasing an impressive debut solo album, *Innu Town*, in 1997, McKenzie sustained serious injury in an automobile accident, and did not record a follow-up album (*Innui*) until a decade later.

Vollant began working on an album of Christmas songs (sung in Innu), following Kashtin's final show in December 1995, but he abruptly stopped the project. Returning to his home in Maliotenam, he took a much-needed break. "I was having trouble with my producers, about the rights of the songs," he said, "so I stopped everything and went back to my family." After a year and a half of this idleness, his loved ones began to be concerned. "My wife looked at me," he remembered, "and said, 'You've got to do something, you can't just sit around thinking about it.'"

Building a recording studio—Makusham (Celebration)—Vollant returned to work. Montreal's French-language newspaper, *La Presse*, acclaimed his first outing, *Katak*, recorded with Zachary Richard and Ray Bonneville in 2003, for its "warm techno rhythms coming from the very heart of the continent."

Resuming and completing the aborted Yuletide album—*Nipaiamianan (Native American Christmas)*—in 2005, Vollant scored a JUNO Award for the year's "Best Aboriginal Recording." A collection of original songs, *Eku Mamu*, followed four years later.

After a separation of fifteen years, Kashtin was reunited at Le Festival Innu Nikamu in Maliotenam and the Aqpik Jam in Kuujjuaq, Nunavik, in 2010. They also recorded an updated, hip-hop version of "Tshinanu," sung in Innu, with Quebec-born Samian (Samuel Tremblay) rapping in French.

Kashtin came together again on June 21, 2012, when Vollant—who has hosted a popular music TV show, on the Aboriginal People Television Network (APTN) since 2009—and McKenzie performed at a free outdoor festival in Winnipeg, on the site of a traditional Ojibwe and Dakota gathering place. Broadcast by APTN, their performance was viewed by more than 200,000 Canadians.

TERESA "BEAR" FOX

A founding member of the Kontiwennenhawi-Akwesasne Women's Singers ("Carriers of the Words"), Teresa "Bear" Fox (Mohawk) has sung traditional songs, and originals based on Mohawk traditions, since 1990. "Our elders are passing away," said the Hogansburg, New York–based mother of five, "and our language isn't as strong as it used to be. Our way of keeping it going is through the songs, so we sing traditional-type songs with the water drum and rattles, and social songs in the Mohawk language."

The youngest of fourteen children, Fox—who got her nickname, "Bear," from the Berenstain Bears children's book series—grew up speaking English. "My mother used to be hit in school for speaking Mohawk," she said, "and she hardly ever used it to speak to us."

Music played a strong role in Fox's childhood home. "My mother loved music," she recalled, "especially country music, like Doug Kershaw, the Cajun fiddle player. She played piano and taught me to play a little, and she played harmonica. I really liked hearing her sing."

Determined to write songs in the Mohawk dialect (Kanienkeha), Fox sought the help of her best friend, Margaret Peters, who spoke the language. Her brothers, who had learned it before she was born, also shared what they knew. "If there were words that I didn't know how to say," Fox explained, "I would ask someone and they would tell me. There were still a lot of Native speakers, and they were all willing to help me."

Fox's brothers, who played in a family musical group, introduced her to the songs of the Mohawk Nation. "They used a water drum," she remembered, "a cylinder that they filled with water, and covered with buckskin. It got its distinct sound based on how much water they used to fill it. My brothers sang with a lot of vibrato. I sang traditional songs because those were the songs that they sang."

Begun as informal weekly meetings led by Fox and her sister-in-law, Katsitsionni Fox, in 1990, Kontiwennenhawi continued to grow. "We were always trying to get more women to join us," said Fox. "Eventually, we had enough women to share our songs."

A fire that destroyed the home that she shared with her ironworker husband, Sky Fox, and their daughter and four sons, in 2001, prompted Fox to write her first English-language songs. "I was going to school to become a teacher," she said, "and didn't have a permanent job, but I wanted to find a way to bring an income to the family, especially after the fire. I started thinking that, if an artist paints, and a potter creates pottery, I could record a solo CD and sell it. I could write songs. Why couldn't I write songs in English [and reach a more diverse audience]?"

Fox's first English-language composition, "Broken," told the heartbreaking tale of a mother who loses her children to the boarding schools. "Rich Girl," the title track of Fox's 2010 debut solo album, followed. Sung a cappella, it celebrated a person's wealth, despite poverty, because of family love. Fox had written the tune as she, and Kontiwennenhawi, traveled to perform at Cornell University in Ithaca, New York. "I was sitting in the back seat," she recalled. "My sister-in-law was driving. All of a sudden, I felt like I needed to write. I grabbed an envelope and a pencil and started writing about how it was growing up on the farm. It was the story of my upbringing. Even though we did not have a lot of money, my mother, and my father, worked hard and made sure that we had clean clothes and plenty of food. I assumed that they were rich."

With the title track from her second solo album (*Diamond*) carrying similarly optimistic sentiment, Fox received a "Songwriter of the Year" NAMMY in 2014. Continuing to teach language and culture at the Mohawk Nation–run Akwesasne Freedom School, she hasn't strayed far from music. "I have so many songs that I haven't recorded yet," she said, "and so many that are left to be written. I really want to get the music out further."

THE BLANCHETT BROTHERS AND PAMYUA

The hand drum–accompanied singing traditions of western Alaska's Yup'ik community are preserved, as well as expanded upon, by Pamyua ("Bum-yu-ah"). On their October 2012 double-CD, *Side A/Side B*—their first in seven years—the Anchorage-based trio celebrated both worlds in which they live. While the first disc featured traditional Yup'ik and Inuit songs, the second updated the same tunes with guitars, bass, drums, keyboards, tenor saxophone, violin, cello, and Philadelphia Soul–style arrangements. "We wanted to honor the traditional drum songs with the Inuit drum and our voices," said Phillip Blanchett (Yup'ik/African American), who formed Pamyua with his brother Stephen, Phillip "Ossie" Kairaiuak (Yup'ik), and Nuuk, Greenland–born Karinna Moeller (Inuit/Dane), "but we wanted to show the other side of our identity too. The songs come from the Yup'ik and Inuit traditions, but we share them in creative and progressive ways. Appreciating both worlds is what's important."

The sons of Philadelphia-born African American David Blanchett and Yup'ik dancer and University of Alaska language teacher, Marie Mead, the Blanchett brothers hail from Bethel, Alaska (population, 6,080), the main port of the

Kuskokwim River on the Yukon Kuskokwim Delta, four hundred miles west of Anchorage. Landlocked from urban centers, the city was undergoing phenomenal change when the brothers were born (Stephen in 1972 and Phillip in 1974). "The Land Claim Settlement Act between Alaska's Native tribes and the United States government was signed in 1971," said Phillip Blanchett. "It was a fresh start for Native people, as we transitioned from tribal people to the corporate world. We still have no roads. We're off the Kuskokwim River, forty miles from the Bering Sea. In the wintertime, once the river freezes, they grade snow on the river as a highway system for vehicles. Otherwise, the only ways to get to other communities are by snowmobile, sixteen-wheeler, or flying. In the summer, after the ice melts, people get around by boat, and flying, but there is a time, in between, when the only way that you can get somewhere is by flying. Flying is our subway system."

The spark leading to Pamyua lit in 1995. "My brother wanted me to teach him a traditional dance," recalled Blanchett, who moved with his parents and brother to Anchorage in the mid-1980s. "I had been dancing with community groups, and performing at Alaska's equivalent of powwows, while he was in college. As I was teaching him the dance, I had to show him how the song went, so he could learn the rhythm and the cadence. He started harmonizing with this simple melody. My first instinct was, 'No, you're doing it wrong,' but before I could complete that thought, both of us realized that we felt something that we had never felt before. We continued to put together a repertoire, just to show our dad. It snowballed from there. I started booking gigs and found that there was interest within our community."

At that point, the brothers reached out to Kairaiuak, who had grown up in Chefornak (population, 395), a traditional Yup'ik village close to Bethel. "In many respects, he's family," said Blanchett. "My family has been trading partners with his for generations. We come from different regions. He's from the coast, and we're from the Tundra. We have fish, and an abundance of animals like reindeer, polar bear, ermine, and caribou. They have sea mammals."

Initially a trio augmented by dancers, Pamyua expanded with the arrival of Moeller in 1996. "We were performing at an international event with artists from the circumpolar regions—Canada, Russia, Alaska, and Greenland," said Blanchett. "She saw us perform and thought that we were going in the direction that she wanted to go artistically. She ended up staying [in Alaska] and joining us. We were married and had two daughters, who traveled all over the world with us, but we divorced many years ago and I have since remarried. We're one big happy family."

Preservation of the Yup'ik language remains essential to Blanchett and Pamyua. "My mother was punished for speaking it as a child," he said. "My brother and I grew up speaking it when we were toddlers, but, in the 1970s, there was a lot of change going on. Our tribe adopted this idea of corporate leadership and we had to accept the American ways, including the English language. My brother and I lost our ability to speak fluently. Ossie, who grew up in the village, is the youngest of ten. Both of his parents are Yup'ik and barely speak any English. That's why we reached out to him."

Whether performing as a quartet, or with a full band, Pamyua energize their shows with masterfully executed choreography. "Our trade secret, within Yup'ik culture," explained Blanchett, "is that the dancing, which is our main form of performance art, has a connection with the audience. There are so many different aspects to dance, but it's about expressing so much that the audiences are absorbed and inspired by what we do. The challenge is to bring that energy to our recordings. There are visual dynamics that come with these drum songs, but, on our recordings, it's the pulse of the drum, the melody of the song, counterbalance of a simple rhythm, and textures of harmony, that give it a level of mystery and intrigue."

Bird and animal calls, punctuated by random shouts, add to Pamyua's sound. "We're actually singing the way that our people have expressed themselves for thousands of years," said Blanchett. "Our songs are about the natural environment, and we're honoring the deeper aspects of our culture."

Pamyua's name derives from a familiar Yup'ik shout. "My mom was a renowned performer," explained Blanchett "and she traveled all over the world. Growing up, I would watch her perform with [Yup'ik dance troupe] Nunamta (People of the Land)." At the end of every dance, the leader of the group would yell, 'pamyua.' When he started a musical group, Blanchett recalled the cry and thought it "appropriate for a group that did Yup'ik dances in a theatrical way." "When I was growing up, it had only one meaning," he remembered. "It meant the end of something, whether it was the tail of an animal or the end of a song. Now, it means four musicians who sing Yup'ik music."

Blanchett and his bandmates initially had reservations about the name. "We worried that it would be difficult for English-speaking people to accept," he recalled, "because it's a Native word and has a 'p' with an unusual pronunciation. At the same time, we wanted to educate people and celebrate our culture. People learn our language just by learning our name. It creates more of a relationship."

The title of Pamyua's 1998 debut album, *Megluni*, derived from the Yup'ik word meaning "beginning." "We didn't plan that," said Blanchett. "On the cover, we're out on the ice, standing in a circle, in a dancing motion. It wasn't until we were working on the graphics that we realized that this was a beginning and an end. We're in a circle that never ends."

One of the tunes on the album, "Reindeer Herding Song," became a hit in 2011 when aired as part of *Flying Wild Alaska*, a Discovery Channel reality-TV show about the owners of a small airline (Era Alaska), Jim and Ferno Tweto, and two of their three daughters. "It was the first song on the first episode of the first season," said Blanchett. "When we started negotiating with the producers, they said that they didn't have any money for us, but could give us credit. We told them that we weren't interested, but they really, really wanted it. We talked so much that we developed this mutually advantageous working relationship. The producer couldn't imagine starting the show without that song. It's become so popular, one of the best-known Yup'ik dances."

One episode of *Flying Wild Alaska* featured an on-screen appearance by Pamyua. A song that Kairaiuak had written after catching a dance student chewing gum in class, "Bubble Gum," was featured, along with a segment on the group's Yup'ik drum making. "We wanted to do a new tune, 'Flying,'" Blanchett recalled, "as a surprise for the Tweto family. We recorded it and, up until the final edit, it was going to be in the show. We use commuter planes all of the time. It's an everyday thing, the way that we live."

In addition to reviving traditional Yup'ik songs, Pamyua has added to the canon with original tunes. On *Side A/Side B*, there are three songs by Kairaiuak ("Bubble Gum," "Ocean Prayer," and "They Sang to Each Other"), a song by Kairaiuak's cousin Vernon John ("Bulldozer"), and a tune by Stephen Blanchett ("His Spear").

One of the oldest songs in the collection, "Pulling," a traditional prayer for strength, is featured four times, including one version that interpolates a sample from a 1973 album, *Eskimo Songs and Stories*, and another that incorporates the voice of the Blanchett brothers' mother.

Pamyua's full-band arrangements represent an unprecedented step in Yup'ik and Inuit music. "We hold a high regard for our American Indian elders, drum makers, and composers," said Blanchett, "but African American music is one of the creative forces of pop music, too, and we hold a high regard for that side of our heritage as well. We pay respect to our elders on both sides."

SUSAN AGLUKARK

Susan Aglukark (1967–) (Inuit) topped the Canadian pop charts in 1955 with "O Siem (Joy in Community)," the debut single from her triple platinum album, *This Child*. With her rendition of Christine McVie's "Songbird" nine years later, the seven-time JUNO-winning songstress not only paid tribute to the Fleetwood Mac keyboardist/vocalist to whom she's often compared, but also chose a tune that described her talents as one of the most successful artists to come out of Canada's Northwest Territories.

Although she mostly writes (and sings) in English, many of Aglukark's songs incorporate phrases, or choruses, in her native tongue (Inuktitut). She recorded a version of "Amazing Grace," as translated into Inuktitut, for her first nationally distributed album, *Arctic Rose* (EMI Canada), in 1994, and followed with *Christmas*, composed of Yuletide classics sung in Inuktitut.

Based in Ottawa, Ontario, since 1991, Aglukark retains ties to Arviat—formerly, Eskimo Point—a remote town (population, 700) along the northwest shore of Hudson Bay, in Nunavut, where she spent most of her young life. "The small town life that I knew, in a lot of ways, is still the same," she said, "but, in other ways, it's so much different. I want to go back to the land, back to the hunting, the fishing, and the camping, back to what I knew, but when I go back to visit, so much has happened too fast."

The fourth of seven children born to a Pentecostal preacher, David Aglukark, and his wife, Dorothy, Aglukark grew up singing in church. Her parents recorded an album, *Inuktitut Gospel Songs*. "There was very little music except for old-time country gospel," she said. "As a preacher's kids, we sang church music. The local radio station had a show at noon and a dinnertime show and played country gospel and bluegrass music; we did not have a record player. There was no nurturing of the music within me. It was a real major learning curve."

Aglukark's father taught her three chords on the guitar when she was fourteen, and a teacher provided a single piano lesson, but that was the extent of her musical training. "I play well enough to write," she said.

The greatest influence came from Aglukark's Christian faith. "I still am very much a believer," she said, "though there were a lot of struggles. I didn't want to be a preacher's kid, as a teenager, but it is a big part of who I am. I don't write Christian or gospel music, but I write with the belief in a greater being."

Aglukark's songs deal with child abuse, poverty, heartbreak, racism, prejudice, and suicide and reflect personal experience. Her grandmother was an alcoholic who froze to death, and five of her cousins committed suicide. Before her tenth birthday, a family friend sexually abused her. Though shame prevented her from speaking about the abuse, she began writing about it in her diary as a young teen. "I wrote about very personal things," she recalled, "things that only my parents knew about. Writing was part of my healing."

Discovering the diary stolen (and her secret revealed), Aglukark refused to write again. "It was such an intrusion into my personal space," she said. "I wasn't ready to go public [about the abuse]. I lost the trust connected to writing and had to get away from it for a while."

Forced to file charges against her abuser, and endure a yearlong court case, Aglukark slowly resumed writing. "It became cathartic for me," she said. "As my life moved on, beyond the court hearings and the consequential conviction, I used it to exorcise my demons."

Bullied in junior high, for her nonconfrontational persona, Aglukark was not looking forward to high school. "In the eastern Arctic, we went to schools in our communities up to the ninth grade," she said, "but, for high school, we had to fly either to the basin region [in western Canada] or the western Arctic in Yellowknife, Northwest Territories. The year that we were ready to go on to high school, Yellowknife was not an option, because they were renovating it. I had no choice."

Starting the school year at Gordon Robertson Education Center (now Inukshuk High School) in August 1985, Aglukark was ready to leave by Christmas break. "I told my father that, if he sent me back to that high school," she recalled, "I'd come home a drug addict. Drugs were that accessible and I knew that I would give in to peer pressure. My father let me drop out."

The following year, the residential high school at Yellowknife was still not ready. Attending Regina Maranatha Christian Academy for a semester, Aglukark was able to make up for the year that she had missed. "When Yellowknife reopened, I went there," she said, "and finished at Sir John Franklin High School."

With her abuser's release after eighteen months in prison, Aglukark felt uneasy in her hometown. Taking a job as a linguist for the Canadian Department of Indian and Northern Affairs in Ottawa, 1,200 miles away, she embarked on what she thought would be a year of healing. More than two decades later, she remains in Canada's capital city. "I don't know if it was such a huge culture shock," she said. "I had lived in Regina, Saskatchewan, for a year, when I went to the Christian school, and I took a semester off [from high school] to work for a member of parliament in Ottawa. I lived on my own when I was seventeen. I had city experience. When I moved [to Ontario], it meant having my own apartment, figuring out the bus system, budgeting, and all the things that I had taken for granted, but I didn't stay out of the fear of going back home. Home was always there for me."

Aglukark worked closely with Ottawa's aboriginal community. "Part of my job was working with those who lived between two worlds," she said, "those who had to leave their homes and relocate elsewhere."

Writing poetry since her senior year of high school, Aglukark was inspired to write a song ("Searching") about her work experiences. When it was included as part of a presentation for her federal employers, "they discussed using it in a short documentary about the effects of living between two worlds. Then, someone suggested that the song be turned into a music video."

The finished video became a heavily rotated hit throughout Canada and went on to win a Much Music award for "best cinematography." Aglukark's life changed in ways that she had never imagined. "I wasn't even a singer-songwriter yet," she said. "It was a poem. I was a preacher's kid, so I knew how to sing, but I didn't consider myself a singer."

Aglukark's rise to stardom was swift. "Within six months of moving to southern Canada," she said, "I was a headliner with a band and a crew. It was very difficult. I didn't have any business sense and had a lot of learning to do very fast."

After releasing a very limited debut album, Aglukark hit her stride with her second effort, *Arctic Rose*, in 1992. "That's when I came to appreciate the difference between poetry writing and songwriting," she said. "I don't read or write music, and I learned English as a second language, but I felt so comfortable transferring personal experiences, feelings, and emotions into three-and-a-half minute stories."

Selling more than 2 million copies, Aglukark's major label debut, *This Child* (EMI Canada), made her a star. "None of us was prepared for how huge a success it was going to be," she said. "I certainly wasn't." The album's first single, "O Siem," became one of the year's best-selling Canadian releases. "I hadn't come to the point, in my artist's mind," said Aglukark, "where I could even fully appreciate what a number-one hit meant, but I knew that it was a wonderful song. It was a great experience from the beginning. Everything about it felt so right. I hadn't transferred all that feeling into writing a song for a radio hit. That never crossed my mind, or my producer's, but, all of a sudden, here we were, with not only a hit song, but also a million-selling album. It all happened so fast."

Despite the popularity of *This Child* in Canada, Aglukark felt unprepared to reach out to audiences beyond the Great White North. "[EMI Canada] wanted to release it in the States," she said, "but I just frankly said, 'I'm not ready to go beyond the border.' I wasn't a good enough singer or good enough on stage yet; I still had a lot of catching up to do."

Aglukark felt increasing pressure to follow the success of *This Child*. "[My next album] *Unsung Heroes* was very difficult," she said. "There was a great deal of expectation for me to create another hit, and I was trying to tell them that *This Child* was a fluke. I didn't know how to write a hit song, but we spent a good two years trying. It was a struggle, but, in the end, the product that came out, we loved."

Aglukark turned the heat up with *Big Feeling* (2003), working with multi-instrumentalist, songwriter, and producer Ben Mink—who, in turn, has worked with k. d. lang, the Barenaked Ladies, Raffi, Jane Siberry, Dan Hill, and Bruce Cockburn. "That was such a wonderful experience," Aglukark said. "I learned so much about moving outside of my self-imposed creative boundaries. Ben was a whole other force. He had his own process and allowed me to tap into it."

Blood Red Earth (2006) showed how far Aglukark had grown as a songwriter and artist. "I was so ready to keep putting out music," she said, "that it was no longer a struggle. I had left [EMI Canada] and taken some time to think, but now I wanted to record and write songs. I was ready to get back into the studio with good musicians. I needed to release that album so that I could move on."

Aglukark released a career-spanning retrospective, *White Sahara*, in 2011. "It's all about my love for the North," she said, "my ongoing love affair with home, culture, history, images, and memories. In addition to my hits, I included some of my favorite 'living stories,' with Indigenous people sharing their memories of back home."

There were three new songs on the disc. "The first single ('Revolution Road') is about how warriors become heroes," said Aglukark, "and heroes become warriors, but they're not the kind of warriors that we imagine—the soldiers—they're everyday people whose personal self-discovery is a form of battle. That's what the song is all about—the struggle of the Aboriginal community, our resilience, and our determination to maintain culture and tradition through it all."

Calling one new tune ("White Sahara") "a love song to Inuit and Arctic culture," Aglukark explained that another ("Where Do We Go From Here") was "about being aware of where we've been but not so sure about our next steps." "How do we combine traditional culture with mainstream?" she asked. "And how do we package it, so that young people choose to stay connected to their culture?"

LEELA GILDAY

Composed during an intertribal gathering in Saskatoon in 2004, Leela Gilday's "One Drum" has become an anthem of unity. "We come from many nations," explained the JUNO-winning singer-songwriter, "but there's commonality among Indigenous people. Since colonization, and especially since the formation of the National Indian Brotherhood of Canada in the late 1960s, people have felt a closer sense of unity and solidarity. We share many of the same struggles. Whatever cultural differences we may have, they shrink next to what we have overcome— colonization—and things that we are still dealing with, like residential schools. 'One Drum' speaks to people on that level. Unity is a very important theme for all Indigenous cultures. We have to work together."

The daughter of a classical trombone player, Gilday (Diné) grew up in Yellowknife, the capital city of the Northwest Territory. "On the map, it looks like it takes up half of Canada," she said, "but, in all of the Northwest Territory, there are only 43,000 people. The capital city is a metropolis of 18,000 people. Fifty percent are Diné. We have a very strong political presence. It's rooted in our relationship with the land and our ancestors."

John Switzer, producer of Gilday's 2002 debut album, *Spirit World, Solid Wood*, previously worked with alt-rockers, including Jane Siberry, Andrew Cash, and the Grievous Angels. "He taught me everything that I know about the studio," said Gilday. "He had a very particular sound as a producer, a really clean sound. He brought that out of me and made me sound great. I still enjoy that record."

Paced by three hits—"One Drum," "Dene Love Song," and "Ride Horseman"—Gilday's second album, *Sedze* was her commercial breakthrough. "I pushed myself," she said. "It was an intense time of growth for me, as a songwriter and an artist, and that album reflected it. It was very different from my first album. I used an upright bass player, and Debashis Sinha played percussion. He brought a very different sound with frame drums and cajón [a box-shaped percussion instrument originally from Peru]. That changed how my songs sounded and spoke to people."

Gilday recorded her third CD, *Calling All Warriors*, in Vancouver. "It has a theme of a call to action," she explained. "Empowerment is the word that describes the album in terms of my messages. It's probably my most important work."

Gilday released her fourth CD, *Heart of the People*, after returning to Yellowknife, following many years in Vancouver, in 2014. "It's very challenging," she said, "but it was a decision I had to make. I'd always wanted to move back home. I'm a northern girl, very tied to my land, my family, and my people. It's where I belong."

LEANNE GOOSE

Of the 60,000 people living in the four regions composing Inuit Nunaat ("Inuit Homeland"), stretching from Labrador to the Northwest Territories, nearly 75 percent are Inuit, Yup'ik, or Aleut. Although the region's Indigenous inhabitants were derogatorily called "Eskimos" (the Algonquin word for "raw meat eater"), and were stereotypically depicted as living in igloos and wearing parkas, there is an exceptionally broad range of rituals, foods, languages, and lifestyles in the continent's coldest clime. "There are sixteen dialects of the Inuit language," said Northwest Territory–based country/blues singer-songwriter and festival promoter Leanne Goose (1966–) (Diné/Inuvialuit). "We're not able to understand people from the eastern Arctic."

The eldest daughter of Canadian country music and rock-and-roll great Louis Goose grew up in the remote city of Inuvik (population, 3,484).[48] "We're at the northernmost end of Canada's highway system," she said, "about 2,400 miles north of Seattle, the closest that you can get to the Arctic Ocean. We're ten degrees north of the Arctic Circle, the sixtieth parallel, just below the tree line, in the McKenzie River Delta Basin, where water flows into the Arctic Ocean."

Accompanying her grandmother, who played guitar and possessed a large collection of vinyl recordings, and grandfather on hunting and trapping expeditions to the bush, Goose spent hours listening to music on the radio. Attending a show by her father's band when she was twelve, she became so spirited that she invited herself onto the stage and began to sing. It was the beginning of her career. "I have eight younger siblings," she said. "My sisters sing, my youngest brother,

Leanne Goose (Diné/
Inuvialiut) brings warmth
(and soulful music) to
the remote regions of
northern Canada.
Courtesy Leanne Goose.

who is thirteen, plays guitar and writes songs. My son is fifteen. He plays guitar by ear; he's quite good. My other son, who's twelve, raps."

Taught clarinet, saxophone, and flute in elementary school, Goose continued to study piano and music theory at the University of Winnipeg. It would be her only lengthy time away from home. After three years in Canada's "Chicago of the North," she returned to Inuvik, where she continues to reside. "Inuvik is a very cosmopolitan place," she said. "We have people from all over the world, all races, and all cultures. We have a mosque, churches, wonderful schools, and a recreation complex (which houses a swimming pool with a slide). We have a curling rink and an ice hockey rink, as well as community dance halls. We have baseball diamonds, so much to see and do."

When we spoke, in May 2012, Goose was preparing for "our twenty-four-hour-of-daylight period (at the beginning of July)." "It'll remain like that until August," she said, "and then it will gradually get darker and darker. By November, we'll be in twenty-four-hour darkness until the first week or two of January. Then, it'll progressively get lighter and lighter."

After apprenticing with her father's band, Goose released her debut album (*Anywhere*) in 2008. "I'm a country and blues artist," she said, "but my roots are very deep in my culture, and the music that comes out is the rhythm of my people. I just express it in a very contemporary way. I sing about my summers at whaling camp, or about going hunting, but the messages are not clear unless you know me. I tell stories during my shows, about growing up in a plywood house with no running water, having to haul water, and cut wood. I was the last generation of my family to attend residential boarding school—and I have a song about my family's experience with that horrific event—but I'm telling my stories in ways that people from all cultures could relate."

For her second album, *Got You Covered* (2011), Goose asked fans for suggestions. "I received over 50,000 requests for the eight songs," she said. "I wanted to do something to honor the people who had been supporting me since I was a wee one."

Although she recruited Gabriel Ayala (Yaqui) to produce her third album, the classical guitarist returned to Tucson during production, and Goose finished the album (*This Time*) with Jason Gordon (Studio 11). "It was an important album to make," she said. "It allowed me the creative freedom to show a side of my home and our lives in the contemporary North."

Despite her busy schedule as a singer, Goose has found time, not only to work for a local hospital (as a physician recruiter), but also to become one of the Northwest Territory's top promoters of music festivals. "I assist in producing the End of the Road Music Festival," she said, "and shows for the Truth and Reconciliation Commissions. I've also produced *Fire in the Sky*, coinciding with the Aboriginal People's Music Awards, in Winnipeg, Manitoba, and *Fire in the Sky*/Toronto, coinciding with the [now defunct] Canadian Aboriginal Music Awards."

RADMILLA CODY

With her 2012 album of songs in the Navajo language, *Shi Keyah: Songs for the People*, Grand Falls, Arizona–raised Radmilla Cody (1975–) became the first American Indian nominee in the Grammy Awards' new Regional Roots category. The product of a short-lived relationship between a forty-three-year-old African American and an eighteen-year-old Diné woman who fled to Georgia shortly after her birth, Radmilla had grown up without running water or electricity on her maternal grandmother's farm on the Navajo Reservation. "She taught me that herding sheep, planting corn, weaving rugs, making traditional foods, and connecting with the land were more important than all the material things in the world," Cody told me in April 2012. "She taught me that was what made us who we were. It's not about us but about everything around us, how we connect with that and create that balance."

As a child, Cody would climb to the top of the sheep corral and sing. "When you're way out in the middle of nowhere," she told NPR in 2010, "herding sheep, and you're spending time jumping over the salt bushes, and sitting around listening to all of the beautiful sounds of nature, something's going to make you open your mouth."[49]

Her grandmother's conversion to Christianity exposed Cody to the hymns of the church. "I remember one particular time," she told the *Los Angeles Times*, "the church had this choir, from I don't recall where, but, man, they sounded so good. I remember thinking in my mind, 'That's what I want to do, that's what I want to sound like.'"[50]

The singing of the late R&B vocalist Whitney Houston also had a profound impact. "I idolized her," Cody told me. "She had such an incredible voice. I wanted to sing like her."[51]

Despite her mixed heritage, Cody entered the Miss Navajo Nation competition in 1997, at the age of twenty-two. "Bi-racial people should not be judged as half of anything," she told *High Country News*. "I went into this competition with a goal that, not only was I going to open eyes, I was [also] going to open doors."[52]

Entrants in the competition, held every September at the Navajo Nation Fair, are judged on the basis of their ability to butcher sheep, fillet the mutton, make tortillas, and card and spin wool as well as their skills in public speaking, their fluency in English and Navajo, and their appearance, attitude, and conduct. "It's sort of like Miss America," Cody explained, "but it's not based on beauty. It's primarily about your knowledge of the Navajo way of life and the life sustaining methods of the Diné."[53]

The position of Miss Navajo Nation carries great responsibility. "It's an honor," Cody said, "a very prestigious title. You travel among your people and speak out on various issues. You speak the Navajo language 95 percent of the time because you communicate with elders, and you have to be on their level. You deal with government officials so you have to be knowledgeable of the government. The media asks your opinion on things. I was pretty vocal about my feelings about various issues."

Cody's win sparked backlash regarding her mixed heritage. In a letter to the *Navajo Times*, Orlando Tom claimed, "There is duty and responsibility to procreate within our own kind so we can perpetuate our existence in the years to come. If we fail in this endeavor, within two hundred years from now, there will be no Indian people. . . . That is why inter-racial unions, and the children [they] bring forth, [are] nothing other than ethnic genocide. . . . Miss Cody's appearance and physical characteristics are clearly black, and thus representative of another race of people."[54]

The racism was nothing new to Cody. "Kids were always teasing me," she told New Zealand music journalist Garth Cartwright. "Black kids doing war whoops, saying all Indians were drunk, and Indian kids calling me 'nigger.' I never took sides when people were rude; I stood up for Navajos and for African Americans."[55]

Cody remembers hostility closer to home. "I dealt with a lot of prejudice on the reservation," she said, "racism from my own family. My own family members and community looked down on me and shunned me for being what I was. My grandmother received critical remarks from people and they asked her why she was raising me and not putting me up for adoption. I shed many, many, tears."[56]

Her grandmother's encouragement helped to ease Cody's worries. "She was there to console me each and every time," she recalled. "She would say, 'My grand baby, don't listen to what other people have to say; the teachings I am instilling [in] you will help you to get through your life and make you a stronger person. You come from two beautiful worlds and you need to embrace them both.'"

Miss Navajo Nation was only a step in Cody's early ascent. Signing with Canyon, she released her debut album, *Within the Four Directions*, in 2000. In addition to "The Star Spangled Banner" in the Navajo language, it included songs about reservation life written by Cody and her uncle Herman Cody, a Navajo language teacher currently working on his doctorate. "We make these albums," said Uncle Herman, "just as grandpa would walk into the hogan, sit down, and start making a moccasin."[57]

Cody opened the 2001 NAMMY ceremonies with her Navajo version of the national anthem. With her second album, *Seed of Life: Traditional Songs of the Navajo*, the following year, she scored a "Best Female Artist" NAMMY.

It had not been clear sailing, though. In September 1998, Las Vegas police arrested Cody. They cited her for wiring $1,000 to her African American boyfriend, Darrell Dwight Bellamy, whom she had met, at the age of nineteen, at Mesa Community College in Phoenix. Because the money was ostensibly for the purchase of marijuana, the police accused her of being involved with money laundering. Violence and intimidation had marked her relationship with Bellamy, who at least once had jammed a gun into her mouth and threatened to shoot. She appeared at some Miss Navajo events with a black eye, telling audiences that she had been hurt in a car accident. "It was a learning process for me," Cody said. "I was very young and impressionable. It was a very painful chapter in my life."[58]

Bellamy had been included on the U.S. marshal's list of fifteen most wanted criminals for having distributed more than 150 kilograms of cocaine since

1993, and for "engaging in a continuing criminal enterprise." The wanted poster described him as "armed and dangerous." "[Bellamy] told her that he was in the car business," Cody's attorney, Stanley Monroe, told the *Arizona Republic* in December 2002, "and she didn't realize until a couple of years later that wasn't his line of work. When she found out about [the drugs], she tried to ignore it. She kept telling herself to get out of the relationship, but only a woman who's been through this can tell you why she didn't leave."[59]

Although she faced a possible five-to-ten-year sentence when she appeared in court in March 2002, Cody pled guilty to the lesser offense of "the actual commission of the felony charge of possession with intent to distribute a controlled substance" and admitted that she had "concealed this knowledge by not letting it be known by authorities." She received a twenty-one-month sentence, followed by a yearlong probation. On January 6, 2003, she entered federal prison in Phoenix. "I had my mom mail me all of my songs," she recalled, "so I wouldn't forget them. I could still sing them while I was doing my time. I shared the songs with girls during our talking circles. That's where three of the songs that I wrote—'Tears,' 'Blessing in Disguise,' and 'Spirit of a Woman'—came from."[60]

Bellamy's arrest (and subsequent imprisonment) put a halt to the abuse that Cody had endured for six years. "At the time that you're experiencing domestic abuse and violence," Cody told me, "it's very difficult to determine that it's an unhealthy way of living. It is a learned behavior, a behavior that I witnessed, not only myself, growing up, in my family, dealing with some of the verbal and physical abuse, but also in my mother. I saw her go through it."[61]

"I witnessed my grandmother go through verbal abuse from some of her children," Cody explained to Jim Largo of the *Navajo Times*, "and I witnessed my mother go through verbal abuse, domestic abuse, and an abusive relationship. It was a very difficult journey for me, from the beginning."[62]

Despite the pleadings of her family, Cody had chosen to remain with Bellamy. "I chose to be blind to the illegal activities that were taking place," she recalled, "because of my love for him."[63]

During her incarceration, Cody found solace in her roots. "I would go out, every morning, and acknowledge the Creator," she remembered. "I would feel the presence of our holy people, and think, to myself, about how many Navajo people were doing the same thing. I knew that they were saying their prayers. I felt the strength. It got me through every day of my time."[64]

As she sat in her cell, Cody reflected on her life. "I knew even while I was doing time," she said to Laurel Morales of Arizona Public Radio station, KNAU, "[that] I needed to get to a place of balance, a place of harmony, a place of understanding, a place of inner peace before I could go out and help others."[65] "I had to face up to the many demons of my past," Cody said, "and understand truly where I went wrong in allowing myself to be part of an unhealthy relationship. I picked up a book on domestic abuse and violence and began educating myself."[66] Resuming her music career following her release from prison, Cody took a major step forward in 2005 with *Spirit of a Woman*, an irresistible mix of traditional Diné songs and contemporary tunes. Toronto Blue Jays pitcher Miguel Batista played Native American flute on the album. "Before I recorded that album," Cody said, "I had it engrained in my mind that I had to start preparing to do an all-English-language album of contemporary songs."

With her fourth CD, *Precious Friend* (2007), Cody turned her gaze to the youngest members of her audience. Accompanying her vocals with the beating of a hand drum and various percussion instruments, she performed Navajo-language songs about colors of the rainbow, fry bread, donkeys, toads, and lambs.

A documentary film produced and directed by Angela Webb, *Hearing Radmilla*, followed Cody's reign as Miss Navajo Nation, and her subsequent legal problems. Covering a decade in the songstress's life, the film premiered during the Pan African Film and Arts Festival in Los Angeles in February 2010. "First-time filmmaker Webb started out to do a documentary about beauty queens," said Leo W. Banks of *High Country News*, "[but] her determination to portray all of the characters as authentically as possible took the film in unexpected directions."[67]

Reaching out to adult listeners, Cody's fifth album (S*hi Keyah: Songs for the People*) scored a Grammy nomination as "Best Regional/Roots Album" of 2012. "[*Shi Keyah*] honors Mother Earth," Cody told Mykel Vernon-Sembach of Northern Arizona University campus newspaper, *The Lumberjack*, "and all that we coexist with on Mother Earth such as the horses, the plants, the land, the people, and the various [Navajo] agencies. . . . Patriotism is certainly in place within this album. It's about life in general, and about everything that encompasses our life today, as Diné people, and as people in general, and how we connect with everything in our life and in our world."[68]

Attending the Grammy Awards ceremony, Cody reconnected with memories of her grandmother, who had passed two months before. "Ever since I was a little girl, I've worn my grandmother's moccasins," she told the *Los Angeles Times*. "The moccasins are what complete this whole exciting time. For me, they are sentimental. I consider them my lucky charm."[69]

A graduate of Northern Arizona University, in Flagstaff, with a bachelor of science degree in public relations, and a minor in sociology, Cody is pursuing a master's degree. She continues to advocate against domestic violence. "As a survivor, I use my personal experiences, and my music, to reach out to those who remain victims," she explained on her official web page, "with [the] hope that they too will embrace the power within themselves to live a healthy, and empowering life, and reconnect [with], and understand, the true meaning of self-value, and love, love, and love. There is hope and you are not alone!"

Cody envisions taking greater strides in contemporary music. "I see myself taking it to the next level," she said, "and performing to a wider audience. I'd like to be able to sing different kinds of songs and more world music; remain connected to the cultural aspects of my music, but reach out to a broader segment of the world."

4 REZ ROCKERS, GUITAR HEROES, AND RASTA MEN

"There are elements from Africa, and the harmonic consistency comes from Europe, but you don't get that thump, that boom, boom, boom in the bass and drums, without the powwow."
— New York–based saxophonist Sharel Cassity (Cherokee)

LINK WRAY

In late 1957, guitarist Fred Lincoln "Link" Wray (1929–2005) gazed from the bandstand to a TV studio audience of teenagers in poodle skirts, bobby sox, and ducktail haircuts. There had been a request for him and his brothers—the house band on *Milt Grant's House Party*, an *American Bandstand*–like teenage dance TV show airing in the Washington, D.C. area—to play "something like 'The Stroll.'" Although the requested tune, one of eight hundred written or co-written by Clyde Ellis, had been a recent top-ten hit for the quartet the Diamonds, Link Wray had spent the past few months in a hospital recuperating from the tuberculosis he had contacted as a soldier in Korea and was one of the few unfamiliar with Ellis's song.

As he waited for his brothers—multi-instrumentalist, lead singer, and bandleader Vernon "Lucky" Wray and drummer Doug—to launch into the song, Wray walked to his amplifier and set the volume control to ten. With his brothers laying down a shuffling rhythm, Wray slammed into his guitar's whammy bar and unleashed a barbed-wire assault of chords that left the studio audience demanding more. The brothers had to repeat the tune three times before the end of the show.

Wray would continue to build on his guitar slinger reputation for another four decades. An inductee of the Rockabilly Hall of Fame and the Native American Music Hall of Fame, he would rank sixty-ninth on *Rolling Stone* magazine's list of top one hundred guitarists. The "father of the electric guitar power-chord," he would inspire Pete Townshend, Jimmy Page, Jeff Beck, Dave Davies (the Kinks), Johnny Winter, Stevie Ray Vaughn, and Brian Setzer, among others.

Wray's repertoire included several pieces—"Shawnee," "Genocide," "Viva Zapata," and "Comanche"—that reflected his Shawnee/Cherokee heritage. "'Comanche' was defiant," Wray's biographer Jimmy McDonough told me, "as tough as nails. It said, 'You can't change me and I won't bow down.' Yet, at the same time, it extended an invitation to dance around the fire."

One of the best of Link's later recordings was a 1990 remake of British songwriter Jerry Lordan's "Apache." British guitarist and vocalist Herbert Maurice William "Bert" Weedon had been the first to record it, but its release had been delayed, and the "British invasion" band, the Shadows, had turned it into an international, chart-topping hit in August 1960. The following year, Danish guitarist Jorgen Ingmann's interpretation reached number two on *Billboard*'s Top 100.

For North Carolina–born Wray, the success spurred by "Rumble," and its follow-up "Rawhide," was a natural step in a life of music. Along with his brothers, he had spent much of his early childhood listening to—and then joining with—his mother Lillian "Mee-Maw" Wray's singing as she picked cotton.

Poverty haunted Wray's childhood. Both of his parents were Holiness Church preachers who held prayer meetings on the street, and his father, who suffered from the lingering effects of being mustard-gassed during World War I, struggled to support the family as a sharecropper.

The first brother to become a performer, Lucky (1924–1979) maintained a feverish pace after moving with his parents and brothers to Portsmouth, Virginia, in 1943. In addition to securing the city's first taxi-driver license and waxing bowling alley lanes (at two cents a lane), Lucky played drums for local orchestras and small ensembles. He would later switch to upright bass, rhythm guitar, piano, and singing lead.

Taught the basics of bottleneck guitar playing, courtesy of a single lesson from an African American carnival worker remembered only as "Hambone," Link joined his siblings in a country-and-western swing trio, Lucky Wray and the Lazy Pine Wranglers, later renamed Lucky Wray and the Palomino Ranch Hands. Dixie Neal, older brother of Gene Vincent and the Bluecaps bassist, Jumpin' Jack Neal, played steel guitar. "Link and his brothers—now, that was real music," said McDonough. "Just listen to Ray's one-note piano tinkle or Doug's tom-toms on a tune like 'Comanche.' They are so right; one does not get that kind of playing with strangers. The way that a couple can finish each other's sentences—Link, Ray, and Doug did that musically. They played as one, those brothers—one sound."

Before "Rumble," Lucky appeared to be the one destined for stardom. After relocating with his younger brothers to Washington, D.C., in 1955, he captured the attention of a local record producer, Ben Adelman, who encouraged him to record as a soloist and promoted him as a teen idol, with his brothers backing him up.

Link's struggles with tuberculosis brought the siblings' partnership to a temporary halt. During the extended break, Doug backed country singer, and TV variety show host, Jimmy Dean. When Elvis Presley appeared on *The Jimmy Dean Show* in early 1957, Doug brought him to the hospital to visit his brother. "Link absolutely loved Elvis," said McDonough. "'Mystery Train' blew his mind."

Shortly after Link's discharge from the hospital, the Wrays reunited on *Milt Grant's House Party*. Link's knife-edged guitar picking had already begun to attract attention. When his older brother signed with Philadelphia-based Cameo Records, Link had gotten a temporary pass out of the hospital to play on the first recordings. The session's engineer and producer were so impressed with his playing that they contacted Archie Bleyer, owner of Cadence Records. "[Bleyer] came down to Fredericksburg, Virginia, to listen to him play at a record hop," Lucky Wray's daughter Sherry told *American Indian News*, "and stayed the whole evening."[1]

The Wrays recorded a fiery rendition of "Rumble" (originally titled "Oddball"), but it would take a rock-and-roll miracle before Bleyer would agree to release it. The ex-music director for ultraconservative pop singer, ukulele player, and radio host Arthur Godfrey, he considered the recording to be "a bad influence on teenagers."

"[Bleyer] strikes me as a pretty square guy," said McDonough. "He probably thought that Ricky Nelson was a punk. Sure, Link looked like somebody who might hotwire your Chevy, but he was quiet and peaceful most of the time. I think his quote 'Be wild, not evil' said it all."

Bleyer's daughter helped to soften his opposition. Finding a similarity between the Wray brothers' recording and Leonard Bernstein/Stephen Sondheim's gang-themed Tony Award–winning musical *West Side Story*, the teen persuaded her father to release the instrumental. It turned out to be a shrewd move. Released in April 1958, the single—credited to Link Wray and the Ray Men—would spend fourteen weeks on the pop charts, peaking at number sixteen, and propel Link to stardom on both sides of the Atlantic. The Library of Congress would add it to its National Recording Registry in 2009.

Despite the record's success, the Wrays' relationship with Cadence ended after Link refused Bleyer's request to tone down his image. "Link Wray without a leather jacket and shades," McDonough said, "is like Batman without a Batmobile. They were his armor. I never knew him to play a show without them."

Fresh from a million-selling hit, Link and his brothers had no trouble finding a more supportive label. Signing with Epic Records, they headed to Nashville to work with the Everly Brothers' production team. The sessions marked the first time that Link would record with the Danolectric Longhorn model guitar that would furnish his signature sound; for "Rumble" he had played a Gibson Les Paul. The resulting single, "Rawhide," was another hard-driving, fuzz-distorted instrumental that would reach the twenty-third slot on the national charts in January 1959. Composed by Russian-born Dimitri Zinoveivich Tiomkin, with lyrics by Pennsylvania-born Ned Washington, it would prove adaptable to a wide range of genres. Introduced by Chicago-born Frankie Laine (Francesco Paolo LoVecchio) in 1958, as the theme of a popular CBS-TV western series starring Eric Fleming and Clint Eastwood, it would be covered by Riders in the Sky, the Dead Kennedys, the Greenbrier Boys, the Jackson 5, Sublime, Oingo Boingo, and Liza Minnelli. Wray's take-no-prisoners version left the others in his dust.

Moving to Maryland in the mid-1960s, Lucky Wray converted a chicken coop into a recording studio where he and his brothers continued to document their musical experiments. "My father was a genius as a recording engineer," said Sherry Wray. "When you listen to Link Wray's music, there's a top, middle, and bottom."[2]

According to rumors, Lucky Wray destroyed the tapes he had made with his brothers after selling the farm in the mid-1990s. Opening a second studio—Wray's Shack Three Tracks & 5—after moving to Arizona in the early '70s, he released several discs under his own name, none of which sold many copies. An actor on several *Gunsmoke* episodes, he made a cameo appearance in the 1974 Martin Scorsese–directed film *Alice Doesn't Live Here, Anymore.*

Although he had minor hits with "Jack the Ripper" in 1961, and "Red Hot" sixteen years later, Link was unable to match the success of the first singles. After recording an album with an orchestra, which failed to chart, in 1969, he moved to San Francisco and hooked up with ex–Quicksilver Messenger Service guitarist John Cippolina, and the rhythm section of Cippolina's band, Copperhead, that is, drummer David Weber and bassist Hutch Hutchinson. He would go on to record a pair of albums and tour with British rockabilly singer Robert Gordon, with Anton Fig on drums. "His seventies' material lacked the attack-dog snarl," said McDonough, "and the just plain weirdness of earlier cuts like 'Hidden Charms' or 'Growling Guts.' Other musicians created very similar music, but nobody but Link could come up with something like 'Genocide.' I can't even listen to the Robert Gordon stuff—an undoubtedly sincere but boring re-creation of the past."

On January 12, 1980, less than seventy-two hours after divorcing his third wife, Wray married Olive Julie Pavlsen, a Danish student of American Indian culture, twenty-five years his junior. Three years later, they would have a son, Christian Oliver Wray.

Wray's relationship with his older brother, Lucky, who controlled his funds, continued to deteriorate. "They had a real love/hate relationship," said McDonough.

"Of course, I heard about it from Link's side. To my knowledge, no one interviewed Ray. He would have had some tales to tell. Family was of utmost importance to Link, but in the end he felt betrayed by his brother."

Never reconciling their differences, Wray was nevertheless heartbroken when his older brother committed suicide in 1979. Five years later, the sudden death from a heart attack of his younger brother, with whom he had remained close, hit him even harder. A year later, he left the United States permanently with his wife and son, and moved to a small island off the coast of Denmark. During the last years of his life, he would maintain little contact with his American family, including his eight children, and old friends. "He had so much paranoia about people from his past," said McDonough. "He'd rather cancel a show then face them. It was a mess and very sad. How much of it was [the fault of his wife] Olive [as many have claimed] and how much of it was Link, I don't know—Link was a pretty paranoid guy."

Recording what would be his final album, *Barbed Wire*, with a Danish rhythm section in 2000, Wray continued to tour until four months before his passing on November 5, 2005. At his funeral, at Christian's Church in Copenhagen, Denmark, eleven days later, Olive and their son, Oliver, were the only family in attendance. Wray's American family and friends were unaware of his passing until weeks after his death.

Producers of film and TV soundtracks and commercials have found Wray's catalogue invaluable. "After my dad died," explained Sherry Wray, who has overseen her uncle's catalogue, "I did a lot of work for many years making sure the rights were what they should be. In the beginning, all the interest I could get was reissues, but in 1983, I got my first call for a movie, *Breathless*, that starred Richard Gere, and they used 'Jack the Ripper' in the pinnacle scene. In 1993, I was sitting in my living room, and a woman called and said she was putting together music for a Quentin Tarantino movie, *Pulp Fiction*, and they wanted 'Rumble' and 'Ace of Spades.'"[3]

A 1994 TV movie, starring David Arquette and Salma Hayek, *Roadracers* included many references to Link Wray. In one scene, Hayek notices one of the guitarist's albums taped to the door of Arquette's apartment and asks, "Is he famous?" Arquette answers quickly, "No, that's why he's cool."[4]

"[Wray] was one of the most original rockers to ever walk the planet," said McDonough, "and he influenced so many. He created such an unholy racket with that guitar. It could be as mournful as a lone wolf's howl at midnight, as angry as a punch in the gut. Nobody else took [listeners] to the places he did—nobody. Just thinking of the little time that I spent with him sends chills down my spine. Whatever rock 'n' roll is—it is Link Wray."

NOKIE EDWARDS AND THE VENTURES

Nole Floyd "Nokie" Edwards (1935–) (Cherokee) helped to transform the Ventures into one of the most successful instrumental bands of all-time, with record sales surpassing 100 million. The 2012 Native American Music Hall of Fame inductee's masterful single-note picking was spotlighted on many of the Seattle-based quartet's top ten hits, including "Walk Don't Run '64," "Perfidia," "Lullaby of the Leaves," "Slaughter on 10th Avenue," "Driving Guitars," "Pedal Pusher," "Sleep Walk," "Let's Go," "Wipe Out," "Pipeline," "Diamond Head," and "Hawaii Five-O."

Playing stringed instruments from the age of five, Edwards acquired an early reputation as one of the Northwest's best young instrumentalists. His notoriety continued to grow as lead guitarist for pre-Buckaroos Buck Owens after the Texas-born country singer and guitarist moved to Tacoma, Washington, as owner of KAYE radio in January 1958. He had not yet achieved the success that he would find after moving to Southern California and pioneering the "Bakersfield Sound," but Owens was already on his way to becoming one of the icons of country music. With the future *Hee-Haw* cohost taking him under his wing, Edwards advanced quickly. "Whenever Grand Ole Opry musicians would be performing in Washington," he remembered, "they would call Buck and ask if he knew any guitar players. He would recommend me. I got to play with people like Ferlin Husky, Lefty Frizzell, and Justin Tubb."

Agreeing to play bass in ex-construction workers Don Wilson and Bob Bogle's new band, the Ventures, Edwards's skills languished on the four-string. His switch with original lead guitarist Bogle became one of the pivotal moments of contemporary popular music. George Harrison, Joe Walsh, Jimmy Page, Stephen Stills, Pete Townshend, Stanley Clarke, Stevie Ray Vaughn, Mark Knopfler, Blondie, the Go Gos, the B52s, and Aerosmith's Joe Perry and Tom Hamilton are among the many acknowledging Edwards's guitar playing—and the Ventures' music—as influences. Inducting the Ventures into the Rock and Roll Hall of Fame in 2008, John Fogerty credited the "audacity of [Edwards's playing]" for "empowering guitarists everywhere."[5]

Often associated with the surf music of the early '60s, the Ventures were so much more. During a recording career spanning more than a half century, their trademark instrumental sound was applied to every imaginable style of popular music, including swamp rock, "switched on" classical music, Latin, jazz, disco, and reggae. *Guitar Player* magazine called them the "quintessential guitar combo in the pre-Beatles era."[6]

Edwards was still playing bass when the Ventures recorded their first hit, "Walk, Don't Run," in 1960. After two unsuccessful singles, both featuring vocals, they had taken a different approach with their third effort, updating an instrumental that they found on a Chet Atkins album. Released independently, "Walk, Don't Run" became a regional hit when a local radio station played it as the lead-in to the news. Reissued by Dolton Records, an affiliate of Liberty Records, had rejected the group's demo, it went on to sell over 2 million copies and reach the runner-up position on the national charts. (Only Chubby Checker's "The Twist" and Elvis Presley's "It's Now or Never" kept it from the top.) "It sold like a number-one record," remembered Edwards, "but it was the payola days, and we didn't do that, so it stayed at number two."

Two years after recording their hit single—in the basement studio of hi-fi enthusiast-turned-engineer Jay "Joe" Boles's Seattle home—the Ventures returned to the top ten with a surf-style interpretation, "Walk Don't Run '64." Additional updated versions came out in 1977 and 1994. The Grammy Hall of Fame inducted the original recording in 1977.

A mostly instrumental band, the Ventures circumvented language barriers. As a result, their popularity soared internationally. Although they toured successfully in England and Australia, Japan provided their greatest setting. Returning to the Land of the Rising Sun on an average of three months a year since 1962, they made the country of 127 million people a second home. They would release more than one hundred albums in the Asian country, outpacing sales of Beatles recordings two to one. "People in Japan loved us," said Edwards. "When we went there for the first time, in 1964, there were 10,000 people waiting for us at the airport. We played at a place that held 5,000 people. It was packed and there were even more people outside who couldn't get in."

As they focused on the Far East, however, the Ventures allowed their popularity in their homeland to fade. "The biggest mistake that we made," said Edwards, "was to not do at least some shows in the United States. We did not have to tour all of the time. We could have done some TV appearances, play[ed] important shows, and kept our name circulated. [Bogle, Wilson, and drummer Mel Taylor] didn't want to do that so we did nothing [here] for ten years. Everyone thought that the Ventures had broken up."

Experiencing a resurgence of their popularity in the United States in 1968, when their recording of the Morton Stevens–penned theme song of the CBS-TV police drama *Hawaii Five-O* became a top-five hit, the Ventures' concentration on their Japanese market continued to frustrate Edwards. As his interests in horseracing increasingly distracted his focus, he handed in his resignation. L.A. session guitarist Gerry McGee replaced him.

Far from idle, Edwards released several solo albums by 1972. Reuniting with his former bandmates the following year, he continued to drive the Ventures for the next nine years with sonic-driven, single-note picking. Cited as an influence by punk and new-wave musicians, the Ventures experienced a revival in the late 1970s and '80s, and again toured extensively throughout the world, including the United States. The Go-Go's would pay tribute to them with "Surfin' and Spyin'," a mostly instrumental tune on their 1982 album, *Totally Go-Go's*.

Edwards continued to pursue outside projects as well. Heading to Nashville, with hopes of becoming a country-music session guitarist, he renewed his friendship with the country-music–singing Frizzell brothers—"Lefty" (William Orville), David, and Allen. He was playing with the Frizzell brothers in July 1975, when Lefty Frizzell, one of country music's songwriting greats, performed his final show before suffering a fatal stroke (prompted by years of alcohol abuse). "It was the strangest thing," Edwards remembered. "Somebody took a photo of Lefty [during the show] and the only thing in the picture that was doubly exposed was his head. Everything else was in focus. He seemed okay, but, of course, I didn't know much about his health."

For a while, Edwards played guitar for Frizzell and West, a country duo that David Frizzell shared with country music great Dottie West's daughter, Shelly. "David and I started running around together in 1961 or 1962," he said. "He was serving in the military on a base that was near where I was living."

Edwards's forays into country music reconnected him with his earliest influences. "I heard Chet Atkins (1924–2001) play when I was five or six years old," he said, "and I wanted to play songs like that too."

During the last five years of Atkins's life, Edwards spent as much time as he could with the influential guitarist and record producer. "We ran around together a lot," he remembered. "One time, I sent him a recording that I had made of Beethoven's 'Ode to Joy.' Sometime later, we were sitting in his office, and he asked me, 'Did you ever put your name on that?' When I answered, 'no,' he said, 'Good, I'm going to cut it just like that.' He had a good sense of humor, I'll tell you."

Edwards continues to honor the memory of his mentor, appearing annually at the Chet Atkins Appreciation Society convention in Nashville. During the July 2012 convention, he memorialized Atkins, and Kentucky-born finger-style guitarist Paul Yendell (1935–2010), with a breathtaking solo demonstration of his still-masterful picking. At the conclusion of the show, Edwards received a replica of rock-and-roll pioneer Buddy Holly's Gibson J-45 from representatives of the Buddy Holly Education Foundation. The following day, he repaid the gesture, recording Holly's "Everyday" for a benefit album.

Jazz, country, and pop guitarist, composer, and inventor Les Paul also had an impact on Edwards's playing. "I didn't know that he was slowing down the tape when he recorded," said Edwards, "but I figured if he could do it, I could do it too. I learned to play without slowing the tape down."

Edwards grew up in a musical family of twelve kids. "Music is in our blood," he said. "Everybody played music. When I was young, all that I knew was bluegrass and country music. I could not understand the first bunch of rock-and-roll records that I bought, so I bought ten more and tried to figure it out. That's how I got into it."

Edwards's talents were apparent early on. "By the time that I was eleven," he said, "I had taught myself to play every stringed instrument."

Shortly after his twelfth birthday in 1947, vigilantes drove the young instrumentalist and his family off their ancestral home in Oklahoma. "My grandmother, on my mother's side, was full-blooded Cherokee," he said. "Before she died, she deeded the property to my mom and made her promise that she would never sell it. After marrying my father, [my mother] settled down to raise a family. My dad cut railroad ties. He had a team of horses and a wagon for hauling. Around this time, someone was going around trying to buy up land. If people refused to sell to him, he would try to run them off, any way he could. One time, my dad came home in the dark, and this man was riding around our house, with a gun, trying to shoot us. My dad had a rifle and shot at him. We quickly put what we could fit into the wagon, started up the horses, and that's how we left Oklahoma."

Edwards and his family didn't look back until they had reached Idaho. "My older brother had gone ahead," he remembered, "and we met up with him. We slept behind billboards at night and stopped at farms, where men were working in the fields, to see if we could work in the house. We would get a little money and some food. Later, my dad traded the team of horses for a car. We looked like the Beverly Hillbillies, with all kinds of things tied to it."

Since the early recordings of the Ventures, Edwards has been on the cutting edge of guitar technology. He used a fuzzy distortion pedal on "The 2000 Pound Bee" in 1962, and applied reverse tracking on the album *The Ventures in Space* two years later. He was among the first to play twelve-string guitar on a rock recording. Initially playing a Fender Jazzmaster Stratocaster guitar, and Fender Precision bass, Edwards switched to a revamped "Ventures model" Mark I guitar, produced by California-based Mosrite, in 1963. His most recent picking has been on an instrument—the Hitchhiker guitar—that he designed and makes available through his website. "By appearance, it resembles the Mosrite guitars," he said, "but it's much better. It uses Seymour Duncan pickups that can be set to fifteen different sounds. It doesn't need batteries, but it has the loudest sustain of any guitar that I have ever played and it stays in tune."

Edwards, who lives in Oregon with his wife, Judy, remains busy. In addition to frequent special guest appearances with the Ventures, he continues to work extensively with St. Louis–born rockabilly guitarist Deke Dickerson, and with his own group, the Venturesmania Band.

JIMI HENDRIX

The great-great-grandson of a full-blooded Cherokee, and the first inductee into the Native American Music Hall of Fame, James Marshall "Jimi" Hendrix (Cherokee/African American) (1942–1970) "sometimes [made] onstage dedications of one of the songs on his debut album ('I Don't Live Today') to the plight of the American Indian."[7]

Two of Hendrix's songs, "Castles Made of Sand" and "Cherokee Mist," reflected directly on his Indigenous roots. "Castles Made of Sand," which debuted on his second album, *Axis: Bold as Love*, in 1967, focused on the loss of dreams. During the first verse, Hendrix recalled his parents' breakup. During the second verse, he remembered growing up American Indian, with lyrics about a young Indian brave (representing his brother) who "played war games in the woods with his Indian friends," only to have his dreams of becoming a "fearless warrior Indian chief" thwarted when "something went wrong—surprise attack killed him in his sleep that night." The third and final verse looked in on an elderly, wheelchair-bound woman (possibly Hendrix's mother) who starts out planning her suicide, but has second thoughts after an undescribed experience gives her hope.

The funky, but melodic, grace of "Castles Made of Sand" made it adaptable to a variety of formats. Pianist, keyboards player, conductor, and occasional Miles Davis arranger Gil Evans recorded it, with a twenty-three piece jazz orchestra, as the centerpiece of his 1974 album, *Gil Evans Plays Jimi Hendrix*. Philadelphia-born, and Boston-based, Vance Gilbert included an acoustic guitar–accompanied interpretation on his 2006 CD, *Angels Castles Covers*. New York–based Native Soul, featuring pianist Noah Haidu and saxophonist Peter Brainin, included a modern jazz rendition on their 2011 CD, *Soul Step*. Public Enemy, A Tribe Called Red, and Frank Ocean sampled it.

Unreleased until 1999, "Cherokee Mist" (aka "The Indian Song") debuted on *First Rays of the New Rising Sun*, a supposed approximation of the album that Hendrix was working on when he died on September 18, 1970. The left-handed guitarist, who played his Fender Stratocaster upside-down, recorded the song more than once between 1968 and 1969, each a highly improvised mix of Mitch Mitchell's powwow-meets-psychedelia drumming; Noel Redding's bottom-heavy bass playing; and Hendrix's broad, sonic textures and imaginative, single notes. One of the unreleased versions featured a sitar, possibly played by Brian Jones of the Rolling Stones.

"Cherokee Mist" was one of the few songs on *First Rays of the Rising Sun* absent from *Voodoo Soup*, the last of four controversial, remixed albums released under the auspices of Alan Douglas, a jazz producer who had become executor of Hendrix's estate following the guitarist's death. Reworking Hendrix's original recordings,

Douglas dropped supporting musicians, overdubbed guitar parts, added female vocalists, and took co-composer credits on several tunes. Shortly after the release of *Voodoo Soup* in 1995, he defended his actions to *BAM* magazine "The focus is on Jimi," he said, "but, by the same token, if the drums don't sound good, then, it makes Jimi sound not so good."[8]

Hendrix's father, who would succumb to congestive heart failure in 2002, and Jimi's adopted stepsister Janie, thought otherwise. After a long legal battle, they gained control of his estate and *Voodoo Soup* was withdrawn from distribution. Hendrix's former engineer Eddie Kramer prepared the original recordings for authorized release as *First Rays of the Rising Sun*.

"Cherokee Mist" lent its name to a 1990s British psychedelic rock band featuring vocalist and guitarist John Redfern and lead guitarist Mo Hone, and it provided the title of Hendrix-phile editor Bill Nitopi's 1994 book, *Cherokee Mist: The Lost Writings*.

Hendrix's interests in his Native roots, and his love of performing, had been fostered by his one-quarter Cherokee grandmother, Zenora "Nora" Hendrix (née Moore) (1883–1984), with whom who he had lived after his parents divorced. A vaudeville performer before marrying Hendrix's grandfather, Nora "had a flamboyant collection of feather hats and flashy costumes," said the late guitarist's stepsister.[9]

Born in Knoxville, Tennessee, Nora Hendrix spent time in Chicago and Seattle before moving to Vancouver with her husband, Ross Hendrix, in 1911. After a few years in Seattle, when the Hendrix brothers were youngsters, she returned to Vancouver, where she worked as a cook at a popular restaurant—Vie's Chicken and Steak House—in the city's African Canadian, Hogan's Alley neighborhood. Black musicians, including Louis Armstrong and Nat King Cole, made the restaurant a favorite haunt. Hitchhiking 2,000 miles to Vancouver after being discharged from the army in 1962, Jimi may have made some of his earliest appearances as a guitarist at the restaurant. Though the restaurant closed in 1976, Vincent Fodera, who purchased, remodeled, and reopened the restaurant in 2005, spoke with neighbors who "remembered hearing the teenage Hendrix practicing after hours at Vie's."[10]

Near the end of his life, Hendrix's fascination with Native culture intensified. According to his stepsister, he traveled to the Tuscarora Reservation in New York State, seeking a cure for sleeping problems. Medicine man Wallace "Mad Bear" Anderson promised to help him, with the provision that he give up the prescription drugs that he had been taking. Hendrix agreed and scheduled a date to return.

The guitarist failed to keep the appointment. A few weeks after his reservation visit, he died, at the age of twenty-seven, in the London apartment of his girlfriend, Monika Dannemann, a German figure skater and artist, allegedly having taken nine of Dannemann's Vesparax sleeping pills—or eighteen times the recommended dosage.

More than four decades after his passing, Hendrix's legacy shows no sign of abating. While his reign as a bandleader lasted a little more than three years, a seemingly endless stream of live albums and boxed sets containing previously unreleased songs, alternate versions, and outtakes have, along with his former drummer Billy Cox's tribute band, Experience Hendrix, continued to keep the guitarist's music alive.

JESSE DAVIS

The only child of a Dixieland jazz drummer and a piano teacher, Jesse Ed Davis (1944–1988) (Comanche/Kiowa) became one of the most demanded studio guitar players of the 1970s and early '80s. His heartfelt bottleneck, slide guitar playing spiced albums by David Cassidy, Albert King, Willie Nelson, Rod Stewart, Leonard Cohen, Keith Moon, Steve Miller, Ry Cooder, Rick Danko, the Four Tops, Marvin Gaye, John Lee Hooker, Harry Nilsson, Van Dyke Parks, Arlo Guthrie, Emmylou Harris, Gram Parsons, and the Fifth Dimension. He recorded with ex-Beatles John Lennon, George Harrison, and Ringo Starr. He played on the Monkees' "Last Train to Clarksville," produced and played on ex-Byrds vocalist Gene Clark's second solo album, provided the bottleneck guitar solo on Jackson Browne's "Doctor My Eyes," and participated in George Harrison's Concert for Bangladesh at Madison Square Garden. Touring with multi-instrumentalist, singer, and bandleader Taj Mahal (Henry Saint Clair Fredericks) (1942–) from 1966 to 1969, he joined Rod Stewart and the Faces for their final American tour in 1975, and recorded two groundbreaking albums with John Trudell (Santee) in the '80s. Honored with a posthumous Lifetime Musical Achievement award, from First Americans in the Arts, in 1998, he entered the Oklahoma State Hall of Fame in 2011.

Davis's solo albums—*Jesse Davis* (1971), *Ululu* (1972), and *Keep Me Comin'* (1973)—featured a superstar array of guest instrumentalists, including Leon Russell, Eric Clapton, Larry Knechtel, Ben Sidran, Mac (Dr. John) Rebennack, Donald Duck Dunn, and Howard Johnson, and background singers Vanetta Fields, Merry Clayton, Clydie King, and Gram Parsons.

Struggles with alcoholism and drug addiction limited his playing, but Davis appeared to be on a rebound after hooking up with Trudell. The three albums that they recorded together—*AKA Graffiti Man* (1986), *But This Isn't El Salvador* (1987), and *Heart Jump Bouquet* (1987)—remain important documents of the

American Indian struggle. "Davis and Trudell's collaboration was one of the milestones of Native music," said Harlan McKosato (Sac and Fox), the former host of radio talk show *Native America Calling.*

More than a quarter of a century after his passing from a heroin overdose, Davis has not been forgotten. "I was always drawn to good Fender Telecaster players," said guitarist Gary Vorgensen (Angela Strehli Band, New Riders of the Purple Sage), "and Jesse Ed was one of the best. He was rough and raw and he played from the hip."

"He had a really different way of playing the guitar," recalled drummer John Ware, who first played with Davis when they were in high school in 1959. "He had a really light touch with both his left hand and his right hand. It had a lasting impression on guitarists. Playing on stage with him could be tough. He tapped his foot completely out of time. You would wonder where he was going, and what he was thinking, but I loved it. People wanted to have him on stage with them because of his solos. He put this odd feel into the tracks."

Born in Norman, Oklahoma, Davis came from a background unlike other musicians with whom Ware had played. "He listened to a lot of jazz," the drummer remembered. "His dad's record collection was seeped in 1950s and '60s jazz. He didn't come out of rockabilly and he didn't have that twang. He could be sloppy, at times, but he was really fluid, even as a fifteen-year-old."

Davis's love of music had a profound effect on his high school friends. "We'd get together at his house on Saturday afternoons," recalled Ware, "and listen to his dad's records—Wes Montgomery and Jim Hall, almost no rock and roll. Some radio stations played four or five hours a day of what they called 'race music' and we got to hear Elmore James and Lightnin' Hopkins. Chuck Berry and Little Richard were played on pop radio, but that was about it."

Until the early 1980s, Davis paid little attention to his Native heritage. "Sometimes, people didn't recognize him as an American Indian," said his former employer, Taj Mahal. "When he was growing up, people called him 'China Boy.' He was a bit conservative [about being Native], but he did sometimes bring it out. He'd talk about how he was part of the first generation of assimilated Indians."

"A lot of people thought that he was Mexican," added Ware. "Not that long ago I was at a recording session in Nashville, and somebody said, 'You used to play with Jesse, that Hawaiian guy.'"

Honing their skills together on the Oklahoma club circuit as teenagers, Ware and Davis continued to renew their collaboration. Briefly separating, while Davis pursued a degree in literature from the University of Oklahoma and toured with country singer Conway Twitty, they reunited in 1965. "He was living at Leon Russell's house [in North Hollywood, California]," said Ware, "and called me to say that Levon Helm was in town. He had left Dylan and did not want to go to

Europe. He was looking for something else to do. He asked if I wanted to be in a band [the Oklahoma Mafia] with them. I said, 'Sure.' We got together in Santa Monica and rehearsed."

The Oklahoma Mafia disbanded after a couple of local bar gigs, but the experience set Ware on his future path. "When we were in Tucson, this seventeen-year-old girl cooked for us," he said. "Two years later, a buddy of mine suggested that I call this singer that he had just met. It looked like she was going to have a hit record, but did not have a band yet. I went to her place to audition, knocked on her door and, when she opened it, she said, 'I know you.' It was Linda Ronstadt—the girl who had cooked for us."

Calling Ronstadt's band "the training ground for L.A. country rock musicians," Ware used his stint with the Tucson-born songstress as a career springboard. After playing drums with ex-Monkee Mike Nesmith's First National Band and Emmylou Harris's Hot Band, he experienced a successful second career as a music documentary and video producer.

Ware renewed his partnership with Davis in 1970, playing drums and keyboards on several tracks on the guitarist's debut album. "He had another drummer that he had brought down from San Francisco," recalled Ware, "but I spent three days in the studio with them, knocking around, and smoking dope, trying to lay down some tracks."

Ware ran into his old friend again a year later. "I was mixing some tracks at the old A&M studios," he said, "and he was recording with Jackson Browne. I knew that the session was on shaky ground because I had bumped into [their drummer] Russ Kunkel as I was entering the building earlier [and he had told me]. It bothered me that he was so wasted, but I heard them running down, what I now know is, 'Doctor My Eyes.' Once again, he was totally on top of his music. I think his solo in that song is one of the best pieces of rock-and-roll guitar ever recorded. It works in fits, and spits, and vicious little snaps that no one has been able to rival."

The last time that Ware and Davis played together came during a 1981 recording session with Emmylou Harris. "He was higher than an air show," remembered Ware, who by then had become part of Harris's management team. "I was concerned, but the music was great. He ran up a six-hundred-dollar phone bill, talking to his wife (Kelly Davis) in Hawaii, but when we listened back to what we recorded, it was so good. It didn't worry me after I heard the music."

Though they never again collaborated, Ware continued to hear from the guitarist. "He called me a couple of times," he said, "asking for money. He told me that he was in [legal] trouble. I called the court and they told me that it was old news. He had already paid his way. He was just surfing old friends for money. I ran into [bassist] Leland Sklar not long after that. He had called him looking for money, too. It was just one of those things. He could have a pocketful of bucks and, then, he would have nothing. That's the way that he lived."

The three years that he spent with Taj Mahal (1966–1969) were the pinnacle of Davis's experiences as a member of a band. An icon of American roots and world music, Mahal still misses the guitarist's playing. "No matter how good my music has been," he said, "I've never gotten that sound again. His playing seemed easy until you put your fingers on a guitar and tried to do it. He was a pleasing arranger, an incredible sideman, very understated."

TAJ MAHAL

When he met Davis, Taj Mahal was already one of the most respected musicians in Southern California. He had started his career in western Massachusetts, playing with R&B bands like Taj Mahal and the Elektras, and sharing a duo with singer-songwriter Jesse Lee Kincaid. Graduating from the University of Massachusetts with a degree in ethnomusicology, he had gone on to play harmonica and sing lead for the Rising Sons, a Los Angeles–based folk-rock group that also included Kincaid, stringed instrument wizard Ry Cooder, and future-Spirit drummer Ed Cassidy. Although they signed with Columbia Records in 1965, more than a quarter of a century would pass before the release of their debut album in 1992.

Following the Rising Sons' self-destruction in 1966, Mahal was determined to begin again. "All of us [in the band] were signed [to Columbia Records] individually," he recalled, "so, when we broke up, we were each still signed to the label, if we chose to do something about it—well, I did."

At first, Mahal had difficulty finding similar-minded musicians. "R&B and blues guys didn't understand that there was another [roots-oriented] scene going on," he said, "that, if you got in on the ground floor, you could build a career and make a mark for yourself."

Mahal wasn't alone for long. "Other musicians were coming up who were as excited as me about playing roots music," he said, "and I played with lots of different people—members of Canned Heat, the Stone Poneys (Linda Ronstadt's band), and the Red Roosters. I was an open, gregarious kind of person and listened to all kinds of music. I had come to L.A. partly to get out of the stodginess of the East Coast. The West Coast seemed more open to people with fresh ideas. They were drawing on stuff from my traditional background."

A mutual friend brought Davis's guitar playing to Mahal's attention. "I had done some sessions with one of Jesse Ed's friends playing harmonica," he remembered. "We were both into fishing, and other things outside of music, and we became good friends. To make a long story short, he came by my house one time for dinner. We sat around jamming. When I told him what I was looking for, he said, 'I've got the guy for you—Ed Davis. He's an Indian from Oklahoma.'"

At the time, Davis was playing in a band with Tulsa-born Jimmy "Junior" Markham (harmonica/vocals) and Leon Russell. Mahal went to see Markham, Russell, and Davis at a small Topanga Canyon club, The Corral. "They blew me away," he remembered, "especially Davis. I got so excited that I called [then-president of Columbia Records] Clive Davis (no relation). I told him that I was on his label and that I had some ideas. I told him that I wanted to produce something by myself, but he said, 'That's not the company policy. I'll send you some producers and we can find someone that you'll like.'"

With Mahal agreeing to compromise, Bob Irwin, the future owner of collector-oriented Sundazed Records, produced the group's debut album, *Taj Mahal*. "He left us alone with the music," said Mahal, "and served as our advocate, working for our best interests with the record company."

Recorded in sixteen hours, the album included an original song by Mahal ("EZ Rider") and updated blues by Sleepy John Estes ("Diving Duck Blues," "Leavin' Trunk"), Blind Willie McTell ("Statesboro Blues"), Sonny Boy Williamson ("Checkin' Up on My Baby"), and Robert Johnson ("Dust My Broom"). "It's raw, raucous, and has a lot of energy," said Mahal, "but it's also got some really nice moments. We didn't do all this jumping up and down, with all kinds of pyrotechnics. Davis used to stand there, with his eyes rolling up inside his head, feeling all the ecstasy that he was putting into his instrument."

"Statesboro Blues" had a profound effect on a young guitar player in Daytona Beach, Florida. "It morphed into Duane Allman's hands," said Mahal. "[Davis] was the one who took the slide-guitar style of Muddy Waters and created a great sound. Duane took it from there."

Mahal and Davis continued their collaboration with two additional albums—*The Natch'l Blues* and the double-LP *Giant Folk/De Old Folks At Home*—in 1969. "By then, we really had the recording process down," said Mahal. "All three albums were done on eight-track recorders with everybody playing at the same time. Other musicians had been getting into overdubbing and their music had gone to sleep. I didn't want any part of that. I wanted to play real music."

"I'd come into the studio," he continued, "play the songs on acoustic guitar, and give the rest of the band some directions. Sometimes we'd listen to the original recordings. I'd play my guitar, or harmonica, and we'd flesh it out. We weren't playing the same shuffles that everyone else was playing. [Drummer] Chuck Blackwell and [bassist] Gary Gilmore were wonderful."

The high point of the three years that Mahal's band was together came with their participation, on December 1, 1968, in the Rolling Stones' Rock and Roll

Circus. "It was clear that there was something happening [in England] that was different than what was happening in the United States," said Mahal. "My personal connection came through Al Wilson of Canned Heat. He was a neighbor of mine when I lived back east, before we came out to California. Whenever he and Canned Heat, along with John Hammond, Ry Cooder, Howlin' Wolf, Sonny Boy Williamson, Muddy Waters, [and] Otis Spann, would go to England, they'd come back talking about how good they had been treated and how much people had loved their music."

The path leading to the trip abroad began at a Sunset Strip nightclub, the Whiskey a Go-Go. "It was a really exciting night," recalled Mahal. "I was onstage playing with my eyes closed. When I opened them, and looked at the dance floor, there was Mick Jagger and Brian Jones of the Rolling Stones dancing, and the Animals' Hilton Valentine and [Jimi Hendrix's manager] Chas Chandler dancing. I thought that, if I had an opportunity to talk with them, I had better take it. When I got off the stage, after the set, I walked over to them. They told me that they had really enjoyed my music. I went right up to Mick and said that if there was ever a project that he could fit us in to let us know. Having said that, it was time to go back to the stage and do the next set. I felt glad that I had spoken to them and made my pitch."

A few months later, Mahal got a phone call from his manager's office. "They told me that the Stones had sent us a first-class round-trip ticket on British Overseas Airways," he said, "so that we could go to England to do something called 'The Rock and Roll Circus.'"

Faced with problems securing work visas, Mahal and the group found a way to circumvent the issue. "The Rolling Stones' office called us," remembered Mahal, "and told us that we'd be coming to England as tourists. I brought some harmonicas, Jesse brought a guitar, Chuck brought his bass, and Gilmore brought his snare and cymbals. They let us [into England], but there was always a worry that the authorities would figure it out."

As guests of the Rolling Stones, the Mahal Band experienced royal treatment. "It was the best that I've been treated in all of the years that I've been in this business," said Mahal. "We had carte blanche. The Stones and Bonnie Raitt are the only ones who have said that they would do something and come through. We were part of everything that went on, with the exception of some rehearsals. We met John Lennon, Eric Clapton, and Pete Townshend. They were very friendly. We met Rocky Dijon, the conga player who played on 'Sympathy for the Devil.' He ended up performing and recording with me for a long time."

Tapes of the Rolling Stones' Rock and Roll Circus remained unavailable until the release of CD and DVD versions in 1996. A remastered DVD followed in 2004.

In addition to a funky blues tune, "Ain't That a Lot of Love," from the original release, it included three additional tracks—Sonny Boy Williamson's "Checkin' Up on My Baby," Sleepy John Estes's "Leavin' Trunk," and the Mahal-Davis collaboration, "Corinna." "'Leavin' Trunk' should not be missed," said Mahal. "[Davis] played a lethal solo on it."

The Rolling Stones' Rock and Roll Circus marked the apex of Mahal and Davis's partnership. "[Davis] started going more towards the bell-bottom, Carnaby Street, British kind of image," said Mahal, "and he became more of a session musician. He didn't want to be traveling so much."

Soon after filming the Rock and Roll Circus, John Lennon came to the United States. Hooking up with Davis, the two musicians began spending time together. One night will go down in rock-and-roll infamy. Stopping for dinner at a Santa Monica restaurant, before heading to an L.A. nightspot, The Troubadour, Davis, Lennon, and Lennon's girlfriend, May Pang, started celebrating early. Lennon got so drunk that, after excusing himself to go to the bathroom, he returned with a Kotex on his forehead, thinking that it was funny. Davis and Pang acted as though nothing was wrong and continued on to the nightclub where Lennon continued his obnoxious behavior. A server soon put the ex-Beatle in his place. Demanding to know if she knew who he was, she quickly retorted, "Yeah, you're some asshole with a Kotex on his forehead."

Davis and Lennon's friendship flowed into their music; the slide guitarist appeared on Lennon's *Wall and Bridges* and *Rock and Roll* albums. He went on to play on Ringo Starr's albums, *Goodnight Vienna* in 1974 and *Rotogravure* two years later. The guitarist's involvement with George Harrison began as a standby substitute for Eric Clapton (who was battling heroin addiction) at the Concert for Bangladesh. Though Clapton managed to play the show, Davis remained onboard. He later played guitar on Harrison's 1975 album, *Extra Texture*, and became the first to cover the ex-Beatle's song "Sue Me, Sue You Blues," which was credited to Harrison's pseudonym, L'Angelo Misterioso.

More than a decade after they last played together, Mahal and Davis reunited, on February 9, 1987, at the Palomino Club, in North Hollywood, California. By that time, Davis had begun performing with Trudell. "He heard that I would be playing there," said Mahal, "and asked if they could open the show."

As Trudell and Davis performed, Mahal watched his former accompanist. "You could see that [the alcohol and drugs] had fouled a little bit of him," he said. "He wasn't as sharp as he had been, but his playing was still on top of it. He had had an auto accident, was walking with a cane, and dealing with a bit of a limp, but he was still doing brilliant work [on the guitar]."

The evening turned into one of contemporary music's most historic events. "It was a night when almost everyone in the audience was a star," said Mahal. "Jackson Browne, Bonnie Raitt, and Maria Muldaur were there."

A massive jam session, with Bob Dylan, John Fogerty, and George Harrison joining Mahal and Davis, concluded the evening. "Dylan was thrilled by what [Davis] was doing [with Trudell]," said Mahal. "That's why he was there that night. He said that it was the best poetry that he had heard."

"Jesse knew that it was going to go down," he continued. "He was a master prankster, with a bold streak. I remember we were once playing at a club on Lansdown Street [in Boston]. We were milling around the crowd, getting ready to play. Some local bikers were there and one of them came by and stepped on Jesse's shoes. The next thing that I knew, they were going down swinging. The bikers beat him pretty badly, but they got more and better than what they gave. When it was time for the set, [Davis] limped onto the stage and played the hardest shit that you have heard in your life. He was just on fire."

Mahal made his final recording with Davis when he hired the guitarist to play on two tracks of his 1987 album, *Taj*. "We hadn't played together for a long time," he said, "but, as far as the depth of his playing, he had his own tone. He was such a fabulous player."

When he heard that Davis had died—with a fresh needle mark on one arm, and burned matches and tinfoil scattered about—Mahal was heartbroken. "I was so mad at him," he said, "but I flew from Toronto to Oklahoma to pay my respects. I remember they had smudged the room with sage. He was [in his coffin] and I walked over. I looked at him and started cursing. They found him, without his moccasins, in the laundry room of the apartment building where he was living. He had taken off all of his rings. I thought that he had gotten away from the demons. I was so pissed, I cursed him out, and, then, I said, 'I hope you're in a better place.'"

Mahal has repeatedly re-recorded "Further Down the Road," one of the songs that he cowrote with Davis. "[When we first recorded it]," he said, "[Davis] had come into the studio without lyrics. I went away, wrote the words, and came back thirty-five or forty minutes later. We recorded it that night. I never fretted over the words. It was a typical R&B groove, kind of like Joe Simon."

"I almost didn't record it a second time," he continued. "I didn't think that you could do it any better than the original. When I recorded it with the International Rhythm Band, we put a more contemporary R&B groove on it. I love the song. I am amazed that people do not hear the subtle parts that Davis put on it. At times, it sounded like three guitars playing. He played with different slides. He really knew his instrument."

A third version of the song was included on Mahal's 2009 album, *Maestro*, celebrating the fortieth anniversary since his first release. "It's a different song with the Phantom Blues Band," he said. "They've got their own tone on it. Eric Clapton is recording it for his next album. I went down to L.A. and put a harmonica part on it."

Mahal's cultural background combines the Cherokee/Creek heritage of his mother, a schoolteacher and gospel singer, and the West Indian/Hispanic roots of his father, a jazz pianist and arranger, and construction company owner. "That's the blend," he said. "One side was going for education and the other was looking for opportunity."

Losing his father in a tractor accident when he was eleven, Mahal found solace in music. "I didn't know that there were places without music," he said. "I couldn't imagine a household without it. Music was like the sea and the water in which I swam. It was great to run into other guys who felt that kind of commitment to music."

After his mother remarried, Mahal and his siblings moved into the home of their stepfather, who owned a guitar. A neighbor, Lynwood Perry, a nephew of blues singer Big Boy Crudup, provided him with lessons.

Music in the Frederick home inspired not only Mahal, but also his younger sister, Carole Fredericks (1952–2001), who moved to France and became a leading gospel and R&B singer. "You didn't hear a peep about her in the United States," said Mahal. "Even when she passed, newspapers couldn't be positive. She was a full-figured woman, and did not look like a Hollywood goddess, but she was a beautiful woman. When she went to Europe, people did not have a problem with it. They heard her voice and said, 'Yes.'"

Separating from Davis, Mahal continued to pursue his own path. "I kept moving on," he said. "I had the tuba band together for two records in the mid-1970s, and then I went back to a solo format for *Recycling the Blues & Other Related Stuff* in 1972, and *Oooh, So Good and Blue* the following year. The soundtrack for the film *Sounder* was kind of a solo project. Starting with *Mo' Roots* in 1974, I went to playing with bands. That was the end of the Columbia Records days and the beginning of the Warner Brothers days. It wasn't until the '80s that I slowed down and went out on the road again as a solo artist."

TOM BEE AND XIT

Opening shows for Three Dog Night, The Beach Boys, Grand Funk Railroad, America, ZZ Top, and Joe Cocker in the 1970s, Indigenous America's first rock group, XIT ("Exit") injected a high-fueled promotion of Indigenous rights and sovereignty to the contemporary mainstream. Their albums remain, according to their Dakota founder and producer Tom Bee (1947–), "as valid today as they were yesterday."

XIT was the first band to address Native issues through contemporary pop/rock arrangements.
Courtesy Tom Bee, SOAR.

XIT's 1972 debut album, *The Plight of the Redman*, shocked executives of Motown subsidiary Rare Earth Records. "They didn't know what to think," said Bee, a Motown staff songwriter when he formed XIT. "I could see that they had tears in their eyes. They said, 'Man, what a great album,' but in the next breath they added, 'What do we do with it?' It was new to them—a concept album dealing with American Indians. I said, 'Just put it out, please.'"

The Plight of the Redman's Indigenous themes, brilliant production, and well-crafted arrangements found an enthusiastic audience everywhere but in the United States. "*Billboard* kept it off their charts," said Bee, "and radio programmers wouldn't play it. They didn't want a 'Native uprising.'"

XIT's troubles with Motown escalated with their second album, *Silent Warrior*, which came out while the occupation of Wounded Knee was taking place. "Berry Gordy sent word to the sales office to hold back on the record," said Bee, "because he didn't want to get involved with that 'political, Native thing,' but, by that time,

Tom Bee (Dakota) has influenced modern American Indian music as producer and leader of the first Indigenous rock band, XIT, and founder of SOAR (Sound of America Records). *Courtesy Tom Bee, SOAR.*

it was too late. They were already advertising it everywhere. The album went on to sell a bunch of records and became a big underground hit on college campuses in the U.S. and all over Europe."

Despite efforts to suppress their music, XIT made a major impact. "We were a big influence on the whole scene," said Bee. "The media labeled us 'the musical ambassadors of the American Indian Movement.' We opened people's eyes on reservations throughout North America. We were cult heroes."

Some non-Natives had a different view. "We were right in their faces," said Bee. "Instead of listening to our album like the story that it was, the minute that they heard the words, 'Go away, white man, this is our land,' it sent red flags to them that this was a militant, antiwar group. They immediately labeled us racists, radicals, renegades, and militants."

Although there were enough tracks for a third XIT album, Bee and Motown had gone their separate ways shortly after the release of *Silent Warrior.* Ten previously unissued songs—augmented by four new tracks—were released in 1977 on the Canyon Records label as *Relocation*.

Adopted by Lakota parents shortly after his birth, Bee grew up in Gallup, New Mexico. "I knew that I was adopted," he said. "When I was in my early teens, my adopted mother sat me down and told me, but I had always suspected it. I didn't look like the other members of the family."

Growing up on the "poor side" of town, Bee found music a refuge. "We lived a block from the Intertribal Ceremonial Grounds," he said, "and every August they would have a four-day powwow ceremony. Tribes from all over the U.S. would come."

The rest of the year, the grounds hosted wrestling matches and rock-and-roll shows. "A couple of the neighborhood kids from Arapaho Pueblo, whose dads worked on the railroad, and I were good friends," said Bee. "We'd set up chairs, and carry them down after the program, and get in for free. I remember seeing the original Ike and Tina Turner Revue, Little Richard, Fats Domino, Chuck Berry, and Buddy Holly."

Music provided personal strength as well. "I was introverted when I was young," remembered Bee, "very bashful, and I didn't have a lot of confidence. I had a speech impediment. I stuttered into my young adult life, but I discovered that, when I sang, I wouldn't stutter. My voice came out normal and I liked it."

Songwriting came naturally. "I was always writing poems and rhymes," said Bee. "Gradually, I turned them into songs. When I first went to Los Angeles, when I was fifteen, I had a book with fifty songs."

After the Jackson 5 recorded his song "(We've Got) Blue Skies" for their 1971 album, *Maybe Tomorrow*, Motown signed Bee to an artist, writer, and producer contract. Smokey Robinson recorded his tune "Just My Soul Responding," complete with Bee's vocable chanting, powwow drum-like percussion, and a string section, for his 1973 solo debut, *Smokey*. R&B singer Michael Edward Campbell included two of his songs—"Roxanne" and "Roll It Over"—on his self-titled album the following year. Two years later, Bee's "Joyful Jukebox Music" provided the title track of Michael Jackson and the Jackson 5's final Motown album.

At the time, Motown was going through transition, with its owner Berry Gordy distracted by cinema. The label had released its first film, *Lady Sings the Blues*, starring Diana Ross, in October 1972, and was in the process of relocating to California. "They were keeping a skeleton crew in Detroit," said Bee, "but they moved everything else to Los Angeles. [Gordy] had done so many things in the music industry that he wanted to conquer other areas of entertainment. He had already shattered all previous sales records and torn down the walls of segregation."

Working at Motown provided Bee with the equivalent of a postgraduate degree in the recording arts. "I really think that I got a degree from the University of

Motown," he said. "I befriended a lot of sales and marketing people and attorneys and they took the time to teach me."

Most American Indian recordings at the time suffered from limited budgets, inadequate recording equipment, and poor distribution. "I looked at the state of Native music," Bee recalled, "and realized that it was a trading post–only genre. I would go into some places and ask if they had any American Indian music. They would think about it for a minute and say, 'We might have some.' Then they would go into the back, come out with a cassette, and blow the dust off. I would laugh and say, 'Someone should start a label and promote the music just like they would any other kind of popular music, not pigeonhole it as American Indian music. They should upgrade the graphics and the sound production, get proper distribution, try to get it into the mainstream, and really do something with it.'"

Bee spent years acquiring the skills needed to make it possible. "I had my own label, Souled Out, in the early 1960s," he said, "and I produced records for Rhythm and Blues acts—Wilson Pickett–type singers with horns. I licensed them to Dot Records, which was part of ABC-Paramount, and we had seven R&B regional hits. I would truck my car up and down Highway 66, selling 45-rpm records. I was involved with concert promotion and management. Even though I liked songwriting, the business end of music really fascinated me. I turned over every stone and didn't leave any stone unturned."

Royalties earned when R&B vocalist Taka Boom, Chaka Khan's younger sister, had a dance hit with his song, "Red Hot," enabled Bee to launch SOAR (Sound of America Records) in 1979. The first four releases included a live album recorded during an XIT concert in Switzerland (*Drums across the Atlantic*), a solo album, and reissues of the albums that XIT had released on Motown. "I bought back the rights," said Bee. "I didn't want them to be prostituted in the bargain bins of Kmart and Walmart for a dollar ninety-nine. I started putting full-page, color ads in Southwestern magazines, the same kind of ads that ran in *Billboard*."

From the beginning, SOAR expanded the possibilities for Native music. "We recorded hip-hop and rap," said Bee, "and some really nice instrumental music. We gave Derek Miller his first break. We have Chester Knight, a great songwriter from Canada, and a Native reggae group, Native Roots. Chief Jim Billie of the Seminole tribe in Florida released two CDs that were produced by John McEuen of the Nitty Gritty Dirt Band."

Some of SOAR's most progressive albums featured the multi-instrumental playing, singing, songwriting, and production of Bee's son, Robbie (1969–). As the leader of Boyz from the Rez, he made his recording debut with *We're the Boyz*, one of the first powwow/hip-hop albums in 1993, and scored a NAIRD (National Association of Record Distributors) award for "Best Independent Video." On his

2005 album, *Legacy*, which he credited to his pseudonym, Santee, Robbie Bee mixed textured electronic keyboard orchestration with guitars, drums, and guest vocalists. Dr. Cornel Pewewardy, Earl Bullhead, and Jack Anquoe (Grayhorse Singers) made appearances. "He's a very intelligent young man," said Bee proudly of his son. "He just graduated from the University of Michigan and he wants to go to law school."

Attempting to get broader recognition for American Indian music, Bee lobbied the National Academy of Recording Arts and Science for a decade before it agreed to add a "Native American Music" category to the Grammy awards in 2001. It seemed fitting when the first award went to *Gathering of Nations Powwow*, a multi-artist album that he coproduced with flutist and recording engineer, Douglas Spotted Eagle (Diné). Recorded at the Gathering of Nations, and released in May 2000, the album included performances by Tha Tribe, Wild Horse, Sage Point, Southern Cree, White Clay, Flying Eagle, Bear Springs, High Noon, Painted Horse, Northern Cree, Trail Mix, and others. "As we were getting ready to go the Grammy ceremonies," he recalled, "my wife opened the Bible randomly and the scripture said, 'Tonight, the Lord will be exalted.' It was like a dream when I walked up to the podium. I felt like I was walking in the clouds. I felt the presence of God all over me."

Members of XIT reunited to play at the Celebrity Palace in the Mystic Lake Casino, in Prior Lake, Minnesota, on May 20, 2000. The show, which included XIT classics, including "We Live," "Christopher Columbus," "Color Nature Gone," and "Reservation of Education," sung by Bee, was filmed with six cameras, and twenty-four track digital audio, and released as a fifty-six-minute-long DVD, *XIT: Without Reservation*, featuring narration by Floyd "Red Crow" Westerman.

Original XIT guitarists A. Michael Martinez and R. C. Garriss, bassist Mac Suazo, and percussionist Lee Herrera continue to play together (without Bee) as OX Boyz. Their 2012 release, *The Red Album*, scored an "Album of the Year" NAMMY nomination. Rock the Vote used their tune "Song of Freedom" during their Southwestern voter registration campaign.

REDBONE

On the February 22, 1974, broadcast of ABC-TV music show *Midnight Special*, the week's guest host, Gordon Lightfoot, introduced a band from Southern California. As the camera zoomed in on a regalia-clad intertribal dancer, stepping to the chopping-beats of a ceremonial drum, bassist/vocalist Pat Vegas Vasquez (1940–) (Yaqui/Shoshone/Mexican) shifted into the funky bass line and led Redbone into their top-five hit, "Come and Get Your Love." Penned by Pat's older brother, guitarist and lead vocalist Candido "Lolly" Vegas Vasquez (1939–2010) (Yaqui/Shoshone/Mexican), it would become one of the best-selling singles of the decade, spending six months in the top forty and being featured on the soundtracks of *To Wong Foo Thanks for Everything* (1995), *Dick* (1999), and *Grown Ups* (2010). A version by the Real McCoy, a German techno-dance group led by rapper and producer Olaf "O Jay" Jeglitza, reached the top of *Billboard*'s dance charts in 1995.

Inducted into the Rock and Roll Hall of Fame, in 2002, and the Native American Music Hall of Fame in 2008, Redbone made an impact far beyond the reservations. They dressed as Plains Indians, but their music had everyone—Native and non-Native—on their feet dancing. Unlike most other groups scoring hits during the Disco era, Redbone was not rooted in Euro-tech dance music but in rock, jazz, R&B, blues, Cajun, and Indigenous traditions. Their self-titled, double-disc, debut album included a slow, funky tune straight out of the Louisiana bayous ("Crazy Cajun Cakewalk Band") and an updating of a centuries-old Creole dance tune ("Dance Calinda"). The influence of New Orleans's R&B and Louisiana's swamp pop was also reflected in their first two hit singles—"Maggie" in 1970 and "The Witch Queen of New Orleans" a year later. Reaching number twenty-three on the charts, "The Witch Queen of New Orleans" paid tribute to Marie Laveau, a late-nineteenth-century Creole practitioner of voodoo.

Beginning with their second album (*Potlatch*), the Native experience infused Redbone's music as Indigenous imagery sprinkled through Pat's original songs, "Light as a Feather," "Chant: 13th Hour," and Lolly's double-time, Native-meets-Zappa instrumental, "Without Reservation." The album also included "Alcatraz," a song that Pat had been inspired to write by the occupation of the former prison site.

In addition to "Witch Queen of New Orleans," Redbone's third album, *Message from a Drum* (1971), included a pair of instrumentals ("Maxsplivitz" and "Perico") featuring the trademark sixteen-notes-on-the-hi-hat-and-snare-drum "King Kong" rhythms of original drummer Pete DePoe, making his final recordings with the band before family obligations forced him to resign. Butch Rillera, Bellamy's cousin, would replace him.

Paced by their success with "Maggie" and "Witch Queen of New Orleans," Redbone opened for Steve Winwood and Traffic, Alice Cooper, and Rod Stewart & the Faces. Their fourth album, *Already Here*, included an eight-minute-plus title instrumental, a Cajun influenced–tune ("Fais-Do"), and a reworking of a Jerry Leiber and Mike Stoller–penned 1950s classic ("Poison Ivy"), but none of its songs touched directly on Indigenous themes.

Redbone, however, was about to make its boldest American Indian statement. Inspired by AIM's occupation of Wounded Knee, which was still going on, "We Were All Wounded at Wounded Knee" put the excitement of dance music to a very topical issue. ABC-distributed Epic Records refused to release it. "We got it out, in five days, by ourselves," Pat Vegas told *Indian Country News*. "We paid five hundred dollars so that we could bring copies with us to Europe. It became the biggest record of the year."[11]

Redbone remained defiant with their fifth album, *Wovoka*. Disco enthusiasts may have bought it because it included "Come and Get Your Love," but they had a sharp awakening when they listened to the title track. Set to a contemporary dance beat, "Wovoka" told of the self-proclaimed Northern Paiute visionary at the center of the Ghost Dance movement in the late 1880s. The tune, however, proved to be Redbone's final hoorah. After their 1974 album, *Turquoise Dreams through Beaded Eyes*, met with disappointing sales, Epic failed to renew their contract. Subsequent releases have featured live tracks and repackaged greatest-hits.

A stroke forced Lolly Vegas to step down in 1995—he would succumb to complications from lung cancer on March 4, 2010—but a series of talented guitarists would continue in his place. "[Lolly] did some amazing things on the guitar," said Raven Hernandez (Diné/Mexican), the California-born guitarist who was the first to replace him. "He played his guitar through a Leslie rotating amplifier and got a really unique sound. He used all kinds of effects that I'm just starting to use today."

"I got to meet Lolly once," said Mark Guerrero, a guitarist, bandleader, and music journalist who played with Redbone in the early 2000s. "He had already had the stroke and his left arm and left leg were paralyzed. He came to see us in [the Vasquezes' hometown] Fresno, California. After the show, we went to his hotel room and talked. The rest of the band had gone, and I was the only one left. We wound up talking for three hours. He told me about his history, and music, and we talked about guitar chords."

The Vasquez brothers' journey began in the cotton fields, and apricot orchards, of Southern California, where they grew up amid migrant workers from their father's Mexican homeland. Determined to make better lives for themselves, they spent whatever spare time they had sharpening their musical skills.

Pat and Lolly were thirteen and fourteen, respectively, when they started backing touring rock-and-roll stars. By their late teens, they were seasoned musicians. When Montreal-born jazz pianist Oscar Peterson needed a guitarist and a bassist for the Monterey Jazz and Pop Festival in 1963, they got the prestigious gig. Encouraged by the crowd's warm reception, the brothers headed to Los Angeles with dreams of musical stardom. Although fame didn't come as quickly as hoped, they were soon two of the most active musicians in Southern California. They played sessions with Odetta, John Lee Hooker, and the Everly Brothers, and backed up Houston-born Dobie Gray on his smooth-soul R&B hit "The 'In' Crowd." They accompanied Elvis Presley in his 1964 film, *Kissin' Cousins*, and they were featured on the soundtrack of *It's a Bikini World*, a musical comedy starring Tommy Kirk, Deborah Walley, and Bobby "Boris" Pickett.

Recording under a variety of names, Pat and Lolly tried staking their claim in surf-rock and hot-rod music, releasing such collectable singles as "Gypsy Surfer," "Wax 'Em Down," and Phantom Surfer" (as the Avantis), "Let's Go" (as the Routers), and "Surf Stomp" and "Batman" (as the Mar-kets). They credited several singles (including "Hot-Rodder's Choice" and "Satan's Chariot") to the Deuce Coup, a band they shared with Glen Campbell, Leon Russell, and David Gates, later of the 1970s pop group Bread.

Whether billed as Vasquez, or Vegas (to obscure their Mexican roots), the brothers played a strong role in the growth of the Hispanic rock of East Los Angeles's Mexican-American community. "Lolly and Pat were a big part of that whole music scene," said Guerrero. "There were so many groups and plenty of venues to play. Cannibal and the Headhunters had 'Land of a Thousand Dances,' and the Premiers had 'Farmer John,' but Lolly's style of Fender Telecaster playing was influential to all of the guitarists."

The brothers had their first breakthrough as songwriters when their song "Niki Hoeky," written with Jim Ford of Johnson County, Texas, was recorded by P. J. Proby (James Marcus Smith), a Houston-born, Elvis Presley–like baritone singer who had been taken under the wing of British producer Jack Good. Aretha Franklin, the Ventures, and Louisiana-born blues/R&B singer Bobby Rush were among those who would cover it. Bobby Gentry would perform it on *The Smothers Brothers Comedy Hour*. Redbone included their version on their debut album.

As members of the Shindogs, the house band for popular ABC-TV music show, *Shindig*, Pat and Lolly performed for a national audience weekly from September 1964 to January 1966. The group, which also included Leon Russell and Delaney Bramlett, backed up guests and performed their own songs. The brothers were featured several times during the show's sixteen-month run. They performed a power-packed medley of "La Bamba" and "Twist and Shout" on one episode, and a Righteous Brothers–like ballad, "Write Me, Baby," on another.

Performing at a popular Los Angeles nightspot, the brothers recorded their first album, *Pat and Lolly Vegas: Live at the Haunted House*, in 1966. With Leon Russell and Dallas-born Thomas Leslie "Snuff" Garrett handling production, the disc's twelve tracks evenly split between original songs and covers of hits by the Rolling Stones, Huey "Piano" Smith, the Four Tops, Wilson Pickett, James Brown, and the Young Rascals.

A backstage discussion with Jimi Hendrix planted the seeds that would grow into Redbone. "Hendrix was a friend of ours," Pat Vegas told *Record Collector* magazine, "and he was half Indian. Once he knew that we were Indian too, he used to come and hang with us. Because of that, Jimi made me aware of my roots. He would say, '[Being] an American Indian is beautiful, man, be proud of that.'"

Taking Hendrix's suggestion as a challenge, the brothers began to conceive of a band that would fuse their R&B and Latin roots with their Native heritage. Tony Bellamy (Yaqui/Mexican American) (1946–2009), a guitarist that they met at Gazzarri's, a popular Sunset Strip nightspot, became their first recruit. Descended from a family of singers and dancers, Bellamy had played guitar for Dobie Gray and had been a member of Peter and the Wolves, a San Francisco–based psychedelic rock band that would evolve into Moby Grape. Renting a house together, the three musicians would spend a year polishing the sound of what would become Redbone. Hired at the suggestion of R&B vocalist Bobby Womack, Pete "Last Walking Bear" De Poe, a drummer from Neah Bay Reservation, Washington, who was a cousin of Leonard Peltier and whose ancestry included northern Cheyenne, Chippewa, Arapaho, Siletz, Roark River, Tututney, Iroquois, French, and German blood, solidified the quartet.

Temporarily disbanding, in 1979, with the Vegas brothers continuing to perform together, as well as separately, Redbone reunited a decade later. On the verge of recapturing their former glory, a stroke forced Lolly to retire. Raven Hernandez took his place. "I had a nine-piece band in high school," said Hernandez, "playing songs by Wilson Pickett and Otis Redding. We built the sound around the horns, the B-3 organ, and the spinning Leslie speakers. In the late '70s, I worked with rock and roll acts like Shirley and Lee, Big Joe Turner, and Joe Houston."

Hernandez's introduction to Indigenous music had come while playing with a top-forty band in the lounge of a Mexican restaurant. "Two women came in," he remembered, "one was [electric guitarist, vocalist, and bandleader] Mary Kaye of the Mary Kaye Trio. I didn't know who she was, but she was descended from Hawaii's last reigning monarch, Queen Liliuokalani, and had been Hawaii's 'first lady of rock and roll' in the 1950s and '60s. The Fender Guitar Company sponsored her with her own model of guitar. When she heard us play, she came over and said, 'I want to hire your band—all but your keyboards player.' She had her own keyboards player who played flugelhorn. I played with her for a year."

A longtime fan of their music, Hernandez had grown up playing covers of Redbone's songs like "Maggie," "Witch Queen of New Orleans," "Come and Get Your Love," and "All Wounded at Wounded Knee." He had given no thought to playing with the band, however, when his telephone rang one night in 1996. When he answered it, "It was a friend saying, 'Do you want to go to a jam session?'" he remembered. "I told him, 'No.' I was comfortable at home, on the couch, and didn't want to go anywhere. He kept trying to persuade me. He told me that he would drive, and even buy me a beer, so I agreed to go with him."

Once they arrived at their destination, Hernandez discovered that "it wasn't the jam session as I thought it was going to be." "It was at a coffee shop,' he recalled, "so much for the beer. We went in and there were twenty people there. Musicians were sitting everywhere. It was completely unstructured. A couple of close friends of Redbone were there, maybe even a cousin of Pat and Lolly Vegas. I got up and jammed with them. I didn't know who they were. I thought they were just a couple of musicians who were jamming. I played 'Play That Funky Music' by Wild Cherry, 'Them Changes' by Buddy Miles, and 'Black Magic Woman' by Santana. Then, we did some I-IV-V blues by Willie Dixon and one of my original tunes. It was kind of a simple format. I wrote it down real quick and we went through the changes. Afterwards, everyone passed out business cards."

A week later, Hernandez's friend called again. "He asked if I remembered the jam session," said the guitarist, "and he told me that there had been some people from Redbone there and they wanted me to come down to audition for the band. I asked, 'When?' and he said, 'Tonight.' That's just the way things happen in life. Sometimes, it's luck, and sometimes, it's fate."

Hernandez loved playing with Redbone. "I got into the statements that their songs were making," he said. "Their commercial hits were good-time, fun songs, but there were a lot of other songs, like 'Alcatraz' and 'Wounded Knee,' that carried important messages. I had played with so many cover bands that I was a human jukebox, but when I started playing with them, I found a new direction. I started writing songs about the environment or a white buffalo. We played at big festivals and concerts. I'd walk onto a stage, play a chord, and have it come out of speakers to 10,000 people. It was so cool. I met many tribal elders and started to feel like an Indian. It really was a part of my heritage. It made a big change in the direction that I was going."

After eight years, it was time to move on. "There were other things that I wanted to do," said Hernandez. "The last year that I was with them, I was working on my second album. I needed to move on and express myself on my own. Pat and Lolly Vegas had been around for a long time, and they were retaining all of their rights and royalties, but I was writing songs [like 'Sacred Land,' 'Happiness,' and 'Civilized Man'] that they were using in their shows. At one point, we discussed recording a new album, but Pat started using session musicians. I respected whatever he wanted to do."

Since 2010, Hernandez has been leading his own Native-rock band, Sacred Land, with Joey Lo Dulce (drums and percussion) and Michael Dominguez (bass and vocals). "We believe in Native culture and the environment," he said, "and about bringing people's attention to certain issues through music."

The son of Chicano music great, Lalo Guerrero, and the leader of East L.A. rock bands, Mark and the Escorts in the 1960s, and Tango in the '70s, Mark Guerrero accompanied Pat Vegas, along with members of Cannibal and the Headhunters, in Sacramento, California, in 2010, and El Paso, Texas, in 2011. He also recorded several tracks with the Redbone bassist. "He has another version of Redbone now," he said of his former boss, "with some musicians from Phoenix. He's in his late-sixties, but he is still on fire musically. He writes all of the time and records his own demos constantly. He has the same enthusiasm that he's always had. He's still creating, still active."

In early 2014, Pat Vegas's twenty-four-year-old son, PJ Vegas, released his debut album, *Priceless*, recorded with Native American flutist Cody Blackbird, as a free Internet download. "When it comes to my music," he told *American Indian Today*, "I want my pain to be felt, my struggle to be understood, [and] my heart to be raw. I want to paint a picture with every verse, every beat."[12]

BLACKFIRE

Hailing from the heart of the land struggle at Big Mountain, Arizona, Blackfire lashed out at mistreatment on the reservations and destruction of the natural environment with punk-rock intensity, angst-driven vocals, sonic-propelled guitars, bone-crushing bass lines, and explosive backbeats.

The offspring of a traditional Diné hatalí (medicine man), Jones Benally (1925–), and the German/Polish ex-folksinger whom he married in 1952, Berta, Blackfire's Klee, Clayson, and Jeneda Benally grew up singing with their parents at powwows and schools as the Jones Benally Family. "[My dad] spent his whole life learning, training, and helping people," said Jeneda.

"He went to a boarding school when he was twenty," added Clayson. "By then, he had learned about the ceremonies and the culture. When the school found out that he could do hoop dancing, they began to send him all over the world to perform. He traveled with a Wild West show; then he became involved with the Hollywood movie scene—John Wayne, Gene Autry, Roy Rogers."

New York–born Berta Benally remained connected to music after moving west in 1969. In support of protests against coal mining on the sacred Big Mountain (Black Mesa, Arizona), close to Flagstaff, where her children were born, she began producing benefit concerts in the early 1980s. "I remember seeing Albert King, Buddy Guy, Taj Mahal, and Ramblin' Jack Elliott," said Jeneda, "all these amazing artists who were friends of our mom."

"I would study the drummers," recalled Clayson (1978–), "and watch what they were doing."

Jeneda's chance meeting with a high school friend led to a career break for Blackfire. After she told her friend about the Native-punk band that she had formed with her brothers, word passed on to C. J. Ramone (Christopher Joseph Ward), bass player for punk-rock originators, the Ramones. Ramone went on to take the siblings under his wing, and produce their debut five-song EP, in 1994, for which they received a "Group of the Year" NAMMY. "We felt a kinship with the energy of punk rock," said Jeneda.

"He looked through our material," added Clayson, "and saw that we had some stuff that was gothic, some that was punk, some rock, and some ska. We even did some klezmer. He said that he was going to choose five of our songs and tell a story with them. From there, he clued us into the Ramones' formula—take it to the highest point, rev up the energy, give people something extremely powerful, end it, and, boom, next song—'one, two, three, four.'"

The Ramones' lead singer, Joey Ramone, who called their music "fireball punk rock," produced Blackfire's first full-length outing, *One Nation Under*, in 2001, shortly before his death after a seven-year battle with lymphoma. Released by Canyon, the album scored a "Best Pop/Rock Recording" NAMMY. "We brought Joey Ramone to play at our reservation," said Jeneda. "There weren't any musical opportunities at the Navajo Nation Fair, so we put on a festival. It was his first concert after the Ramones retired. He played with a band that he called 'Joey Ramone and the Resistance' and did songs about empowered youth."

Blackfire's double-disc 2005 album, *Beyond Warped*, included a pair of Ramones tunes ("I Believe in Miracles" and "Planet Earth 88"), originally recorded for an Argentinean tribute album (*Todos Somos Ramones*), and live tracks recorded during the skateboard shoe manufacturer–sponsored Vans Warped Tour. "We did a lot of Ramones covers," said Clayson, "including 'Lobotomy.' I remember telling Joey that we played it because we usually played serious music and, every once in a while, we liked to do a song for the kids to get mindless to. He said, 'No, no, no, this is actually a very political song. It's about people who go into institutions and have no representation.' I think he was speaking from his own history, something definitely brought on that song."

Blackfire toured Europe twelve times, and performed in 2003, along with Malians Ali Farke Toure and Tinariwen, and Led Zeppelin's Robert Plant, at the Festival in the Desert in Essakne, Mali. Their performance of "What Do You See" was included on the live album of the festival.

The Benally Family collaborated with R. Carlos Nakai, and (then-conductor of the Flagstaff Symphony Orchestra) Randall Craig Fleischer, on an orchestral piece, "Triumph," premiered in 2009. "We spent two years working on it," said Clayson. "It incorporated traditional Diné songs and dances. We used [Nakai's] flute as an orchestral sound."

Nakai played a guiding role during the young Benallys' lives. "It goes back to when we were children, performing at the Grand Canyon," said Clayson. "In the summer, he would come up and share the stage with us. He gave us our first PA. Before there was Native rock, he would say, 'Let's get together and play pow-wow rock.'"

Blackfire was among many artists invited to compose music for lyrics written by America's great folk songwriter, Woody Guthrie. "We have a strong connection to Woody's kinfolk," said Clayson. "We've gone to Okemah, Oklahoma, met his family, and played at Woody Fest. We had the honor of opening the 100th year celebration of his birth in Germany."

Blackfire would release *Woody Guthrie Singles* in 2003, featuring their adaptation of Guthrie's "Mean Things Happenin' in This World" and his Native-themed "Indian Corn Song," which they renamed "The Corn Song." Janeda and Clayson re-recorded "Mean Things Happenin' in This World" for their debut album as Sihasin (*Never Surrender*). "We wanted to keep the spirit of Woody Guthrie alive," said Clayson. "He wrote songs about the Dust Bowl and unions, but he also wrote about American Indian issues."

Following their Woody Fest performance of "Mean Things Happenin' in This World," Guthrie's old friend Pete Seeger approached them. "He said, 'I listened to the song,'" recalled Clayson. "'You did a great job. It sounded nothing like the original.' We hadn't had any guide other than [Guthrie's] words, but we wanted to do complete justice to the song. Later, Cyril Neville recorded our version, which was a huge honor."

Blackfire instantly connected with Guthrie's "Indian Corn Song." "Woody wrote about women's rights, Indigenous people's rights, and the issues that were happening within communities," said Clayson. "'The Corn Song' talks about wastefulness and how Indigenous people are . . . living off the planet in a balanced way. It was always one of my favorite songs to play."

Blackfire's double-CD second album, *[Silence] Is a Weapon*, the NAMMY's "Best Recording of 2007," celebrated the dual worlds in which they lived. While one disc featured power-driven Native-punk, and included an updating of Peter LaFarge's "I'm an Indian, I'm an Alien," the other featured Diné songs. "We wanted to inspire youth to learn the traditional songs," said Janeda, "as well as our culture, dances, and ceremonies."

The political commitment of the Benally brothers and their sister extended beyond their music. For much of the first decade of the twenty-first century, they were involved with an unsuccessful struggle to prevent the Arizona Snowbowl, a ski resort on the western flank of sacred San Francisco Peaks in north-central Arizona, from using reclaimed wastewater to make snow. Jeneda and her mother joined with the Save the Peaks Coalition—a group with which Klee Benally is involved—and other individuals to file suit against the National Forest Service in 2007. After a five-year legal battle, the Ninth Circuit Court of Appeals dismissed their complaint in February 2012. The wastewater snow began to flow nine months later.

Klee, who had produced a documentary film, *The Snowball Effect*, about the conflict, faced charges for his participation in a protest that caused a work stoppage. Coconino Country Justice Court judge Howard Goodman, who had used his film when he taught a class, found him guilty of "resistance to desecration," sentenced him to community service, and billed him for the ninety-nine dollars and twenty-four cents lost by construction workers. To satisfy his sentence, Klee helped to teach a class, "Investigating Human Rights," at Northern Arizona University.

With the focus of their older brother, lead singer, guitarist, and songwriter distracted, Jeneda and Clayson faced a dilemma; Blackfire had a full schedule of shows booked. "Jeneda and I played a couple of shows [as a duo]," said Clayson, "and it was really interesting. There was a piece missing, without Klee, but there was so much creative new energy."

SIHASIN

Klee's younger brother and sister were soon writing new songs from a different perspective than Blackfire. "We already had ideas for most of the songs," said Clayson. "It was like putting together a puzzle. Jeneda would have a melody and I would have something that fit with it. We started pulling all of these elements together. Songs just naturally grew. It was like putting a seed in the ground, watering it, and having instant gratification."

The duo's new approach necessitated a name change. "In the Diné language, Sihasin means 'hope,'" said Jeneda. "It's one of our values, as Diné people, to think in a positive way. My brothers and I have always expressed that anger is a tool for attacking negativity and instilling motivation, but what we wanted to focus on, musically and creatively, was what happened after the anger."

Released on Tacoho Records, the label on which Blackfire had released two EPs and three CDs in October 2012, *Never Surrender* introduced a more diverse sound than Blackfire's punk-infused music. "We sang about border issues ('Move Along'), the call for peace ('Mean Things'), and the idea of never surrendering," said Clayson. "People have to compromise on a daily basis, but we wanted to remind them to find their own strength and take a stand."

"Creating this album was a form of therapy," added Jeneda, "to help me heal and to help me grow. Emotionally, I was the most depressed that I had ever been. We had lost our lawsuit against the United States Forest Service to protect children

Sihasin (Diné/German/Polish) is a brother-and-sister offshoot of Native-punk rockers Black-fire. *Courtesy Sihasin.*

from eating reclaimed wastewater snow on a holy mountain. I've always just been a bass player, singing a little in the background, but I needed to vocalize the sadness that I was feeling."

Janeda wrote one of the strongest songs on the album, "Take a Stand," as she waited at a bus stop for her daughter. "I started singing this melody into the recorder of my cell phone," she recalled. "It really resonated with my six-year-old daughter. She heard it once and did not forget it. She kept singing it back to me. It talks about how our ancestors have never left us—all that cultural knowledge, that deep spiritual connection that we have towards our homeland is very powerful. It is something that we cannot see, but can certainly feel. The breath that we have, our heartbeat, all of who we are, comes from our ancestors. That song has given me a lot of hope. Whatever we can do to help our global community, and our people, to feel empowered, that is what we want to do."

As a bassist, Jeneda stepped out with a spectrum of unique tones on *Never Surrender*. "I'd been playing for over twenty years," she said, "but had never experimented much before. I like the sound of a naked bass, with just a little distortion, but we had a wonderful engineer, the late Capt. Chris Mix, who created a special box for me that split my bass into a bass amp and a guitar amp. There's no guitar, but it's a new sound."

Jeneda first took notice of the bass at the age of thirteen. "I was listening to some music," she recalled, "and I can't even tell you what song it was, but the sound of the bass resonated with me. It was the greatest sonic emotion that I had ever felt. Something about the vibration, and the tones of the notes, spoke to my soul."

As a female bass player, Jeneda faced considerable opposition. "I had to deal with sexism and racism," she remembered. "It was very frustrating. People told me that I would have to cut my hair and that women were not anatomically correct for the bass. That gave me some fire."

Clayson altered his style of playing drums for Sihasin. Rather than sitting down, and playing—as he had with Blackfire—he stood up, holding his drumsticks backwards, with rattles in his hands, as well as his sticks. "Sihasin is the opposite of Blackfire," he explained, "where the focus was on the historical events, the suffering, and the pain. I wanted to do something that reflected the positive. I used a powwow drum (for my floor tom), and my mother's Taos Pueblo drum. I started using the rattle with Blackfire, and it had become something that I loved. It enhances in so many ways. I like to do triplets, and complicated rhythms, that you typically need to be sitting down to do, but I felt like dancing—being upright, projecting, and singing."

Much of the siblings' recent attention has focused on cinema, from both sides of the camera. The coordinator of the Native American Film and Video Festival at the Museum of Northern Arizona in 2004 and 2005, Klee has been involved with a number of community media projects, including Indigenous Action Media and Outta Your Backpack Media. Clayson starred in the pilot of a TV soap opera, *The Rocks*, filmed in Sedona, Arizona, while Jeneda made her film debut as a space commander on a mission to Mars, in a Diné science fiction film, *The Sixth Sense*. "We have to be ambassadors for our culture," she said, "and make sure that we're presenting accurate portrayals and protecting the things that are sacred, making sure that we're going to leave a true impression of who we are—for our children to pass on to their children."

RAGGAE INNA HOPILAND

Surrounded by the Navajo Reservation, and less than ten times its size, the 2,531,773-square-mile Hopi Reservation in northeast Arizona became the epicenter of Native-reggae in the late 1970s. Lured by their love of Bob Marley's music, many of the reservation's young people had been making regular trips to

Phoenix, about four hours away, to catch reggae bands. "We'd drive down in the afternoon," Gerry Gordon, an elementary school teacher in Hopi Land for more than two decades before moving to the Phoenix school system in 2000, told the *New York Times*, "go to a show, get back at 4 A.M., and go to work that morning."[13]

Tiring of the long trip, Gordon and Burt Poley, a wood carver known for his spirit-representing kachina dolls, formed an organization—Culture Connection—to produce reggae concerts closer to their home. After testing the market with a show by the Phoenix-based Sons of Captivity in an elementary school gymnasium, they launched a much bigger, ongoing series—Reggae Inna Hopiland—featuring internationally touring reggae bands, at the 2,500-seat Hopi Civic Center.

CASPER LOMA-DA-WA

For Winslow, Arizona-born Casper Loma-Da-Wa, or Calvin Arthur Lomayesva, (1967–), the first Reggae Inna Hopiland concert, which featured Freddie McGregor and the rub-a-dub vocal group Michigan and Smiley, was a revelation. "I had been into the rap scene and slam poetry," said the Ojibwe/Yaqui vocalist and songwriter, "but I can remember watching the show and thinking, 'That's what I want to do.'"

Loma-Da-Wa became an avid attendee of the reggae concert series. "I saw so many great shows," he said, "Yellowman, Dennis Brown, Burning Spear, Black Uhuru, and Bob Marley's boys—Stephen, Damian, and Ziggy. If Bob Marley was alive, he would have made the trip to Hopi."

"I really liked the messages of the songs," Loma-Da-Wa continued. "They were talking about things that happened in Jamaica that we could relate to in Hopi—things like police brutality."

Listening to reggae, however, wasn't enough. Loma-Da-Wa yearned to experience the music's roots for himself. Gathering his passport, a thousand dollars in cash, and his tent, he headed to Jamaica, for the first of many trips, in 1991. "I went for a full month," he said. "I wanted to feel the essence of what it was to be on the island. I learned so much about the culture, the history, and Rastafarianism. I've always been intrigued by Jamaica's Indigenous people—the Arawak, the original inhabitants."

Loma-Da-Wa has been singing since his earliest memory. "[My grandfather] would discipline me by putting me in a fifty-gallon barrel," he recalled, "but, instead of crying, I'd sing a combination of powwow songs, things that I heard on the radio, and my own stuff. I was five years old."

Writing hip-hop songs since high school, Loma-Da-Wa easily made the transition to reggae. Shortly after launching Third Mesa Records with his first album,

Original Landlord, in 1997, he and the Mighty 602 Band debuted at the Sierra Nevada Music Festival. "I was on the telephone with one of the promoters, who kept asking me for the band's name," he said. "I looked at a telephone book and told him, 'the Mighty 602 Band,' after the area code in Tempe, Arizona—602."

Nearly forty musicians have passed through the Mighty 602 Band, but the group's nucleus has remained stable. "Most of the original lineup is still with me," said Loma-Da-Wa. "William 'King Roach' Banks started on bass, but he's moved to the guitar, and his son, Justin, plays bass, now. He's only twenty-three years old, but he was with us from day one. As a kid, he used to go to the shows and help us."

Tunes on *Original Landlord*, including "Why" and the title track, addressed the suffering of the Hopi and called for unity between all people. "Hundred Years of Redemption" reflected on a century of Hopi-Navajo land disputes.

The flames literally burned hotter on their next album, *The Sounds of Reality*, in 2000. "We recorded it in the summer," said Loma-Da-Wa, "when the temperature reaches 120 degrees Fahrenheit. We didn't have air conditioning in the storage unit where we rehearsed. Everybody stripped down to boxers. Our female vocalist was in her panties and her bra, but it turned out to be our best album."

The opening track on *The Sounds of Reality*, "How the West Was Won," presented a history lesson through Native eyes. "Hopiland Winter" took a grim look at the continuing poverty among the inhabitants of the Hopi Reservation. "Jealousy," featuring British reggae singer and DJ Tippa Irie, viewed envy within the Hopi community. "As Native people, and human beings," said Loma-Da-Wa, "we're our own worst enemies. We're like a bucket of crabs. When one crab tries to get out, the others pull him back. We are selfish and blinded by the ways of the Pahana, or white people. We want to have iPhones and access to the Internet. We want to have hi-definition TVs. We're not supposed to be envious, but we are."

Another song on *The Sounds of Reality*, "Crossing Borders," explored one of the biggest problems plaguing American Indians. "It talks about the reservations surrounded by cities," said Loma-Da-Wa, "especially the Salt Lake River Reservation, outside of Phoenix. They have one of the highest crime and murder rates per capita. I believe that it's because the city is right across the border. Youth have nothing happening on their reservations, but they have access to everything in the cities. There's gang violence, crime, drug abuse, and alcoholism."

"Love Life" presented a more optimistic view. "Our youth have so many problems on the reservations," said Loma-Da-Wa, "but I wanted to tell them that there's more to life—they hadn't even scratched the surface yet—they shouldn't be lethargic, hanging out on the reservation, smoking pot all day. They have to motivate themselves."

A seven-and-a-half-minute-long piece, with musically accompanied, spoken word by John Trudell, "No Indian" presented a funky, brass-driven look at modern Hopi life. "I caught [Trudell] in the middle of a four-month world tour," said Loma-Da-Wa. "He had just gotten back from Spain, and had one day off before flying back to Europe. He flew to Phoenix, did the track, flew back to Los Angeles that night, and then flew off to Europe the next day, for three months. It was cool that he made time for me."

"I was coming from a Christian perspective," he continued. "My grandfather was a Christian, and he taught me a lot, but John is an atheist and I wanted his version too. I wanted a religious view and a reality view. I like his version better than mine. It is so deep. I could have never come up with the lines that he wrote. They are just beautiful. "

Loma-Da-Wa's friendship with Trudell developed slowly. "Early in my career, I reached out to him," he said, "but he doesn't trust too many people. It took six or seven years for him to trust me. I would see him at music festivals and give him bowls of fruit. I never rushed him or pushed myself too much. After seven years, I handed him the fruits, but, this time, instead of opening his hand to receive them, he grabbed my hand and said, 'Sit here, Casper, and talk with me.' We have been friends since."

Still in diapers during the occupation of Wounded Knee, Loma-Da-Wa learned much about the era from Trudell. "He gave me the full rundown on Alcatraz and Leonard Peltier," he said, "and he warned me to be careful about the websites that I went to and what I said over the phone. He said, 'You're the new generation.' I had never looked at it like that. I'm a working stiff, I go to school, and I'm not trying to create any problems. All that I am trying to do is entertain people with my music. He said, 'That's what makes you dangerous.'"

Having also built a close friendship with Milton "Quiltman" Sahme, Loma-Da-Wa invited Trudell's longtime accompanist to appear on his 2010 album, *Honor the People*. "He's an extremely spiritual person," said Loma-Da-Wa, "very in tune with the Earth. You don't have to teach him about recycling or alternative medicine. He's already doing it."

In addition to singing on the title track, Quiltman appeared on "Brother Leonard (Set Him Free)," Loma-Da-Wa's tribute to Leonard Peltier. "As that man sits in prison, and the older generation leaves us," said Loma-Da-Wa, "his legacy leaves with them. It's my responsibility, as an artist, to educate this new generation about his sacrifice."

Although reggae remained its foundation, *Honor the People* incorporated a wider range of influences. "We dabbled in different kinds of music," said Loma-Da-Wa. "People were pigeonholing me as a Hopi reggae artist and, though I didn't mind being associated with reggae, I did not want to be known as an 'American Indian musician.' I'm a musician who just happens to be Hopi."

The harsh life portrayed in his songs reflects Loma-Da-Wa's childhood memories. One of five boys and five girls born to a Hopi father and a Diné mother, he was steeped in Hopi traditions. "My father used to take me to ceremonies," he said, "and we would watch the katsinas (supernatural spirits) dance. My mom still prays in the traditional way."

Loma-Da-Wa's father, however, was an alcoholic, and his parents divorced before his teens. For the next few years, he went back and forth between his dad's home on the Hopi Reservation and his mother's home on the Navajo Reservation.

Turning to alcohol himself, Loma-Da-Wa was in danger of following his father's lead. Arrested for a minor offense, and sentenced to probation, he wound up in the Vision Quest Recovery Facility, a group home in Vancouver, B.C., for at-risk teens. It turned out to be the best thing that could have happened to him. In addition to receiving counseling and job training, he was able to participate and excel in sports. Enrolled in a school wilderness program, he lived in a tipi. He later rode a ten-speed bicycle from Tucson to St. Joe, Missouri, more than thirteen hundred miles away.

With his parents focused on their own difficulties, Loma-Da-Wa got most of his elder advice from his grandfather, Sankey Lomayesva. "He was a very kind man," he recalled, "always concerned with others. What he passed onto me was humility. He told me, 'You could be on top of the world, but, if you're not humble, you're not going to make it. You don't want to live like the Pahana [white man], but in tune with your spirit.' He taught me that. He was very instrumental in me finding myself, many times."

Loma-Da-Wa's grandfather endowed him with the nickname Casper. "I come from the Ghost Clan," he said, "but my grandfather gave me that name because he said that I would disappear. I still do it to this day. I might be hanging out with you one minute, and, if you turn around, by the time that you turn back, I will be gone. I am a social butterfly and cannot be in one place for too long. I want to experience life to the fullest."

One of the greatest breaks in Loma-Da-Wa's career came when he joined Micki Free (Cherokee/Comanche) and Crystal Shawanda (Anishnabekwe) for *Native Music Rocks*, a national tour of Hard Rock Cafés in 2009. The Seminole tribe of Florida—owners of all the Hard Rock Cafés but the one in Las Vegas—sponsored the tour that lasted from January to June. "Their operations manager, Tina Osceola, saw us at the Ah-Tah-Thi-Ki Seminole Indian Museum in Big Cypress, Florida," said Loma-Da-Wa, "and asked us to take part in President Obama's first inauguration. That was our introduction to the Seminole tribe."

In the midst of the *Native Music Rocks* tour, Loma-Da-Wa received an invitation to join a dozen other American Indian artists at Madison Square Garden in celebration of Pete Seeger's ninetieth birthday in May 2009. "It was one of the most amazing experiences of my career," he said. "I had played at the Jazz and Heritage Festival in New Orleans, twice, and the Kennedy Center, and Smithsonian [Institution], in Washington, D.C., but being on stage with the likes of Bruce Springsteen, Ben Harper, Dave Matthews, Michael Franti, Tom Morello, Kris Kristofferson, and Mr. Seeger, was incredible."

With his fourth album, *Brother's Keeper*, in 2011, Loma-Da-Wa reflected on deeply personal issues. "The title track talks about watching someone close to you die from alcoholism," he said. "I've lost six cousins, an uncle, and two brothers from alcoholism in the course of seven years. I lost an uncle, on my mother's side, from suicide. My younger brother Isaac's friends murdered him. They were high on crystal meth and alcohol. They got into a fight and beat him to death."

The father of two daughters, born in 1986 and 1988, and the husband of a hospice nurse, Loma-Da-Wa supplemented his music with full-time work as a land surveyor. Laid off in the economic recession, after working for an engineering company for fourteen years, in 2011 he returned to college in pursuit of a degree in child psychology. "The classes that I'm taking, sociology and psychology," he said, "coexist with what I've been putting out for years in music. My songs talk about things that I see going on around me."

JOHN WILLIAMS AND NATIVE ROOTS

The cofounder of Albuquerque, New Mexico–based Indigenous reggae band Native Roots, John Williams remembers driving to the Reggae Inna Hopiland shows from his Phoenix home, forty-five minutes away. "I saw so many top-notch reggae acts," Williams told me in September 2012, "people like Jimmy Cliff, Burning Spear, and Don Carlos."

Williams first heard reggae, in Cypress, California, as a high school exchange student. "I was staying in a Jamaican family's home," he said, "and they asked me if I had heard reggae music."

When he innocently replied that he knew about [New York–born calypso revivalist] Harry Belafonte, the family took Williams to where it kept its record player. For the next couple of hours, he got a crash course in Jamaica's music. "They played me Bob Marley, Jimmy Cliff," he remembered, "and Toots and the Maytals."

The intensifying wave of Native activism inspired Williams, who was a high school sophomore during the occupation of the Pine Ridge Reservation. "Our parents taught us to stand up for our rights," he said. "We were involved with changing the school system to where we weren't learning white man's history anymore. We wanted to learn about tribal government and the reality of where we are and who we are today. We took over the schools and the district offices and got the schools to change."

Environmental issues also drove Williams, especially the conflicts over the development of a ski resort—the Arizona Snowbowl—on San Francisco Peaks, north of Flagstaff, long revered as sacred by the Navajo and the Hopi. "We supported that struggle," said Williams, "along with the idea of being able to pray in our own way."

William's passion for reggae intensified as a member of AIM. "The movement latched on to Bob Marley," he said, "and everything that he stood for. We'd go to Flagstaff, spend the day in meetings singing powwow and AIM songs, then we'd jump into my pickup and listen to reggae."

As a youngster, Williams dreamed of playing drums. "I visualized everything in my head," he said, "so that, when I got my first drum set, I already knew how to play. No one had to show me what to do."

Years would pass, however, before Williams picked up his first drumsticks. "My mom forced me to play the piano," he recalled. "I hated it. When you grow up on a reservation, and you're a boy who plays the piano, you're asking for ridicule. I didn't want anyone to know about it, but, if she hadn't forced me to play, I wouldn't have gotten good at it. She felt that it was important for me to learn."

Believing that he would get a chance to play drums as a sixth grader, Williams could barely wait for that school year to begin. "I was so looking forward to it," he remembered. "Four days before school started, I came to audition for the school band and ran over to the drums. I was so happy, but the band director came over to me and said, 'You're not going to play drums. We already have too many drummers. You're going to play trombone.'"

Despite his protesting, the trombone expanded Williams's musical skills. "It strengthened my ear for music," he said. "As a trombone player, you learn to adjust the slide to the sound that you want, like with a violin or any other fretless instrument. I learned pitch very well."

When he finally got his chance to play drums in his late teens, Williams felt an instant affinity for the skank, offbeat rhythms of reggae. "When you listen to something so much," he said, "it becomes natural. Even when I was playing with a country band, I would drop the accents on the three whenever I could. No one knew; they would be dancing away. I'd get a few funny looks from the lead singer, but he didn't complain."

Williams's passion for syncopation remains at the heart of his keyboards playing. "I'm not like a pianist," he said, "going up and down the scales. I play it like a drum, with different rhythmic variations. A music teacher told me that Stevie Wonder plays the same way."

A Native Studies student at Phoenix College by day, Williams played bass with reggae groups, including the Roots Rebels, at night. "We were the first Native-reggae band," he said. "We were an instant hit. We played at the Grand Canyon, the Navajo Nation fairs, and the Apache celebrations."

Although he experienced success amid Phoenix's thriving music scene, family obligations forced Williams to move to Albuquerque. "My dad was nearing retirement age," he said, "and my parents were wondering where they were going to move. I was in Phoenix and my two sisters were in Albuquerque—I was outvoted."

Williams remained involved with a variety of musical projects, including producing recordings of Joy Harjo's spoken-word and early experiments with her band, Poetic Justice, and demos of his original tunes. Sending a rough cut of "The Place I Call Home," a song that he had written before leaving Phoenix, to an Albuquerque radio station, he received a phone call from a deejay, informing him that the record had aired and that the feedback had been amazing. Among the many calls that the deejay received was one from Emmett "Shkeme" Garcia of Santa Ana Pueblo, a budding singer and lyricist. Acting as an intermediary, the deejay passed Garcia's telephone number along to Williams, who invited Garcia to jam with him. "Right off the bat," Williams remembered, "it was 'boom!' A week later, we had four songs."

Raised in a small village eighteen miles north of Albuquerque, Garcia studied social work in Lawrence, Kansas, at Haskell Indian Nations University and at the University of Kansas. A skilled storyteller, he's authored several children's books. Polishing his skills as a vocalist by singing along to cassette tapes, he further whetted his distinct sound as a member of the Rio Grande Singers and the Gathering of Nations Dance Troupe. "I'm more into being the musician," said Williams, "taking care of the melodies, harmonies, rhythms, and the production, and he's into the lyrics and the singing. It makes for a really great combination."

With the addition of Williams's sister, Poetic Justice's ex-drummer Susan Williams; second lead guitarist and bassist Carlo Johnson; and Johnson's father, rhythm and lead guitarist Willie Bluehouse Johnson, Native Roots launched shortly after Williams and Garcia's meeting. The elder Johnson had been a member of XIT. "I had never heard anything integrating rock and Native music before XIT," said Williams. "They used American Indian beats with lyrics that were out of this world. Redbone was cool, but they looked like sellouts when you stood them next to XIT."

Willie Johnson's guitar playing figured prominently in Native Roots' early work, but his background was in blues and rock, not reggae, and the band's music often frustrated him. With his departure, Jason Garduno, a non-Native guitarist who had played with Bob Marley's son, Ky-Mani, and Peter Tosh's son, Andrew, replaced him. "We missed the natural, funky element [of Johnson's playing]," said Williams, "but Jason's guitar playing made up for it."

Although they added a second non-Native member when Joey Evans replaced Susan Williams on drums, Native Roots' message remained the same. "Some bands get into reggae music," said Williams, "because it's an opportunity. We never saw it that way. We play reggae because it's our choice of music."

A high school American Indian Studies teacher since 1984, Williams takes pride in Native Roots' academic achievements. "When my sister and Willie Bluehouse Johnson were still in the band," he said, "we represented the balance between education and art with an attorney on drums, a judge on guitar, and a high school teacher, with a master's degree, on bass and keyboards."

Releasing its debut album, *Place I Call Home*, on Warrior Records, a subsidiary of Sound of America Records (SOAR), in 1997, Native Roots hit its stride with its second effort, *Rain Us Love*—scoring a NAMMY as the "Best World Beat Recording of 2002." With their third album, *Celebrate*, five years later, they further solidified their standing as one of Indigenous America's top acts. In addition to scoring a NAMMY as "Best World Beat Recording," they received the award for "Group of the Year." "Each of our CDs has been a step up in terms of production," said Williams. "We're tighter than ever, but we're still not in a position to rest. We have to be constantly improving."

Preparing to record their fourth album, Native Roots has been debuting new songs at their concerts. "Our second CD was a little more produced than our first," said Williams, "and the third album got a little more into jazz, but we're reggae musicians and we want to go back to our roots. That's where our hearts are."

CLAN-DESTINE

Reggae, hip-hop, blues, salsa, funk, jazz, rock, and tribal influences converge through the music of Phoenix-based Clan-destine. One of the busiest bands of the late 1990s and early 2000s, they opened for country music artists like Willie Nelson, Alabama, Billy Ray Cyrus, Lorrie Morgan, and Pam Tillis, and appeared at powwows and art galleries throughout Indian Country. "We were able to put together some really cool sounds," said founding member, lead singer, percussionist, and didgeridoo player Juan "Cano" Sanchez (1970–) (Lakota), "and inject Native culture and spirituality into rock and roll."

Receiving a "Best Pop/Rock Album" NAMMY for their second album, *Deeply Roots*, in 2000, Clan-destine toured Germany twice. The reign of the band's original

Clan-destine continues to break into the mainstream with a fiery mix of reggae, hip-hop, blues, salsa, funk, jazz, rock, and tribal influences. *Courtesy Clan-destine.*

lineup, though, was brief. Shortly after releasing their third album, *Amajacoustic*, they disbanded, with members going in diverse directions. Multi-instrumentalist and songwriter Frank Poocha and his first cousin, guitarist Chuck Harris, continued to stir excitement as coleaders of the Native-rock band DAWA until late 2013, while a resurrected Clan-destine, organized by Cano Sanchez in late 2008 following an eight-year hiatus, continues to build on the original group's legacy.

Despite appearances by founding members, David Montour (Mohawk/Cayuga/Potowatomi), Harris, and Sanchez, the reorganized Clan-destine's debut album, *Operation Peace*, showed that much had changed. "It was a conscious choice," said Sanchez. "We wanted to write songs that showed off Native culture, but we wanted to say something meaningful too—close your eyes, look up at the sky, put your hands to the sky, [and] be at peace with the world and everyone around you—that's what *Operation Peace* is about."

Among the hottest topics addressed was sexuality, a theme threading several tunes. "My ancestors walked around naked," said Sanchez, "with no shame. They lived in lodges with the whole family living together in one room. I have a psychiatric background, and I've worked in hospitals with handicapped children, facilitating groups. I've seen teenaged pregnancy, Natives with a higher rate of AIDS, and a higher suicide rate. What we wanted to address was that American Indians were human."

One of the more-uplifting songs on *Operation Peace*, "We're on Our Way to Sugar Lake," was set to a Brazilian groove. "It's about a lake in Minnesota," explained Sanchez, "where Natives would come, in the spring and summer, and camp. The song is about driving there, but it's also about trying to preserve memories. Things are so hard and people are so tired, scared, and broke that it is important to remind them to open up, be their true selves."

Aiming for crossover, mainstream success, Clan-destine II updated its predecessor's sound with contemporary music influences. "We're still doing songs that we did before," said Sanchez, "but they are much different. We added a deejay/turntablist, Matthew Vaiza; a new drummer, Mike De La Torre, who knows about Afro-Latin, Afro-Cuban, and Afro-Brazilian beats; and a female vocalist, Rachel Villa. It gives us a whole different feel."

One of seven brothers and four sisters, Sanchez grew up listening to his siblings' record collections. "I remember listening to Led Zeppelin, Rick James, and Sly and the Family Stone," he said. "I remember getting into David Bowie's album, *Let's Dance*, because of the musicians that he used, especially Stevie Ray Vaughn. There was a hip-ness to it, yet it was still pop."

Sanchez dreamed of becoming a performer. "I remember wearing a suede jacket with fringes on it," he said, "and dancing around, pretending that I was Elvis Presley, when I was six years old."

The passion that Sanchez felt for rock and roll balanced with a lifelong involvement with traditional music. "I can remember hearing Apache songs played on the water drum," he said, "and I can remember that, when I'd be approaching a powwow, the drums in the distance would evoke something in me. It was more than a novelty. It was in my heart and I was drawn to it."

Though he launched his career with an American Indian dance troupe in Hawaii, Sanchez was encouraged to listen to a broad range of music. "My mother and father didn't differentiate between different kinds of music," he said. "They'd play a Johnny Cash record, a Beatles record, or a Freddy Fender record. Being of Spanish descent, my dad listened to Nortñeo records [from Mexico]. It was very mixed."

Sanchez remembers being rebellious as a child. "As soon as you'd tell me not to do something," he said, "I'd be doing it. If you told me not to go somewhere, I wanted to look through the keyhole and see why not. If someone told me not to drink or do drugs, I wouldn't take their word for it. I had to get the experience. I remember drinking when I was fourteen years old. I got into a lot of trouble and was sent to facilities."

Sanchez's "outlaw" period was brief. Arrested for public intoxication in his mid-teens, he made life-changing choices. Sitting alone in a jail cell, he became determined to turn things around before it was too late. "I haven't had a drink since," he said.

After singing with local rock and pop bands, Sanchez's path intersected with that of David A. Montour, one of Indigenous America's truly eclectic artists. As skilled in the visual arts as he is in music, Montour was an artist-in-residence at the Heard Museum for more than a decade, and received acclaim for his sculpting in stone and bronze, jewelry making, and Native American flute making. As a musician, he played flute for Keith Secola's Wild Band of Indians.

At the time he met Montour, at a community celebration in Tempe, Arizona, Sanchez was building momentum with his band, Rainbow Tribe. Releasing an independently produced EP, they had started fielding invitations to open shows for nationally touring acts. Montour's seemingly unlimited creativity, though, fascinated him. "I had broken my leg in a motorcycle accident," Sanchez remembered of their first meeting, "and it was the first day that I was able to walk after the accident. A friend had gotten me out of the house. I ended up sitting at a table, talking with David. We chatted for a moment, and, when I started walking away, he said, 'Hey, are you a singer?' Being young and cocky, I said, 'Yeah, did you see my band?' 'No, I just had a feeling.' From there, he told me that he was trying to put a group together. We scheduled a jam for the following week."

Disbanding Rainbow Tribe, Sanchez focused on his collaboration with Montour. "His concept," he explained, "was similar to what I was trying to do."

Assembling the original lineup of Clan-destine, the vocalist/dancer and the flute player drew musicians from Phoenix's thriving music scene. A graduate of the Musician Institute in Hollywood, California, Chuck Harris was a highly respected guitar instructor. Non-Native drummer Steve Gatlin had played with Rainbow Tribe.

For their most accomplished member, Frank Poocha, Clan-destine represented a chance to explore original music. A skilled saxophone, trumpet, keyboards, powwow drum, rattles, and bells player, and a passionate powwow singer, Poocha toured with (and produced) Joy Harjo and Poetic Justice and had been a founding member of the Rasta Farmers, one of the earliest Native reggae bands. "I write a lot of music," he said, "so I jumped at [Sanchez and Montour's] invitation. In the beginning, about 80 percent of the music was mine. I already had the songs complete in my head. I had the bass line and the rhythm and I knew what I wanted the melody to sound like. I just showed the others what to play."

First cousins Poocha and Harris grew up together on the Hopi Reservation. "We went to the same ceremonies to dance and sing," said Poocha. "He went to music school in Los Angeles, and I studied music education at Pima Community

College in Tucson, Arizona, but we knew that we would play together. He's an excellent guitarist and flutist and I do a little bit of everything."

The youngest son of a Pima mother, who taught fifth grade, and a Hopi father, who was a principal, Poocha learned the importance of education. "I do a lot of cultural awareness workshops for schools and other organizations," he said. "I sing powwow songs, and songs in Pima, Navajo, and Hopi, and I play traditional instruments, like drum, rattles, and bells. Music is a valuable teaching tool. My mom and dad not only taught me to share our culture, but to learn about, and respect, other religions and cultures too."

Poocha's love of music was evident early on. "My older brother played trumpet in high school," he said. "I used to sneak his trumpet out of the closet when no one was around, and try to play it."

In addition to playing with junior high and high school bands, Poocha marched with the Navajo Tribal Band and the Hopi Tribal Band. Although he began college as a business administration major, he realized his "mistake" after joining the school's jazz band, and transferred to music education. "I learned music theory," he said, "how to play the guitar and piano, and I built on my trumpet playing."

From the start, Clan-destine aimed for widespread success. "We didn't want to be just another Native band," said Poocha, "with musicians standing around and jamming. We wanted to move all over the stage and be choreographed and dynamic. We were one of the first Native bands to do that. The sky was the limit. We did not put any limitations on what we did. It was an art form."

Clan-destine performed many of their early shows at American Indian venues, where Montour would be hired to play and the rest of the band would accompany him. "People wanted to hear Native-oriented things," said Sanchez. "We played a lot at the Heard Museum. Whenever they'd have a reception, guests wanted to hear Native beats, flutes, and chants."

Clan-destine's fan base continued to expand. "We had a regular gig at the Electric Ballroom," said Sanchez, "a 2,500-seat, two-room club. When we started, we played to almost nobody. Dave was very entrepreneurial when it came to promoting our shows, though, and, before we knew it, we were packing the place. There'd be a line out the door."

Signing with Canyon, Clan-destine was extremely hopeful when their eponymous-titled debut album was released in 1996. "[Canyon] had approached Dave to do a flute record," said Sanchez, "but he didn't want to do that. He felt that, for him, it would be too one-dimensional, so he pitched the band."

Clan-destine recorded the album as a live performance on a soundstage, with few overdubs. "It was mostly done in one take," said Sanchez. "We recorded and mixed everything in two days."

Members of Clan-destine had a harsh awakening when the album failed to sell. "Canyon was very limited as to where they could promote us," said Sanchez, "and by how much of a budget they had. We had gotten offers from Warner Brothers and Sony Music, but they wanted us to be a novelty act. We were paying homage to our ancestors and didn't want be a novelty."

The disappointment left some members of Clan-destine disillusioned with the music business. "We learned that you needed money for promotion and distribution," said Sanchez. "It doesn't need to be a million dollars, but a few thousand would have been nice."

Preparing to record a follow-up album—*Deeply Rooted*—Clan-destine spoke with several labels before electing to release it on their own Rezdawgs label. "It turned out great," said Sanchez. "We ended up getting gigs, being able to tour, and making a decent living, without having to sign everything away."

With the addition of Derek Davis, a seven-time world champion, hoop dancer, Clan-destine reached new heights as an American Indian band. "It helped launch us into what we had aspired to be," said Sanchez, "the new day warriors, using music as a vehicle."

Released in late 1999, *Deeply Rooted* took Native America by force. "I'm still amazed at how much respect we got," said Sanchez. "We took what everybody had been feeling and added elements of music that Natives were listening to—rock, blues, Waila, and powwow. When we integrated the Native spirit into rock and reggae, people could listen to it and have the best of both worlds."

Clan-destine continued to celebrate their heritage at the NAMMY ceremonies when *Deeply Rooted* was named "Best Pop/Rock Album of 2000." "At the time, we had been learning honor songs," recalled Sanchez. "Derek was showing us more aspects of our culture and getting us to incorporate more traditional beats. When we went up to receive the award, I didn't want to give the same speech that I hear everyone give every year, so we just put our hands together, raised the award in the sky, and sang an honor song. The reaction was amazing."

Clan-destine's third album, *Amajacoustic*, in December 2000, emphasized traditional roots and included old-world-meets-the-new tunes, including "Rez Dawgs," "Blue Flute," and "Song for Suwaime." The group's spirit, though, had begun to wane. "We had been touring for a decade,' said Sanchez, "and we had our suitcases always packed. We would do things like flying back from Germany at 6 A.M., Phoenix time, running to the rehearsal warehouse, picking up our gear, driving to a show, playing for 8,000 people, packing up, taking the equipment back to the warehouse, repacking our suitcases, and flying out the next morning to Michigan. We did things like that nonstop."

"We were making a living," he continued, "but in order for our families to not be living hand-to-mouth, we had to make so much money. Dave and I pushed to get corporate funding, and we did some shows for Coca-Cola, but, everybody was just too tired."

Poocha was the first to leave. "It was a management thing," he said. "We started making a whole lot of money opening for major acts—$7,500 to $10,000 a show, for a forty-five-minute set. I was trying to hold the management accountable for the funds, but I never got any straight answers. I started questioning the money trail and finally got fed up with it and left."

Chuck Harris followed shortly afterwards. With Clan-destine in splinters, Sanchez did what he could to keep things going. "We still had contracts for gigs," he said, "and some endorsement deals. I performed for another three years with pickup musicians. We even toured with Willie Nelson. We didn't record, but we were still staying very valid as a live act."

Discussions with Tom Bee, who wanted to release the band's next album on SOAR, fell apart over artistic differences. "He wanted us to do a hard-rock record," said Sanchez, "something like Guns and Roses."

Instead, Sanchez gathered four original tunes—"What UC," "Nightflight," "Make It Right," and "Is It Enough"—and recorded an EP, *Cano Huma*, with help from Clan-destine members.

The founding bandmates next came together for a special concert at the National History Museum of the Smithsonian Institution, in Washington, D.C. "They wanted the original members," said Sanchez, "so I made some phone calls and got everyone back together. We played some shows, and then we really started working together again and getting stuff going."

Although the reunion progressed into Clan-destine II, Poocha and Harris, who had performed as a duo since their departure from the group, yearned to return to their own music. After several aborted attempts to put together a new band (DAWA), the cousins succeeded in assembling a solid lineup that included bassist/guitarist/vocalist Rudy Chavez (Pasqua Yaqui), drummer/vocalist Johnny Laurence (Hopi/Assiniboine), bassist/percussionist Jon Allen "Brad" Black (Cherokee), and lead singer/keyboardist/percussionist Patrick Murillo (Chicano). "We rehearsed a lot," said Poocha, "and got an arsenal of music together before doing our first shows. We set ourselves up to be successful."

DAWA's debut video, *A Joyful Defiant Tone*, premiered in February 2012. "It came from one of the hurricanes that hit the Caribbean islands," said Poocha. "Chuck came up with the title when he was watching TV. He saw the city obliterated and people out in the streets. The news showed a group of women—mothers and grandmothers—singing in their language. No matter what hit them, nothing could take away the happiness and joy that they had for their families and children.

They were going to sing, and be joyful, but they were also going to be defiant. If they were knocked down, they would just get back up and sing louder."

INDIGENOUS

Fiery guitar playing, powerhouse rhythms, and dusty, baritone vocals have propelled Mato Nanji (Mah-toe Nan-gee) and Indigenous into contemporary music's mainstream. "I have a different take on rock and the blues," said the Lakota/Dakota guitarist/bandleader. "It's a mixture of all of the old guys—Jimi Hendrix, Stevie Ray Vaughn, and Carlos Santana—and newer, edgier stuff."

Releasing an independent album, *Live Blues from the Sky*, in 1995, Indigenous continued their ascent with *Love in a Mist* a year later. With the release of *Things We Do*—their first album recorded at Pachyderm Recording Studios in Cannon Falls, Minnesota, thirty-five miles south of the Twin Cities—in 1999, they broke through nationally. Released on the studio's label, it spawned three hit singles—"Things We Do," "Got to Tell You," and "Now That You're Gone"—and reached the twenty-second slot on *Billboard*'s Mainstream Rock chart. Indigenous received a NAMMY for "Best Album," "Best Group," and "Best Pop Group." Amazon named them "Blues Artist of the Year." "It was a special record," said Nanji, "the first time that we had gone into a great studio with a producer. We had done recordings that we'd sell out of our car, but this was the first time that we were able to concentrate on getting it done the right way."

A video of the title track received a "Best Music Video" award at the American Indian Film Festival in San Francisco. "We performed the song [at the award ceremonies]," said Nanji. "It was pretty cool, a lot of fun."

A summer-long tour as opening act of B. B. King's Blues Festival brought Indigenous further exposure. "We did sixty shows across the country," said Nanji. "Tower of Power was [on the bill]. Taj Mahal did a few dates, Robert Cray, Jimmie Vaughn, and Kenny Wayne Shepard. We were in a different city every night. It was awesome, a really good experience."

Indigenous, which originally included Nanji's brother, "Little Buffalo Man" (Ptehcaka "Pte" [peh-TEE] Wicasa) on bass; his sister, "Good Eagle Woman" (Wanbdi [wan-ba-DEE] Waste Win) on drums; and their cousin, Tasunka (or Horse) on congas, timbales, bongo, and tambourine, followed *Things We Do* with a live-in-the-studio album, *Live at Pachyderm Studio 1998*. Going on to score a "Best Blues Album" NAMMY, the album included a twelve-plus-minute-long rendition of Jimi Hendrix's slow blues classic, "Red House." "It didn't say it on the album," said Nanji, "but [the recording session] was a private party. A bunch of people came into the studio and we played."

Indigenous reached its commercial peak, as an independent artist, with *Circle* in 2000. Produced by Texas songwriter Doyle Bramlett, the album reached number twelve on the *Billboard* charts, with two top ten AAA singles—"Rest of My Days" and "Little Time."

Moving to a major label, Sony-owned Zomba/Silvertone, in 2003, Indigenous veered toward a broader sound. Their eponymous-titled debut for the label was a throwback to the power blues-rock trios of the early 1970s.

Indigenous released a self-produced EP, *Long Way Home*, with five new originals, and a live recording of "Things We Do," in 2007, but band members were no longer as enthusiastic as they had been in the beginning. "Everybody was slowing down," remembered Nanji. "My brother wanted to start his own group and my sister didn't feel like touring anymore. It was time to make a move."

With his sister and cousin going their separate ways, Nanji was determined to keep Indigenous going. Signing a three-album deal with Vanguard Records, he hired studio musicians and recorded *Chasing the Sun* in 2006. "My brother played bass," he said. "It was one of the last records that we did together. We brought in a great drummer from Minneapolis, Michael Bland, who used to play with Prince. For me, it was a cool experience. I was able to play with different musicians and get a whole new flavor."

Continuing to write songs with his wife, Leah, with whom he had cowritten most of the songs on *Indigenous*, Nanji accumulated a backlog of material. Recording twenty songs during the *Chasing the Sun* sessions, he had a dozen songs left over for *Broken Lands* in 2008.

Broken Lands signaled a departure from Indigenous's original hard rock and blues sound. "The Eagles were a big influence on me," said Nanji. "The way that they approach their music is really soulful. It has a feeling that you cannot really explain. If it feels good, and makes you feel good, that's what it's supposed to do."

The Acoustic Sessions, released in 2010, further emphasized Nanji's subtler influences. With his wife on background vocals; producer/engineer Jamie Candiloro (Ryan Adams, REM, Willie Nelson, the Eagles) on keyboards, percussion, and background vocals; and Lisa Germano on violin, the album featured stripped-down versions of songs spanning Indigenous's first decade. "I had never recorded a full acoustic album before," said Nanji. "It provided a look at what I do when I'm sitting down and writing a song."

The album also included Nanji's interpretation of Roy Orbison's 1989 top ten hit, "You Got It." "I've always loved Roy Orbison," he said, "and I've always been a fan of Sam Cooke. I've always loved great singers."

Hailing from the Yankton Indian Reservation in southeastern South Dakota, Nanji and his siblings were home-schooled and immersed in Native culture. "I love hearing Navajo flute playing," he said. "It's such a beautiful musical instrument. I've used traditional flute licks and melodies and they've added a creative aspect to my playing."

From an early age, the Nanji children were encouraged to create their own music. Their father, Greg Zephier, who had played guitar with a Native rock band, the Vanishing Americans, was happy to teach them what he knew. "We had old amps and guitars in our basement when I was growing up," recalled Nanji. "That's where I got into it."

As they grew into teenagers, Nanji and his siblings became more serious about music. "We started becoming a band when I was fifteen or sixteen years old," said Nanji. "Of course, my sister wanted to play the drums and sing."

Though they showed natural talent, Zephier was determined that they sharpen their skills before bringing their music to the public. "My dad cracked down on us," remembered Nanji, "and made us practice for a year. We spent most of our time at home, rehearsing, and learning songs."

The discipline paid off. Once they were "allowed" to perform their first show, Indigenous was off and running. "We started playing in clubs around the area— Nebraska, Minnesota, Iowa, and, even here in South Dakota," said Nanji. "We couldn't really go to a lot of bars without our parents being there. We were all underage."

An electric album, *Indigenous Featuring Mato Nanji*, in 2012, represented a step toward the future, while the return of Nanji's brother, Pte, brought things full circle. "He's been coming on the road with us and playing percussion," said Nanji. "It's so good to have him back, playing music with me again."

Since regrouping, Nanji and Indigenous have continued to gain steam. Their 2013 album, *Vanishing Americans*, received a "Blues Album of the Year" NAMMY, with Nanji being named "Artist of the Year."

Nanji has continued to pursue outside projects. He toured with Chicago-born neo-blues visionary Otis Taylor, whose 2013 album, *My World Is Gone*, focused on Native issues. With recharged energies, and a growing repertoire of great tunes, Nanji is aiming to take Indigenous's music far from the reservation. "We've got such a huge Native fan base," he said, "but we want to be color-blind. We want to reach an international audience and tour worldwide."

THE PLATEROS

Indigenous America's newest guitar hero is Levi Mitchell Platero (1994–), leader of the exciting blues-rock trio the Plateros. Before his twenty-second birthday, Platero (Diné) is already a veteran of more than a dozen years as a top string-slinger.

"When I was young, I listened to a lot of Jimi Hendrix, Iron Maiden, Black Sabbath, and Buddy Holly," Platero told me in October 2011. "I was into Ritchie Valens and Santana, but, once I got into playing the guitar, my interests shifted to metal bands because of the riffs and the clean sweep of guitar leads. Mainstream music caught my ear, things like Smashing Pumpkins, Weezer, and John Mayer, but I seem to have grown out of that and gone back to the music's source."

A family band, the Plateros includes the young guitarist and his cousins, Douglas Platero on drums and Bronson Begay, who replaced his father, Murphy Platero, on bass. "Music just flows out of us," he said. "We've never sat down and said, 'Let's make up a good riff.' It comes out of the moment. We're cousins, but we've grown closer together and we're more like brothers."

Platero grew up on the Tohajiilee Indian Reservation, the eastern agency of the Diné Nation, about thirty-five miles from Albuquerque, where he still lives. "I consider it more a community than a reservation," he said. "We're so far away from the big Navajo reservation. I never got around to knowing the people in the community. I would see them at the store, in Albuquerque, but I never really knew them. Most of the people that I knew were family."

The roots of Diné music greatly influenced Platero's playing. "I love listening to the Navajo flute," he said. "It's such a beautiful musical instrument. I've used traditional licks and melodies as a creative aspect of my playing."

Gospel music provided an additional foundation. "My dad's mom and dad were in the first Diné gospel group to accompany their singing with musical instruments," said Platero, "but it never occurred to me that that was anything unusual. I thought every family was like that, though I now feel blessed to have had that history. It molded the music that I play. A spiritual side takes over. It's a feeling that can't be explained through words, but it's a feeling that I want to show the world."

Teaching himself to play drums and guitar, Platero's father, Murphy (1963–), joined his parents and uncle's musical ministry at the age of eleven. Together with his brother Eugene, who is Douglas's father, he formed a country-rock gospel group, the Harvesters, later known as the Morning Star Band, in 1984.

When they separated to start families, the two brothers began ministries of their own. Eugene and his wife, Marita, moved to the Navajo Nation township of Kenyenta, Arizona, and started a band, while Murphy and the former Janice Yazzie formed a Christian country-rock group, Hidden Manna.

Levi started playing drums at the age of seven. "Sometimes, I'd sit in for my dad's drummer," he said. "My mom usually played bass. I did that for two years."

Warned by his father that there were already "enough drummers in the world," Platero switched to the guitar before his tenth birthday. His experience as a

The Plateros (Diné) is a power-rock trio led by teenage guitar wiz Levi Platero.
Courtesy the Plateros.

drummer helped him to advance quickly. "It gave me rhythm," he said. "I had beats incorporated into my mentality. I learned very early that, if you do not have rhythm, you are just hitting a bunch of notes. I transferred what I knew from the drums to the guitar. It helped a lot."

Stevie Ray Vaughn provided an early influence. "The first song that I learned was Stevie Ray's 'Pride and Joy,'" said Platero, "and the next was 'Crossfire.' It had no rhythm guitar on it, just a series of licks, but I experienced what being a lead guitarist felt like. When I went back to playing rhythm, the low E chord, shuffling boogie, came naturally to me. I was able to play lead and rhythm, at the same time, after about a year, but I kept pushing myself."

Platero made his debut as a guitarist when he joined his father's band in a small church in Birdspring, Arizona. "I remember my dad telling me to come up to the stage," he said. "It was nerve wracking, but I told myself, 'This is what I want to do.'"

Cousin Douglas soon joined the pubescent guitarist. "When I first started playing guitar," remembered Platero, "I'd set up my amp and play for a couple of hours. Douglas would hear me jamming. Sometimes, he would come over and set up his drums. Once we started getting it together, my dad picked up his bass and started jamming with us. We learned four or five songs and that was it—the Plateros."

The Plateros made the first of what would become semiregular appearances at the Gathering of Nations with a twenty-minute set in April 2005. "It was my first time performing at a gathering" recalled Platero, who had not yet reached his thirteenth birthday, "or, even, a powwow, but once we got on the stage, it flowed. I had as much fun as I could. I was a pre-teenager, but I wasn't cocky, I just wanted to play music."

After the senior Platero retired from the band in 2010, in order to focus on its management, Bronson Begay replaced him on bass. "He comes from close to Kansas," said Levi. "The first time that we played together, it clicked, but I went back to playing with my dad. We kept in touch. He came up for a couple of months and started playing organ and piano for us. We became a quartet for a while. Then, when my dad stepped down, he took over the bass. He's a great guitar player, one of the best blues players I have heard in a long time. He's also a great backup singer. His pitch is high and he can harmonize really well."

Despite his success as a musician, Platero continued his education. "My mom would have killed me [if I had dropped out]," he said. "It came to a point where I wasn't going to graduate, but my mom told me, 'You could do it.' She said, 'I want you to graduate. You can't do anything without a high school diploma.'" I just sat and sat, with my nose in the books. Everyone in my family doubted me, but I pushed the extra two miles and got it done."

Platero was almost as excited about graduating from high school as he was about music. "I went to the administrator's office, and got my diploma," he said. "I looked at it, looked at everybody in the room, and, as soon as they said, 'Congratulations,' I took the diploma and ran out of the school as fast as I could go—I had a gig to get to."

5 DIVAS, HIP-HOPPERS, AND ELECTRONIC DANCE MASTERS

"We've always done everything on our own. That's the way we like it. It gives us a great sense of pride. We've never had to sell out to any degree."

—Darren Brulé, ex-Reddnation (Cree)

FELIPE ROSE AND THE VILLAGE PEOPLE

Formed in Greenwich Village in 1977, the Village People dominated late '70s and '80s pop music with disco hits, including "Macho Man," "In the Navy," "Go West," and (as any sports fan or cover band knows) "YMCA." Chosen as much for their dancing and theatricality as for their singing, members dressed as stereotypical characters—the police officer, the soldier, the construction worker, the cowboy, and the biker. "We were blazingly in people's face," said the Village People's Brooklyn-born "Native American," Felipe Rose (1954–).

Rose's portrayal was more than an act. His mother, a nightclub dancer in the 1940s and '50s, was a Puerto Rico–born, part-Taino Indian who moved to New York at the age of seven. His father was full-blooded Lakota from Colorado. "It was who I was," explained Rose, "and everything that I knew. I can't change what happened with our ancestors, or if the United States belonged to American Indians and treaties were broken, but I can be a representative of what's to come."

In collaboration with coproducer and multi-instrumentalist Frosty Lawson (Frost Bite Productions), Rose used respites from the Village People's schedule to explore his Indigenous roots. Launching an independent production company (Tomahawk), he released the first of an ongoing series of Native American–infused dance singles—"Trail of Tears"—in 2001. The NAMMY named it the year's "Best Historical Performance," with Rose and Lawson also sharing "Best Producer"

Felipe Rose (Lakota/Taino/Hispanic) rose to international fame as the stereotypical "American Indian" of disco superstars the Village People, but his portrayal reflects his own roots. *Courtesy Felipe Rose.*

honors. "It's such a dynamic tune, incorporating modern dance, and pop, with Native American influences," said Lawson. "We did it for the pure joy of writing it."

Inspired by John Ehle's book, *Trail of Tears: The Rise and Fall of the Cherokee Nation,* the song had deep personal meaning for Lawson. "My great-great-grandmother's parents died on the Trail of Tears," he said. "We had already written the song when I found out that my ancestors had actually been there."

Historical references are sprinkled throughout the tune. "At one point, [Rose] sings about 'Cherokee Rose,'" said Lawson. "That refers to the legend that wherever Native Americans died on the Trail of Tears, flowers grew for every tear that was shed."

Rose's performance of "Trail of Tears," with accompaniment by Native and non-Native instrumentation and a stage full of regalia-clad dancers at the NAMMY ceremony in September 2002, still resonates with those lucky enough to have experienced it. "They still haven't topped it," said Rose. "The most amazing part of that evening," he continued, "happened when I was waiting to take my seat after the performance. I was standing behind Keith Secola. For me, he's like Bob Dylan. I managed to tell him that. He said, 'Really? Wow, cool, man.' We became friends and hung out together in Arizona. It was nice to reconnect with that part of my world and heritage."

Released the following year, Rose's second solo effort, "We're Still Here—The Virginia Indians Tell Their Story," scored a "Song/Single of the Year" NAMMY. Inspiration for the tune had sparked as Rose and Lawson worked on a tribute album for Thomasina "Red Hawk" Jordan (1940–1999), a songwriter, poet, and hip-hop rapper who had been active in the struggle for federal recognition of Virginia's American Indian tribes. "I celebrated her life through music," said Rose.

Rose's third solo single, and his third straight NAMMY winner, "Red Hawk Woman," paid further homage to Jordan's memory. "We took a portion of [Jordan] reading one of her children's stories," said Lawson, "and put it onto the track."

When we spoke in July 2012, Rose and Lawson had been working on their next single, "Lost Bird at Wounded Knee," for two years. "It's based on the December 1890 massacre," said Lawson. "When the firing began, a mother tried to protect her baby [Lost Bird, or Zinka Lanuni], but she was shot and killed. As troops were going through the aftermath, they heard the baby's cry. Gen. Leonard Colby, who found her, adopted her. She went through a lot of abuse, had a very tough life, and died at twenty-nine. We wrote about it, and it turned out to be a grandiose production. The material is so emotional; it hits really hard."

A month after the Village People received a star along Hollywood's Walk of Fame in November 2008, Rose gained admittance into the Native American Music Hall of Fame. "That was a doubly good time," he said to me. "I've been very blessed."

Though his American Indian heritage connects with his paternal roots, Rose knew little of his father. "He and my mom met in Manhattan," he said. "He had relocated to New York to work as a welder in the 1950s. My mom was on her way to dance at a club when she saw him, at a construction site, on a steel girder."

The romance was brief. "When he found out that [my mother] was Puerto Rican," said Rose, "he ran to the hills. Actually, it was because her Pentecostal family did not understand American Indians. They had come from Puerto Rico and they knew nothing about Native culture. As far as they were concerned, he was an alien."

After his parents divorced—before his second birthday—Rose continued to live in his mother's Puerto Rican–influenced home. "Latin and Salsa dancers and musicians, like Mongo Santamaria, Pepé Castillo, and August San Juan, would hang out and party," he remembered.

Rose remained connected to his Hispanic roots. During a two-year break from the Village People in the mid-1980s, he performed with the Latin music superstar

Tito Puente (1923–2000) at the Red Parrot Disco in midtown New York. "That was exciting," he said. "I danced a salsa/Apache kind of dance with Sheree Rodriguez, and he backed us up. At the rehearsal, I was so nervous that we weren't going to have enough time. I thought that we'd need at least a couple more hours of rehearsal, but he broke it down and made it easy. That was his genius."

One of his father's sisters, who lived in New York, provided Rose with a connection to his Native roots. "She told me that I had to celebrate that side of my heritage, too," he remembered. "She said that I was a shadow walker and that I should know that I'm from both worlds."

Rose's early passion for music was sparked when he heard Michael Jackson's chart-topping theme for *Ben*—the 1973 sequel to the Daniel Mann–directed horror film, *Willard*, of the previous year. "When I heard that song," he recalled, "I knew I wanted to be in the music business. I grew up listening to the Jackson 5. There was something about that song, and the way that he sang it, that connected with me."

Dance also drew Rose's attention. Sponsored by a scholarship, he danced with Downtown Ballet of Puerto Rico, a New York–based group directed by choreographer Pascal Guzman. "We did a ballet," said Rose, "*Julia de Burgos*, at Lincoln Center."

During weekend breaks, Rose transformed into an American Indian. "I'd put on my Native gear," he said, "and dance in clubs, balancing both worlds. It was everything that I wanted to be and how I wanted to live. They called me a 'dancer/percussionist.' You could hear the sleigh bells that I wore around my ankles."

Even amid New York's burgeoning nightlife, Rose stood out. When French producer Henri Belolo, who had discovered the Philadelphia-based disco superstars the Ritchie Family, saw the regalia-clad dancer, sparks flew. "He wanted me to play bells on a Ritchie Family album," said Rose. "Then, he said, 'No, no, forget it. I have a bigger idea.' That turned out to be the Village People. I was at the right place at the right time."

The Village People brought international fame and financial security, but Rose was uncomfortable with the stereotyping. "Casablanca Records wouldn't use my whole heritage in our publicity," he said. "There aren't many things that I would have changed, but that was one of the things that I should have insisted on."

Rose's recent projects include a comic book, *Swift Arrow*, illustrated by Lawson's daughter, Morgan, with text by Vincent Schilling, in which his animated likeness portrays a superhero defender of the environment. "I wanted to embrace the cartoon side of myself," Rose explained, "and use it to address some serious situations. If I did it in the real world, people would think I was speaking out of line, so I did it as a comic book character."

JANA MASHONEE

Born a year before the Village People formed, Jana Maria Mashonee (1976–) rose to the apex of contemporary dance music in the mid-1990s. Her first releases included a top forty *Billboard* Hot Dance Music hit ("What Am I to You"), a *Billboard* pop single of the week ("Ooh Baby Baby"), and an infectious, techno-dance tune ("More Than Life") that would be included on numerous compilations and sell more than a million copies. For her fourth single, she transformed Led Zeppelin's "Stairway to Heaven" into a fiery disco tune that reached number seven on *Billboard*'s Hot Dance Singles charts. "I'm an urban Indian," Mashonee told me, "walking in two worlds. We have our traditional culture and we go to ceremonies, powwows, and sweats, but we're also lawyers, doctors, and people living in a society that's not on the reservation."

Mashonee's repertoire includes mid-tempo ballads, pop tunes, digitized rock, and modern Native American originals. "My forte is not up-tempo," said the eight-time NAMMY recipient. "I'll reserve the dance stuff for people who remix my songs. They can speed them up."

The daughter of a Lumbee father and Lumbee/Tuscarora mother, Mashonee has balanced mainstream recordings with musical explorations of her cultural roots. Her second album, *American Indian Christmas* (2005), featured holiday classics translated and sung in a variety of Native languages. "A lot of preparation went into researching the songs," she said, "and deciding what languages to do them in. I went through tribal councils to make sure that it was okay. Then I had to find ten language advisers to translate them and help me with the pronunciations. I'm not fluent in any of the languages."

Blending powwow drums, Indigenous flutes, and electronic instruments, choral chanting, and soaring lead vocals in English, Native languages, and vocables, Mashonee's third album, *American Indian Story* (2006), is one of modern Native America's masterpieces. The recipient of a NAMMY as the year's "Best Pop Album"—with "Producer of the Year" honors going to Mashonee's manager/accompanist/collaborator/producer Stephan Galfas—and a Grammy nominee as well, it told the fictitious, coming-of-age tale of a young American Indian girl at the time of the First Encounter. Transformed into a book, which was coauthored with Galfas, Mashonee's story published in 2012. "[Sha'kana] comes from the past," she said, "but she's contemporary, too, like me."

A video of one of *American Indian Story*'s most dynamic songs, "Enlightened Time," received a NAMMY for "Best Short Form Music Video," a Queens International Film Festival award for "Best Domestic Music Video," and a Native

Jana Mashonee (Lumbee/ Tuscarora) became the first American Indian to score a *Billboard* top-ten dance hit, but she's alternated between pop recordings and album-length celebrations of Indigenous roots. *Courtesy Jana Mashonee.*

American Film and Video award for "Best Music Video." "It's a very positive tune," said Mashonee, "very uplifting and spiritual."

Mashonee's embracing of her roots contrasts with how she viewed her heritage as a child. Born in the tri-racial Robson County city of Lumberton, in southeastern North Carolina, where she was one of 45,000 assimilated American Indians, she grew up in Baltimore, Maryland, and Charlotte, North Carolina, where she felt alone. "I hated being Native American," she remembered. "I didn't appreciate the culture; I resented it. I would have to do my 'Native thing' and hang out with other Native kids, make my regalia, and do things that were Native, but I did not like it. It made me different, which I did not want to be."

Despite her protests, Mashonee's parents were determined she experience her culture. "Religious music is a big part of the Lumbee community," she said, "and there's a unique interplay between traditional music and gospel music. I grew up singing in the church."

Mashonee's father, who sang with a Beatles-like band, the Sparks, encouraged her love of music. "He's a great singer," she said, "with a deep, Elvis Presley–like vibrato. He could have been a Sinatra-like balladeer, but the Sparks did up-tempo rock and pop songs. They had a couple of regional hits in North Carolina."

As a youngster, Mashonee studied jazz and tap dancing, tried her hand at guitar, and learned to play Native flute and piano. "It helps that I'm a well-rounded musician," she said. "I'm not as versatile an instrumentalist as I'd like to be, but I write on the piano and play flute during my shows. I tried to play my brother Jamison's drums, but I couldn't do it. For many years, I hated him for playing so well."

The "professional" rivalry, however, had little effect on the siblings' respect for each other. "If I asked Jamison to come with me on a big tour," Mashonee warned, "and he told me, 'no,' I'd disown him as a brother."

Mashonee made her stage debut—as Jana Marie—with a weekend cover band, Peace and Love, in the clubs of Charlotte, North Carolina. "The guy who played bass was from [Atlanta-based R&B band] the Voltage Brothers," she said. "We played R&B and funk. I love soulful music. It was such a fun time."

During a performance with Peace and Love, Mashonee caught the ear of Rodney Shelton, a drummer, keyboardist, songwriter, and producer who, as a member of an R&B group, Curio, released an album—*Special Feeling*—on Motown in 1990. He had also penned Keith Washington's chart-topping 1991 R&B hit, "Kissing You." "[Shelton] came up to me," recalled Mashonee, "not because he wanted me to be his next artist, but because he wanted me to demo his artist's record. She already had a record deal."

Mashonee agreed to work with Shelton as a demo singer. "It was an opportunity to be in a studio," she said. During one session, Mashonee delivered a jaw-dropping take of a song that she was demo-ing. "[Shelton] liked my version so much," she recalled, "that he said that he would see if he could get me a record deal. I thought that was hilarious. I had not thought about anything like that. I was still in school, going to Davidson College, near Charlotte, and studying psychology. I was in my junior year."

Much to Mashonee's surprise, Shelton came through. Curb Records agreed to sign her. The songstress, however, was not quite ready. "I could have quit school," she said, "and moved to Los Angeles, where the record company was, but I felt that it was important to get my education. I had one more year left. They waited for me and did not release the record until I graduated. For me, it was more important to get my degree."

For the first of four singles, label executives persuaded Mashonee to cover Smokey Robinson and the Miracles' 1965 hit, "Ooh Baby Baby." "I think it's superficial," she said, "the ultimate teenybopper song; I wanted to gag. I sang it because I needed the studio experience. I didn't know that they were going to release it, but it got me the most airplay of any song I have ever had. It's easily digestible."

Mashonee proposed the revamped "Stairway to Heaven." "I wanted to do something that was completely off-the-wall," she said. "When I first did it, especially in the New York area, people couldn't believe it, but it got me a lot of attention."

Returning to the more mainstream sound of her 2005 debut album, *Flash of a Firefly,* Mashonee's fourth outing, *New Moon Born* (2010), was the first release on Miss Molly Records, the SONY-distributed label that she started with Galfas. It incorporated a wide range of influences. "It's more bluesy and soulful," she said, "and more introspective. I grew up listening to Barbara Streisand. She's my number-one singer. The mastery of her vocal technique—how she holds notes and phrases things—astounds me. I like Alicia Keys, too; she's so soulful and truthful about her music."

With the release of the CD's first single, "A Change Is Gonna Come," featuring guitarist Derek Miller (Mohawk), Mashonee expanded on the immortal Civil Rights ballad. "Sam Cooke's recording can't be re-created," she said, "but I wanted to do my own version. It was important to me; it provided the motif for the album. We were finished with the studio, and had done all of the songs that we had planned, but I begged them to let me do it."

Mashonee's persistence paid off. Debuted as part of her performance at President Obama's Inauguration Ball in January 2009, her interpretation went on to score "Best Song/Single" and "Best R&B Recording" NAMMYs.

Appearing in a romantic comedy, *Dream Weaver,* starring Wes Studi (Cherokee), in 2002, Mashonee had a cameo in Holt Hamilton's independent comedy, *Blue Gap Boy'z,* six years later. She also appeared in *Raptor Ranch,* a campy, sci-fi comedy that premiered at the Berlin Film Festival in February 2012. "We shot it in Texas and Russia," she said. "It's definitely not an Academy Award–winner. That's for sure."

PBS-TV filmed Mashonee, along with percussionist Tony Redhouse (Diné) and flutist Mary Youngblood, during a November 2010 performance in San Jose, New Mexico, as part of a yet-to-be-aired series, *Pure Native,* spotlighting modern Indigenous musicians. "We're supposed to do a part two," she said, "and we're crossing our fingers that Buffy Sainte-Marie will be involved, as well as Crystal Gayle."

The first American Indian–owned label sold in Walmart, Miss Molly Records took its name from Mashonee's grandmother. "I thought it was cool to pay homage to her," she explained. "She was such a wonderful woman. The logo is a photo of her."

Miss Molly continues to build on its roster of artists. "We have a Spanish-speaking artist (Marre) who's like Shakira or Avril Lavigne," said Mashonee. "She's just finishing her album. We also have a Janis Joplin–meets–Sarah McLaughlin singer, Beth Hart, who performs a lot in Sweden and Europe. She was the *Star*

Search winner in 1998 and had some hits in the United States. We're always looking for new talent."

Mashonee has garnered nearly as much acclaim as a fashion stylist as she has with her music. "I used to make jewelry," she said. "It was just simple beadwork that I thought would be fun to do, but it got to the point where it was taking up a lot of my time and I stopped. I have worked with other clothing designers, but I know what I like and what looks good on me. I like to be involved with every aspect of who I am as an artist."

Since 2002, Mashonee has called Connecticut home. "I'm traveling so much," she said, "I could be just about anywhere. I just need an airport."

LITEFOOT

American Indian youth were among the first to embrace hip-hop and rap. As founders of Grandmaster Flash and the Furious Five, the Cherokee Glover brothers—Melvin "Grandmaster Melle Mel" and Nate "Kidd Creole"—may have been the first Native American hip-hoppers to record, but Upland, California–born, and Tulsa, Oklahoma–raised, Gary Paul "Litefoot" Davis (1969–) was the first artist to express Native concerns through rap. With his poetic wordplay set to masterfully produced hip-hop beats, the Eastern Cherokee rapper continues to shock listeners with razor-tongued diatribes against five hundred years of mistreatment. "Young Native people didn't have a musical way to hear about important points of view," he explained, "and I thought I could be that voice and use my music to express the Native American experience. If [African American rap group] Public Enemy could express what they were going through, I could too."

Litefoot made his initial impact through film, portraying a two-inch "toy" Native American (Little Bear) in *Indian in the Cupboard*, the 1995 Frank Oz–directed adaptation of Lynne Reid Banks's children's book. His portrayal earned him a Best Actor award from First Americans in the Arts. He would go on to star in *Mortal Kombat Annihilation* (1997), *Kull the Conqueror* (1997), *Song of Hiawatha* (1997), *Adaptation* (2002), and *29 Psalm* (2002), and guest on TV shows, including *CSI: Miami* and *Any Day Now*.

Indian in the Cupboard changed Litefoot's life. "As a musician, especially one focused on a niche market—Indian country—I had been very shoestring-budgeted," he recalled, "but the first time that I got off the plane [for a reading of the script in New York], there was this person with a sign, and a limo, waiting for me. It blew me away. Then, when I got to where I was going to do the reading, they gave me an envelope with five one hundred dollar bills in it. 'What's this?' 'This is for your food.' I had just come from trying to make a meal last."

Although his early interests were in athletics, especially football, Litefoot recalls music being "a huge part of my upbringing." "I remember my parents asking me what I wanted for my birthday," he said. "I was probably two years old; we still lived in California. I told them that I wanted to see [jazz-rock band] Chicago, so they took me to the Hollywood Bowl."

Litefoot was immersed in popular music and R&B as a youngster. "I listened to a diversified, contemporary soundtrack," he said, "everything from Chicago and Tower of Power to the Jackson 5, the Vanilla Fudge, the Temptations, the Spinners, the Four Tops, and Barry White. I remember going to my grandparents' house and hearing Hank Williams, Jr., on the country music radio station."

An aspiring vocalist, Litefoot's sister provided entry into the world of recording. "She didn't trick me to go into the studio," he said. "I went there to see what she was doing. She asked me to write a song. I was definitely inclined, from a poetic point of view, to write stories and poetry. I hadn't yet crossed over to music, but I wrote the song for her, a little sixteen-bar rap."

Although he didn't consider himself a singer, Litefoot agreed to record a demo of the song. "The producer said that they needed to know the cadence," he explained, "and how I meant it to sound. I hesitantly went in [the studio] and did it. Then, they said, 'Can you do it a little more like this?' I did it again. Then they said, 'Cool. That was your first rap recording.'"

Litefoot's defiant stance and profanity-laced lyrics scared established record labels. "Record executives told me to tone down the Native American aspect of my music," he remembered.

Releasing his debut album, *The Money*, on his independent label, Red Vinyl, in 1992, Litefoot continued to release a new album nearly every year for the next decade. Four of those albums—*Good Day to Die* (1996), *The Life & Times* (1998), *Rez Affiliated* (1999), and *Triple Boogie* (2001)—scored "Album of the Year" NAMMYs. "I was a workhorse," he said, "but there were things that I wanted to say. I had to come out with a record that had a strong theme that was very pro-Native, and then do a record that had some of that, but was Mainstream. That set up the next record, and I came back with a message again. I knew my community, Indian Country, enough to know that, if you keep forcing it down their throat, they're going to choke on it, but, if you give them just enough, they'll come along with you."

Released after the premiere of *Indian in the Cupboard*, Litefoot's sixth album, *Good Day to Die*, met with a confused reception. "The music that I was making was ahead of its time," he said, "and the messages were definitely ahead of their time. There was a lot of frustration with people not getting the subject matter. I heard radio people saying that they could not play me on the air because I was promoting suicide. They did not understand that 'a good day to die' did not mean that you should kill yourself. It meant that, if you are living the way that the Creator planned for you to live, and doing the things that you are supposed to be doing, then, if that day, you happen to meet your end, it's a good day to die. It was frustrating to have my own people be that oblivious of Native concepts."

Litefoot's message cut through with barbed intensity. "When you get into hip-hop," he said, "you have to be clever with your wordplay. You have to say things in ways that are very poignant and profound, but you have to add more levels to it and say it in such a fashion that people listen. It has to have double entendre and metaphors that make people think."

Litefoot parlayed success into a variety of projects. The president and CEO of the National Center for American Indian Enterprise Development (NCAIED), a nonprofit organization dedicated to Native American economic self-sufficiency through business ownership, he oversees an empire (Litefoot Enterprises) that produces a line of clothing (Native style), sneakers (Litefoot Flex Arrow), books, and hip-hop recordings. Since 2005, he's joined his wife, Carmen Davis (Makah/Yakama/Chippewa Cree), in providing "revitalization, inspiration, sustainability, and empowerment" to Native American reservations. As part of the Reach the Rez project, they were instrumental in creating a nonprofit organization, the Association for American Indian Development, to bring Native American public figures and community leaders to reservations to work with young people.

DARREN BRULÉ AND REDDNATION

Many young American Indians followed Litefoot and the Glover brothers into the world of urban beats and rhythmic wordplay, but "you could count on one hand the number of Native people doing hip-hop" when High Prairie, Alberta–born Darren Brulé (aka Ill Logical) discovered rap during the summer of 1994. "There were less than a half-dozen [Native] groups rapping in the U.S. and Canada," he said.

Brulé, a Cree, first heard a Native rapper on the Sucker Creek First Nation Reserve, about three and a half hours north of Edmonton, where he grew up. "One of the guys that I went to high school with was touring with a Native dance theater company," he recalled. "At a youth conference, summer of 1994, he presented a workshop and did some rapping. It was the first time that I saw a Native person rapping."

With his passion sparked by the performance, Brulé immersed himself in the quickly expanding hip-hop scene. When his friend invited him to join his new Indigenous rap group, Full-Blooded, in Calgary, he jumped at the chance. "We performed at schools and conferences," he recalled. "We had traditional dancers, break dancers, and a deejay/turntablist; it was a mix of elements—from traditional culture to hip-hop."

Evolving into Reddnation in 2000, the group shifted its focus. "My vision was to be an aboriginal hip-hop group," Brulé explained, "and get rid of the traditional elements of our performance. I felt conflicted about blending the two worlds together. It didn't feel right. We were profiting off our culture, and we didn't feel comfortable about it. We felt like we should just leave it where it is—the powwow dancing with the powwow and the hip-hop with the pop music."

The move proved fortuitous. "Doors started opening," said Brulé. "It wasn't long before we started getting shows outside of Grand Prairie. We started doing shows in the Northwest Territory and it just grew and grew and grew. We were playing in British Columbia, Saskatchewan, all across Canada, within two years."

SHADOWYZE

Possessing an undergraduate degree in anthropology from the University of West Florida in Pensacola, Shadowyze (Shawn Enfinger) (1972–) applied a political edge to his rap songs after living with Indigenous people in the Mexican state of Chiapas. Recalling the brutal killing of the Mayan people by Mexico's military at the turn of the twentieth century, the title track of his debut album, *Murder in Your Backyard*, received a "Best Hip-Hop Song" NAMMY in 2005.

Opening shows for Ice-T, Digital Underground, and Queen Latifah, Shadowyze continues to spread his message. In 2013, he voiced his objection to the controversial name of Washington's NFL football team with "Say No to the R Word," written with guitarist and songwriter Oliver Tuthill. The track opened and closed with audio snippets of AIM cofounder (and 2014 Native American Music Hall of Fame inductee) Russell Means (1939–2012). "[Means] was against mascots and logos that depicted us as cartoonish," said the Muskogee Creek/Cherokee/Irish/Scottish rapper to *Indian Country Today*, "and against racial slurs like the 'R-word.'"[1]

Combining rap, original song, and Jim Pepper's "Witchi-Ta Toe," Shadowyze scored a "Best Hip-Hop Song" NAMMY in 2014.

DALLAS ARCAND AND KRAY-Z-KREE

On the opening track of Dallas Arcand's debut 2008 album, *REZalationZZ*, credited to his pseudonym Kray-Z-Kree, the Edmonton, Alberta–based producer, flute player, songwriter, and singer, who includes French, Métis, Sioux, and Cree in his heritage, declared that he "put the Cree in creativity." The recipient of a "Producer of the Year" Aboriginal People's Choice Award, Arcand broke new ground with dance-inducing tunes like "Pow Wow Danze Party," "Native Pride," "Pow Wow Trailz," "Tribal Danze," and "Wild West (Way High Hi)." Hip-hop, however, represented only one segment of the creative vision of this Mount Royal University behavioral science graduate.

Arcand's first album under his own name, *Picking Sweetgrass*, in 2009, represented a 180-degree reversal. Solos played on the Indigenous flute or accompanied by gently strummed guitar, bass, and drums replaced the dance rhythms, electronic beats, and fast-tongued poetry of *REZalationZZ*. There was even an original song about sweetgrass. The recipient of a Aboriginal People's Choice Award as the year's "Best Flute CD" and "Best Instrumental CD," *Picking Sweetgrass* also received a "Best Flute CD" Canadian Aboriginal Music Award.

Setting Native American flute to the funky, dance grooves of electric guitar, bass, drums, percussion, and electronic keyboards, Arcand again defied expectations on his third CD, *Modern Day Warrior*, in October 2010. Tunes like "Happy Sundance," "Groovy," "Indian Trance," and "Feel the Rhythm" made it impossible to sit still while listening. Ontario-based Dawn Desmarais (Métis) added vocables to three songs—"Cedar Tree Jungle, "Indian Trance," and "Muskwa Dance"—with Saskatchewan-based round-dance singer, Quinton Tootoosis (Cree). As electrifying as anything to hit the twenty-first century dance floor, *Modern Day Warrior* pointed to the future. "It's about breaking the stereotypes," said Arcand, "and giving people a taste of reality—showing them what it's really like to be an aboriginal person."

FRANK WALN AND NAKE NULA WAUN

Frank Waln (1990–) became the youngest recipient of a "Producer of the Year" award in the history of the NAMMY with "Always Ready," a hip-hop track included on a popular summer 2010 mix tape. The Sicangu Lakota rapper/producer followed with a second NAMMY, for "Best Hip-Hop Recording," a year later, with the debut album (*Scars and Bars*) by his band, Nake Nula Waun (Nah-kay Noo-Lah Wah-OOn). He scored an *Indian Country Today* Music Award in 2013, as the year's "Best Male Artist." "Something big is on the horizon," Waln assured me in November 2011, during a break from his audio production and music design classes at Chicago's Columbia College. "I feel it in my gut, and my heart, and I know that I'm on the right path. I owe it to my ancestors to not waste my gift of music."

Raised on the Rosebud Reservation, in south-central South Dakota, Waln grew up with Lakota music. "There was no modern music of any kind," he said.

"There was the powwow scene and traditional music, but that's where it ended."

Playing piano from the age of three, Waln found emotional refuge through music. "My mom and dad split when I was four," he said. "It was pretty ugly. I saw my dad beat my mom. He threw my Christmas presents at me. That was the last time that I saw him for fifteen years. It caused a lot of inner turmoil."

Waln's mother, and an aggregate of what he remembers as "strong women," instilled a sense of family and community, themes that continue in his songwriting. Though baptized a Catholic, he was encouraged to participate in sweat lodges, ceremonies, and Sun Dances.

Waln's introduction to hip-hop came through fate. "I was walking on a gravel road by my house," he recalled, "and saw something sparkling in the sun. I walked over and saw that it was a face-down CD, all-scratched up. I thought, 'There's no way that this is going to play,' but I picked it up, brought it home, and put it on my CD player."

Not only did the CD—*The Marshall Mathers Album* by Kansas City, Missouri–born hip-hopper Eminem (Marshall Bruce Mathers III)—play, but it also had a life-changing effect. "Hearing Eminem talking about his childhood trauma with his mother and father," recalled Waln, "I could relate to everything that he was saying. He was telling my story in a creative way. When you added the powerful feeling of that pulsating beat, it connected with me."

Other artists expanded Waln's vision. "I was drawn to [Brooklyn-based rappers] Nas [Nasir Olu Dara Jones] and Jay-Z [Shawn Casey Carter]," he said. "They were poets reciting over beats, talking about things that I was experiencing, even though they grew up in a different place."

Aspiring to become a medical doctor from the age of five, Waln shunned alcohol and drugs and dedicated himself to his education. Graduating from White River High School as valedictorian, he received a full scholarship to study pre-med at Creighton University, a private Jesuit college in Omaha, Nebraska. Campus life was a culture shock. "A fish doesn't know the water he's living in," he said, "until he's out of the water. All I had known, up to that point, was the reservation. When I went to college, kids were coming from rich families and they had gone to the best high schools that money could buy. It made me realize how rough our experiences on the reservation were, but, at the same time, how unique and special our culture was."

Between classes, Waln expanded his repertoire. "I had only listened to hip-hop," he said, "but something spurred me to listen to other types of music. One of the first things that I got into was the Beatles. I knew who they were, but I had never before dug into their music. It was the start of an amazing adventure. This whole other world opened to me. It led me to a lot of different music—the Rolling Stones, the Black Keys, and the Doors."

Starting out with an electronic keyboard, obtained in the third grade, Waln built an arsenal of instruments and recording equipment. "My cousins would go cruising in their cars," he said, "and I'd be in my room making music and beats. I figured out how to use a drum machine I bought in a pawnshop by myself. It came with a manual, but it took me two months, sitting in my room every day, to figure out how to program it."

Working a summer job at a reservation hospital, Waln grew frustrated by the indifference of the medical administration. Dropping out of school, despite four straight semesters on the dean's list, he turned to music. Meeting Andre "Dre" Easter, a soulful-voiced, Richmond, Virginia–born rapper who had married Waln's cousin, at a family Christmas party, in 2008, he found a kindred spirit. "We talked for a while," Waln remembered, "and then, he joked, 'Here's my producer.' It was more prophetic than either of us could have imagined."

The two hip-hoppers quickly took steps toward Nake Nula Waun. "We started making music in his basement," said Waln, "just messing around. I had a studio and made beats. He rapped. He grew up singing in church and has a great Southern style of rap. It's a great mixture."

Nake Nula Waun took a lead forward when Thomas Schmidt, who had joined as a third member, enlisted in the U.S. Marine Corps. Kodi Denoyer replaced him, although she had not sung in public before joining the group. "She was really quiet and shy," said Waln. "I knew her through her mother, who worked for a tribal program that we did shows for. Her mother was always telling me, 'Oh, my daughter, she plays guitar, she plays bass, she sings.' At the time, we were trying to put a band together and needed a bass player, so I spoke with her mom and she came to one of our practices."

During a break, Denoyer stepped to the mic and started singing. "I don't know if she knew if we were paying attention," said Waln, "or even if we were in the room, but it was obvious that she had an amazing voice." It took two weeks of persuasion before Denoyer would agree to sing with the group. "We finally got her into the studio," said Waln. "Dre and I had already written the lyrics and we had the beats ready. We weren't sure of what was going to happen, but she really came through. She's sung before thousands of people since and her mom is always telling me, 'I'm so glad that you got Kodi out of her shell.'"

When it came to recording *Scars and Bars*, Waln assumed production and mixing duties. "We did the whole thing in two months," he said. "We didn't sit down and think about the structure of the songs. Instead, we did each tune the way that we felt was right. The kick drum, hitting on the one-two-three-four beat, pounding away at that constant rhythm is the heartbeat of the people, and I put that heartbeat into the programmed drums too. It added to the energy and passion of the music."

Nake Nula Waun's name, which translates into English as "I am always ready, at all times, for anything," is a familiar phrase in the Lakota language. "It goes back thousands of years," said Waln. "It was used to describe Lakota warriors before they went into battle. They would stake themselves out with a rope, or a piece of cloth, and not leave that place until the battle was over, or until they died. They were ready to die for their people. It was the way of life on the reservation. Everyone still has it rough, but we are all in it together, and we come together through the music. The band is a way of life."

Through their songs, Nake Nula Waun presents American Indian youth with positive messages of hope and encouragement. "If I hadn't had music," said Waln, "I probably would have killed myself. The reservation has the highest suicide rate in the world. There's a lot of domestic abuse, a lot of drugs and alcohol, but our music is healing. I got a message from a kid who said that he was going through tough times, and our music gave him hope that everything was going to be okay. That was more rewarding than winning an award or getting radio airplay."

Waln became involved with protests against the proposed Keystone XL tar sands pipeline running between the western Canadian sedimentary basin in Alberta and oil refineries in Nebraska, Illinois, and Texas. During a protest rally in Washington, D.C., in April 2014, he introduced a new track, "Oil 4 Blood." "If you look at the chorus," he told indianz.com, "when I say, 'Soil my love,' I mean 'You're destroying the earth,' and when I say 'My mother,' I'm talking about the earth. Our word for nature means 'mother,' so we look at the earth very much the way we look at our mother. In the verses, I'm talking about issues we face on the reservation. . . . We have a lot to worry about already. We don't need this pipeline poisoning our land."[2]

IDLE NO MORE

A liquid-diet hunger strike by Attawapiskat First Nations chief Theresa Spence, protesting a legislative act (Bill C-45) that threatened aboriginal sovereignty and environmental protection, inspired Nina Wilson, Sheelah McLean, Sylvia McAdam, and Jessica Gordon to organize the grassroots activist group Idle No More in November 2012. Starting out with teach-ins and rallies in Saskatchewan on December 10, 2012—Canada's National Day of Action and Amnesty International's Human Rights Day—the protest swept through Canada. Using social media, Idle No More gathered supporters for rallies, mass marches, and flash-mob round dances. Solidarity protests erupted in Stockholm, London, Berlin, Auckland, and Cairo. There were also demonstrations in various states—Minnesota, Michigan, Ohio, New York, Arizona, Colorado, Maine, New Mexico, Vermont, South Carolina, Washington, Indiana, and Texas, as well as Washington, D.C. "It is abundantly clear that Aboriginals are getting the worse deal of any minority group in Canada," said Tristin Hopper of the *National Post*. "It's conceivable that many Idle No More protests were not spurred by any particular piece of legislature, but by the simple frustration that something is clearly very wrong."[3]

A TRIBE CALLED RED

Ottawa-based DJ collective A Tribe Called Red dedicated a 2013 track, "The Road," to Chief Spence. "I wouldn't call myself an activist," said A Tribe Called Red cofounder Bear Witness (Aaron Thomas) (Cayuga) to *Metro Ottawa*'s Samantha Everts, "[but] just making music is political when you're doing it as part of the aboriginal community."[4]

Combining archival Drum recordings with electronic keyboards, scratch-able turntables, hip-hop beats and dubstep rhythms, A Tribe Called Red has melded the musical traditions of the powwow into an exciting style of electronic dance music (EDM). "We're making club music for aboriginal people," Witness told me.

Frustrated by the absence of Indigenous music in Ottawa's dance clubs, A Tribe Called Red organized their first aboriginal dance party in the spring of 2008. The event, promoted as "The Electric Powwow," was a phenomenal success. "We packed [the Babylon Nightclub] the first night," said Witness. "People told us that it was something that was needed."

Encouraged by the response, A Tribe Called Red continued to plow new ground. Performing at West Fest, a large music festival in Ottawa, they introduced a new dance style that they called "the Powwow Step." "We wanted to do something different," said Witness. "Ian (DJ NDN) knew a Grass Dance song that was open—with no drumming—for the first round. We could throw a track right under it. It was about 140 bpm (beats per minute), which was just right for dubstep—an electronic dance music style that originated in London, England, in 1998. We tried a track ('The General') and it clicked. Dubstep and powwow drums went together perfectly. It was a real 'aha' kind of moment."

As they premiered their "Powwow Step," accompanied by intertribal dancers, Witness and DJ NDN caught the attention of Dan General, who, as DJ Shub, had performed earlier in the day. "He was living in Fort Erie, a seven-hour drive from the festival," said Witness, "but, he was so knocked out by what we had done that, the next night, he sent us a track—'Electric Powwow.' It became the title track of our first album."

General joined A Tribe Called Red shortly afterwards. "Working with Dan has been amazing," said Witness. "He has the ability to take an idea and run with it. He's taken what we were trying to do, in our makeshift fashion, and turned it into something amazing."

A Tribe Called Red has created an exciting new style of EDM (electronic dance music) that melds DJ scratching, hip-hop grooves, and archival powwow drum recordings.
Photo by Brudder Falling Tree, courtesy A Tribe Called Red.

Cooperative interplay remains the key to A Tribe Called Red's artistic success. "We operate more like a band than three deejays taking turns," said Witness, "and we get all kinds of sounds happening at the same time. One of us will layer tracks, somebody will play samples from movies, comedy bits, or archival recordings, and someone will scratch a turntable."

"Each of us comes from a different background in music," he continued, "with very different tastes and completely different skills. DJ Shub is a two-time Canadian EDM champion—a real turntablist. He represented Canada at the world championships two years in a row. He has the biggest production background. He has produced hip-hop beats for groups in his community for years. He was able to transfer his hip-hop production skills to what we were doing. DJ NDN was the drummer in a well-known punk band (the Rip-Cords) for two or three years, and he had a background as a youth powwow drummer."

A Tribe Called Red's message goes beyond its music. Along with DJ NDN (Ian Compeau), and DJ Shub (Dan General), Witness uses the trio's mashups to promote realistic views of American Indians. "We want to take the power away," he explained, "from metaphors that are racist and one-dimensional."

The son of a Buffalo, New York–born photographer, Jeff Thomas, and the grandson of Gloria Miguel, cofounder of New York's Spiderwoman Theater, Witness, who grew up on the Six Nations Reserve of the Grand River Iroquois Confederacy in Ontario, was no stranger to pejorative Native imagery. "[My father] did a lot of work around powwows," he said, "photographing people in and out of regalia, and he photographed aboriginal people living in urban landscapes. He also worked with historical photographs by Edward S. Curtis, with the idea of looking beyond the fact that they were setup photos—these were real people."

Witness's maternal great-grandparents sang original American Indian–sounding songs in Coney Island sideshows. "They weren't traditional," he said. "My great-grandfather was a Kuna Indian, from the San Blas Islands, off the coast of Panama, but he wore a Plains Indian headdress. He and my great-grandmother performed for tourists."

Given a camera by his grandfather, Witness immersed himself in Ottawa's thriving nightclub scene. As a video deejay, he became part of a small coterie that would evolve into A Tribe Called Red. "There were originally four of us," he remembered, "deejays who just happened to also be Native. DJ NDN was the only one who knew all of us."

A Tribe Called Red's debut album, *Electric Powwow*, was released in March 2012 as a free Internet download. "That's where the music industry is right now," said Witness. "It's not about selling records, but about using our music to promote ourselves. We recorded it in our home studio. All that it cost was our time. We could give it away as a promotional tool. The more people that we got to talk about it, and listen to it, the more shows we got booked to play. We have to give a lot of respect to our manager on that one."

Short snippets of Drum recordings flavored most tracks, but the album's apex came with "Red Skin Girl," an unrelenting electro-Native dance track that featured A Tribe Called Red's wizardry—and dance rhythms—applied to a round-dance song sung in English by the Northern Cree Singers. "DJ NDN brought Northern Cree's recording to the group," said Witness, "and we knew right away that we had to do a remix of it. Dan (DJ Shub) started running with it right away. In a couple of days, we popped out with it. It was one of our most exciting tracks. Our manager wanted to release it as a single and started the process of getting in touch with [Canyon Records, Northern Cree's] label and clearing the samples."

On their second album, *Nation II Nation*, A Tribe Called Red remixed tracks by Black Bear, Sitting Big, the Chippewa Travelers, Smoke Trail, Northern Voice, Eastern Eagle, and Sheldon Sundown. "A big part of what we do is exposing people to how alive and strong powwow music and culture is," Witness told *Metro Ottawa*. "These aren't old historical recordings [we're sampling from]; most of the guys are under thirty."[5]

Witness produced a series of videos, *The Javier Trilogy*, in collaboration with Javier Estrada, a Monterey, New Mexico–based deejay/producer doing similar work with Aztec and Mayan music. "One of the videos is a remix of one of Estrada's tracks," he explained. "There's a track that A Tribe Called Red did with him and there's one of his tracks, where he remixed the theme song of the Sergio Leone–directed 1965 film, *For A Few Dollars More*."

A Tribe Called Red's future projects include "an EP—*A Tribe Called Redbone*, with remixes of Redbone tracks," said Witness, "and we just got some tracks from Ulali and Pura Fé [that we're going to remix]. We're also going to start making new recordings of powwow groups. We got a grant to bring them into the studio and pay them as session musicians. All of the singers will get credit."

A Tribe Called Red continues to host "The Electric Powwow" at the Babylon Nightclub the second Saturday of each month. "They're a lot of fun," said Witness. "We get up to 350 people into a medium-sized club with a big, hot, sweaty dance floor. Everybody knows our music, not only at our Electric Powwows, but also at our shows away from here. People know the songs and they know the vocables."

6 DEPICTING AND DEFYING STEREOTYPES

"I played the Kennedy Center a few years ago, and a woman came up to me and said, 'Indians should just play Indian music. They should play flutes and drums and sing about feathers'—How racist can someone be?"
—Singer-songwriter Darryl Tonemah (Kiowa/Comanche/Tuscarora)

DEPICTING STEREOTYPES

The Philadelphia-born composer of more than five hundred songs, including "Listen to the Mockingbird" and "Die Deitcher's Dog (Where, Oh Where, Has My Little Dog Gone)," Septimus Winner (1827–1902) scored one of his biggest hits with a counting song, "Ten Little Indians." Winner's deceptively innocent song would be popularized by E. P. Christy and his blackface troupe, Christy's Minstrels, during their tour of Great Britain in 1860, and recorded by a lengthy list of artists, including the Beach Boys, Harry Nilsson, Bill Haley & the Comets, Kevin Roth, and the Peter Pan Singers. "Asking children to sing 'Ten Little Indians' is pure racism," claimed Barbara A. Gray-Kanatiiosh, author of Indigenous-themed children's books. "The song is an Indian annihilation song that the pioneers sang to their children to soothe their fears."[1]

Between 1883 and 1916, William Frederick "Buffalo Bill" Cody's Wild West shows spread a glorified image of the American West—cowboys, Rough Riders, and Plains Indians—across the United States and Europe. At a time when American Indians were restricted from practicing their religions and traditional cultures, Cody's show provided an outlet for their fervor. "They adopted the performance encounter," said anthropology professor Linda Scarangella McNenly in *Native Performers in Wild West Shows: From Buffalo Bill to Euro Disney*, "as a space in which to maintain and express aspects of their warrior identity by modifying war songs for this new context."[2]

One of America's truly iconic characters, Cody (1846–1917) was an expert equestrian, sharpshooter, scout, showman, and heroic star of numerous dime novels. As originator and guiding force behind Buffalo Bill's Wild West show, he would both promote tribal culture and mold the stereotypical image of American Indians that persists among some non-Natives to this day. "They reduced Westernness and Nativeness," said McNenly, "to archetypical performances that became viewed as authentic representation of history and culture; they constricted stereotypical images of Indians as exotic, noble savage warriors."[3]

Buffalo Bill's Wild West shows commenced with the full-cast procession that would evolve into the Grand Entry of today's powwows. "For my grand entrance," said Cody, "I made a spectacle which comprised the most picturesque features of Western life. Sioux, Arapahoes, Brulés, and Cheyennes in war paint and feathers led the van, shrieking their war whoops and waving the weapons with which they were armed in a manner to inspire both terror and admiration in the tenderfoot audience."[4]

After the procession, a soldier carrying a U.S. flag would ride into the arena, present "the Stars and Stripes as an emblem of the friendship of America to the world,"[5] and lead the audience in singing "The Star-Spangled Banner," helping to promote Francis Scott Key's song decades before Congress named it the national anthem.

At every stop along the show's itinerary, the Cowboy Band's brass instruments and drums would lead a morning parade through city streets. During matinee and evening performances, the Western-regalia-clad group would accompany acts with "popular songs of the day, all kinds of dance music, from the waltz to the ragtime cakewalk, medleys of opera and operetta tunes, descriptive and novelty pieces, and transcriptions from the standard orchestral literature."[6]

Most of the fifteen-piece Cowboy Band was recruited from New York's Musicians Union. Cornet player William Sweeney, known for synchronizing orchestrations to horses' gaits, led the group from Cody's rodeo-like extravaganza, "The Old-Glory Blowout," in 1882, until the Wild West show's "Farewell Tour" in 1913.

Sweeney's successor, Ohio-born cornet and baritone player Karl Lawrence King directed Cody's band for the Sells-Floto Circus and Buffalo Bill's Wild West Combined show from 1914 to 1915. He would go on to compose twenty-two overtures, twelve gallops, twenty-nine waltzes, and one hundred and eighty-five marches—including the Ringling Bros. and Barnum & Bailey's theme "Barnum & Bailey's Favorite."

Kansas-born cornet player Merle Slease Evans ("the Toscanini of the Big Top") directed the music for the Buffalo Bill and the 101 Ranch Combined show, Cody's final tour, in 1916. Evans would go on to direct Ringling Bros. and Barnum, &

Bailey's circus band for a half century. "He wanted his music to have the zip that went with the sawdust," said the *New York Times*, "the beat of hoofs, and the cheers of excited children."[7]

In addition to "authentic" war dances, performed by Native cast members (mostly Lakotas, but also Arapahos, Pawnees, Cheyennes, and Crows), Buffalo Bill's Wild West shows included orchestrated "Indianist" pieces played by the Cowboy Band. Karl King's heavily stereotypical "On the Warpath" featured during the Sells-Floto Circus and Buffalo Bill's Wild West Combined Grand Entry in 1914. A more somber piece, "The Passing of the Red Man," musically depicted the interplay between American Indians and non-Natives during the nineteenth century. It would become a favorite of Cody's, and he would often request that it be played.

As director of the National Conservatory of Music in New York from 1892 to 1895, Antonin Dvořák (1841–1904) spent much of his time researching what would become Symphony No. 9 in E minor (Opus 95), subtitled "From the New World" and popularly known as the New World Symphony. "I have simply written original themes embodying the peculiarities of the Indian music," the Czech composer told the *New York Herald* before the piece's premiere on December 15, 1893, "and, using these themes as subjects, have developed them with all the resources of modern rhythms, counterpoint, and orchestral color."[8]

Following Dvořák's lead, other non-Native composers, including Edward McDowell, Charles Wakefield Cadman, and Arthur Farwell composed "Indianist" symphonies and chorale pieces based on Native themes. Even John Philip Sousa orchestrated Native melodies. "They were coming from an outside perception," pointed out Jerod Impichchaahaaha Tate. "They weren't Native classical composers, but white Americans using American Indian music in their own music. It's a big difference."

Popular songs—including "Red Wing" (1907), a melodic source for Woody Guthrie and Bob Dylan; "Golden Arrow" (1909); and "Silver Star" (1911)—built on the idealistic "noble savage" image of American Indians as peaceful, spiritual, and naturalistic, yet still uncivilized. "Nothing is so gentle as man in his primitive state," wrote Jean Jacques Rousseau (1712–1778), the Geneva-born philosopher, writer, composer, and originator of the noble savage concept, "when placed by nature at an equal distance from the stupidity of brutes and the fatal enlightenment of civil man."[9]

Broadway shows and films reinforced the stereotyping. Protesters picketed Richard Rodgers and Oscar Hammerstein II's musical *Annie Get Your Gun* in 1946, for its inclusion of "I'm An Indian, Too," one of the songs that Irving Berlin penned for the show, along with "There's No Business like Show Business," "Doin' What Comes Naturally," and "Anything You Can Do." Sung on Broadway by "the undisputed first lady of the American musical theater," Ethel Merman, its lyrics included references to totem poles, tomahawks, and peace pipes.

Disney's 1953 animated film, *Peter Pan*, based on Scottish author and dramatist Sir J. M. Barrie's 1904 play, took things further. As "What Makes the Red Man Red," by Sammy Kahn, Frank Churchill, Sammy Fain, and Ted Sears, is sung, cartoon American Indians, voiced by New Orleans–born Candy Candido and the Mellomen, clap their hands to their mouths, make "wa-wa-wa-wa, wa-wa-wa-wa" sounds, smoke a peace pipe, and use stereotypical words like "paleface," "Injun," "squaw," and "how."

Derogatory imagery continued to spread. Wooden, storefront Indians ("Kaw-Liga"), lonesome Indian braves ("Little Bear"), and bloodthirsty warriors ("Mr. Custer") seemed the norm. Rex Allen scored a top-five country hit with "Don't Go Near the Indians" in November 1962.

A rock band that dressed in Revolutionary War–era uniforms, and possessed a name recalling an eighteenth-century colonist, Paul Revere and the Raiders topped the pop charts in 1971 with "Indian Reservation (The Lament of the Cherokee Reservation Indian)." Penned by Nashville songwriter J. D. Loudermilk and recorded during a solo session by lead singer, Mark Lindsay (whose mixed ancestry includes Cherokee), it recalled the forced relocation of the Trail of Tears. Released under the band's moniker, it sold more than 6 million copies and remained Columbia Records' top-selling release for almost a decade.

The first to cover "Indian Reservation (The Lament of the Cherokee Reservation Indian)," Marvin Rainwater (1925–) renamed it "The Pale-Faced Indian" before recording it in 1959. "I made a terrible mistake when I changed its name," confessed the Wichita, Kansas–born country music/rockabilly pioneer in October 2012. "I don't know what got into me. I have always had weird ideas come out of my mind, but this was the dumbest thing that I ever did. 'Pale-Faced Indian'—what does that have to do with the song? I just went out of my mind and defeated myself."

Although he scored his greatest success with rockabilly tunes, including "Boo Hoo," "Hot and Cold," and "Whole Lotta Woman," Rainwater dressed in Native regalia and included many Indian-themed songs in his repertoire. He had a top-twenty hit with Loudermilk's "Half-Breed" (no relation to Cher's hit more than a decade later) and covered Hank Williams's "Kaw-Liga" and the J. P. "Big Bopper" Richardson–composed (and Johnny Preston–popularized) "Running Bear." "There might be some Indian in me," he said, "but I don't really know."

Viewers of CBS-TV's *Sonny & Cher Comedy Hour* on September 12, 1973, witnessed one of the indelible images of early '70s television. Astride a motionless stallion, the show's barely buckskin-clad cohost, Cher (Cherilyn Sarkisian

LaPiere), introduced her latest single, "Half-Breed," bemoaning the suffering she had endured as the product of mixed parentage. The song, by Al Capps and lyricist Mary Dean, reached the top of *Billboard*'s Hot 100 and became the El Centro, California–born songstress's second solo number-one hit. Although she would omit it from her set list for more than a quarter of a century, it would make a comeback during her *Do You Believe* tour in 1999, and *Living Proof: The Farewell Tour* in 2002. "I hated that song," remembered Keith Secola, "because it was real. I grew up with prejudice. I can remember bullies calling me 'half breed.'"

Many non-Natives have since embraced a more realistic view of American Indians, but the stereotyping continues. Mississippi-born country singer Tim McGraw, the son of former baseball great Frank "Tug" McGraw, had his breakthrough with his 1994 recording of Tommy Barnes, Jumpin' Gene Simmons, and John D. Loudermilk's "Indian Outlaw." Reaching number eight on *Billboard*'s Hot Country Singles and Tracks chart and number fifteen on its Hot 100, it was sung from the perspective of a "half Cherokee and Choctaw" in pursuit of a "Chickiwawa," and was laden with stereotypical imagery, including peace pipes, bows and arrows, and tipis. According to *Billboard*'s Deborah Evans Price, the recording "pushes relations back two hundred years."[10]

Anaheim, California–based ska-rockers No Doubt stirred controversy immediately with the November 2012 debut of their video for "Looking Hot," the second single off their sixth album (and first in a decade), *Push and Shove*. Set in the American Wild West, the clip featured lead singer Gwen Stefani as a Pocahontas-like Native princess, dressed in fringed white buckskin. As the rope-bound captive of "cowboys" portrayed by drummer Adrian Young and guitarist Tom Dumont, the platinum blonde songstress waits for a "tribal chief," played by London-born bassist Tony Kanal, the son of Indian emigrants, to rescue her. As she smiles seductively at her captors, she sings, "Do you think I'm looking hot?"

Offensive to most women, the video was particularly insulting to America's original inhabitants. In an open letter, the director of UCLA's American Indian Studies Center, Angela R. Riley (Potawatomie), claimed the video perpetuated the myth that "American Indians are near historical relics, frozen in time as stereotypically savage, primitive, uniquely spiritualized and—in the case of Native women—hyper-sexualized objects to be tamed."[11]

Withdrawing the video the next day, No Doubt issued a public apology on their website. "As a multi-racial band," they explained, "our foundation is built upon both diversity and consideration for other cultures. Our intention with our new video was never to offend, hurt, or trivialize Native American people, their culture, or their history."

Non-Native "wannnabes" continue to bowdlerize Indigenous culture. "If all of these people were actually Native American," said Sal Serbin (Assiniboine), director of American Indian Movement–Florida, "we would have easily outnumbered the Cavalry in the American Indian Wars and this country would have been run by different tribes."[12]

"[These 'wannabes'] have seen *Dances with Wolves* too many times," said John White Antelope (Arapaho), a direct descendent of White Antelope, the Southern Cheyenne chief who was killed and mutilated during the November 29, 1864, Sand Creek massacre while attempting to secure a truce. "They only associate the romantic and spiritual with being a Native American. They think we're these mystical creatures. They don't see my nine-to-five job."[13]

DEFYING STEREOTYPES

Misappropriation of culturally significant symbols, including headdresses, tipis, totem poles, and pipes, are, according to A Tribe Called Red's Ian Campeau (DJ NDN), "creating a false idea of what it means to be Indigenous today. It's robbing the First Nations of their nation-hoods and nationality, making us all 'Indian' instead of recognizing us as Anishinaabe or Ojibwe. Also, it gives the impression that Natives are something from the past—not here today. . . . We, as First Nation people, have never had control of our image in colonial media since its birth."[14]

"We call this the 'leather, feather, teepee, and tomahawk syndrome,'" explained Barrie Cox-Dacre, executive director of the International Resource Centre and Lenni Lenape Resource Centre in Edinburgh, Scotland. "A lot of people think they can put on an inaccurate plastic bonnet, and some grease paint, and that it's okay—it's not."[15]

Concerned that non-Natives were exploiting American Indian ceremonies, especially the Sun Dance, the Lakota held the four-day Summit V in 1993. Five hundred representatives of forty tribes and bands of the Lakota drafted, and approved, *A Declaration of War against Exploiters of Lakota Spirituality*. "We have to put a stop to it," the declaration demanded. "We were the ones who were given these ceremonies so that [our] people would remain together and strong. We were told to take care of these ceremonies so that our children and their children would have a future."[16]

In July 2014, the Bass Coast Music Festival in British Columbia banned attendees from wearing feather headdresses in respect of "the dignity of aboriginal people." "We understand why people are attracted to war bonnets," read an official statement. "They have a magnificent aesthetic, but their spiritual, cultural, and aesthetic significance cannot be separated."[17]

The stereotyping has not been universal. Many non-Native songwriters have presented empathetic views of Indigenous America. Ottawa-born Bruce Cockburn's "Stolen Land" addressed Indigenous suffering "from Tierra del Fuego to Ungave Bay," while Holly Near's "Broken Promises" equated the broken promises and disease-infested blankets given to American Indians with the bombing of Vietnam. Toronto-born Neil Young has based several songs on Indigenous history. "Cortez the Killer" portrayed Spanish conquistador Hernando Cortez and his men as brutal destroyers of the highly civilized Aztec Empire, while "Pocahontas" led listeners from the massacre of an Indian tribe by European settlers to a fictitious meeting—at the Astrodome—with Pocahontas and Marlon Brando.

Forty-one years after his top-two country (and top-fifty pop) album *Bitter Tears: Ballads of the American Indians*, Johnny Cash's son, John Carter Cash, coproduced *Badlands: Ballads of the Lakota* for his father's former sideman and son-in-law, John Martin "Marty" Stuart. Focusing on the Oglala Lakota on the Pine Ridge Indian Reservation, Stuart's country-folk tunes tore through idealistic images to confront the realities of tribal poverty and historic suffering.

In recognition of Australia's 2009 apology to the aborigines, and the United States's Native American Apology Resolution a year later, Carlos Santana dedicated his band's mostly instrumental thirty-sixth album, *Shape Shifter*, to Indigenous people around the globe. "One thing I love about American Indians," the Mexico-born but San Francisco–based bandleader told *Guitar World* in July 2012, "is how they always say, 'You can't break my spirit. You may steal my land—you may do this or that to me—but you can't break my spirit.'"[18]

GABRIEL AYALA

The greatest counter to the pejorative imagery is provided by Native musicians defying stereotypes and creating innovative music. "I've never tried to sell myself as an American Indian classical guitarist," said two-time "artist of the year" NAMMY recipient, Gabriel Ayala (1972–) (Yaqui). "When my career was starting, I'd show up at a concert and people would ask where my flute was. I'd say, 'I left it home. This is how I choose to express myself; I hope you'll enjoy it.'"

Building his early reputation with masterful solo guitar arrangements of western classical music, Ayala continues to expand his musical vocabulary. His 2009 album, *Tango*, featured guitar adaptations of Argentinean accordionist Astor Piazzolla's tango masterpieces and received a "Best Instrumental Album" NAMMY.

The first (and so far, only) classical musician signed by Canyon, Ayala released the first of the three albums that he would record for the label's Explorer subsidiary, *Portraits*, in 2009. The CD included arrangements of Bach's "Toccata and Fugue in

Gabriel Ayala (Yaqui), with his classically trained proficiency, transforms the acoustic guitar into an instrument of beauty and imagination.
Courtesy Gabriel Ayala.

D minor" and Spanish guitarist/composer Fernando Sor's early eighteenth-century variations on "O Cara Armonia" from Mozart's *The Magic Flute*.

After a solo guitar album, *Remembrance*, in 2010, Ayala left Canyon and launched Deez Mas Records. It turned out to be a shrewd move. His first release on the new label, *Shades of Blue*, in 2012, reached the top slot on the CD Baby charts, where it remained for more than four months. "I realized that the only one who would really take a risk on me was me," said Ayala. "No one could promote my music better. Some people still think that leaving Canyon was a crazy idea, but my CD went to number one and that was better than any of my earlier albums had done. I think it was an incredibly smart decision."

Songs on *Shades of Blue* were extremely intimate. "They're soundtracks to very important times in my life," said Ayala. "I wanted to show people a different side of my playing, that I didn't have to play everything as fast as possible and show off. I wanted to show expressive-ness and my musicality, as a musician, not as a guitar player. I have a degree in music and can read music. I can notate music. I can write for a symphony. I wanted to infuse all these genres—from classical to jazz to flamenco—and take listeners on an emotional roller coaster. I wanted them to not know what the next song was going to be."

Born in Corpus Christi, Texas, Ayala comes from a large family. He has sixteen aunts and uncles on his mother's side, and eleven on his father's, along with one hundred first cousins. "We had goats and chickens for milk and eggs," he told Lee Allen of *Indian Country Today*. "Sometimes a pet would be missing and when I asked about the animal's whereabouts, my grandmother would say 'in your stew.'"[19]

Ayala's grandmother, who raised him from infancy, shaped his view of the world. "She taught me how to be a man," he said, "but she also showed me how to sew, how to cook, and how to clean, and she reminded me that I should never think that I was above a woman. I was never too good to mop a floor or peel potatoes. They were very humbling lessons."

"She shared traditional stories with me," he continued, "and told me about my grandfather, what it was like when they were growing up. [She was born in 1908.] We'd sit on the swings in front of her house and talk."

The connection with his grandmother helped Ayala to compensate for the absence of his parents. "My father and I met. We exchanged a few words," he said, "and had a couple of meals together, but I can count on my two hands the number of times that I've seen him. It is what it is; it made me the man that I am. I take everything for what it is and move on, try to cope, and do the best that I can with what I have."

Ayala's mother played a role in his upbringing. "My mom was an integral part of my life," he said. "She just wasn't there with me. She was living and working in another city but she'd send money to help us survive."

Although they kept in touch, and occasionally reunited, Ayala and his mother knew little about each other. During one of his mother's visits, he overheard her mistakenly bragging that he could play the guitar. "I could already play several instruments," he said, "including the cello, saxophone, and piano, but she thought that I played the guitar. She was telling my aunts and uncles about how great her son was, boasting that 'he could even play the guitar.' I just went along with it, not knowing that a week later, she would buy me a guitar for my birthday."

When she learned that he had misled her about his guitar playing, Ayala's mother was furious. "For a full year, she kept telling me to sell the guitar," he recalled. "She really milked it and made me feel bad. I finally said to her, 'One day, I'm going to be a famous guitar player; I can't sell it.'"

Putting new strings on the long-languishing guitar, Ayala began to strum. "It changed everything about me," he remembered. "I heard the sound of the instrument that I was meant to play. I became literally addicted to it, and had to have it near me. There are photos of me, passed out, with the guitar on my chest. It is such an intimate instrument. You caress it; embrace it next to your body. It physically touches your heart. Your arms surround it. I don't want to get overly spiritual and say that it's because it's made of cedar, and cedar is sacred, but it is."

Learning the fundamentals of guitar playing in school, Ayala sharpened his skills with popular rock tunes. "When you start playing the guitar," he said, "you play whatever's popular—things that you hear on MTV or the radio. I was a product of the 1980s, listening to rock and roll, and thinking that I was going to be a rock star."

Ayala's vision of music changed forever when he heard his guitar instructor playing a classical piece. "It stopped me in my tracks," he said, "and made me fall in love with the instrument all over again."

When he told the instructor that he wished to learn the piece, the educator's response disheartened him. "He told me, 'You'll never be able to play this. This music is too hard for you,'" Ayala remembered. "I stopped studying with him right away. I needed someone who was a positive influence, someone who knew what they were talking about."

Though he transferred to an instructor whose background did not include classical music, Ayala found a more encouraging reception. "If I would have had the money," he said, "I would have definitely gone to a classical instructor. It was a general course on guitar basics, learning to play chords, and reading sheet music, but when I told [the instructor] that I wanted to get more in depth into classical music, he started buying books, and we learned together."

Planning to study music performance in college, Ayala auditioned for the two-year Del Mar College, in Corpus Christi, Texas. It did not go well. "In high school, I was a big shot," he said. "Everybody wanted to hear me play the guitar, but, when I showed up for my college audition, and heard some of the other people auditioning, it was eye-opening. They were incredibly talented musicians playing at a very high level. They'd been playing since they were in primary school and had ten years on me."

After auditioning for a committee of music professors, Ayala learned he had not passed. "They felt that I wasn't good enough to be a music performance major," he recalled. "They said that I could be a music education major, which was still great—they were still going to give me a scholarship—but it was very disappointing. Again, it was somebody telling me that I couldn't do something, that I wasn't talented enough."

Determined to show the committee that they had made a mistake, Ayala gave up his entire social life to focus on the guitar. "I practiced ten hours a day," he said. "If I had a few minutes between classes, I'd jump into a practice room and play scales nonstop. Then I would run to class. It just took over everything."

The dedication paid off. When he auditioned again the following semester, Ayala received a more positive response, and the committee approved his entry into the music performance program. "I was very, very happy," he remembered, "but, at the same time, I was disappointed that they had made me wait. I looked at them, said, 'I told you that I was serious about music five months ago,' and walked out of the room. As soon as I closed the door, I said to myself, 'What an idiot you are; you could have just lost your scholarship.'"

Ayala prepared himself. "I waited for them to come out," he recalled. "When they did, I said, 'I meant no disrespect, but I'm really passionate about music.' They said, 'Gabriel, we see that. We're very happy about it, and glad that we inspired you to do better, but, please, don't do that again.' They let it go . . . luckily."

From that point, Ayala proved an ideal student. "Everything was 'Yes, sir,' 'No, sir,' and 'What can I do for you, sir?'" he remembered. "I took my lessons very literally. When the professor told me that I needed to learn a Bach sonata, I went home and learned it that evening. When I came to my lesson, I was prepared. I told him that I had learned the piece and was ready to perform it. This was in a week's time—a fourteen-page piece of music. I was that dedicated to showing that my passion for music wasn't going to fade."

Transferring to Texas A&M University after two years at Del Mar, Ayala became, at the age of nineteen, the youngest adjunct faculty member in the school's history. "I didn't have my music degree yet," he said, "but I was teaching my colleagues how to play the guitar. Some had been playing ten to fifteen years longer than I had. It was very humbling. It showed me that, with perseverance, anything was attainable."

As a classical guitar student, Ayala maintained a disciplined regiment. "It's incredibly difficult," he said. "You're constantly practicing and keeping the foundation of your technique at a very high level. That means playing scales, or arpeggios, reading sheet music, keeping on top of musical genres, and being in touch with all kinds of music. It means being a well-rounded musician. Fortunately, I love to practice and can play scales for two or three hours at a time. I love to have a guitar in my hands."

After graduating from Texas A&M University, Ayala was determined to continue his studies. "I auditioned for many universities," he said. "I was asked to come to schools like Cologne University, in Germany, and Austin Peay University in Clarksville, Tennessee, and a few other places, but, being in the Southwest—around my own tribe, my own people—was important to me. Arizona was a place where, after I had my degree, I could make my home."

Approaching directors of the University of Arizona's postgraduate music department, Ayala explained his reasons for wanting to come to the school. An audition was scheduled. Choosing a complicated piece by Italian composer Mario Giulani

(1781–1829) for his audition, he prepared to show off his instrumental mastery and gain admittance to the school.

As Ayala began to play, the instructor picked up a telephone and made a call. "I was playing an immense, nine-page piece," remembered the guitarist, "but it was only five minutes long. It was blazingly going by. I was putting 200 percent into it. I started thinking, 'How rude is this? This guy is really going to make a phone call while I'm trying to audition for him? This is awful.'"

Ayala listened as the instructor spoke into the phone. "He said, 'Hi, this is so-and-so. I want you to know that I have just accepted Gabriel Ayala as a master's degree candidate and want him on full fellowship.' I stopped playing the guitar and looked at him dead in the face. He looked at me, smiled, and said, 'Keep playing. I like that song.' I was stunned. Then I heard him say, 'I'll drop him off after his audition. Get the paperwork ready.' It was that simple. I stood up, shook his hand, and said that I didn't know what to do. He said, 'Finish the song.' I played it like I had never played it in my life."

During the two years that he spent studying for his master's degree, Ayala took advantage of the school's recording studio. "It's where I made my first recording," he said. "I needed an audition tape for an international guitar competition in Malibu, California. More than 150 guitarists applied. They chose twenty-two. I was one of them."

Launching a professional career in music after graduating from the University of Arizona (with a 4.0 grade point average) in 2003, Ayala scored the first of many NAMMY nominations with his independently released debut album.

For his second album, *I'll Be Home for Christmas*, Ayala turned to the Yuletide season for inspiration. "Christmas is my favorite holiday," he said, "not for religious reasons, but because people are a little nicer around Christmastime. The spirit of Christmas moves them. They are more courteous. As I started touring more and more, I told people not to worry, that I'd be home for Christmas, no matter what happened, even if it was only in my dreams."

Ayala included more than twenty reinterpreted holiday classics. "My friends said that I was crazy," he said, "that I shouldn't put all of them on one CD; I should do a volume one and a volume two, and make twice the money. But I said, 'That's a rotten idea. I'm not playing music to become a millionaire. I'm playing to share this gift that the Creator has given me.'"

The 1992 Martin Brest–produced film, *Scent of a Woman*, starring Al Pacino and Chris O'Donnell, inspired Ayala's third album, *Tango* (2008). "There was an incredible tango scene in the middle of the movie," he explained. "When I heard the song, it took over my body. The music just overwhelmed me. I needed to adapt it into my style of playing. I wished that the piece [performed in the film by accordionist Astor Piazzolla] had been written for the guitar."

The more he thought about it, the more determined Ayala became to interpret Piazzolla's music on the guitar. "I went online and bought the piano sheet music," he said, "and, thirty minutes later, I was playing it on the guitar. I played it the following night at a concert, and people went crazy. I started adding more tango compositions to my repertoire and doing arrangements that no one had done before. It was new and exciting."

Ayala has since introduced a new musical approach that he calls "jazzmenco," fusing Spanish classical music, flamenco, and jazz. "When I hear a guitar," he said, "I don't hear it as a guitar. I hear it as a condensed symphony. When I play, I hear horns. I hear percussion. I hear woodwinds. I hear reed instruments and brass."

Despite the global range of his repertoire, Ayala's roots remain at the heart of his playing. "My music instills cultural beliefs," he said. "It could be in the title of a song—some of which are in my language—or in the reason why a piece was written. Sacred sites have inspired some."

Ayala's tunes reflect the song traditions of the Yaqui community. "I'm a singer for my tribe," he said, "and I sing for our ceremonies. When I compose songs, I don't run to the guitar, I start singing."

Natural sounds of the Southwest also provide inspiration. "I'll be sitting out in the desert," said Ayala, "with a tall glass of iced tea, listening to the coyotes singing back and forth to each other, until a melody comes to me. It changes the way that I compose music. I don't need my guitar to create something."

Ayala wrote a recent piece, "Whispers from Eagle Hill," while visiting extended family on the Kahnawake Reserve in Canada's Mohawk Country. "I was sitting by this lakefront," he recalled, "and listening [to the sounds of the night]. I had my guitar in my hands, but I didn't play it. When I came back to the house, people said, 'You were out there for a couple of hours.' It seemed like I had only been gone for minutes. I had heard so many voices within the trees, within the waves of the water crashing back and forth, and within the wind."

Although he approached Canyon Records about recording him before releasing three independent albums, Ayala encountered resistance. "They told me that they were a Native American label," he remembered, "I said, 'Luckily for you, I'm Native American.' Then they said, 'We only record American Indian music.' I said, 'That's so disappointing, but I'm an American Indian.' They kind of laughed it off."

Following a well-received appearance at the John F. Kennedy Center for Performing Arts in Washington, D.C., in 2009, Ayala renewed his pitch. This time, the label responded differently. "They e-mailed me back," Ayala remembered, "and asked me to come to the studio to talk."

Soon afterwards, Canyon signed Ayala to a new subsidiary label, Explorer, created exclusively to release his music. "They had to justify why they could record me," he said, "even though it wasn't traditional American Indian music."

Recording his first album for the label (*Portraits: Music for Classical Guitar*) solo, Ayala began to reach out to other musicians, recording *Passion, Fire, & Grace* in 2010 with percussionist Will Clipman. "I wrote the compositions out," said Ayala, "and told Will how I wanted him to play—which rhythms, which instruments. There was some artistic freedom on his part, but I could already hear the end result in my head."

Ayala's next album, *Sonoran Nights*, featured the guitarist and percussionist joined by tenor saxophonist, guitarist, and vocalist (and Mary Redhouse's brother) Vince Redhouse (Diné). "It was a great opportunity to collaborate with other musicians," said Ayala, "and to see if they inspired me. They were all musicians that I deeply respected, with careers thirty years longer than my own. The fact that they wanted to play with me was an incredibly humbling experience. They liked my music so much that they wanted to be a part of it."

Just as his career seemed to be taking off, an auto accident en route to a concert in New Mexico left Ayala seriously injured. "I was on the freeway, going seventy-five miles an hour," he remembered, "when somebody cut me off. It almost took my life. I couldn't move for four days. I had bruises all over my chest from the impact of the steering wheel. It was hard for me to breathe. I didn't want to do anything but sleep and pray that the pain would go away."

Forcing himself out of bed after four days, Ayala grabbed his guitar and began to play. "I was inspired to write '12–19,' based on the day of the accident—December 19," he said. "It was like a birthday for me, another chance at life. I wrote the entire composition the first time through. It was as though I had been perform- ing it for years. I stopped myself afterwards and thought, 'Did I steal that song from someplace?' I started looking through my CDs for the melody or the chord progression. How could I know a song that well without having played it before? I came to the realization that it was a gift from the Creator. Through tragedy, good things come. For me, it was that gift of music, once again."

"When I closed my eyes, I could see the accident reoccurring," he continued. "I could see the heads of the children in the other car, as they banged into the window, the glass starting to fly. I could see the fillings in the driver's mouth as she looked at me and realized that she had done something wrong and was about to be impacted by my vehicle. It was incredibly difficult to even want to play the song live. It brought up feelings that I didn't want to relive, but I realized, for healing to begin, I needed to share. I recorded it to show the real-ness of life to people. It could all be gone in an instant."

Ayala's latest music reflects a growing interest in improvisation. "I love to improvise," he said, "but it wasn't until three and a half years ago that I began. I was of the school of music where, if it's not on the paper, you don't play it. If it says, 'crescendo,' you get louder. If it says, 'pianissimo,' you play quietly. When I started listening more to jazz and flamenco, I said, 'These musicians are playing whatever notes they want to play. What are they doing? Don't they know that they're breaking the rules?'"

"But I fell in love with the idea of breaking the rules," he continued. "I was on tour in Venezuela and said, 'Tonight, I'm going to improvise a whole song.' It was one of the serious moments of my life. I had no idea how to end the song. What I thought would be a two- or three-minute composition ended up being a six-minute song. Later, I recorded it. It was an expression of how I felt. From there, improvisation became a very important part of my career. Nowadays, when I perform, I play the written melody of a piece, and, from there, I improvise. As I play the notes, I sing the melody in my head. It's music on a whole other realm."

Having become one of Indigenous America's most respected artists, Ayala is aiming for the mainstream. "Some people ask me what's next," he said, "and I jokingly tell them 'global domination,' but I really do want to perform for people in Germany, France, and Sweden, all over the world. It's important that the message gets through."

CODA

As I worked on this book, people asked about my heritage. The truth is I don't know. My paternal roots go back to Russia and Austria, but my mother was adopted as an infant, and my brother, sister, and I have not subjected to DNA tests. Speaking with American Indian musicians, listening to their music, and conducting research, however, I came to believe that there are really only two kinds of people: those who believe in harmony between human beings, the natural world, and the supernatural world and those who believe that human beings have an inherent right to subjugate, dominate, and exploit the other worlds. It's that adherence to balance that connects American Indians with hippies, New Agers, and others concerned about the planet. Race, religion, and heritage are secondary. As for me, it doesn't matter who or what you are, or where you came from, if you're committed to living harmonically, we stand united. If not, may you be swallowed by the Earth as Toviba predicted more than a century and half ago. We'd all be the better for it.

In late 2012, I received a copy of a two-page letter that Robert Doyle had written to Neil Putnow, president of NARAS (National Academy of Recording Arts and Sciences). In the letter, the Canyon Records owner and president responded to the announcement that the Grammy Award's Native American category was combining with Hawaiian, Zydeco/Cajun, and Polka to create a new Regional Roots Music category. Acknowledging that the consolidation was not "discriminatory, considering that changes were made to mainstream, high profile categories as well," he went on to say, "the loss of the Native American category diminishes everyone."

NARAS's decision is but one more obstacle faced by Indigenous musicians. The economic recession has made a drastic impact. SOAR, Silver Wave, and Indian House Records are concentrating more on their back catalogues than on releasing new music. Makoche has turned its full-time attention to its recording studio. And after years of prosperity, Canyon Records has been facing a steeper climb.

"When I was a kid, Native American records were pretty basic," remembered Wayne Silas, Jr. "You'd see them at trading posts, powwows, and hardly anywhere else. But [then] it became really exciting. We'd go into record stores, like Virgin Records in Times Square, and there would be a Native American section with our CDs. Now, it's making another change, with all the digital downloading. The music world is changing."

The outlook for American Indian music, though, is far from bleak. Innovative musicians are constantly breaking new ground, creating unique sounds while preserving traditional roots. At the fifteenth Native American Music Awards celebration, in November 2014, many of the artists in this book were represented. Tha Tribe's *Stoic* was named "best powwow recording," while Theresa "Bear" Fox was honored as "songwriter of the year." Indigenous's *Vanishing Americans* was named the year's "best blues recording" with Mato Nanji named "artist of the year." Joanne Shenandoah's "Native Dance" scored as "best world music recording," while her daughter Leah was named "debut artist of the year." In recognition of her Christmas album, Rita Coolidge was named the year's "best female artist." A Tribe Called Red received a "best music video" award for "Sister," featuring Northern Voice. The Aboriginal DJ collective has continued to push the sounds of Indigenous America even further, collaborating with Buffy Sainte-Marie on a track, "Working for the Government," released in July 2015.

After more than half a millennium of stereotyping, cultural suppression, economic poverty, forced assimilation, and urbanization, the music of Native America (like the people) remains invincible, continuing to burn with hope, promise, and determination. Isn't it time that we listen?

NOTES

INTRODUCTION

1. Bartolome Las Casas, *History of the Indies* (New York: Harper & Row, 1971), www. gutenberg.org/cache/epub/20321/pg20321.html.
2. Alice Cunningham Fletcher, *A Study of Omaha Indian Music* (Lincoln: University of Nebraska Press, 1994), 9.
3. United Nations Permanent Forum on Indigenous Issues (UNPFII), *Declaration on the Rights of Indigenous People*, 2007.

CHAPTER 1. THE HEARTBEAT

Epigraph. Melba Blanton, "The Rainmaker's Secret Weapon," *Occult*, October 1973, 32–35.

1. Jake Saltzman, "Two-day Pow-wow Celebrates Native American Culture," *Patriot Ledger* (Quincy, Mass.), May 25, 2014.
2. Patty Talahongva, "Powwow 101," *Native Peoples*, July–August 2004, 28.
3. Ibid.
4. Tara Browner, *Heartbeat of the People: Music and Dance of the Northern Pow-Wow* (Champaign: University of Illinois Press, 2004), 21.
5. Alice Fletcher, "Hae-Thu-Ska Society of the Omaha Tribe," http://omahatribe.unl.edu/ etexts/oma.0015/.
6. Blanton, "Rainmaker's Secret Weapon," 32–35.
7. L. W. Wilson, with Lucy Cherry, Writers Project Administration (WPA), November 26, 1937. http://digital.libraries.ou.edu/whc/pioneer/papers/12276%20Cherry.pdf.
8. Matt Gilbert, "Potlatch: Perspective on the Alaska Way of Life." www.newsminer.com/ features/sundays/community_features/potlatch-perspectives-on-the-alaska-way-of-life/ article_5b012c2a-e924–11e3-a04b-0017a43b2370.html. Accessed June 2, 2014.
9. Thomas E. Mails, *Fools Crow: Wisdom and Power* (San Francisco: Council Oaks Books, 2001), 89.
10. Fred W. Voget, *Shoshoni-Crow Sun Dance* (Norman: University of Oklahoma Press, 1998), 78.
11. Jeffrey Zelitch (Anpetu Oihanke Wanica), "The Lakota Sun Dance," *Expedition* 13, no. 1 (September 1970), University of Pennsylvania Museum of Archeology and Anthropology.

12. Frederick Schwatka, "Among the Apaches," *Century Magazine*, May 1887, 28.
13. Alice Cunningham Fletcher, "Sun Dance of the Ogallala Sioux," in *Proceedings of the American Association for the Advancement of Science* (Washington, D.C.: Government Printing Office, 1883).
14. Ibid.
15. David Busch, "Southern Ute Indian Tribe Spiritual Leader Eddie Bent Box Walks On: Read Part of His Story Here," *American Indian Today*, October 9, 2012. http://indiancountrytodaymedianetwork.com/2012/10/09/southern-ute-indian-tribe-spiritual-leader-eddie-bent-box-walks-read-part-his-story-here.
16. James McLaughlin, *My Friend, the Indian* (New York: Houghton Mifflin Co., 1910), 202.
17. Ibid.
18. James Mooney, "The Ghost-Dance Religion and the Sioux Outbreak of 1890," *Annual Report of the Bureau of American Ethnology* (Washington D.C.: Government Printing Office, 1894.
19. Ibid.
20. Ibid.
21. Mooney, "Ghost-dance Religion."
22. Ibid.
23. McLaughlin, *My Friend*, 210.
24. Ibid., p. 210.
25. Curtis, *Indians' Book*, 198.
26. Black Elk, as quoted in John G. Neihardt, *Black Elk Speaks: Being the Life Story of a Holy Man of the Oglala Sioux* (Albany: State University of New York Press, 2008), 218.
27. Mark A. Michaels, "Indigenous Ethics and Alien Laws: Native Traditions and the United States Legal System," *Fordham Law Review* 66, no. 4 (1998), 1565.
28. Robin Fisher, *Contact and Conflict: Indian-European Relations in British Columbia, 1774–1890* (Vancouver: University of British Columbia Press, 1977), 189–90.
29. John Tierney, "The Potlatch Scandal: Busted for Generosity," *New York Times*, December 15, 2008.
30. Ibid.
31. Richard Pratt, "Kill the Indian, Save the Man," given at the Nineteenth Annual Conference of Charities and Correction, Denver, Colo., 1892. Reprinted in Richard Pratt, *Americanizing the American Indians: Writing by the "Friends of the Indian," 1880–1900* (Cambridge, Mass.: Harvard University Press, 1973), 260–71.
32. John Collier, *Annual Report of the Secretary of the Interior for the Fiscal Year Ended June 30, 1938* (Washington, D.C., Government Printing Office, 1938).
33. "Native Americana: 10 Recent Albums from Canyon Records," *No Depression*, November 25, 2013. http://nodepression.com/article/native-americana-10-recent-albums-canyon-records.

CHAPTER 2. THE WARBLE

1. Bryan Burton, *Voices of the Wind: Native American Flute Songs* (Wauwatosa, Wisc.: World Music Press, 1998), 6–8.
2. Stephen R. Riggs, *The Gospel among the Dakota* (Chicago: W. G. Holmes, 1869), 98.

3. Mary Crow Dog and Richard Erdoes, *Lakota Woman* (New York: Harper Perennial, 1990). http://facultyfiles.deanza.edu/gems/delaneyanthony/LakotaWoman.pdf.

4. Anna Kisselgoff, "New Graham Work Revisits Native America," *New York Times*, October 15, 1988.

5. Peter Ellersten,"'SynthacousticpunkarachiNavajazz'—What Does It Sound Like?" *Hogfiddle*, March 31, 2010. http://hogfiddle.blogspot.com/2010/03/hum-221-r-carlos-nakai-what-does-xxxx.html.

6. O. W. Jones, *Native American Flute Maker*, video, Canyon Records, Phoenix, Ariz., 2010.

7. Ibid.

8. "The Legendary Musician of the Native American Flute Performs at the Mind Body Spirit Expo," *New Visions*, Fall 2011, 18.

9. Kristine Morris, review, "Dancing into Silence," *Spiritualty & Health*, January–February, 2011. http://spiritualityhealth.com/reviews/dancing-silence.

10. Review, "Carry the Gift," *All Music Guide*. www.allmusic.com/album/carry-the-gift-mw0000199099.

11. Review, "Dancing into Silence," *Arizona Network News*.

12. John Malkin, review, *Spirituality & Health*, September–October 2013, http://spirituality-health.com/reviews/awakening-fire.

13. Ibid.

14. Kat McReynolds, "Ready for Reunion: Carlos Nakai and Peter Kater Plan Concert Series," *Mountain Xpress* (Asheville, N.C.), November 19, 2014.

15. Sandra Hale Schulman, review, "Totemic Flute Chants," *Indian Country News*, December 8, 2007.

16. *Echoes*, NPR, March 5, 2008.

CHAPTER 3.TRIBAL VOICES

Epigraph. Randon A. Perry, "An Evening with Radmilla Cody," *Indianapolis Reporter*, March 10, 2011.

1. Alice Cunningham Fletcher, aided by Francis LaFlesche, *A Study of Omaha Indian Music* (Cambridge, Mass.: Peabody Museum of Archeology and Ethnology, 1893), 10.

2. Curtis, *Indians' Book*, 60.

3. Henry A. Schoolcraft, *Historical and Statistical Information Relating the History, Condition, and Prospects of the Indian Tribes of the United States: Collected and Prepared under the Direction of the Bureau of Indian Affairs, per Act of Congress of March 3, 1847*, 6 vols. (Philadelphia: Lippincott, 1851–1857).

4. Curtis, *Indians' Book*, 60.

5. Jay Courtney Fikes and Margaret Runy Castaneda, *Carlos Castaneda, Academic Opportunism, and the Psychedelic Sixties* (Victoria, B.C.: Millenia Press, 1993).

6. Omer Call Stewart, *Peyote Religion: A History* (Norman: University of Oklahoma Press, 1987), 45.

7. James Sydney Slotkin, "The Peyote Way," *Teaching from the American Earth: Indian Religion and Philosophy* (New York: Liveright, 1975), 102.

8. Edward Ellsworth Hipsher, "American Opera and Its Composers" (Philadelphia, Pa.: Theodore Presser, 1927), 86.

9. Curtis, *Indians' Book*, xii.

10. Ibid.

11. Frances Densmore, "The Study of Indian Music," *Musical Quarterly* 1, no. 2 (April 1915), 187–97.

12. Willard Rhodes, liner notes, *Music of the American Indian of the Southwest*, Folkways, 1951.

13. Manuel Archuleta, as told to Ilon Barth, "The Chants of My People," *Desert Magazine*, October 1949.

14. Ibid.

15. *Arizona Republic* (Phoenix), October 29, 2000.

16. Antonino D'Ambrosio, *A Heartbeat and a Guitar: Johnny Cash and the Making of Bitter Tears* (New York: Nation Books, 2009), 75.

17. Ibid.

18. Gordon Friesen, "Indigenous Folk Singer: Peter LaFarge," *Broadside*, October–December, 1976, 6.

19. Julius Lester, Peter LaFarge obituary, *Village Voice*, January 1966.

20. Peter LaFarge, liner notes, *Many a Mile* (New York: Vanguard, 1965).

21. John Einarson, *Four Strong Winds: Ian and Sylvia* (Toronto: McClelland & Stewart, 2011), 122.

22. Ibid.

23. Buffy Sainte-Marie, *The Buffy Sainte-Marie Songbook* (New York: Grosset & Dunlap, 1971), 16.

24. Gale Courey Toensing, "Language Restoration a Top Priority at Mashantucket Conference," *American Indian Today*, April 5, 2006. http://indiancountrytoday medianetwork.com/2006/04/05/language-restoration-top-priority-mashantucket-conference-107319.

25. Review, "Coincidence and Likely Stories," *Rolling Stone*, November 26, 1992.

26. Lenny Stoute, "Buffy's Back with the First Album in Fifteen Years," *Toronto Star*, September 20, 1992.

27. Michel Martin, "Floyd 'Red Crow' Westerman Balanced Acting with Activism," NPR, December 17, 2007.

28. Michael Carlson, "Floyd Red Crow Westerman," *The Guardian*, New York, December 24, 2007.

29. Roger Moody, *The Indigenous Voice: Visions and Realities* (London: Zed Books, 1988), 324.

30. Joanne Shenandoah, liner notes, *Nature Dance*, self-produced, 2013.

31. Robert Baird, "Trial by Fire: American Indian Movement Co-Founder John Trudell Finds a Life Line in Words and Music," *New Times* (Phoenix), June 17, 1992.

32. Cynthia Oi, "Front Man: John Trudell Doesn't Box Himself In with Labels Like Migrant Musician, Poet, and Activist," *Star Bulletin* (Honolulu), February 22, 2001.

33. Don Snowden, "Rock Meets Indian Tradition," *Los Angeles Times*, July 18, 1992.

34. CD review, *The New Industrialist*, May 1994, 46.

35. Jim Bessman, "Trudell Lets Words Do the Talking," *Billboard* (New York), June 13, 1992.

36. Anthony Goulet, "What Is a Good Man? A Conversation with John Trudell, Human Being," Good Men Project, October 28, 2014. www.goodmenproject.com.

37. Buddy Seigel, "Walking Tall down 'the Red Road': Native American Singer Bill Miller's Music Celebrates His Heritage While Soothing the Pain of Racism," *Los Angeles Times,* August 27, 1994.

38. Ibid.

39. Mark Crawford, "Spotlight: Bill Miller," *Cowboys & Indians,* October 2012. www.cowboysindians.com/Cowboys-Indians/October-2012/Spotlight-Bill-Miller/.

40. Bill Miller, liner notes, *Chronicles of Hope,* 2010.

41. Alex Simon, "Hollywood Interview: Robbie Robertson," *Venice Magazine,* December 1998. http://thehollywoodinterview.blogspot.com/2008/03/robbie-robertson-hollywood-interview.html.

42. Lorraine Alterman, "Rita Coolidge Fall into Spring," *New York Times,* June 1977, 86.

43. Robert Christgau, *Rock Albums of the '70s: A Critical Guide* (New York: Da Capo Press, 1981), 91.

44. Megan Disken, "Murder-Suicide Victim Was Sister of Rita Coolidge," *Ventura (Calif.) County Star,* October 4, 2014.

45. Ayesha Morris, "Pura Fe, Soni Moreno, and Jennifer Elizabeth Kreisberg," *Washington City Paper,* January 29, 1999. www.washingtoncitypaper.com/blogs/artsdesk/?s=Ulali.

46. Ulali, *Mahk Jchi* liner notes, Corn, Beans, and Squash Records, 1994.

47. CD review, www.bluesweb.com.

48. Northwest Territories, Bureau of Statistics, 2006.

49. "Two Cultures, One Voice," *Morning Edition,* NPR, May 10, 2010.

50. John M. Glionna, "Radmilla Cody, Navajo Singer from Arizona Is Ready for the Grammys," *Los Angeles Times,* February 6, 2013.

51. Craig Harris, "Radmilla Cody," *Dirty Linen,* June–July 2007, 28–32.

52. Leo W. Banks, "An Unusual Miss Navajo," *High Country News,* March 7, 2011. www.hcn.org/issues/43.4/an-unusual-miss-navajo.

53. Harris, "Radmilla Cody," 28–32.

54. Orlando Tom, "Sense of Identity," *Navajo Times* (Window Rock, Ariz.), December 23, 1997.

55. Garth Cartwright, *More Miles Than Money: Journey through American Music* (London: Serpent's Tail, 2009), 122.

56. Ibid.

57. Banks, "An Unusual Miss Navajo." www.hcn.org/issues/43.4/an-unusual-miss-navajo.

58. Harris, "Radmilla Cody," 28–32.

59. Mark Shaffer and Dennis Wagner, "Radmilla Cody: Ex-Miss Navajo Nation Heading for U.S. Prison," *Arizona Republic* (Phoenix), December 13, 2002.

60. Harris, "Radmilla Cody," 28–32.

61. Ibid.

62. Jim Largo, "Offerings to the Holy People," *Navajo Times* (Window Rock, Ariz.), March 23, 2012.

63. Harris, "Radmilla Cody," 28–32.

64. Ibid.

65. Laurel Morales, "Navajo Singer Radmilla Cody Nominated for First Grammy," KNAU, February 7, 2013.

66. Harris, "Radmilla Cody," 28–32.

67. Banks, "An Unusual Miss Navajo." www.hcn.org/issues/43.4/an-unusual-miss-navajo.
68. Mykel Vernon-Sembach, "NAU Alumni Radmilla Cody Nominated for Grammy Award, *The Lumberjack*, Northern Arizona University, February 7, 2013.
69. Glionna, "Radmilla Cody," *Los Angeles Times*, February 6, 2013.

CHAPTER 4. REZ ROCKERS, GUITAR HEROES, AND RASTA MEN

1. Kara Briggs, "Power Source behind Link Wray's Chords: His Family," *American Indian News*, June 14, 2011.
2. Ibid.
3. Ibid.
4. Ibid.
5. John Fogerty, Induction speech, Rock and Roll Hall of Fame, New York City, March 10, 2008.
6. "20 Who Mattered," *Guitar Player*, January 1987, 64.
7. Richie Unterberger, *The Rough Guide to Jimi Hendrix* (London: Rough Guides, 2009), 25.
8. Michael Davis, "Alan Douglas: Hendrix Producer under Fire," *BAM*, August 25, 1995. www.me.umn.edu/~kgeisler/ad.html.
9. "Jimi Hendrix's Patchwork Coat Heads to the Museum of the American Indian," *Washington Post*, April 29, 2010.
10. Steven Chua, "Vancouver Hendrix Shrine Rocks On for Second Year," *Toronto Sun*, July 11, 2012.
11. Vincent Schilling, "'Come and Get Your Love' at 40: Pat Vegas Reflects on Redbone's Ride," *Indian Country News*, April 1, 2014.
12. Vincent Schilling, "PJ Vegas, Son of Redbone's Pat Vegas, Teams with Cody Blackbird," *American Indian Today*, January 27, 2014.
13. Bruce Weber, "Reggae Rhythms Speak to an Insular Tribe," *New York Times*, September 19, 1999.

CHAPTER 5. DIVAS, HIP-HOPPERS, AND ELECTRONIC DANCE MASTERS

1. Genesis Tuck, "Rapper Shadowyze Says 'Say No to the R Word,'" *Indian Country Today*, November 4, 2013.
2. "Interview: Frank Waln on His Keystone XL Pipeline Protest Song," indianz.com, May 9, 2014.
3. Tristin Hopper, "In the Beginning: A Look at the Causes behind Idle No More," *National Post* (Toronto), January 5, 2013.
4. Samantha Everts, "A Tribe Called Red: Aboriginal Group's New Album Is All Politics and Sponge Bob," *Metro Ottawa*, May 23, 2013.
5. Ibid.

CHAPTER 6. DEPICTING AND DEFYING STEREOTYPES

1. Barbara A. Gray-Kanatiiosh, 'Racism & Stereotyping: The Effects on Our Children, on Our Future. www.tuscaroras.com/graydeer/pages/racism.htm.
2. Linda Scarangella McNenly, *Native Performers in Wild West Shows: From Buffalo Bill to Euro Disney* (Norman: University of Oklahoma Press, 2012), 194.
3. Ibid.
4. William Frederick Cody, *An Autobiography of Buffalo Bill* (New York: Farrar and Rinehart, 1920). http://www.gutenberg.org/files/12740/12740-h/12740-h.htm.
5. Ibid.
6. James R. Smart, liner notes, *The Sousa and Pryor Bands: Original Recordings, 1901–1926* (New World Records, New York, 1976).
7. Wolfgang Saxon, "Merle Evans Is Dead: Former Band Leader at Ringling Brothers," *New York Times*, January 3, 1988.
8. James Creelman, review, *New York Herald*, December 15, 1893.
9. Jean Jacques Rousseau, *Discourse on the Origin of Inequality* (Indianapolis, Ind.: Hackett Publishing Co., 1992). http://www.gutenberg.org/files/11136/11136.txt.
10. Deborah Evans Price, "For Curb's Tim McGraw, Success Isn't 'Too Soon,'" *Billboard*, August 19, 1995, 6.
11. Angela R. Riley, "UCLA American Indian Studies Open Letter to No Doubt," November 6, 2012. http://www.aisc.ucla.edu/news/aisc_openletter.aspx.
12. Chris Anderson, "Indian War: Men Feud over Native American Heritage," *Herald-Tribune* (Sarasota, Fla.), January 27, 2012.
13. Chad Garrison, "Going Native," *Riverfront Times* (St. Louis), November 1, 2006.
14. Trevor Risk, "A Tribe Called Red Want White Fans to 'Please Stop' Wearing Redface 'Indian' Costumes to Shows," *Huffington Post*, July 12, 2013.
15. "No Doubt's Native American Video: Why It Wasn't Looking Hot," *The Guardian* (New York), November 5, 2012.
16. Lakota Summit V, "A Declaration of War against Exploiters of Lakota Spirituality," June 10, 1993. http://www.aics.org/war.html.
17. Sean Michaels, "Canadian Festival Bans Native American-Style Headdresses," *The Guardian* (New York), July 26, 2014.
18. Alan Di Perna, "Interview: Carlos Santana Discusses His New Album 'Shape Shifter,'" *Guitar World*, July 20, 2012. http://www.guitarworld.com/node/16344.
19. Lee Allen, "Music 'Addict' Gabriel Ayala Plays for Pope and President," *Indian Country Today*, December 10, 2012.

BIBLIOGRAPHY

Sources interviewed by the author are listed at the end of the bibliography.

BOOKS, ARTICLES, THESES, SPEECHES, AND LINER NOTES

Allen, Lee. "Music 'Addict' Gabriel Ayala Plays for Pope and President." *Indian Country Today*, December 10, 2012.

Alterman, Laurie. "Rita Coolidge Fall into Spring." *New York Times*, June 2, 1974.

Anderson, Chris. "Indian War: Men Feud over Native American Heritage." *Herald-Tribune* (Sarasota, Florida), January 27, 2012.

Archuleta, Manuel, as told to Ilon Barth. "The Chants of My People." *Desert Magazine*, October 1949.

Baird, Robert. "Trial by Fire: American Indian Movement Co-Founder John Trudell Finds a Life Line in Words and Music." *Arizona Republic* (Phoenix), October 29, 2000.

Banks, Leo W. "An Unusual Miss Navajo." *High Country News*, March 7, 2011.

Bessman, Jim. "Trudell Lets Words Do the Talking." *Billboard*, June 13, 1992.

Blanton. Melba. "The Rainmaker's Secret Weapon." *Occult*, October 1973, 32–35.

Braine, Susan. *Drumbeat . . . Heartbeat: A Celebration of the Powwow (We Are Still Here)*. Minneapolis, Minn.: Lerner Publishing Group, 1995.

Briggs, Kara. "Jazz Sax in a Native Key." *American Indian News*, April 20, 2010, www.americanindiannews.org/2010/04/jazz-sax-in-a-native-key/.

———. "Power Source behind Link Wray's Chords: His Family." *American Indian News*, June 14, 2011, www.americanindiannews.org/2011/01/music-link-wray/.

Brown, Dee. *Bury My Heart at Wounded Knee: An Indian History of the American West*. New York: Holt McDougal, 1970.

Browner, Tara. *Heartbeat of the People: Music and Dance of the Northern Pow-Wow*. Champaign: University of Illinois Press, 2004.

Burton, Bryan. *Voices of the Wind: Native American Flute Songs*. Wauwasota, Wisc.: World Music Press, 1998.

Busch, David. "Southern Ute Indian Tribe Spiritual Leader Eddie Bent Box Walks On: Read Part of His Story Here." *American Indian Today*, October 9, 2012.

Carlson, Michael. "Floyd Red Crow Westerman." *The Guardian* (New York), December 24, 2007.

Carney, George O. and Hugh W. Foley, Jr. *Oklahoma Music Guide: Biographies, Big Hits, and Annual Events*. Stillwater, Okla.: New Forums Press, 2003.

Cartwright, Garth. *More Miles Than Money: Journey through American Music.* London: Serpent's Tail, 2009.

Carver, Jonathan. *Travels through the Interior Parts of North America, in the Years 1766, 1767, and 1768.* London: C. Dilly, H. Payne, J. Phillips, 1781.

Christgau, Robert. *Rock Albums of the '70s: A Critical Guide.* New York: Da Capo Press, 1981.

Chua, Steven. "Vancouver Hendrix Shrine Rocks On for Second Year." *Toronto Sun,* July 11, 2012.

Claypoole, Antoinette Nora. *Who Would Unbraid Her Hair: The Legend of Annie Mae.* Lawrence, Kans.: Anamcara Press, 1999.

Cody, William Frederick. *Autobiography of Buffalo Bill.* New York: Farrar & Rinehart, 1920.

Collier, John. *Annual Report of the Secretary of the Interior for the Fiscal Year Ended June 30, 1938.* Washington, D.C.: Government Printing Office, 1938.

Cooper, James Fenimore. *Last of the Mohicans: A Narrative of 1757.* London: John Miller, 1826.

Cordova, Randy. "Musician Radmilla Cody's Life Is a Rich Tapestry." *Arizona Republic* (Phoenix), February 8, 2012.

Courtwright, Julie Renee. *Taming the Red Buffalo: Prairie Fire on the Great Plains.* Ann Arbor, Mich.: ProQuest, 2007.

Crawford, Mark. "Spotlight: Bill Miller." *Cowboys & Indians,* October 2012.

Crow Dog, Mary, and Richard Erdoes. *Lakota Woman.* New York: Harper Perennial, 1990.

Curtis, Natalie. *The Indians' Book: Authentic Native American Legends, Lore, and Music.* Houston, Tex.: Portland House, 1996.

D'Ambrosio, Antonino. *A Heartbeat and a Guitar: Johnny Cash and the Making of Bitter Tears.* New York: Nation Books, 2009.

Davis, Michael. "Alan Douglas: Hendrix Producer under Fire." *BAM,* August 25, 1995.

de Champlain, Samuel. *Voyages of Samuel de Champlain, 1604–1618.* New York: Charles Scribner & Sons, 1907.

de Najera, Pedro de Castaneda. *The Journey of Coronado, 1540–1542, from the City of Mexico to the Grand Canon of the Colorado and the Buffalo Plains of Texas, Kansas, and Nebraska.* New York: A. S. Barnes & Co., 1904.

de Vaca, Alvar Nunez Cabeza. *The Journey of Alvar Nunez Cabeza de Vaca also His Companions from Florida to the Pacific, 1528–1536.* New York: Allerton Book, 1904.

Disken, Megan. "Murder-Suicide Victim Was Sister of Rita Coolidge." *Ventura County (Calif.) Star,* October 4, 2014.

Duncan, Jim. "Ponca Hethuska Society." Master's thesis, Northeastern State University, Tahlequah, Oklahoma, 1997.

Einarson, John. *Four Strong Winds: Ian and Sylvia.* Toronto: McClelland & Stewart, 2011.

Ellis, Clyde. *A Dancing People: Powwow Culture on the Southern Plains.* Lawrence: University Press of Kansas, 2003.

Ellis, Clyde, Luke Eric Lessiter, and Gary H. Dunham. *Powwow.* Lincoln, Neb.: Bison Books, 2005.

Everts, Samantha. "A Tribe Called Red: Aboriginal Group's New Album Is All Politics and Sponge Bob." *Metro Ottawa,* May 23, 2013.

Field, Gary S. *American Indian Music Traditions and Contributions.* Portland, Ore.: Portland Public Schools, 1993.

Fikes, Jay Courtney, and Margaret Runy Castaneda. *Carlos Castaneda, Academic Opportunism, and the Psychedelic Sixties.* Canada: Millenia Press, 1993.

Fisher, Robin. *Contact and Conflict: Indian-European Relations in British Columbia, 1774–1890.* Vancouver: University of British Columbia Press, 1977.

Fletcher, Alice Cunningham. "Sun Dance of the Ogallala Sioux." Proceedings of the American Association for the Advancement of Science, Washington, D.C., 1883.

————, and Francis La Flesche. "The Omaha Tribe." In 27th Annual Report, Smithsonian Institution, Bureau of American Ethnology, Washington, D.C., 1905–1906.

————, aided by Francis LaFlesche. *A Study of Omaha Indian Music.* Cambridge, Mass.: Peabody Museum of American Archeology and Ethnology, 1893.

Fogerty, John. Speech at the induction of the Ventures, Rock and Roll Hall of Fame, March 10, 2008, New York.

Friesen, Gordon. "Indigenous Folk Singer: Peter LaFarge." *Broadside*, October-December, 1976, 6.

Garrison, Chad. "Going Native." *Riverfront Times* (St. Louis), November 1, 2006.

Giddings, Howard A. "The Natchez Indians." *Popular Science Monthly*, June 1891.

Gilbert, Matt, "Potlatch: Perspective on the Alaska Way of Life," June 2, 2014, http://www.newsminer.com/features/sundays/community_features/potlatch-perspectives-on-the-alaska-way-of-life/article_5b012c2a-e924-11e3-a04b-0017a43b2370.html.

Glionna, John M. "Radmilla Cody, Navajo Singer from Arizona Is Ready for the Grammys." *Los Angeles Times*, February 6, 2013.

Goulet, Anthony. "What Is a Good Man: A Conversation with John Trudell, Human Being." Good Men Project, October 28, 2014, http://www. goodmenproject.com.

Gray-Kanatiiosh, Barbara A. *Cahuilla (Native Americans).* Minneapolis, Minn.: Abdo Publishing, 2007.

Greeley, Horace. *An Overland Journey, from New York to San Francisco, in the Summer of 1859.* New York: C. M. Saxton, Barker, 1860.

Hall, Roger A. *Performing the American Frontiers, 1870–1906.* Cambridge, U.K.: University of Cambridge Press, 2001.

Harjo, Joy. *Crazy Brave: A Memoir.* New York: W. W. Norton, 2013.

Harris, Craig. *The Band: Pioneers of Americana Music.* Latham, Md.: Rowman & Littlefield, 2014.

————. *The New Folk Music.* Crown Point, Ind.: White Cliff Media, 1991.

————. "Radmilla Cody." *Dirty Linen*, June–July 2007, 28–32.

Hipsher, Edward Ellsworth. "American Opera and Its Composers." Philadelphia, Pa.: Theodore Presser, 1927.

Hopper, Tristin. "In the Beginning: A Look at the Causes behind Idle No More." *National Post* (Canada), January 5, 2013.

Howard, James. "The Ponca Tribe." *Bureau of American Ethnology Bulletin* 195, 1965.

Kisselgoff, Anna. "New Graham Work Revisits Native America." *New York Times*, October 15, 1988.

LaFarge, Peter. Liner notes. *Many a Mile.* New York: Vanguard, 1965.

Lakota Summit V. "A Declaration of War against Exploiters of Lakota Spirituality." *News from Indian Country*, 1993.

Largo, Jim. "Offerings to the Holy People." *Navajo Times* (Window Rock, Ariz.), March 23, 2012.

Las Casas, Bartolome. *History of the Indies.* New York: Harper & Row, 1971.

Lester, Julius. Peter LaFarge obituary. *Village Voice*, January 1966.

Lewis, Meriwether, and William Clark, *Journals of Lewis and Clark*, 1804–1806. New York: Penguin Classics, 2002.

Lewis, Robert M. "Wild American Savages and the Civilized English: Catlin's Indian Gallery and the Shows of London." *European Journal of American Studies*, Spring 2008, http://ejas.revues.org/2263.

Lumholtz, Carl Sofus. *Unknown Mexico: A Record of Five Years' Exploration among the Tribes of the Western Sierra Madre in the Tierra Caliente of Tepic and Jalisco and among the Tarascos of Michoacao.* New York: Scribner's Sons, 1902.

Mails, Thomas E. *Fools Crow: Wisdom and Power.* Tulsa, Okla.: Council Oaks Books, 2001.

Malkin, John. CD review. *Spirituality & Health*, September–October 2013, http://spirituality health.com/reviews/awakening-fire.

Marquette, Father Jacques. *Travels and Explorations of the Jesuit Missionaries in New France 1610–1791.* Cleveland, Ohio: Barrows Brothers, 1849.

Martin, Michel. "Floyd 'Red Crow' Westerman Balanced Acting with Activism." NPR, December 17, 2007.

Matthiessen, Peter. *In the Spirit of Crazy Horse.* New York: Penguin Books, 1980.

McLaughlin, James. *My Friend, the Indian.* New York: Houghton Mifflin, 1910.

McNenly, Linda Scarangella. *Native Performers in Wild West Shows: From Buffalo Bill to Euro Disney.* Norman: University of Oklahoma Press, 2012.

McReynolds, Kat. "Ready for Reunion: Carlos Nakai and Peter Kater Plan Concert Series." *Mountain Xpress* (Asheville, N.C.), November 19, 2014.

Means, Russell. *Where White Men Fear to Tread: The Autobiography of Russell Means.* New York: St. Martin's Griffin, 1996.

Michaels, Mark A. "Indigenous Ethics and Alien Laws: Native Traditions and the United States Legal System." *Fordham Law Review* 66, no. 4 (1998).

Miller, Bill. Liner notes. *Chronicles of Hope.* 2010.

Moody, Roger. *The Indigenous Voice: Visions and Realities.* London: Zed Books, 1988.

Mooney, James. "The Ghost-Dance Religion and the Sioux Outbreak of 1890." *Annual Report of the Bureau of American Ethnology.* Washington, D.C.: Government Printing Office, 1894.

Moore, Francis. *A Voyage to Georgia; Begun in the Year 1735.* St. Simons Island, Ga.: Fort Frederica Association, 1983.

Morales, Laurel. "Navajo Singer Radmilla Cody Nominated for First Grammy." KNAU, February 7, 2013, http://knau.org/post/navajo-singer-radmilla-cody-nominated-first-grammy.

Morris, Ayesha. "Pura Fe, Soni Moreno, and Jennifer Elizabeth Kreisberg." *Washington City Paper*, January 29, 1999.

Morris, Kristine. Review. *Dancing into Silence. Spiritualty & Health*, January-February, 2011, http://spiritualityhealth.com/reviews/dancing-silence.

Nakai, R. Carlos, and James Demars, *The Art of the Native American Flute.* Phoenix, Ariz., Canyon Records, 1997.

"Native American: 10 Recent Albums from Canyon Records." *No Depression*, November 25, 2013. http://nodepression.com/article/native-americana-10-recent-albums-canyon-records.

Neihardt, John G. *Black Elk Speaks: Being the Life Story of a Holy Man of the Oglala Sioux.* Albany: State University of New York Press, 2008.

Oi, Cynthia. Front Man: "John Trudell Doesn't Box Himself In with Labels like Migrant Musician, Poet, and Activist." *Star Bulletin* (Honolulu, Hawaii), February 22, 2001.

Percy, George. "Observations Gathered out of a Discourse of the Plantation of the Southern Colony in Virginia by the English, 1606." In *Jamestown Narratives: Eyewitness Accounts of the Virginia Colony, The First Decade, 1607–1617.* Champlain, Va.: Roundhouse, 1998.

Perry, Brandon A. "An Evening with Radmilla Cody." *Indianapolis Reporter,* March 10, 2011.

Pratt, Richard. "Kill the Indian, Save the Man." Nineteenth Annual Conference of Charities and Correction, Denver, Colorado, 1892. Reprinted in Richard Pratt, *Americanizing the American Indians: Writing by the "Friends of the Indian" 1880–1900.* Cambridge, Mass.: Harvard University Press, 1973, 260–71.

Price, Deborah Evans. "For Curb's Tim McGraw, Success Isn't 'Too Soon.'" *Billboard,* August 19, 1995, 6.

Riggs, Stephen R. *The Gospel among the Dakota.* Chicago: W. G. Holmes, 1869.

Risk, Trevor. "A Tribe Called Red Want White Fans to 'Please Stop' Wearing Redface 'Indian' Costumes to Shows." *Huffington Post,* July 12, 2013.

Roberts, Chris. *Powwow Country: People of the Circle.* Helena, Mont.: Far Country Press, 1992.

Rousseau, Jean Jacques. *Discourse on the Origin of Inequality.* Indianapolis, Ind.: Hackett Publishing Co., 1992.

Sabo, George, III. Paths of Our Children: Historic Indians of Arkansas. Arkansas Archeological Survey, 1992.

Sainte-Marie, Buffy. *The Buffy-Sainte Marie Songbook.* New York: Grosset & Dunlap, 1971.

Saltzman, Jake. "Two-day Pow-wow Celebrates Native American Culture." *Patriot Ledger* (Quincy, Mass.), May 25, 2014.

Saxon, Wolfgang. "Merle Evans Is Dead: Former Band Leader at Ringling Brothers." *New York Times,* January 3, 1988.

Scales, Christopher A. *Recording Culture: Powwow Music and the Aboriginal Recording Industry on the Northern Plains* (Refiguring American Music). Durham, N.C.: Duke University Press, 2012.

Schilling, Vincent. "'Come and Get Your Love' at 40: Pat Vegas Reflects on Redbone's Ride." *Indian Country News,* April 1, 2014.

———. *Native Musicians in the Groove.* Summertown, Tenn.: Native Voices Books, 2009.

———. "PJ Vegas, Son of Redbone's Pat Vegas, Teams with Cody Blackbird." *American Indian Today,* January 27, 2014.

Schoolcraft, Henry A. *Historical and Statistical Information Relating the History, Condition, and Prospects of the Indian Tribes of the United States: Collected and Prepared Under the Direction of the Bureau of Indian Affairs, per act of Congress of March 3, 1847.* 6 vols. Philadelphia: Lippincott, 1851–1857.

Schulman, Sandra Hale. Review, "Totemic Flute Chants." *Indian Country News,* January, 2008.

Schwatka, Frederick. "Among the Apaches." *Century Magazine,* May 1887.

Seigel, Buddy. "Walking Tall Down 'the Red Road': Native American Singer Bill Miller's Music Celebrates His Heritage While Soothing the Pain of Racism." *Los Angeles Times,* August 27, 1994.

Shaffer, Mark, and Dennis Wagner. "Radmilla Cody: Ex-Miss Navajo Nation Heading for U.S. Prison." *Arizona Republic* (Phoenix), December 13, 2002.

Simon, Alex. "Hollywood Interview: Robbie Robertson." *Venice Magazine,* December 1998, http://thehollywoodinterview.blogspot.com/2008/03/robbie-robertson-hollywood-interview.html.

Slotkin, James Sydney. "The Peyote Way." In *Teaching from the American Earth: Indian Religion and Philosophy.* New York: Liveright, 1975.

Smart, James R. Liner notes. *The Sousa and Pryor Bands: Original Recordings, 1901–1926.* New York: New World Records, 1976.

Smith, Paul Chaat, and Robert Allen Warrior. *Like a Hurricane: The Indian Movement from Alcatraz to Wounded Knee.* New York: The New Press, 1997.

Snowden, Don. "Rock Meets Indian Tradition." *Los Angeles Times,* July 18, 1992.

Stewart, Omer Call. *Peyote Religion: A History.* Norman: University of Oklahoma Press, 1987.

Stoute, Lenny. "Buffy's Back with the First Album in Fifteen Years." *Toronto Star,* September 20, 1992.

Strachey, William. *Historie of Travaile into Virginia Britinia.* London: Hakluyt Society, 1849.

Talahongva, Patty. "Powwow 101." *Native Peoples,* July–August, 2004, 28.

Tierney, John. "The Potlatch Scandal: Busted for Generosity." *New York Times,* December 15, 2008.

Toensing, Gale Courey. "Language Restoration a Top Priority at Mashantucket Conference." *American Indian Today,* April 5, 2006.

Tom, Orlando. "Sense of Identity." *Navajo Times* (Window Rock, Ariz.), December 23, 1997.

Troutman, John W. *Indian Blues: American Indians and the Politics of Music, 1879–1934.* Norman: University of Oklahoma Press, 2009.

Trudell, John. *Lines from a Mined Mind: The Words of John Trudell.* Golden, Colo.: Fulcrum Publishing, 2008.

Tuck, Genesis. "Rapper Shadowyze Says 'Say No to the R Word.'" *Indian Country Today,* November 4, 2013.

Turner, Frederick. *Portable North American Indian Reader.* New York: Viking Press, 1973.

United Nations Permanent Forum on Indigenous People (UNPFII). *Declaration on the Rights of Indigenous People.* New York: United Nations, 2007.

Unterberger, Richie. *The Rough Guide to Jimi Hendrix.* London: Rough Guides, 2009.

Vernon-Sembach, Mykel. "NAU Alumni Radmilla Cody Nominated for Grammy Award." *The Lumberjack.* Northern Arizona University, February 7, 2013.

Voget, Fred W. *Shoshoni-Crow Sun Dance.* Norman: University of Oklahoma Press, 1998.

Walker, J. R. "The Sun Dance and Other Ceremonies of the Oglala Division of the Teton Dakota." *Anthropological Papers of the American Museum of Natural History* 16, part 2. New York: American Museum of Natural History, 1917.

Weber, Bruce. "Reggae Rhythms Speak to an Insular Tribe." *New York Times,* September 19, 1999.

Wilson, L. W., with Lucy Cherry. Writers Project Administration (WPA), November 26, 1937, http://digital.libraries.ou.edu/whc/pioneer/papers/12276%20Cherry.pdf.

Wood, William. *New England's Prospect.* Amherst: University of Massachusetts Press, 1994.

Wright-McLeod, Brian. *The Encyclopedia of Native Music: More than a Century of Recordings from Wax Cylinder to the Internet.* Tucson: University of Arizona Press, 2005.

Zelitch, Jeffrey (Anpetu Oihanke Wanica). "The Lakota Sun Dance." *Expedition* 13, no. 1, September 1970.

AUTHOR INTERVIEWS

The records of these interviews are in the author's possession.

Interviewee, Date Interviewed

Susan Aglukark, September 2011
Walter Ahhaitty, September 2013
Bryan Akipa, September 2011
Don Amero, March 2012
Dallas Arcand, October 2011
Marcos Arcentalis, March 2012
Gabriel Ayala, May 2012
Howard Bad Hand, April 2013
Keith Bear, September 2011
Tom Bee, February 2011
Jay Begaye, November 2011
Tiinesha Begaye, December 2011
Clayson Benally, December 20112
Jeneda Benally, December 2012
Phillip Blanchett, December 2012
Douglas Blue Feather, July 2011
John Brown, June 2011
Darren Brulé, October 2011
Stephen Butler, March 2013
Michael Buyere, November 2011
Radmilla Cody, April 2012
Paula Conlon, October 2011
Rita Coolidge, January 2012
Charlie Cozad, July 2011
Antonino D'Ambrosio, July 2013
Gary Paul "Litefoot" Davis, November 2011
Mary Helen Deer, September 2013
Robert Doyle, December 2011
William Eaton, May 2012
Nokie Edwards, May 2011
Pura Fé, October 2011
Joseph Fire Crow, February 2013
Vince Fontaine, November 2011
Bear Fox, December 2011
Leela Gilday, October 2011
Leanne Goose, May 2012
Clint Goss, January 2014
Mark Guerrero, March 2011
Joy Harjo, July 2011

Sarah Hattman, April 2012
Mary Kay Henderson, March 2013
Raven Hernandez, January 2012
Tony Isaacs, December 2011
Julia Keefe, October 2014
Frosty Lawson, July 2012
Kevin Locke, July 2011
Casper Loma-Da-Wa, April 2012
Taj Mahal, March 2012
James Marienthal, September 2012
Yolanda Martinez, October 2011
Jana Mashonee, August 2011
Derek Matthews, May 2011
Barbara McAlister, October 2011
Jimmy McDonough, March 2012
Harlan McKosoto, October 2011
Bill Miller, July 2011
Robert Mirabal, October 2011
Louis Mofsie, October 2011
R. Carlos Nakai, June 2012
Mato Nanji, October 2011
A Paul Ortega, February 2012
Jamie K. Oxendine, June 2014
Terry Paskemin, April 2013
Levi Platero, October 2011
J. Poet, March 2014
Frank Poocha, December 2012
Aziz Rahman, September 2013
Marvin Rainwater, February 2012
Robbie Robertson, May 2013
Felipe Rose, July 2013
Buffy Sainte-Marie, July 2011
Cano Sanchez, March 2012
Vincent Schilling, November 2011
Sandra Schulman, February 2012
Keith Secola, October 2012 and July 2012
Joanne Shenandoah, October 2011
Kathy Sierra, March 2012
Wayne Silas, Jr., July 2011

Gary Stroutsos, August 2011
Cree Summer, October 2011
David Swenson, December 2011
Jerod Impichchaahaaha Tate, October 2011
Darryl Tonemah, October 2011
Terry Tsotich, November 2011
Florent Vollant, December 2011
Gary Vorgensen, April 2012
Frank Waln, November 2011

John Ware, December 2013
Chenoa Westerman, August 2011
Terry Wildman, April 2013
John Williams, September 2012
Bear Witness, April 2012
Steve Wood, July 2011
Malcolm Yepa, August 2012
Mary Youngblood, August 2011

INDEX

Page numbers in italic type refer to illustrations.